M

HOLOCAUST JUSTICE

MICHAEL J. BAZYLER

HOLOCAUST JUSTICE

The Battle for Restitution in America's Courts

New York University Press • *New York and London*

NEW YORK UNIVERSITY PRESS
New York and London

© 2003 by New York University

Library of Congress Cataloging-in-Publication Data
Bazyler, Michael J.
Holocaust justice : the battle for restitution in America's courts /
Michael J. Bazyler.
p. cm.
Includes bibliographical references and index.
ISBN 0-8147-9903-5 (cloth : acid-free paper)
1. Holocaust survivors—Legal status, laws, etc.—United States.
2. Holocaust survivors—Claims.   3. Restitution and
indemnification claims (1933-   ).   I. Title.
KF6075 .B39 2003
940.53"18144—dc21   2002154298

New York University Press books are printed on acid-free paper,
and their binding materials are chosen for strength and durability.

Manufactured in the United States of America

10 9 8 7 6 5 4 3 2 1

Contents

In memory of Leopold (Paul) Page

Acknowledgments

Many individuals made this book possible.

I am especially grateful to all those who took time to read drafts and provide me with comments, some quite detailed. Without their critical advice, this book would not have been possible. They are Michael Berenbaum, J. D. Bindenagel, Michael Bradfield, Roy Carlin, Rabbi Abraham Cooper, Vivian Curran, Sam Dubbin, Paul Dubinsky, Monica Dugot, John Fishel, Eric Freedman, Agnieszka Fryszman, Linda Gerstel, Lloyd P. Goldenberg, Judah Gribetz, Karen Heilig, Marilyn Henry, Paul Hoffman, Steve Hunegs, Sarah Jackson, Danny Kadden, Frank Kaplan, Miriam Kleiman, Thomas Kline, David Lash, Ivy Lee, Jody Manning, Vartkes Marootian, Kevin Murphy, Burt Neuborne, Owen Pell, Jonathan Petropoulos, Morris Ratner, Leo Rechter, Shari Reig, John K. Roth, Lucille Roussin (who is also a most wonderful editor), Moshe Sanbar, Randy Schoenberg, Nat Shapo, Howard Spiegler, Lisa Stern, Deborah Sturman, Harriet Tamen, Gideon Taylor, Leslie Tick, Anne Webber, Richard Weisberg (who also recommended this project to NYU Press), Eric Wollman, and Arie Zuckerman.

I am also grateful to the various attorneys and their clients involved in the Holocaust restitution suits who allowed me to interview them and provided invaluable data and documents about the litigation discussed in this book.

This book was also made possible through the various visits I made to other institutions, which gave me both the time and opportunity to write the book. These included a sabbatical semester in London, arranged by Lord Janner, head of the Holocaust Educational Trust; a semester at Chapman University School of Law, arranged by President Jim Doti, Professor Marilyn Harran, and Dean Parham Williams at Chapman University in Orange, California, where I taught my Holocaust and the Law course for the first time; and a semester in New

York at Brooklyn Law School, made possible by Dean Joan Wexler, which allowed me to complete the book. My colleagues at Whittier Law School and Brooklyn Law School offered critical reviews and helped flesh out some of the important themes of the book during the faculty colloquia I gave at both institutions.

My colleagues and friends at Whittier Law School, my home institution, offered critical support throughout this project. I want to note especially the assistance of Curt Jones of the Whittier Law Library, who graciously and expeditiously responded to even my most obscure research requests and was successful *every time* in locating the source for which I was searching. Karl Friedrich of Faculty Support Services was a wonder, not only typing the manuscript through its various stages, but also providing valuable editorial input. His colleague Henrietta Johnson, head of Faculty Support Services, was most gracious and kind despite all the deadlines she faced, from both me and other faculty members.

I want to acknowledge the enormous support and enthusiasm for this project by Dean Neil Cogan, without whom this book would not have been possible. I also want to recognize our late dean, John Fitzrandolph, a dear friend and backer of the annual international law symposia at Whittier, including the March 1998 Nazi Gold symposium, at which this book had its origins. I deeply miss him.

My research assistants at both Whittier Law School and Brooklyn Law School were wonderful and included Noelle Clark, Gregory Diamond, Julia Kunina, Derek Nicoletto, Pavani Thagirisa, and Adrienne Scholz, whom I asked for help after she received a perfect "100" in my Holocaust and the Law course. Ms. Scholz proved to be the best research assistant I have had during my more than twenty years of teaching. She has a great legal future ahead of her.

I am forever grateful to Bonny V. Fetterman, my independent editor, who taught me how to write a book. Jennifer Hammer, my editor at NYU Press, not only provided critical editorial assistance but also guided this project over a difficult period in the aftermath of September 11.

Finally, and most importantly, I note the moral support of my fellow board members at The "1939" Club, that heroic group of Holocaust survivors (and their children) who, with their youthful energy and passion, gave me inspiration and motivation for this project. To all of them, my *hartsikn dank* (heartfelt thanks).

Preface

The Holocaust was both the greatest murder and the greatest theft in history. Not only were six million Jewish men, women, and children murdered, but historians estimate that the Nazis stole assets worth between $230 billion and $320 billion in today's dollars from the Jewish population in Europe. American military historian and World War II scholar Allan Millett has labeled the Third Reich a "kleptocracy." The Nazis, he explains, "were lowbrow guys with highbrow pretensions. They stole everything in sight: art, jewelry, artifacts, paintings of the masters. Basically, they had a taste for expensive stuff, but they didn't want to pay for any of it."[1] For more than half a century since the end of World War II, most of these losses remained uncompensated. Beginning in the 1950s, postwar West Germany paid reparations of approximately $70 billion to some Jewish victims of Nazi persecution, but the amounts to each individual were small and came nowhere close to compensating for the suffering endured by the victims or the actual monetary losses suffered by European Jewry.

The financial books of the Holocaust are being settled only now. Surprisingly, the accounting is not being done in Europe, where the Holocaust took place, but in the United States. Why here?

The answer lies with the American legal system. Diplomacy, individual pleas for justice by Holocaust survivors and various Jewish organizations for the last fifty years, and even suits in foreign courts, have not worked. It is only now, with the intervention of the American courts, that elderly Holocaust survivors throughout the world are starting to see their hopes for compensation at last being realized.

The beginning of this phenomenon—of Holocaust survivors and their heirs bringing successful suits in U.S. courts—can be traced to October 1996 with the filing of three federal class action lawsuits in New York. Surprisingly, these suits were not against the German government or German companies but against the three largest Swiss banks for failing to return the money deposited with them on the eve of and during World War II.

Since then, the floodgates of litigation have opened. European insurance companies have been sued for failing to honor insurance policies purchased before the war by people who became Holocaust victims. German companies and companies with German-based subsidiaries have been sued for using slave labor during World War II. Like the Swiss banks, banks in Germany, Austria, and France have been accused of stealing money deposited with them by Holocaust victims. Finally, museums worldwide, including those in the United States and even Israel, have been found to be holding art looted by the Nazis.

The arena for resolving all these claims has been the courts of the United States. In August 1998, the Swiss banks settled for $1.25 billion, which at that time was the largest settlement of a human rights case in U.S. history. In December 1999, that settlement was topped by a $5 billion settlement with Germany, to resolve suits for slave labor and related claims against private German companies.

European insurance companies have also come to the bargaining table, creating an international insurance commission to settle the Holocaust-era insurance lawsuits against them. Some American companies, sued for doing business with the Nazis through their European subsidiaries, also have joined these settlements. Others are still denying responsibility.

The real hero of this story is the American justice system. It is a tribute to the U.S. system of justice that American courts were able to handle claims that originated more than fifty years ago in another part of the world. The unique features of the American system of justice are precisely those factors that made the United States the *only* forum in the world where Holocaust claims could be heard today. These unique principles include

1. The ability of foreign citizens to file suit in the United States for human right abuses committed in foreign lands.
2. The recognition of jurisdiction over foreign defendants that do business in the United States, even over claims that occurred abroad.

3. The recognition of class action lawsuits.
4. The ability of lawyers to take cases on a contingency basis, thereby giving Holocaust claimants top-notch legal representation when filing civil suits against European and American corporate giants.
5. A legal culture in which lawyers are willing to take high-risk cases with a low probability of success, in order to test the limits of the law.
6. Fixed and affordable court filing fees when filing a civil lawsuit.
7. The ability to have a jury trial in civil litigation.
8. The existence of an independent judiciary that does not "take marching orders" from the political branches of government.

The purpose of this book is to explain the Holocaust restitution movement, its long-delayed genesis, its successes, and its failures. As a professor of law, I have been examining, writing, and lecturing about the unfolding restitution story almost full time for the last five years. My interest in documenting this extraordinary story has both personal and professional roots.

The subject of the Holocaust is very close to my heart. I grew up in postwar Poland, in the city of Lodz. We lived near the site of the infamous Lodz ghetto, where a quarter of a million Jews were interned during the war and from where they were deported to the death camps in Chelmo and Auschwitz. I still remember, as a young boy during the 1960s, walking past streets where remnants of the barbed wire from the Lodz ghetto remained.

Both my parents were Holocaust survivors. Teenagers when World War II began, they escaped death by fleeing eastward to the Soviet Union. My father's family was not so lucky; all of them were killed by the Nazis. As the sole surviving member of his family, my father was obsessed by the Holocaust. His obsession was channeled into collecting photographic books on World War II. Since the Nazis avidly recorded in thousands of photographs the humiliation and destruction they committed on the Jews of Europe, such photo journals were plentiful in postwar Poland, which itself was obsessed with recording the horrors of the Holocaust. The books my father favored were large, coffee table–size albums. They were neatly stacked on our one bookshelf, readily available for perusal by his children. He never us told his story. Rather, we had to learn it ourselves by viewing those horrific photographs. The now-famous photograph of the little boy with his arms held up in surrender as a Nazi soldier with a rifle stands behind him, smiling for the camera, that little boy—I felt in my heart—was I.

My mother was more fortunate. She escaped eastward with her entire family when the Nazis attacked the Soviet Union in June 1941. She did talk about her experiences, including her flight on a horse-drawn wagon during bombing raids by the Luftwaffe. Her one wish at that time, she told me as we looked out the window of our Polish apartment, was never again to have to monitor the sky for planes with bombs intended for her and her loved ones.

Most of my parents' friends were Holocaust survivors, the small remnant of a once dynamic Jewish community in Poland that was almost wiped out. As a child, I thought nothing strange of seeing numbers tattooed on the arms of adults visiting our home. My parents always feared another war in Europe, another destruction that—this time—would not spare them and their children. The language spoken at home was Yiddish, and one of the first words I learned was *melhume*, "war." Many years later, as an adult, I was surprised to learn that it was a Hebrew word borrowed by Yiddish.

My parents' fear finally led us to emigrate from Poland to the safety of America. Arriving in the summer of 1964, at age eleven, I was sent to a Jewish summer camp to learn to speak English before the start of the new school year. Looking at the other children, I remember noting something different: the young Jewish boys and girls here did not look like victims. They were nothing like the Jews in the black-and-white photographs of the books that my father carried with him on our journey or the classmates in the Jews-only segregated school I attended in Lodz. Strong, confident, and not afraid to express their Jewishness, they were part of American society. I had arrived on another planet.

I relate this story because it explains how I came to write this book. As an American-educated law professor, I had put the Holocaust behind me. Instead, my focus was on writing about—and litigating—contemporary human rights abuses: the killing fields of Pol Pot's Cambodia, the starving children in Mengistu's drought-stricken Ethiopia, the torture victims of the military junta regimes in Argentina and Chile.

Just as the rest of the world tried to forget about the Holocaust, shunning the elderly victims still alive, so did I. I purposely avoided joining the various Holocaust groups formed by the sons and daughters of Holocaust survivors. I once went to a meeting of one such Los Angeles–based group and never returned.

In my role as educator, I organized yearly international law symposia at my home institution, Whittier Law School, which focused on human rights issues. After one such symposium in 1997, I began looking for next year's topic. My co-organizer, then the board chair of Amnesty International USA, suggested a program focusing on the rights of refugees. I offered an alternative theme: the emerging issue of restitution for Holocaust survivors.

The media had been reporting on the serious allegations being made against Swiss banks for keeping money over the last half-century that had been deposited with them by European Jews on the eve of World War II. In the 1930s and 1940s, thousands of Jews across Europe took advantage of the Swiss banks' secrecy laws to protect their assets from the Nazis by depositing them with those banks. In fact, the private Swiss banks urged their government to pass such laws specifically to entice Jews into bringing their assets to Switzerland. Even more sensational were the claims that both the Swiss banks and the Swiss government did extensive business with the Nazis during the war, acting as a conduit for assets stolen from Nazi-occupied Europe. Most shocking, these assets included gold stolen by the Nazis, including gold ripped from the mouths of Jews in the death camps. "Nazi gold," a term that came into usage at this time, refers not to gold belonging to the Nazis but to gold stolen by the Nazis from their victims, as well as a range of other wartime thefts.

The "Nazi gold" story captured the popular imagination. The American media were constantly reporting on the subject: the $20 billion class action filed in New York by elderly Holocaust survivors against the Swiss banks, the Swiss contortions in trying to explain away their wartime acts, and the special interest that the American government was taking in the issue. President Bill Clinton appointed a special assistant, Deputy Assistant Secretary of State Stuart Eizenstat, a Jewish American lawyer from Atlanta, to search the United States' wartime archives for proof of Swiss complicity with the Nazis. The U.S. Senate Banking Committee, under the leadership of its scrappy chairman,

Senator Alfonse D'Amato, grilled Swiss bank executives during hearings scheduled on the issue. At these hearings, elderly Holocaust survivors were finally given a public forum to talk about the struggle they had been quietly carrying on for the last fifty-five years. Their stories were heart wrenching: emaciated survivors making their way after the war to Switzerland to collect the money deposited by their dead parents and being turned away for lack of a death certificate, which the Nazis, of course, did not issue; desperate letters sent by now-destitute survivors to the banks, which remained unanswered or, when answered, denied their claims in bureaucratic language; calls by survivors for accountability that were largely ignored for fifty years.

The Swiss were not the only villains in the now-emerging Holocaust restitution saga. Another group of financial perpetrators was revealed: the European insurance companies that failed to pay on policies bought by Jews before the war. Such policies were called the "poor man's Swiss bank account." Again, the locus of the action was the United States. The same German, French, Swiss, and Italian insurers that had profited from the Holocaust had now become owners of brand-name U.S. insurance companies: Farmers Insurance, Fireman's Fund, The Equitable Companies, Kemper, and many others. The National Association of Insurance Commissioners had set up a Holocaust insurance task force to look into the issue, and some insurance commissioners were holding hearings in their states, similar to the D'Amato hearings regarding the Swiss banks. Here, too, the European executives were being put under bright lights and hard questioning with the intent of making them explain their actions and what they planned to do to remedy the situation. And of course, there was the litigation: in March 1997, a class action lawsuit was filed in a New York federal court against sixteen European insurance companies, seeking $1 billion from each for refusing to pay out the policies.

A third Holocaust restitution issue pertained to art that had been stolen by the Nazis from private collections before making its way to the United States, the largest art market in the world. Some experts were claiming that many American museums held art with suspicious origins, likely to have come from Jewish private collections looted by the Nazis.

In March 1998, I held at Whittier Law School the first conference in the United States to deal with these three issues which, at that time, comprised the entire world of Holocaust restitution. Holocaust historians, public officials, attorneys, and Holocaust survivors addressed a standing-room only crowd. The event, called "Nazi Gold and Other Assets of the Holocaust: A Search for Justice," was covered by both the national and the international media and included a story in *Time* magazine.

In organizing the conference, I began to search for financial support to cover the travel expenses of those speakers whom I would be bringing to the event. I contacted the largest and most active Holocaust survivors' organization in Southern California, The "1939" Club. The organization was created in 1952, the year I was born, and began as a social club for Jewish survivors from Poland who had arrived in Los Angeles from war-torn Europe. Its name is a reminder to future generations that 1939 was the year of the beginning of the Holocaust, when Nazi Germany invaded Poland. Although the members then were in their twenties and thirties, the organization now had on its board fewer than a dozen of the original members. Among them was Paul Page, a former president of the organization and a survivor of Schindler's factory who convinced Thomas Keneally to write the book *Schindler's List* and Steven Spielberg to make the film based on it. In 1978, the organization, now involved in civic activities, created the first chair in Holocaust studies, at UCLA, whose present holder is the renowned Holocaust historian Saul Friedländer.

Not only did The "1939" Club help me with funding, but the members invited me to speak at one of the luncheons they held at the Beverly Hills Hotel, where I danced to Yiddish tunes, with my mother joining me as a guest. After my speech, I was approached by Paul Page, who eagerly told me about his "post-Schindler" life in America. Paul was adamant: Holocaust restitution was taking too long. Survivors are dying at a rate of 10 percent each year; something had to be done now. Sadly, I could not offer him hope of a speedier settlement.

Under the constant but gentle prodding from William Elperin, a child of survivors who became the first "second-generation" president of The "1939" Club, I soon became a board member and officer. A new life had opened for me, but a familiar one. The Holocaust had again become a daily part of my life. I was again with survivors with tattoos on their arms, many of them even from Lodz. But these survivors were not victims but proud individuals who, phoenix-like, had risen from the ashes of the death camps and rebuilt their lives in America. And so I had come full circle. The Holocaust had again become a daily part of my life.

This time, however, I was able to examine it in the context of the human rights work I had been doing for the previous two decades.

In looking at the Holocaust restitution efforts, my mission has always been to include the views of the survivors themselves. Too often, the opinions of the survivors have been ignored. Books about the Holocaust fall into two types: scholarly treaties written, especially today, by writers who, for the most part, did not experience the Holocaust, or memoirs written by now-elderly survivors who focus primarily on their experiences during the war. At conferences, the survivors are either completely ignored or shunted aside in favor of the so-called scholarly experts.[2] In public debates, when the survivors are given a forum in which to speak, they most often assume the role of a background chorus. In this book, I focus on the Holocaust restitution movement as both a legal story and a human drama about individual Holocaust survivors. I will not pretend that I can speak for any of them. But my background and work over the last five years have made me an "insider" of sorts. I have tried hard to earn the trust and respect of the survivors and, most important, to listen to them. Holocaust survivors are far from a monolithic group. In fact, some of the most bitter fights in the restitution arena have been among the survivors themselves. Where there has been disagreement, I have tried to elucidate it.

One word of caution: As you read about the various machinations of the Swiss banks, the European insurance companies, and even the German industry's financial collusion with the Nazis, you should remember that the greatest evil of the Holocaust was mass murder. The financial crimes, while serious and worthy of examination, pale in comparison with the industrialized killings committed by the Nazis themselves, which were on a scale unparalleled in world history. A focus on the nefarious actions of European and American business during the war should never be used merely to spread the blame or to lessen the responsibility of Hitler and the other Nazi architects of genocide.

The restitution now being received by elderly survivors—more than a half-century later—is just a small step toward closing the financial books for the most heinous crimes committed during the twentieth century. It cannot bring back the six million people who died.

■

Paul Page, no. 173 on Schindler's list, died on March 9, 2001, after a long illness. Like tens of thousands of other Holocaust survivors who waited over the last half-century for the Swiss, German, Austrian, Italian, French, and American companies to acknowledge their wrongdoing through some measure of compensation, he died while awaiting payment. At the time of his death, the Holocaust restitution claim forms were just being sent out to survivors. The following month, PBS television stations throughout the United States screened Spielberg's *Schindler's List*. The screening was dedicated to Paul Page. And so is this book.

I

Suing the Swiss Banks

THE HOLOCAUST RESTITUTION MOVEMENT had a curious beginning. While the major perpetrator of crimes against the Jews during
World War II was Germany, the movement for restitution began with
accusations against Switzerland, a country that had remained neutral in
the war.

Suddenly a nation that had both cultivated and maintained an
image of evenhandedness and neutrality—to the point of not even joining the United Nations—was being accused of engaging in terrible financial misdeeds during the war. Switzerland no longer was viewed as
a "land populated by peace-loving burghers and peasants, watchmak-
ers, bankers and hoteliers, committed to upholding Switzerland's 'ever-
lasting neutrality,'" wrote Amos Elon in a *New York Times Magazine* article; the image of Switzerland as "the land of Heidi and the home of the
International Red Cross, 'Europe's pharmacy' and perpetual aid first-
aid station" was disintegrating.[1] Rather, it now was being viewed as a
nation that, as a result of its financial dealings with the Nazis, was
guilty of profiting from the death and misery of others as well as pro-
longing the war. As chillingly put by one commentator: "History has
caught up with William Tell and exposed him as a pimp."[2]

In June 1999, Switzerland unexpectedly lost its bid for the 2006
Winter Olympics. The loss was blamed on negative publicity generated
by its Holocaust-era events. Swiss Sports Minister Adolf Ogi complained, "I never even dreamed that we had such a bad reputation. I
heard delegates say they wanted the Swiss to lose. People don't like
Switzerland."[3]

How did the Swiss get into such a mess? Accusations that neutral
Switzerland had profited from trade with the Nazis had surfaced even
during the war. Immediately following the cessation of hostilities, researchers working for the Allied armies came across records of the

Swiss government's nefarious dealings with the Nazis. As a consequence, Switzerland and the Allied nations signed the Washington Accord in 1946 which forced a reluctant Switzerland to return a portion of the gold that the Nazis had stolen from the treasuries of the nations they conquered and that they either had deposited in Switzerland for safekeeping or sold directly to the Swiss. For Switzerland, the Washington Accord ended the matter of its wartime complicity.

Destitute Holocaust survivors whose families had deposited money with private Swiss banks for safekeeping on the eve of the Nazi onslaught and who demanded its return were easier to ignore. Letters from survivors living abroad inquiring about the fate of the deposited funds were never answered. After being liberated from the death camps, some of the survivors traveled to Switzerland, showing up at the banks' doorsteps seeking the return of their deposited funds. But the banks set up bureaucratic obstacles. A favorite method was to ask the survivor to produce a death certificate confirming that the parent who had deposited the funds was indeed dead. The Nazis, of course, did not issue death certificates for the six million Jews they killed. Most survivors, eager to get on with their lives, simply gave up, and the Swiss banks ended up keeping the funds. The dormant accounts became a forgotten footnote of World War II.

New rumblings about the Swiss erupted in the mid-1990s. After researchers working for the World Jewish Congress (WJC) made him aware of the issue, Edgar Bronfman Sr., the billionaire scion of Seagram's liquor empire and head of the WJC, first approached the Swiss banks in 1995 about the dormant accounts. Then in 1996, the U.S. Senate Banking Committee, headed by Senator Alfonse D'Amato, began holding hearings on the matter.

Investigative journalists launched the story, and books exposing the tawdry details of Swiss complicity began to appear. The book titles themselves revealed the new, negative image of the Swiss:

Nazi Gold: The Full Story of the Fifty-Year Swiss-Nazi Conspiracy to Steal Billions from Europe's Jews and Holocaust Survivors

Hitler's Silent Partners: Swiss Banks, Nazi Gold and the Pursuit of Justice

Hitler's Secret Bankers: The Myth of Swiss Neutrality during the Holocaust

The Last Deposit: Swiss Banks and Holocaust Victims' Accounts

Swiss Banks and Jewish Souls
The Swiss, the Gold and the Dead: How Swiss Bankers Helped Finance the
    Nazi War Machine[4]

The last title was particularly painful to the Swiss, since it was written by one of their own, Swiss sociologist Jean Ziegler, who also happened to be a member of the Swiss parliament. After the book was published, calls were issued in Switzerland to strip Ziegler of his parliamentary immunity and try him for treason.[5]

The popular media riveted the public's attention to the issue. *Time* magazine ran a cover story, "Echoes of the Holocaust," detailing the stories of Holocaust survivors whose claims for deposited funds were being rejected by Swiss banks.[6] Its evocative cover depicted gold bars shaped in the form of a swastika, imposed on a background photo of emaciated death camp survivors. PBS aired a *Frontline* documentary describing the accusations against the Swiss, and A&E's *Investigative Reports* devoted two hours to the emerging story.

Even more damaging to the Swiss was a report issued in May 1997 by the U.S. government, which had begun reexamining its own archives the year before for a fresh look at Switzerland's behavior during the war. Eleven government agencies participated in the study, including the State, Treasury, and Defense Departments; the CIA; and the National Security Agency. Commonly known as the first Eizenstat report,[7] for Stuart Eizenstat, the assistant secretary of state selected by President Bill Clinton to head a commission to examine the issue, the 212-page report accused Switzerland and the other neutral nations of "profit[ing] handsomely from their economic cooperation with Nazi Germany, while the Allied nations were sacrificing blood and treasure to fight one of the most powerful forces of evil in the annals of history."[8]

The Eizenstat report was a bombshell, highly publicized in both the United States and Europe.[9] Focusing on the issue of gold stolen by the Nazis (the so-called Nazi gold) and its subsequent fate, the report estimated that the Nazis looted approximately $580 million ($5.8 billion in today's dollars)[10] of gold from the nations they conquered. This consisted of both gold taken from the treasuries of the Nazi-occupied nations ("monetary gold") and an unknown amount taken from individual victims, including gold coins, wedding rings and other jewelry, and gold tooth fillings from Holocaust victims, some of it removed from the remains of death camp victims and therefore known as "victim gold."

While the Eizenstat report found no evidence that the Swiss bankers knew the gruesome origins of victim gold, the report concluded that the bankers were well aware of the source of the Nazis' monetary gold transfers made within Switzerland.

> The Swiss National Bank and private Swiss bankers knew, as the war progressed, that the Reichsbank's own coffers had been depleted, and that the Swiss were handling vast sums of looted gold. The Swiss were aware of the Nazi heists from France of Belgian gold, as well as from other countries.[11]

The report estimated that the total amount of gold the Nazis funneled through Switzerland amounted to $185 million to $289 million (approximately $1.8 billion to $2.8 billion in today's dollars). It also found that at the end of the war, Switzerland held approximately $500 million in other German assets. Examining the efforts by the United States after the war to have Switzerland return the Nazi-stolen assets to their rightful owners, the report stated, "The Swiss raised one objection over another" to such demands.

When the Washington Accord was finally signed in 1946, Switzerland agreed to return $58 million, thereby keeping more than half its wartime booty. But even then, Switzerland failed to abide by its promise. The report continued: "U.S. negotiators concluded by 1950 that the Swiss had no intention of ever implementing the 1946 Washington accord. Secretary of State Dean Acheson remarked that if Sweden was an intransigent negotiator, then Switzerland was intransigence 'cubed.'"[12]

The Eizenstat report further acknowledged that the Truman administration missed a critical opportunity to enforce the agreement by unfreezing Swiss assets in the United States shortly after the war. "Most leverage was lost before Switzerland had met its obligations," the report affirmed. The Truman administration could have imposed sanctions on Switzerland for failing to honor the agreement but chose not to do so. By 1952, in the face of Switzerland's stonewalling, the United States and other allies agreed to a total payout of "only $28 million—far less than the agreed [-upon amount]."

The Swiss were caught by complete surprise by these attacks, and their initial responses made matters even worse. They made their first mistake in December 1996, when Jean-Pascal Delamuraz, the economics minister and the outgoing Swiss president, labeled the attacks as "blackmail" by Jewish groups to extort money from Switzerland. Delamuraz later apologized for his remarks.

A month later, Switzerland's ambassador to the United States, Carlo Jagmetti, resigned because of a leaked document in which he likened the accusations to a "war" against Switzerland being conducted by Jewish organizations in the United States. Such Swiss missteps eventually led one commentator to charge that the Swiss "never miss an opportunity to miss an opportunity."[13]

I personally encountered the Swiss's inability to come to grips with the issue in late 1997 while organizing a symposium at Whittier Law School concerning a broad spectrum of issues associated with Nazi gold. This was the first academic conference to deal with the subject.[14] Since the program was being held at a law school, where debate and critical discourse are the norm, I wanted all sides to be represented. My letters to the Swiss banks, inviting them to send a speaker, at first went unanswered. Finally, one of their attorneys called in response to my invitation letter. He was scheduled to make a presentation on the controversy at the Holocaust museum in Houston and said that he was eager to appear on our program. But his enthusiasm faded the moment he learned that lawyers for the claimants would also be present. At that point, he curtly declined.

The Swiss government initially agreed to send a representative but then changed its mind as well. I forwarded two complimentary admissions to high-ranking representatives of the Swiss government, with the suggestion that they at least send someone to participate in our question-and-answer sessions. To my surprise and relief, they did and were so pleased with the conference that they asked me to organize an event in which they could make a formal, albeit late, appearance.[15] Eight months later, in November 1998, Ambassador Thomas Borer, the Swiss envoy for Holocaust-era issues, along with a Swiss government historian, appeared at an all-day program to present the Swiss side of the story.[16] The most interesting part of the November postscript was Borer's appearance at Friday night services at a local synagogue where, with a *yarmulke* on his head, he delivered a passionate defense of the Swiss.

The appointment of Borer as a special envoy on these issues in October 1996 and the creation of a special World War II task force headed by Borer were important steps for the Swiss government to show that they were now taking the issue seriously. Another was the creation of a humanitarian fund in 1997 totaling approximately $180 million (to which the Swiss banks contributed $70 million) to aid destitute Holocaust survivors worldwide.[17] Officially called the "Swiss Fund for Needy Victims of the Holocaust," this goodwill and public relations gesture did not address the issue of stolen assets and did not stop the emerging restitution movement. The Swiss took two other important steps to deal with their wartime record.

In May 1996, the Swiss Bankers Association (SBA), the trade body of the Swiss banks, created the so-called Independent Committee of Eminent Persons (ICEP) and convinced Paul Volcker, the former chairman of the U.S. Federal Reserve Bank, to become its head.[18] The SBA then gave the ICEP an open-ended budget to audit the records of the Swiss banks to ferret out the wartime dormant accounts. In December 1996, the Swiss government created a nine-member historical commission, headed by Swiss historian Jean-François Bergier, which included historians from the United States, the United Kingdom, Poland, and Israel. The Bergier Commission's agenda was to assess anew the role of Switzerland during World War II.[19] By that time, however, it was a matter of too little too late. The Swiss were now coming face-to-face with the weapon that would prove the most effective for resolving not just the allegations against the Swiss but all other ensuing Holocaust-era claims: the American class action lawsuit.

OCTOBER 1996: THE BEGINNING OF HOLOCAUST RESTITUTION LITIGATION

The first lawsuit was filed by Edward Fagan, the most colorful and controversial of the attorneys involved in Holocaust litigation. But Fagan's high profile and irascibility made him a prime target for negative and, at times, unfair reviews by the media.[20] His full-time engagement with the Holocaust restitution campaign came about through sheer coincidence. In the mid-1990s, Fagan did some unrelated legal work for Gizella Weisshaus, an energetic Holocaust survivor born in Romania. The grateful Weisshaus became a mother figure, delivering homemade food to Fagan's office every week. During one of her visits, Weisshaus told Fagan about her attempts to collect the money deposited by her father in Switzerland before the war.

Weisshaus was nine years old when the war began. She and her family, all Hasidic Jews, lived in Romania, initially an ally of Nazi Germany but later occupied by it. In 1944, Weisshaus's father was arrested by the Nazis. Before he was shipped off to the camps, he informed the then fourteen-year-old Gizella and her six siblings that he had opened a Swiss bank account a few years earlier at the Union Bank of Switzerland (UBS).

After the war, Weisshaus, who herself was a survivor of Auschwitz, made three trips to Switzerland seeking the return of the funds, all without success. The UBS demanded documentation, including an account number, which she did not have. In 1950, she immigrated to the United States.

Fagan had been reading about the criticism of the Swiss banks over the wartime deposits and showed Weisshaus an article from the *New York Times* on the subject. Listening to her story, Fagan became excited. Always ready to venture into new legal territory, as he explained later, he realized, "Oh my God, I have a plaintiff. I don't know if she's real, but I have a plaintiff."[21]

Almost two weeks later, Fagan filed the first class action lawsuit against the Swiss banks, seeking $20 billion in damages and listing Gisella Weisshaus as the lead plaintiff. The *Weisshaus* lawsuit, filed on October 3, 1996, marked the beginning of the Holocaust restitution movement in the U.S. courts.

A solo practitioner in New York City, Fagan had little previous experience with international matters or class action litigation. He therefore turned to two experienced practitioners for assistance: New York University Law School professor Burt Neuborne and Philadelphia attorney Robert Swift. Neuborne is a constitutional and human rights scholar with impeccable credentials, and in the 1980s, he served as a legal director of the American Civil Liberties Union (ACLU). Neuborne agreed to come on board as a tribute to his deceased daughter, a rabbinical student who in September 1996 had died suddenly from a congenital heart defect. Swift had acquired experience in international human rights litigation in the early 1990s when he sued former Philippine dictator Ferdinand Marcos, after Marcos went into exile in Hawaii, for human rights abuses committed on Philippine citizens when Marcos was ruling the country.

At the same time that Fagan was readying the *Weisshaus* lawsuit, another lawyer was busy preparing his own lawsuit against the Swiss banks. Michael Hausfeld had a law practice quite different from Fagan's. Hausfeld is a name partner in a Washington, D.C., firm described by the *Corporate Legal Times* as "probably the most effective class-action firm in the country for lawsuits dealing with a strong social and political component."[22] Hausfeld is one of the firm's shining stars. In 1996, he concluded what was at that time the largest class action settlement in the United States, $141 million paid by Texaco to settle accusations of race discrimination in its workforce.

Hausfeld's involvement in Holocaust litigation came through a friendship with Martin Mendelsohn, a partner in a powerful Washington, D.C., firm which lists Bob Dole and George Mitchell as senior counsels. For many years, Mendelsohn had been representing the Los Angeles–based Simon Wiesenthal Center, led by two dynamic and politically connected rabbis, Marvin Hier and Abraham Cooper. In the mid-1980s, Hausfeld and Mendelsohn were part of a team of lawyers working with the center on behalf of Leon Handel, a Holocaust survivor from Yugoslavia. Handel filed a civil lawsuit in a Los Angeles federal court against a former high-ranking official of fascist Croatia, a puppet state created by the Nazis after their conquest of Yugoslavia. The official, Andrija Artukovic, had immigrated to the United States after the war and, like Handel, was living in Southern California. As a prelude to the work they would be doing fifteen years later, the lawyers styled the suit as a class action and sought compensatory and punitive damages from Artukovic for his involvement in persecuting Jews in wartime Croatia. But in the 1980s, American courts were not ready to hear suits stemming from the Holocaust, and *Handel v. Artukovic*[23] was summarily dismissed. Seeking to avoid a repeat of their earlier experience, Hausfeld and Mendelsohn worked for more than half a year to develop their case against the Swiss banks.

In a highly unorthodox move for a law firm, Hausfeld hired Holocaust historians on a full-time basis to collect evidence for the lawsuit. His chief historian was Miriam Kleiman, a young researcher who, while working part-time for the WJC, had first stumbled on some of the most incriminating documentation of Switzerland's role during World War II. Her most valuable discovery was a report identifying Jewish depositors by name at one Swiss bank and listing the exact amounts of each deposit. In September 1996, Hausfeld enticed Kleiman to work for him. He then sent her across the Potomac River to the U.S. National Archives in College Park, Maryland, to search for documents dealing with

Switzerland's wartime role. For the next four years, Kleiman became an invaluable member of the Holocaust restitution litigation legal team, uncovering a number of "smoking guns" against the Swiss.

With its experience in gathering wartime data, the Simon Wiesenthal Center also used its team of researchers to gather evidence implicating the Swiss. The WJC, D'Amato's Senate Banking Committee, and the U.S. Holocaust Memorial Museum likewise sent researchers to pore over the dusty, yellowing files. Not to be outdone, the Swiss government, the Swiss banks, and their lawyers sent their own teams to learn what other embarrassing materials might be hidden in the U.S. Archives. Suddenly, these long-forgotten wartime documents, numbering about 10 million pages and 5,000 cubic feet of paper, became gripping reading material for the swarm of researchers who descended on College Park. As Kleiman commented to the *Washington Post;* "It's a boom time for Holocaust researchers. Everyone's out there looking through boxes."[24]

To Hausfeld, the historical documents became important pieces of legal evidence that he would use later against the Swiss banks to push them into a settlement. If the Swiss banks did not settle, Hausfeld was ready to introduce these documents as prime exhibits during trial. This marriage of Holocaust historians and class action lawyers, which Hausfeld initiated, was something new. For the first time in U.S. legal history, historians became the experts who would make or break the case for the trial lawyers. The only other similar scenario in which Holocaust historians played such a leading role was in the 1999 defamation trial in London by the "Holocaust denier" David Irving against Deborah Lipstadt. There too, historians played a critical role, producing evidence for the English barristers and solicitors defending Lipstadt that convinced the British trial judge that David Irving indeed was a "Holocaust denier."

The historical research proved invaluable, not only in litigation against the Swiss, but in all subsequent Holocaust lawsuits. The historians repeatedly unearthed documents that implicated both European and sometimes even American corporations in wartime financial misdeeds. As part of their public relations campaign, the lawyers shared each incriminating document with the press as soon as it was discovered.

In October 1996, Hausfeld was ready to file his complaint. By that time, he had also enlisted Melvyn Weiss, one of the nation's most savvy class action lawyers, to join his legal team. Weiss's firm, Milberg Weiss

Bershad Hynes & Lerach, earned its reputation by winning multimillion-dollar awards in securities suits filed on behalf of disgruntled investors.[25] As the litigation developed against the Swiss banks and other European corporate defendants, Weiss brought along Deborah Sturman, an aggressive young attorney who for a time lived in Germany and had a knack for compacting historical facts into cogent legal arguments. Sturman eventually moved from Los Angeles to New York specifically to work on the Holocaust suits. The Hausfeld team also included another young attorney who played an important role in the litigation. Morris Ratner was a young partner at Lieff, Cabraser, Heimann & Bernstein, a San Francisco law firm whose senior partner, Robert Lieff, had been co-counsel with Hausfeld on previous cases, during which the two experienced lawyers developed a good working relationship. The prestige and experience of Lieff, Cabraser were equivalent to that of Hausfeld's firm, but its base of operations was on the West Coast, where some of the Holocaust restitution lawsuits would soon be filed.

Hausfeld's diligent, methodical approach, however, caused him to lose the race to the courthouse. His suit was filed on October 21, 1996, more than two weeks after Fagan's, a scenario that was repeated as the Holocaust litigation movement expanded into other areas. Fagan had the uncanny ability to file the first lawsuit on behalf of one group of survivors and thereby open a new front in the Holocaust restitution movement. Hausfeld and his lawyers would then follow with a lawsuit of their own, filed on behalf of another group of survivors asserting similar claims.

Acrimony between the lawyers arose at the outset of the litigation. Referring to Fagan's suit, Hausfeld recalls, "It angered us, because here we were taking all this time, and he writes this sloppy ten-page thing and makes this silly demand for $20 billion."[26] The $20 billion demand may have been unrealistic, but it worked wonders for publicity purposes. Invariably, a story discussing the litigation against the Swiss banks would mention that the Swiss banks were being sued for $20 billion.

Unlike Fagan and his team, Hausfeld and his lawyers took on the case against the Swiss banks on a *pro bono* basis, but this was last time they would do so. In all subsequent Holocaust restitution suits, they charged for their work.

In January 1997, a third class action was filed against the Swiss banks by yet another set of lawyers. This time, the claimants were not individual survivors but the World Council of Orthodox Jewish Communities, an organization based in the United States claiming to be the heir to Jewish religious institutions destroyed by the Nazis in Europe.

Three separate lawsuits were now pending in a Brooklyn federal court against the Swiss banks. As a result of the different sets of lawyers recruited by each legal team, twenty-eight firms were participating as plaintiffs' counsels.

Some streamlining was clearly needed. In April 1997, the three cases were consolidated before one judge, Edward R. Korman, and collectively titled *In re Holocaust Victim Assets Litigation.* The plaintiffs' lawyers formed an executive committee consisting of ten firms, with Hausfeld and Swift appointed as cochairs of the executive committee.

At Judge Korman's urging, Neuborne was selected in February 1997 as special counsel to plaintiffs. Trusted by all sides, he was the glue that held together the various plaintiffs' legal teams, preventing the acrimony among the lawyers from spilling into the open. In private and sometimes even in public, Fagan and Swift on one side and Hausfeld, Weiss, and Mendelsohn on the other bristled over differing styles, approaches, and claims.

THE WORLD JEWISH CONGRESS AND THE DORMANT SWISS BANK ACCOUNTS

The lawyers filing the lawsuits were essentially following the headlines. By the time they came into the picture, in October 1996, the issue had already been raised with the Swiss. The person responsible for doing so was Edgar Bronfman Sr., the head of Seagram's spirits business who in the 1970s took over the helm of the WJC, an organization founded in the 1930s for the defense of Jewish rights.[27] Bronfman learned of the issue through his deputy, Israel Singer. Singer, then secretary-general of the WJC, is an ordained rabbi and a former political science professor and himself the son of survivors.[28] He first began thinking about looking further into the wartime role of the Swiss banks in 1994 after reading a historically based novel, *The Swiss Account.*[29] In the story, Swiss banks conceal assets deposited with them during the war. Singer asked Bronfman for permission to look into the issue and began by examining the wartime documents in the U.S. Archives, which Kleiman and other WJC staffers found for him in College Park. The WJC staffers brought him a treasure trove. First were reports by U.S. wartime intelligence of Swiss banks purchasing gold from the Nazis and trading for Swiss francs, as well as Allied efforts, mostly unsuccessful, to stop the practice. Then came the records of postwar negotiations to have the Swiss government and private Swiss banks give up the gold and other assets that had been stashed away by the Nazis in Switzerland. Finally, Singer began hearing stories of the Swiss banks stonewalling requests by families of Holocaust victims to return the deposits that had been placed in Switzerland for safekeeping during the Nazi years.

With Bronfman's support, Singer and another WJC leader, Elan Steinberg, at the time the organization's executive director, became the WJC's frontline foot soldiers in the Holocaust restitution struggle. The negotiations they began in 1995 with the Swiss banks expanded into a worldwide campaign involving most of Europe's governments and numerous corporations. That campaign can be traced to a fateful meeting on September 12, 1995.

Bronfman and Singer met on that day in Bern, Switzerland, with the board of the Swiss Bankers Association to discuss the dormant accounts question. Singer laid out for the bankers the Jewish survivors' claims to the long-sought funds deposited with the Swiss banks under the inducement of the Swiss banks' secrecy laws. He then presented them with damning evidence of the banks' role as bankers for the Nazis, including a postwar U.S. government report that concluded that the Nazis had transferred approximately $6 billion in gold and other looted assets to Switzerland for safekeeping. That conclusion was reached by the Tripartite Commission for the Restitution of Monetary Gold, an agency created in 1946 by the United States, the United Kingdom, and France to return so-called monetary gold stolen by the Nazis from the treasuries of occupied Europe. After the war, the story of Switzerland and "Nazi gold" was soon forgotten. But in 1989, American historian Arthur Smith Jr. resurrected it in a little-known book entitled *Hitler's Gold: The Story of the Nazi War Loot*.[30] In the book, Smith explained how the Nazis seized approximately $625 million in gold (approximately $6.25 billion in today's dollars) from the central banks of occupied countries. Only $330 million was recovered, leaving, by Smith's estimates, another $295 million in the "bank vaults of neutral

Europe. Evidence clearly points to Switzerland as the recipient of the largest amount of looted monetary gold."[31] Bronfman raised the issue of these wartime thefts in his tense meeting with the Swiss Bankers Association.

As Bronfman relates the story, the Swiss bankers, confronted with the evidence, became quite rude and claimed that their investigation revealed only 774 dormant Jewish accounts in the Swiss banks. They then offered to turn over $32 million to the WJC to resolve the claims. Bronfman saw this as a bribe. "They had bought off groups before, and this was just a bigger bribe. I realized what they really wanted us to do was to take the money and run."[32]

Most galling to Bronfman was the Swiss bankers' lack of civility. They didn't even offer their visitors a seat, preferring to discuss matters standing. "I don't think it occurred to them that there was not a chair. From my viewpoint, you do not treat people that way."[33] As Bronfman tells it, that missing chair cost the Swiss banks $1.25 billion, the amount the Swiss finally settled for in August 1998.

In 1995, however, Bronfman's response was that he was not looking for a lump-sum settlement, because no specific dollar figure could be discussed until the Swiss banks opened their records to reveal how much they held in the dormant accounts. What Bronfman wanted, as he explained in an interview, was "a proper accounting, not a payoff."[34] Frustrated by the Swiss banks' intransigence, Bronfman turned to the United States' political system for relief.

The Swiss banking industry was dominated by three large banks—Union Bank of Switzerland, Credit Suisse, and the Swiss Bank Corporation—and all three had offices in the United States. Fortuitously for Bronfman, as it turned out, the head of the U.S. Senate Banking Committee was New York Senator Alfonse D'Amato. *Time* magazine described the situation as follows:

> The Republican from Long Island was down in the polls back home . . . [and] desperate for an issue that would refurbish his image. Bronfman brought him a heaven-sent gift certain to appeal to his large bloc of Jewish voters. When Bronfman told him about the Swiss banks' stalling, D'Amato offered public hearings by his Senate Banking Committee. With the in-your-face D'Amato aboard, the war was about to begin in earnest.[35]

Since the Swiss banks had a major presence in the United States, Bronfman and Singer realized that they had some truly powerful leverage.[36] In April 1996 and again in October of that year, D'Amato's Senate Banking Committee held hearings on the Swiss banks' dormant accounts issue.

Bronfman did not stop there. On April 8, 1996, a day before he was to testify at D'Amato's first hearing, Bronfman approached First Lady Hillary Rodham Clinton, who agreed to arrange a meeting with the president.[37] President Clinton turned the matter over to Stuart Eizenstat, then the undersecretary for international trade at the State Department. Eizenstat had little inkling of the job he was taking on. For the next five years, Holocaust restitution became his chief preoccupation, and he continued to work on the matter even when he became the number two person in the Treasury Department during Clinton's second term.[38]

In July 1997, two months after the Eizenstat report was issued, the Swiss banks announced that their investigation had now yielded 1,756 accounts. A list containing the names and nationalities of the account holders was published in full in newspapers throughout the world. According to the banks, this list represented "all known World War II–era accounts of non-Swiss individuals." This soon appeared to be incorrect. Three months later, in October 1997, the banks were forced to add more than 3,500 names to the list. The banks were now stating that the two lists, containing 5,570 dormant accounts with an aggregate value of approximately $45 million, were a complete listing of dormant accounts of foreign nationals held by the Swiss banks.[39] But few people believed them, especially since the families of various survivors with proof of Swiss wartime accounts did not appear on either list. Equally disconcerting, the lists contained, alongside the victims' names, the names of the Nazi war criminals who opened bank accounts during the war. The Swiss banks, hoping that the publication of the lists would relieve them of the pressure they were facing, were sorely disappointed. If anything, by the end of 1997, their reputation had sunk even lower. The once mighty Swiss banks, it now appeared, could not do anything right. Two other embarrassments were still to come before the litigation was settled.

ESTELLE SAPIR: HOLOCAUST HEROINE
OF THE SWISS BANK LITIGATION

The first hero of the Holocaust restitution movement was Estelle Sapir. Born in Warsaw in 1927, Sapir was the daughter of Josef Sapir, a wealthy Jewish investment banker who relocated his family to Paris on the eve of World War II. In 1941, after the Nazis conquered France, the teenaged Estelle was separated from her father when he was arrested by the Nazis and taken to a detention camp in southern France. She also soon arrived there and was able to speak to her father through the barbed wire. According to Sapir, as she held her father's finger through the wire, he told her, "You have to survive. You'll be OK, because there's money in the bank." He then drilled her repeatedly on the names of banks in Switzerland, England, and France where he had opened accounts. "Many times," Sapir recalled in a newspaper interview, "he said, 'Repeat this. Repeat this.' And I remember the names of the banks. I remember."[40] Shortly thereafter, Josef was shipped off to the Majdanek concentration camp in Poland, and Sapir never saw her father again.

In 1946, Sapir, now nineteen, made her way to the Geneva branch of Credit Suisse, the Swiss bank where her father told her he had deposited money. She brought with her a ledger that Josef Sapir had kept in his own handwriting, showing that he had deposited the equivalent of $82,875 with Credit Suisse in Geneva in 1939.

The branch manager refused to even search for the funds, claiming that Sapir needed to produce a death certificate for her father and records of his deposits. Her other documentation—a letter in French her father wrote from Majdanek on the last day of his life, photographs of him on a train full of Jews bound for Majdanek, and Nazi records showing that he was transported there on March 6, 1943—were deemed not sufficient.

> It was like dealing with the Gestapo all over again. They insisted I needed a death certificate. I pleaded with them. I told them there were no records from the camps. I started to scream at a bank manager, "What do you want me to do? Find Hitler and Himmler and ask them to sign my father's death certificate?" They just looked at me blankly.[41]

In contrast, the banks in England and France had promptly returned to her the money deposited by Josef Sapir before the war. Still, Estelle Sapir did not give up. For the next ten years while living in Paris, Sapir made twenty trips to Credit Suisse. Each time, the bank refused to deal with her.

In the late 1960s, Sapir immigrated to the United States. Never married, she lived alone in a one-room apartment in Queens and worked for twenty-seven years in a drugstore before retiring. During all that time, she continued to write to Credit Suisse, seeking the return of her family's funds.

In April 1996, when the Senate Banking Committee scheduled hearings on the issue, Sapir, now frail and elderly, was one of its most prominent witnesses. Her struggle became a powerful symbol of the Swiss banks' refusal to deal with the wartime dormant accounts when, in 1997, her story was prominently featured in two television documentaries on Switzerland's role during World War II. As she related in the documentaries, during Senate hearings, and in frequent interviews, "I promised my father the last time I saw him in the concentration camp . . . that I would find his account with the Swiss. Before I die, I must do this."[42] In May 1998, fifty-two years after her first attempt to recover the funds, Credit Suisse finally admitted that it had found documentation of a prewar bank account opened by a "J. Sapir" but that "it could not determine how much the account may have once contained."[43] Embarrassed by the negative publicity generated by its handling of the claim, Credit Suisse took the extraordinary step of settling with Sapir, who was represented by Fagan, even while continuing to deny payments to the other class action plaintiffs. Although it insisted that the settlement terms remain secret, various media sources reported that Credit Suisse paid $500,000 to settle the matter.[44] To make it clear that it did not intend the Sapir settlement to set a precedent, "the bank went out of its way . . . to describe it as an exceptional case."[45] According to the *New York Times*,

> by settling individually with Miss Sapir, who is down to 65 pounds and clearly in poor health, Credit Suisse has taken care of one of the most visible examples of its failure to investigate accounts opened by Holocaust victims. . . . [Sapir] became a 4-foot-9-inch symbol of the Holocaust survivors whom the Swiss banks summarily dismissed."[46]

The next year, in April 1999, Estelle Sapir died. A true heroine, she remains a symbol of the struggle by elderly Holocaust survivors to obtain long-delayed justice from the Swiss banks and other European institutions. Even though she enjoyed her settlement for less than one year, she lived long enough to see not only a personal victory of her claim but also the Swiss banks' acknowledgment of the claims of the other Holocaust survivors.

In a 1998 interview, after her lawsuit against Credit Suisse was settled, Sapir remarked, "I felt that my father was always behind me and with me. When I die and go to heaven, I will see him and say, 'I accomplished it.'"[47]

CHRISTOPH MEILI: CATCHING THE UBS IN THE ACT OF DESTROYING EVIDENCE

At the New York press conference on August 12, 1998, that announced the class action settlement with the Swiss banks, Estelle Sapir and Senator Alfonse D'Amato appeared with another hero of the Holocaust restitution movement, former Swiss bank guard Christoph Meili. On the night of January 8, 1997, Meili had committed an act of such courage that his life was forever changed. As a result of those actions, over the next three years he was snatched from a quiet life in Zurich, Switzerland; dropped into the epicenter of the Holocaust restitution movement in New York; and eventually again found relative anonymity, though this time in an quiet suburb of Southern California.

Meili worked as a guard for a security company in the Zurich branch of the Union Bank of Switzerland (UBS), the largest bank in Switzerland and one of the largest in the world. While going about his duties on the graveyard shift on that fateful January night, he discovered something strange. In UBS's basement shredding room lay reams of pre–World War II financial documents awaiting shredding the next morning. Meili took some of the documents, put them in his knapsack, and brought them home, where he shared the find with his wife, Guissi. Together, they decided to contact the Israeli consulate, which, matter-of-factly, told them to put the documents in the mail. Next, they contacted the local Jewish community center in Zurich. Werner Rom, the head of the Jewish community, took the documents but felt obliged to turn them over to the police. As Rom later explained in a *Dateline NBC* segment, "This was hot stuff."

Meili was fired from his job, and the Zurich police opened a criminal investigation against him for violating Swiss bank secrecy laws. Shortly thereafter, charges were also brought against UBS and its chief archivist for allowing the shredding of such documents. Some months earlier, in reaction to the furor over the dormant accounts, the Swiss parliament had enacted a law making it illegal to destroy prewar financial documents.

Ten months later, in October 1997, the criminal investigation against Meili was dropped. The Zurich district attorney's office likewise dropped all charges against UBS and its personnel. By that time, however, the Meilis, facing death threats at home, had fled to the United States. Senator D'Amato arranged for Meili to testify at one of his Senate Banking Committee hearings, and a newspaper account related Meili's testimony:

> Meili, a bespectacled baby-faced man of 28, sits behind a long oak table. Staring up into the glare of TV lights at D'Amato's sympathetic face . . . Meili speaks in German while an elderly woman translates. The scene is oddly reminiscent of the Nuremberg trials, where Nazi war criminals were judged a half-century ago, except that it is not Meili but his country that is on trial. After his testimony, the stereotype of Switzerland as a land of ski slopes, yodelers and watchmakers will be shattered. From now on, Switzerland must live down its collaboration with the dark forces of Adolf Hitler.[48]

In July 1997, Congress passed special legislation that was signed by President Clinton, granting Meili and his family permanent residency in the United States.

I first met Meili in March 1998, a little over a year after his heroic act, when he accepted my invitation to appear at the Nazi Gold conference at Whittier Law School. A shy young man, he related his story in halting English before taking questions from the audience. At his side was Ed Fagan, the scrappy Holocaust lawyer who plucked Meili out of Switzerland and brought him to New York when the shredding saga reached its peak in Switzerland. By that time, Fagan had filed suit on behalf of Meili against UBS for wrongful discharge and did not want him to say anything to jeopardize the case. In answer to one question, Meili

Former Swiss bank guard and "whistleblower" Christoph Meili and his family receiving an American flag from Senator Alfonse D'Amato upon obtaining permanent residency in the United States in July 1997 under a special law passed by Congress and signed by President Bill Clinton. *Courtesy of AP Photo / Ed Bailey.*

explained what made his situation unique. "I have become the first Swiss person to seek and acquire political asylum in the United States."[49] That was the banner headline carried by *Time* when it published a story about Meili and his appearance at Whittier.[50]

Meili told the audience what had made him perform such a courageous act. Once a troubled youth, he had escaped his checkered past by turning to Christianity. He had married, and he and his Italian-born wife had become struggling parents with two small children. He knew no Jews; in fact, he had never met a Jew. But as a history buff, he had read stories in the Swiss press about the ongoing saga of the Jews' claims to prewar dormant accounts. He also had seen the movie *Schindler's List* and had been deeply moved by it. Discovering the documents in the shredding room, Meili recalled the scene from the film when Schindler watches the roundup of the Jews by the Nazis and decides to take action. At that moment, Meili felt he had to do the same. At the end of his presentation, the audience, primarily Holocaust survivors, gave Meili a standing ovation. For the first time, the young man smiled. I have seen this scene repeated many times since. Wherever Meili speaks, the audience spontaneously rises to its feet to applaud.

Meili's story, at least for a time, had a happy ending. Sitting in the audience at the Whittier law symposium was William Elperin, president of The "1939" Club, the same William Elperin who had encouraged

Edward Fagan, attorney for Holocaust survivors, confers with Michael
Bazyler (*middle*) and Christoph Meili (*right*). *Courtesy of the Whittier Law School.*

me to join this Holocaust survivors' organization when I asked it for
support for this symposium. Listening to Meili that afternoon, Elperin
was surprised that this defender of the Jewish people was now living
with his wife and children in a cramped New Jersey apartment and was
again supporting himself by working as a security guard, this time in a
Manhattan high-rise. Elperin took action. The "1939" Club began a fund
drive to send him to college, and Elperin asked me to cochair the drive.
As soon as we announced our mission, three universities in California
offered Meili a scholarship. Meili and his family moved to Southern
California in July 1999, where he enrolled as a full-time student at
Chapman University in Orange County.[51] In April 1999, the state of Israel honored Meili at the Holocaust Memorial at Yad Vashem by designating him, like Schindler, a "Righteous Gentile." The United States be-
stowed on him its own honor: In July 1998, Meili appeared on Oprah
Winfrey's television program.

Unfortunately, the Meilis separated and divorced three years after
moving to California. The pressure on Meili and the attendant publicity
of the family were too much. Guissi and their two young children now

live alone in the house that The "1939" Club rented for them and where, shortly after their arrival, we took a busload of survivors for a Sunday barbecue to welcome the Meili family to California. Christoph still attends Chapman and in 2002, as an act of patriotism toward his new country, joined the U.S. Navy Reserves. On March 15, 2002, Judge Korman directed that Meili receive $775,000 from the Swiss settlement fund, part of the $1 million allocation agreed to by the plaintiffs' representatives in August 1998, to reward Meili for his courageous behavior and the consequences he suffered for it. The largest portion of the funds went into an educational trust fund for the Meili children.

ALAN HEVESI: THE GODFATHER OF
HOLOCAUST RESTITUTION SANCTIONS

Along with class action litigation, the Senate hearings held by Senator D'Amato, pressure by Jewish groups, and the steady stream of bad publicity, another component proved critical to the resolution of the Swiss bank claims: the threat of financial sanctions. The person overseeing the various sanctions threatened against European business entities for failing to resolve Holocaust restitution claims was Comptroller Alan Hevesi, the chief financial officer of New York City. Hevesi began working on the issue in December 1997. Confronted with the Swiss banks' intransigence in recognizing the dormant account claims, Hevesi organized a conference on Holocaust restitution, inviting fellow financial officers at the state, county, and city levels throughout the United States to come to New York City to look into the Swiss bank issue. At the conclusion of the conference, which carried the impressive title of "International Conference on the Recovery and Return of Dormant Holocaust-Related Swiss Bank Accounts and Hidden Assets," Hevesi created the innocuous-sounding Executive Monitoring Committee, whose stated aim was to monitor "international efforts at restoring stolen, lost and looted property to Holocaust survivors and victims' heirs."[52]

Sanctions have always been an important part of American foreign policy. Today, the United States imposes some form of sanctions against more than two dozen nations. But common wisdom currently holds that sanctions do not work.[53] For example, the embargo against Cuba, which has lasted for more than forty years, has failed to bring down the

Castro government. The Holocaust restitution movement, however, offers a perfect example of a successful use of sanctions. Before the campaign against the Swiss, the only prior instance of a successful use of sanctions was in helping end the apartheid regime in South Africa. Hevesi and the other supporters of sanctions against the Swiss often cited the South Africa example as a precedent.

Most interesting about the sanctions against the Swiss banks is that they were used not only in the face of vehement objections by Switzerland—which filed formal diplomatic protests with the U.S. government—but also in the face of opposition by the Clinton administration. All during the movement, the federal government urged the state and local governments not to impose sanctions. The most vocal critic of the sanctions was Stuart Eizenstat, Clinton's "point man" on the Holocaust restitution issues. Eizenstat argued that the sanctions were counterproductive, but time and again, he was wrong. The sanctions worked and became a much-used tool in the claims against subsequent defendants in the Holocaust restitution movement. Sanctions were either used or threatened against Austrian and French banks, European insurance companies, and German firms. In each instance, they worked magnificently either to invigorate long-ignored World War II claims or to break impasses over stalled negotiations.

THE SWISS BANKS COME TO THE BARGAINING TABLE

In the summer of 1998, the Swiss banks, under intense pressure, decided to pursue a settlement. In trying to resolve the claims, the banks, however, made yet another horrible misstep. Rather than privately meeting with the plaintiffs' lawyers and the WJC representatives to negotiate a settlement, the banks publicly announced in a press conference on June 19, 1998, that they were ready to settle the claims for $600 million. This amount, they insisted, was their top offer.

Jewish leaders were outraged, calling the amount insultingly low. At this point, Hevesi moved into action. Along with New York State Comptroller H. Carl McCall, Hevesi announced at a press conference on July 2, 1998, in Manhattan, his system of so-called rolling sanctions, specifically "designed to pressure Swiss banks into reaching an agreement with Holocaust victims who claimed the institutions held their assets for decades."[54] Officials in other states urged that sanctions against the Swiss banks be imposed immediately. California Treasurer Matt Fong, then running on the Republican ticket for the U.S. Senate, called for the immediate pullout of California investments from the Swiss banks. Hevesi urged otherwise.

Hevesi brilliantly figured out that a more useful club to wield against the banks would be merely to threaten sanctions and to announce a plan for their actual imposition in the future. Thus, Hevesi's "rolling sanctions" would be implemented as follows: (1) if a settlement was not reached by September 1, 1998, the New York state and city comptrollers would stop depositing their short-term investments with the Swiss banks and would bar Swiss banks and investment firms from selling state and city debt; (2) if a settlement still was not reached by November 1, 1998, private investment managers investing for the state and city would be instructed to cease trading through Swiss firms; and (3) finally, other unspecified sanctions would follow if the matter was still pending.

The Swiss government joined the Swiss banks in protesting the sanctions. The Swiss business community placed full-page ads in the *New York Times* and other papers to gather public support against the moves against the Swiss, warning of a trade war between the two nations. Eizenstat, under instructions from the federal government, called the move "counterproductive" and urged Hevesi to drop it. Testifying before the Senate Banking Committee, Eizenstat explained:

> Mr. Chairman, I get paid to make judgments about how our actions affect foreign countries. I can assure you that far from helping Holocaust survivors achieve a just and fair settlement, sanctions can delay and retard the process—making it more difficult for us to get a measure of justice for Holocaust survivors.[55]

Hevesi and McCall held firm.

A month later, the Swiss banks capitulated. In August 1998, they reversed their earlier position and raised to $1.25 billion what they had insisted two months earlier was their first and last offer of $600 million. The plaintiffs' attorneys, demanding $1.5 billion, agreed to accept this amount, and the case was settled.

Asked to explain the banks' sudden reversal of their position, Rabbi Marvin Hier, head of the Simon Wiesenthal Center, explained: "It was for only one reason: they were pressured into it. Without the pressure, without Senator D'Amato's banking committee, without the threat of sanctions, the Holocaust survivors would have gotten nothing."[56]

In a story examining how the Swiss settlement was achieved, the *Financial Times* came to the same conclusion:

> The clearest lesson from the Swiss banks' $1.25 billion settlement with Holocaust survivors is this: threatening to impose sanctions can work. Every important breakthrough in the negotiations came soon after threats from U.S. local government officials to impose sanctions. . . . The settlement itself came two weeks before a threat to start the sanctions and a week after Moody's, the rating agency, published a report saying that UBS, Switzerland's (and Europe's) biggest bank, might lose its triple-A rating if sanctions were imposed.[57]

With this victory, Hevesi and his Executive Committee had now become a potent force in the Holocaust restitution movement. Subsequent settlements—with the German and French banks, with German industries over the wartime use of slave labor, with the European insurers—all carry the stamp of Hevesi's efforts.

Why did sanctions work for Hevesi, a local city official, when they were so ineffective when wielded by the U.S. government? The main difference was that Hevesi's sanctions were not applied against a foreign government but against private banks. True, in terms of wealth, these banks are more powerful than most of the world's nations and so should have been able to withstand the financial losses imposed by the sanctions. However, as corporate multinationals, the banks ultimately are rational decision makers. Faced with the likely possibility of substantial financial losses from the threatened sanctions, the banks, looking at the economic bottom line, made the rational choice that it would be cheaper for them to settle than to continue to fight the claims. "Without a doubt," one commentator noted, "the Swiss banks were pushed into a settlement because of their fear of being shut out of vital U.S. markets."[58] Rulers of foreign governments, on the other hand, and especially the megalomaniacs on whom sanctions are most often imposed, do not necessarily follow the rational model. Although pride, quest for power, and various other noneconomic factors are used by government rulers in the face of outside pressure, all of these were absent among the bankers sitting in the Swiss boardrooms coolly deciding how to deal with the Holocaust-era claims.

In addition, the sanctions against the Swiss banks were threatened for a single, limited purpose: to affect the outcome of a particular lawsuit. Never before have sanctions, either in the United States or abroad, been applied with such a narrow focus. Second, while their legality has never been tested in court, since the case settled before any court challenge to them was heard, it is quite possible that the sanctions would have been illegal. Indeed, sixteen months later, the U.S. Supreme Court issued a decision severely limiting the power of states and local officials to issue sanctions. The case involved the so-called Massachusetts Burma Law. To express its displeasure with Burma's dictatorial regime, Massachusetts severely restricted the ability of its state agencies to purchase goods and services from companies doing business in Burma. The Supreme Court struck down the law on the ground that it unconstitutionally infringed on the federal government's exclusive power over foreign affairs.[59] This was the very same argument made by Eizenstat in urging New York to drop the threat of sanctions against the Swiss.

THE $1.25 BILLION SETTLEMENT

The negative publicity generated by Estelle Sapir's accusations against Credit Suisse, the embarrassment of the Union Bank of Switzerland (UBS) over the Meili episode, and, of course, the threat of sanctions from Hevesi were critical factors leading to the resolution of the Swiss banks' settlement.

Before the settlement was completed, however, the plaintiffs' attorneys had to take one more step. In June 1998, they opened a second front in the litigation against the Swiss banks by filing an additional lawsuit in a California state court. The Swiss banks now had to defend themselves on both coasts of the United States. One day before filing the California action, the attorneys filed yet another lawsuit, this time against the Swiss National Bank (SNB), the Swiss government's central bank.

The litigation against SNB stemmed in large part from an interim report issued a month earlier by the Bergier Commission, the multinational panel of historians created by the Swiss government and headed by the Swiss historian Jean-François Bergier.[60] The report's findings were devastating. Like the U.S. government's Eizenstat report, issued a year earlier, the Bergier report completely negated the image of wartime innocence that Switzerland had created for itself. This time, however, the findings were made by a Swiss government historical commission, not a foreign body. (In 2002, the Bergier Commission issued its final report, which went even further than this interim study in implicating Switzerland and its industries for their wartime financial dealings with the Nazis and other activities that helped perpetuate the Holocaust).

In a gesture of a painful mea culpa, the commission found that "Switzerland was the leading center of German gold transactions abroad during World War II and the [SNB] was the biggest client, buying 1.2 billion Swiss francs' worth, or about $280 million at wartime prices . . . worth more than $2.5 billion today." It further found that part of the gold that the SNB had purchased from the Nazi Reichsbank included "119.5 kilograms of fine gold (worth $1.2 million at today's prices) that could be identified as being melted down by the Nazi bankers into gold bars from teeth fillings and wedding rings torn away from the victims in the Nazi concentration camps." Most serious, the commission declared that the SNB was fully aware of the origins of the gold it was buying from Nazi Germany:

> There is no longer any doubt. The governing board of the National Bank was informed at an early point in time that gold from the central banks of occupied nations was being held by the Reichsbank, and the Swiss National Bank was also aware of other methods used by the Germans to confiscate gold from private individuals before and after the outbreak of the war.

"Other methods," of course, was a euphemistic way of referring to the brutal ways in which the gold was taken from the Jews, including ripping gold teeth from the victims. The report concluded: "Although it was plain for all to see that Germany was acquiring gold by illegal means, the [Swiss] authorities appear to have remained wedded to 'business as usual.'" In a country where the private banks and the government bank are viewed as parallel institutions, the Bergier Commission's report was as damaging to the private banks' image as to the SNB.

As mentioned earlier, on June 19, 1998, the bank defendants came to the bargaining table offering $600 million to settle the class action litigation. By this time, UBS had merged with Swiss Bank Corporation, and so UBS would be paying two-thirds of the amount, with Credit Suisse responsible for the other one-third. To buttress their position, the U.S. heads of the two banks submitted an editorial to the *Washington Post* entitled "What's Right with the Swiss Banks' Offer," characterizing the offer as "substantial."[61] The two banks maintained that they would not engage in any further negotiations. The $600 million was their first and last offer. Two months later, on August 12, 1998, the banks settled for $1.25 billion, more than twice that amount.

The person most responsible for putting the deal together was Judge Edward Korman, the Brooklyn federal judge presiding over the litigation. His successful efforts in both the settlement and the all-important implementation phase of the agreement have made him one of the champions of the Holocaust restitution movement.

In August 1998, almost two years after the lawsuits were filed, the cases had hardly moved forward. Initially, the Swiss banks, like other major corporations facing lawsuits, hired top-notch legal counsel. The defense lawyers' standard response was to challenge the suits on procedural grounds. Rather than answering the lawsuits and thereby allowing the cases to proceed to trial, the banks' lawyers filed extensive motions to dismiss (totaling more than five hundred pages of briefs and supporting documents), presenting every conceivable reason why the suits should be thrown out of court. The banks argued that American courts lacked jurisdiction over the cases; that the claimants who sued had no right to represent the class of Holocaust survivors on whose behalf they were attempting to file the class actions; that the suits were time barred (had come too late); that the suits should be transferred to Swiss courts; and, finally, that the litigation was unnecessary, since the banks already had in place a nonadversarial mechanism in Switzerland, the Volcker Committee, to handle the claims. Swiss Ambassador Alfred Defago also wrote to Judge Korman, urging dismissal of the suits. According to Defago, "The most effective and just means for dealing with these matters are in Switzerland, not in a United States court. . . . The Government of Switzerland urges the Court to dismiss the lawsuits."[62]

In turn, the plaintiffs filed their own voluminous responses, arguing that the suits should be allowed to go forward. By the time that all the papers and exhibits were filed, they totaled more than two thousand pages. Rather than rule on all the motions, Judge Korman, in a brilliant tactical move, let both sides stew for a while by not issuing a decision.

Meanwhile, Hevesi and other state and local government officials put pressure on the banks by calling for a boycott of the Swiss banks.

On July 28, 1998, sensing that the timing was right, Korman called a meeting of the attorneys representing both sides. Rather than meeting in chambers, he selected a more conducive venue. In an unorthodox move, Korman invited the parties to meet for dinner at Gage & Tollner, a restaurant in Brooklyn near the courthouse. Also present was Rabbi Israel Singer, the WJC representative who had first brought the dormant accounts issue to the attention of Edgar Bronfman Sr. While the attorneys and Judge Korman feasted on crab soup, steak, and broiled salmon, Singer did not eat. Gage & Tollner was not kosher.

Korman allowed both sides to make their best case before him. He listened and then tried to fashion a settlement. It didn't work. The dinner guests paid their separate checks and left the restaurant without a deal. But Korman did leave the parties with two proposals. Each offered a different way to settle the cases. The plaintiffs' attorneys, who demanded $20 billion in their lawsuits, revealed to Korman that they would settle for $1.5 billion. The banks were still stuck at $600 million. The negotiations continued over the next two days, with Korman stepping in when necessary. Senator D'Amato also joined the talks.

The Swiss banks preferred Korman's proposal, according to which they would not have to make one lump payment. Instead, they agreed to divide the settlement into four equal installments, the first to be paid upon settlement, with the remaining three over the next three years. With revenues in the billions, the banks had no problem, of course, making one lump-sum payment, but it was a matter of principle.

On August 12, 1998, a final figure was reached: $1.25 billion, with the banks receiving a credit for payments made by any Swiss bank for dormant accounts traced by the Volcker Committee. Then, a misunderstanding occurred. The banks believed that they would not have to pay any interest on the three annual installments. Not so, according to the plaintiffs' attorneys. The talks were on the verge of breaking down over the interest issue. Judge Korman implored both sides to continue. Eventually, D'Amato came up with a figure of 3.78 percent, a rate whose rationale "is one of the enduring mysteries of the world," according to one source in the talks. Interest would begin accruing on

January 2001, after the third installment was paid, and would also accrue on the fourth and final installment, due in November 2001.

The deal was announced in open court on August 13, 1998, with a tired but pleased Judge Korman presiding.

SORTING OUT THE SETTLEMENT

As the settlement with the Swiss banks was coming to a close, one lawyer intimately involved with the negotiations worried that in the allocation process following the settlement, the worst was yet to come:

> You've got the general European Jews, the Eastern European Jews. You've got the government of Israel; you've got thousands of individual survivors; you've got all kinds of other groups, arguing that portions of the money should be aside for different purposes in the Jewish community. It's not going to be an easy task. The fight against the Swiss is going to be nothing compared to the attempt to mediate the various interests.[63]

Unfortunately, the lawyer was right, but only partially. It took more than three years to complete the settlement and distribute the money to the claimants, longer than the actual litigation against the Swiss banks. Some of the delays were avoidable; others were not. Although many factors contributed to the delays, infighting was not one of them.

As the parties envisioned the settlement in mid-August 1998, the distribution of the funds to survivors would start soon after the Swiss banks made the first of their four installment payments, beginning with the first on November 23, 1998. The elderly claimants, however, would not have to wait to collect their funds until November 23, 2001, when banks were to make the final installment. Professor Burt Neuborne, special counsel for the plaintiffs whom Judge Korman in February 1999 appointed as the plaintiffs' lead settlement counsel, strongly believed at the time of the settlement that the banks would make their payments ahead of schedule, thereby putting the matter behind them.

Nothing of the sort happened. While the Swiss banks dutifully made their four scheduled payments, they nevertheless interjected significant obstacles that delayed their distribution. As a result, the money remained stuck in a court-created escrow account as the parties continued to wrangle over the fine points of the settlement. By the time the first payments went out in late 2001, many of the survivors who joyously hailed the settlement in mid-1998 had died while waiting for their check. Others just gave up, exasperated not only by the numerous delays but also with the complicated forms they were made to fill out in order to receive the settlement proceeds.

Some of the seeds causing the long delays were planted at the time of the settlement. Essentially, the parties failed to work out many of the critical details when they announced the historic settlement in August 1998, and these details later came back to haunt them. Of course, with the September 1, 1998, deadline for issuing further sanctions against the Swiss banks looming just two weeks away, the parties in the litigation cannot be blamed for settling the case without first working out these thorny issues. This mentality of "let's just take the money and run," however, created a host of problems that haunted Judge Korman and all the parties over the next three years.

Other delays could not be avoided, being the usual consequence of having to follow U.S. court rules, especially those dealing with class action litigation. These rules, with their emphasis on ensuring fairness and avoiding prejudice against any actual or potential claimant, naturally slowed down the postsettlement process and delayed the distribution of any settlement funds. Lawyers are used to these postsettlement delays, but the survivors found them frustrating. As Morris Ratner explained, "What you call delay, I call ensuring that due process was served." Ratner pointed out that the victims had input into the allocation of the settlement, which both slowed down the payments and ensured a democratic process. "The amount available to be paid to most of the victims was symbolic," he asserted. "It was just as important, symbolically, that they have a role in their own settlement."[64]

The postsettlement resolution process had an inauspicious start, a sign of worse things to come. To complete the written settlement agreement, it took the parties more than five months after the settlement was orally agreed on and tentatively approved by Judge Korman in open court in August 1998.

After the settlement agreement was finally signed, on January 26, 1999, Judge Korman laid out a timetable according to which the more than one million potential beneficiaries, the class members on whose behalf the suits were filed, were to be notified of the settlement. These nearly one million potential claimants were not only Jews. Neither were they restricted to individuals whose relatives had deposited money in a Swiss bank before the war. Rather, because the Swiss banks were accused in these lawsuits not only of wrongfully keeping such deposited funds but also of earning money by trading with the Nazis in goods made by slave labor and in possessions looted from victims (including gold), the beneficiaries of the Swiss banks had to include victims of these Nazi policies as well.

The class action notices went out in early summer 1999. A potential claimant had until October 22, 1999, to opt out of the settlement if he or she still wanted to pursue an individual action against the Swiss banks.

The duty to notify potential beneficiaries of a class action settlement is legally required for all U.S. class actions. In this case, however, the notification process was, as described by the *Los Angeles Times*, "the most ambitious effort ever to notify potential beneficiaries of a legal settlement."[65] Since the potential recipients of the Swiss funds could be anywhere in the world, advertisements announcing the settlement were published in five hundred newspapers, in more than forty countries, and in languages ranging from Albanian to Yiddish. Toll-free telephone information lines were created in each of the countries. For the computer literate, an official Web site was created, www.swissbankclaims .com, in which every court document, beginning with the January 1999 settlement agreement, was posted. The Web site itself used twenty languages. A Portland–based company specializing in class action notification was hired as a notice administrator to interface with the claimants, and another company in Wisconsin was made responsible for community outreach. As Ratner asserted, "No one has ever reached out to as many survivors as we did."[66]

Judge Korman allocated $25 million, or 2 percent of the $1.25 billion settlement, for notification and other distribution expenses. Before the case was finally concluded, the entire $25 million had been spent.

On June 9, 1999, Professor Neuborne, the chief settlement counsel, sent the first in a series of letters to the claimants. In the letter, Neuborne apologized for the delays that had already taken place and advised them of further impediments in the future:

> All of us who have worked on this Settlement regret that we cannot move more quickly in distributing the funds. It is our duty, however, to assure that everyone affected by the Settlement is given a chance

to comment on its fairness, and to have an opportunity to express an opinion about the fairest way to allocate and distribute the funds. That takes time. . . . Because we all feel so deeply about the Holocaust, we want this process to treat every survivor with scrupulous fairness.

Two days later, on June 11, 1999, the official "Notice of Pendency of Class Action and Proposed Settlement and Hearing," likewise required by class action court rules, was mailed to every person responding to the newspaper notices or contacting the Web site. The notice contained an "Initial Questionnaire," which claimants were asked to fill out in order to register their claim.

The questionnaire immediately came under heavy criticism. It was long and complicated; worst, it asked claimants to recount in detail their Holocaust experiences. Elihu Kover, director of a New York agency helping aging survivors fill out the questionnaire, complained, "Clients look at this 20-page thing and they don't understand it. It's not like filling out a welfare application. It's an emotional issue. This is pretty complicated and stressful."[67] In fact, it was only six pages long, but as one critic told me, "It sure seemed like 20 pages."

An elderly couple in Los Angeles, both survivors of Auschwitz, asked me to help them fill out the form. It took a few hours. The wife started to cry when she began to recount her arrival and the selection process at Auschwitz. That was the last time she saw her mother and infant nephew, who perished in the gas chambers. We all were exhausted when the evening ended.

Eventually, a total of 580,000 Initial Questionnaires were submitted, with less than 20 percent claiming restitution of a Swiss dormant bank account. Of those, only 6 percent could name the particular Swiss bank purportedly holding the prewar money deposited by their relatives. All the other applicants were survivors asking for compensation because they had been slave laborers under the Nazis or had their possessions looted, or both.

On November 29, 1999, Judge Korman held a "fairness hearing" to determine whether the $1.25 billion settlement was "fair, adequate, and reasonable"—again, a requirement of class action rules. Of course, in this case the result was pretty much preordained. Since Korman had already approved the settlement in principle in August 1998, he was unlikely now to reject it, unless, of course, the final terms differed radically from the settlement presented to him by all sides a year earlier. They did not.

Nevertheless, the hearing brought up problems that had not been envisioned when the parties had completed their deal. For example, individuals appeared at the hearing claiming that the Swiss were still holding Nazi-stolen art belonging to them. Under the settlement agreement, these art claims would be extinguished through the Swiss banks' settlements. In response, Judge Korman modified the settlement to keep open these art claims (see chapter 5 for discussion of Holocaust looted art claims). In addition to the hearing in his Brooklyn courtroom, Korman also scheduled a few weeks later a hearing for the Holocaust survivors in Israel. The hearing was held through a teleconference, so the Israeli survivors would not have to come to the United States to be heard.

On August 9, 2000, two years after the initial settlement, Korman signed his final order and judgment approving the settlement agreement as fair, adequate, and reasonable. But it almost did not happen, for at the last moment, the Swiss banks threatened to pull out of the deal. After Judge Korman reminded the Swiss banks that they must "act responsibly,"[68] they retracted their threat.

The thorniest issue now was how to allocate the $1.25 billion. To assist him with this task, Judge Korman in 1998 selected Judah Gribetz, a respected Jewish community leader and New York attorney who had served as counsel to New York Governor Hugh Carey, as "special master" to work out an allocation plan. Gribetz's unenviable task was to receive written suggestions about how to divide the funds and to issue a plan of allocation that Korman would then approve. Anyone could submit a suggestion, and Gribetz received more than one thousand comments on how to allocate the funds.[69] In September 2000, Gribetz submitted to Judge Korman his Proposed Plan of Allocation and Distribution. The plan was more than nine hundred pages long.

I confess to having pored over the plan for days, attempting to make full sense of it. It was a daunting task. To help with the process, Gribetz issued a thirty-eight-page overview and a seven-page summary of the plan.[70]

In drawing up his allocation plan, Gribetz did not have free rein over how to distribute the $1.25 billion. Rather, he was constrained by the limitations on distribution already spelled out in the settlement agreement signed by the parties in January 1999.

That agreement contained terms that both surprised and angered many who were following the litigation. Most curiously, the agreement did not limit the eligible claimants to Jews. Rather, in addition to Jewish victims or their heirs, it added four other groups persecuted by the Nazis who would share in the settlement proceeds: (1) homosexuals, (2) physically or mentally disabled or handicapped persons, (3) the Romani (Gypsy) peoples, and (4) Jehovah's Witnesses. These five categories of eligible claimants were given the lauded status in the agreement of "Victims or Targets of Nazi Persecution" (VTNP).[71]

Throughout the course of the litigation, the common understanding was that the lawsuits against the Swiss banks were filed on behalf of Jewish victims. All the named plaintiffs in the lawsuits before Judge Korman were Jewish survivors.[72] Also, only Jewish groups participated in the litigation and settlement negotiations. Last, the parties' briefs uniformly labeled the class members as being victims of "the Holocaust," the term referring to the killing and persecution of European Jewry during the war. This belief—that only Jews would recover in the Swiss class action litigation—continued even at the time of the August 1998 settlement. Press releases announcing the settlement praised the benefits that Holocaust survivors would be receiving from the resolution of the litigation.[73]

Little attention was paid, however, to the fact that the class of plaintiffs designated in all but one of the complaints against the Swiss banks (the World Council of Orthodox Jewish Communities was filed on behalf of Jewish victims only), categorized the claimants as being both Jewish and non-Jewish. Credit—or blame—goes to the plaintiffs' lawyers. Not able to predict which categories of plaintiffs would ultimately succeed in the litigation, the lawyers took the safest route when filing the suits and defined as broadly as possible the class members on whose behalf they were suing.

Having opened the door for non-Jewish victims to share in the Swiss settlement, the settling parties, however, excluded groups who rightly also fit the label "Victims or Targets of Nazi Persecution." Most significantly, the settlement excluded the entire category of Slavic peoples—primarily Poles and Russians—who suffered horribly at the hands of the Nazis.[74]

The decision to include some non-Jewish victims and exclude others was made exclusively by the plaintiffs' lawyers and senior WJC officials. The included groups did not lobby to be included in the settlement. Professor Burt Neuborne explained how the cutoff was determined:

> We had to walk a fine line between everyone harmed by the Nazis—which is virtually all of Europe—or only the Jews. . . . Both extremes were unacceptable. The first would have so diluted the recovery it would have rendered the whole suit meaningless. . . . The second would have made it unfairly parochial.[75]

The excluded victims, such as non-Jewish ethnic Slavs from eastern Europe, had to console themselves with the hope of future recovery from the ongoing slave labor litigation against the German firms. As it turned out, the actual distribution of funds from both the Swiss and German settlements occurred at about the same time, even though the Swiss banks settled a year and a half before the German firms did (see chapter 2). Because of the various delays in distributing the Swiss settlement funds, the non-Jewish VTNPs in the Swiss settlement did not receive their checks any sooner than the non-Jewish beneficiaries of the German settlement did. The Jewish survivors, eligible to receive funds from both the Swiss and German settlements, received their settlement checks almost at the same time, even though the Swiss litigation concluded eighteen months earlier. Gribetz's actual dollar figure allocations for each VTNP class also closely followed the categories of claimants set out in the settlement agreement.

The first set of claimants who had sued the Swiss banks were persons seeking to recover money deposited with the Swiss banks for safekeeping before or during the war. Claimants to these dormant accounts were designated in the settlement agreement as the "Deposited Assets Class." Since the original purpose for the Swiss bank litigation was to obtain the return of these funds, Gribetz felt bound to allocate the largest portion of the settlement—up to $800 million—for this class of claimants. Since less than 20 percent of the 580,000 people who completed the Initial Questionnaires made a claim for deposited bank assets, it appears that the entire $800 million will not be used for payments to this class. But to cover that contingency, Gribetz recommended that any unused portion of the $800 million be allocated through a secondary distribution to the other groups of claimants.

While the original gravamen of the complaints was to accuse the Swiss banks of failing to return money deposited with them for safe-keeping, the complaints also blamed the banks for engaging during wartime in three other types of wrongful conduct.

First, the Swiss banks were accused of knowingly trading with the Nazis in goods made by slave labor by either purchasing those goods directly from the Nazis or financing the importation of such goods into Switzerland. These allegations were based on the various books published at the time exposing the Swiss banks as being the secret bankers for the Nazis. This class was designated in the settlement agreement as "Slave Labor I Claims."

Second, the lawsuits also alleged that some Swiss companies directly owned or controlled factories in Germany or Nazi-occupied Europe that used slave labor. Those persons who worked for such Swiss-run companies were designated as a separate class, known as "Slave Labor II Claims."

Third, the Swiss banks were also accused in the suits of helping the Nazis launder profits that they earned from goods looted from Jews. This class was designated as the "Looted Assets Claims."

In their pleadings, the plaintiffs alleged that the defendant Swiss banks earned more than $75 million by knowingly trafficking in looted assets and assets produced by Nazi slave labor and that the current value of such profits earned by the defendant banks was in excess of $1 billion.

Finally, the Swiss government had earlier admitted that it denied entry to Jews and other persecuted groups fleeing the Nazis. The private Swiss bank defendants insisted that this so-called Refugee Class be included in the settlement. Their goal was to extinguish all World War II–related claims against Switzerland and its industries through this settlement. Now came the hardest part: dividing up the remaining $450 million and accrued interest of approximately $100 million among these non-deposited-assets groups.

As already noted, almost all the 580,000 persons who returned the Initial Questionnaires made claims based on these latter allegations, and not for the return of money deposited in the Swiss banks. Since the worldwide advertising campaign encouraged anyone with a likely claim to fill out the questionnaire, it turned out that many of the applications for these nondeposit claims came not from the survivors themselves but from people claiming to be their heirs.

Gribetz, along with Neuborne, quickly realized that the list of eligible persons for these latter claims would need to be drastically reduced. As they explained,

> There is simply not enough money available to make direct payments to most heirs in the slave labor, refugee and looted assets classes. Otherwise, so many payments would be required and so much of the Settlement Fund would be used up for costly eligibility determinations that everyone essentially would get nothing.[76]

Another practical problem was that none of the Holocaust survivors named as plaintiffs—or, for that matter, any other survivor—could prove that the benefits the Nazis earned from their slave labor or looted assets made their way into the Swiss banks' coffers.

To avoid these practical difficulties, Gribetz recommended that every person who was a former slave or forced laborer under the Nazis—and who fit one of the VTNP categories—receive the same amount: somewhere between $500 and $1,000, the final figure depending on the number of VNTP claimants applying for these funds. The actual amount turned out to be closer to $1,500 for each VTNP slave laborer. Judge Korman initially authorized payouts of $1,000 and then in September 2002 added an additional $450 when Gribetz informed him that enough interest had been earned on the still-undisbursed funds to increase the payment to each VTNP claimant by 45 percent. The claimant did not have to prove the link to the Swiss banks; proof of being a forced or slave laborer under the Nazis would suffice.[77] The heirs of such former laborers would be excluded, with one exception: if an eligible claimant was alive on February 15, 1999, but subsequently died, the decedent's heirs could collect the payment.[78]

For the looted claims, Gribetz took another tack. Concluding that every VTNP claimant must have had some assets stolen from them by the Nazis and that tracing such assets or proceeds to benefits earned by the Swiss banks from the Nazi-stolen loot was impossible, the proposed plan simply excluded payments to claimants seeking compensation for looted assets. As Gribetz explained:

> There is hardly a victim of the Nazis who was not looted, and on nearly an incomprehensible scale. . . . Plundered loot took a variety of paths once it had been seized. . . . It is neither justifiable nor appropriate to

select which looting victims may be entitled to recompense from this U.S. $1.25 billion Settlement Fund based entirely upon the happenstance of where the Nazi Regime chose to direct which loot, which records of plunder happen to survive, and which items one may hazard a guess may have found their way to or through Switzerland.[79]

Instead, Gribetz allocated $145 million to this category, which was then disbursed through existing charity programs to needy VTNP survivors. Most of the funds went to aid elderly Jewish survivors in the former Soviet Union, the so-called double victims, since they had been excluded from earlier German reparations programs while living behind the Iron Curtain and were now in dire need in the aftermath of the economic collapse of the former Soviet republics.

Those refugees who were still living and who were denied entry into, or expelled from, Switzerland during wartime were allocated $3,625 each. This group was small, totaling no more than a few thousand, and so each one eventually received a greater amount.

On November 20, 2000, Judge Korman held a second court hearing, this time to get reactions to Gribetz's allocation plan. At the hearing, various VTNP groups argued that their share of the proceeds should be increased. Other groups, not included in the distribution (such as heirs of the VTNPs or non-VTNP groups), claimed that they should be included in the settlement. Korman rejected all the objections or proposed modifications and approved Gribetz's Plan of Allocation and Distribution in full two days later.

DISTRIBUTING THE SETTLEMENT

With an allocation scheme in place, the next step was to begin the claims process and, when that was completed, to begin the actual distribution of the funds. Unfortunately, more delays arose.

The Swiss banks refused to issue a complete list of possible dormant accounts. Volcker's audit of the Swiss banks determined that 4.1 million bank accounts had been opened in Switzerland between 1933 and 1945. Of these, 53,886 accounts could have belonged to victims of Nazi persecution, with 21,000 probably so linked. Volcker's report urged that the names of all these account holders be published.[80] But the Swiss banks balked, arguing that they would be flooded with doubtful claims. The banks' position was untenable. Without a full disclosure of all suspected dormant accounts, potential heirs would never know whether money belonging to them might be sitting in a Swiss bank. Only with the publication of a complete list of names could those believing that they might be entitled to dormant account money determine whether a deceased relative had in fact opened an account with the Swiss banks. Previous experience had already born this out. In 1997, when the Swiss Bankers Association published two lists of prewar dormant accounts, Madeline Kunin, U.S. ambassador to Switzerland, discovered her mother's name on the list. Secretary of State Madeline Albright likewise found out that her Czech grandparents, who perished in the Holocaust, had opened a bank account in Switzerland before the war.

Judge Korman agreed that the Swiss banks should publish their dormant account list and chastised the banks for failing to do so:

> On March 30, 2000, after an inordinately long and unexplained delay
> . . . the Swiss Federal Banking Commission ("SFBC") authorized publication of . . . 26,000 of the accounts referred to in the Volcker Report that were identified as a having a "probable" link to Holocaust victims. No authorization was given by the SFBC for the publication of the approximately 28,000 remaining accounts identified in the Volcker Report as "possibly" related to Holocaust victims. . . . Perhaps even more disturbing was the failure of the SFBC to mandate the creation of a central database of 4.1 million accounts that were opened in Switzerland between 1933–45. . . . The unwillingness of the SFBC to mandate compliance with the recommendations of the Volcker Committee is inexplicable. . . . It also amounts to nothing less than a replay of the conduct that created the problems addressed in this case.[81]

Korman also reprimanded the nondefendant Swiss cantonal and private banks, which wanted to be included in the settlement but refused to reveal information about their dormant wartime accounts. "It is disturbing, to say the least," he commented, "that having participated in creating the problem that the Volcker Committee was attempting to address, the Swiss private and cantonal banks do not feel a moral obligation to the victims of Nazi persecution."[82]

Unfortunately, there was no leverage to apply against the banks. In February 2001, after some hard-fought negotiations, the Swiss banks agreed to publish only the names of the 21,000 probable account holders, in addition to the two lists of names of dormant account holders published in 1997. As a compromise, a person could still make a claim even if his or her name was not on the list, and such a claim would be investigated. To process the dormant account claims under the settlement, Judge Korman brought onboard the Zurich-based Claims Resolution Tribunal (CRT), created in 1997 by the Swiss Bankers Association and led by Paul Volcker to process the claims stemming from the banks' publication of their initial two lists. Judge Korman formally made the CRT part of the court settlement process by appointing Volcker and Michael Bradfield, his chief legal counsel, as special masters for resolving the dormant account claims.[83]

Disputes about disclosure arose also with regard to the class of claimants entitled to compensation for having worked for a Swiss-owned or controlled company that may have used slave labor. Swiss companies did not employ slave labor in Switzerland during the war; however, many Swiss companies had branches in Germany or Nazi-occupied Europe and were suspected of having used slave laborers. The plaintiffs' representatives wanted the Swiss to publish the names of all such companies. They argued that a former slave laborer most likely would not have known whether the company for which he or she was forced to work was, in fact, Swiss owned or controlled. Again, the Swiss objected to full disclosure. To move the process forward, in April 2001, the Swiss published a partial list as well as another partial list of refugees expelled from or denied entry into Switzerland during the war.

In mid-April 2001, five months after Korman approved Gribetz's plan, the claims process for the Swiss settlement formally began. Unfortunately, claimants in all categories were required to complete another form to apply formally for funds, even if they earlier had completed the Initial Questionnaire.

Two sets of appeals also had to be dealt with before distribution could begin. In September 2000, the Second Circuit dismissed an appeal by a Polish American organization that argued that ethnic Poles should be included in the settlement.[84] In July 2001, the Second Circuit dismissed an appeal by three Jewish survivors who claimed that Gribetz's plan of allocation was unfair.[85]

In July 2001, five years after the start of the litigation against the Swiss banks and close to three years after the settlement was announced at the Brooklyn federal courthouse, payments of approximately $1,000 finally began to dribble in to aging survivors. By then, all involved were thoroughly exhausted by the ordeal.

As of this writing, the distribution of the Swiss settlement funds is continuing, albeit more slowly than expected. By the summer of 2002, CRT II had processed fewer than 200 claims out of the 32,000 filed, 12,000 of which matched a name on one of the dormant account lists published by the Swiss banks. Out of the $800 million allocated by Gribetz and approved by Judge Korman, less than $20 million had been distributed by CRT II, administered by Volcker and Bradfield.

In June 2002, Judge Korman, as overseer of the settlement, took matters into his own hands. He issued a new set of rules aimed at speeding up the payments to the dormant account claims. The rules consisted of new, relaxed, presumptions that the CRT II staff had to apply when assessing the claim. Under these presumptions (available on the CRT II Web site, www.crt-ii.org), if evidence of an account were found, the CRT II must assume that the money in the account had not been paid and was due to the claimant, unless there was clear evidence to the contrary. The presumptions were triggered by the Final Report issued by the Swiss government's Bergier Commission in March 2002, which found that the Swiss banks had engaged in the wholesale destruction of their records after the war (see the following discussion). These relaxed presumptions allow claimants to receive payment of the discovered account even if records regarding payment are not available. Moreover, the same presumption of nonpayment applies to claims on Holocaust-era insurance policies (see chapter 3).

The overhaul of CRT II helped. Five months later, in November 2002, the total tally for both the number of claims processed and the amount of funds awarded had doubled. More than four hundred claims had now been processed, and the total amount awarded to dormant account claimants had risen to $53 million, including one monumental award: 7,117,236 Swiss francs, or more than $4.8 million, issued on November 8, 2002.

The seventy-seven-year-old claimant, who requested that her identity remain secret, is one of the three daughters of Dr. Otto Fuchs, a well-to-do Czech patent attorney from Brno, the second largest city in the Czech Republic. Dr. Fuchs, who was Jewish, was arrested after the Nazi takeover of Czechoslovakia and sent to a concentration camp. He survived the war, along with two of his three daughters, including the claimant. Dr. Fuchs died in Czechoslovakia in 1957. The other daughter died in 1998 and was survived by her own daughter, the claimant's niece.

Dr. Otto Fuchs had an unmarried sister, Maria Fuchs, who perished during the war. She was a concert singer and lived in Berlin. After Hitler came to power, Maria fled to Brno where she was arrested by the Germans and shipped off to a concentration camp in Poland, from which she never returned.

In 1999, the claimant, still living in Brno, filed two Initial Questionnaires under the Swiss bank settlement. She indicated that she believed that her father might have opened a Swiss bank account before the war because he had had business connections with Swiss colleagues at that time. The CRT II investigators found a demand deposit account for an Otto Fuchs from Brno, which was closed in March 1941, two years after the Nazi takeover of Czechoslovakia. The bank records did not show the amount in the account or whether, or to whom, the proceeds of the account were paid. But there also was no evidence that Dr. Fuchs ever closed the account or received the funds. Without additional information, the CRT II applied the above-mentioned presumption that neither Dr. Fuchs nor his family ever received the proceeds of the account. Since the amount of the account could not be determined, the CRT II also applied its rule that in such an instance, it would use the average value of the same or a similar type of account in 1945. The average value figure that the CRT II used for a demand deposit account of the type held by Otto Fuchs was 2,140 Swiss francs.

The story of the Fuchs family does not end there. During their investigation, the CRT II staffers discovered that Otto Fuchs was the brother of the listed account owner, Maria Fuchs, who had opened accounts at another Swiss bank. (The CRT II would not identify either of the two Swiss banks where Otto Fuchs and Maria Fuchs had accounts.) The ICEP's list of "probable or possible" Nazi victim account holders contains the names of both "Frl. Maria Fuchs" from Germany and "Otto Fuchs" from Czechoslovakia (the list also contains eight other individuals with the last name of "Fuchs"). Further research showed that Maria Fuchs had seven different accounts at this unidentified Swiss bank, which the Swiss authorities froze during the war. The ICEP auditors surmised that the bank had closed the accounts after the war. Five of the accounts listed actual values; one account held an unknown value; and the last was tied to a safe deposit box, which Maria Fuchs had opened in February 1938. The bank forced open the box in March 1946. It contained an envelope with 1,000 Swiss francs marked "for Dr. Ing. Otto Fuchs" and listing his exact address in Brno. (The box also contained gold coins valued at 20,000 Swiss francs and 5,000 Swiss francs.)

In sum, no evidence existed that any member of the Fuchs family ever received Maria Fuchs's funds, and all indications are that the bank simply kept the money and the contents of the safe deposit box. Based on this and other persuasive evidence, the CRT II concluded that an award should be made to the claimant for the bank account opened by Otto Fuchs in the amount of 2,140 Swiss francs and for the seven accounts owned by Maria Fuchs totaling 590,963 Swiss francs, for a final award of 593,103 Swiss francs. After this amount was multiplied by 12 to arrive at the present value of the Fuchs's eight accounts, the claimant received an award of 7,117,236.00 Swiss francs, or $4,808,493.26, which she is sharing with her niece.

The Fuchs award was the largest payout on any Swiss dormant bank claim. It confirms what the plaintiffs' representatives had been saying all along, that before the war, Jews had deposited substantial funds for safekeeping in Swiss banks, but after the war, the banks had failed to return the funds. The critics' claim that the Swiss bank settlement was nothing more than a form of organized blackmail conducted by Jewish groups and American lawyers, with no evidence that the banks had cheated depositors or their heirs of money rightfully due to them, is directly contradicted by the Fuchs award. As the award decision explains, "After the War, account holders and their heirs would not have been able to obtain information about such accounts due to the Swiss banks' practice of withholding or misstating account information in their responses to inquiries because of the banks' concerns regarding double liability."[86]

How many more Fuchs-type awards remain unpaid? When I posed that question to Michael Bradfield, Judge Korman's special master with Paul Volcker at the CRT II, on the day that the Fuchs award was issued, he replied:

> There is not enough experience to make an estimate, but I can tell you the current value for twelve thousand of the accounts for which there is a match between an account and a claimant. For these accounts, using values in bank records, and average values for those accounts for which there are no values in bank records, and adjusting these

1933-to-1945 values to current values by multiplying by a factor of 12, the total value for these accounts is 925 million Swiss francs, or about $618 million. This is a useful number, but it does not tell you either the total number or the total amount of the awards, as a lot more analysis of these claims is necessary for an award to be determined.

The plan now is for the CRT II to complete in 2003 the claims process for the other outstanding claimants. But the tribunal has a long way to go: more than eleven thousand claims that match names on the Swiss banks' published account list must still be investigated, and $750 million (of the $800 million allocated by Gribetz) remains undisbursed. If the total amount of the dormant account claims does not use up the $800 million fund, a secondary distribution will be made. Gribetz again may be called on to recommend to Judge Korman how to distribute these leftover funds. As chapter 6 discusses in detail, this matter already is generating strong controversy.

THE AFTERMATH: WAS IT WORTH IT?

Was the Swiss banks' settlement worth it? Since the heart of the litigation against the Swiss banks was to recover money wrongfully kept by the banks for more than a half-century, the answer is definitely yes. The banks were made to give up these funds, and the funds were eventually—though much more slowly than anyone expected—distributed to the rightful claimants. In recognition of Switzerland's wartime financial alliance with Nazi Germany, those survivors not lucky enough to have had money left for them in secret Swiss banks accounts before the war—meaning almost all the survivors—also received some payouts from the settlement. The injuries to refugees denied entry to Switzerland and laborers forced to work as slaves for Swiss companies operating in Nazi Germany also were recognized, and compensation was paid to them. One hundred million dollars of the Swiss bank funds also went to provide immediate assistance to "neediest of the needy" Holocaust survivors, especially those in the former Soviet Union.

Having painted the beneficial consequences of the Swiss banks litigation, I concede that not all is so rosy. Other than the lucky few survivors who could lay claim to a dormant Swiss bank account, most elderly survivors received only a token sum of $1,000, which Judge Korman later raised to $1,450 on Gribetz's recommendation. (As of November 1, 2002, approximately 115,000 survivors had received this payment.) For this amount, they had been made to dredge up once again their painful wartime horrors.

From a legal point of view, the low payouts were justifiable. The essence of the Swiss bank litigation was to recover money kept by the banks after war, and so the only proper claimants to these funds were the actual account holders or their heirs. For this reason, Gribetz allocated the major portion of the $1.25 billion settlement—$800 million—for these claims. When this distribution allocation and the exclusion of other groups from the settlement were challenged on appeal, the Second Circuit twice upheld the settlement and found that of all the applicants, the dormant account claimants had the strongest legal case.[87] However, during the claims process, few survivors understood this. All were encouraged to apply for funds, and their expectations were raised and then lowered as the harsh reality sank in that the payments received by almost all the applicants would be minimal. Neuborne, in correspondence, defended the results:

> I share your concern over the limited recoveries going to Jewish slave laborers. Of course, the amount is too low. But, to be fair, you should note that the $1,000 figure was chosen because the German Foundation will provide an additional $7,500 to each slave laborer [see chapter 2] and that additional distributions are highly likely if the bank account fund is not fully exhausted. It is also unfair to characterize the Swiss recovery as $1,000 per survivor, when many thousands of bank account recoveries will be far greater.[88]

Nevertheless, the reality of how little each survivor was to receive was made even more painful when compared with the benefits received by other parties involved in the Swiss bank claims, none of whom were the actual victims of the wartime misdeeds.

First, the lawyers. In late 2002 and early 2003, Judge Korman awarded approximately $6 million in attorneys' fees, amounting to approximately one-half of 1 percent (0.05%) of the settlement. Korman set the fees based on recommendations made to him by Professor Burt Neuborne in his role as special settlement counsel. Neuborne pointed out that these awards were substantially lower than the amounts lawyers usually receive in successful class action cases, which would be "between 15% and 20% of the benefits generated by their efforts."[89] With this $1.25 billion settlement, Neuborne explained, the lawyers "could be expected to receive fee awards of between $200 and $300 million."[90] Three of the principal lawyers who litigated the Swiss bank case and led the negotiations—Neuborne himself, Michael Hausfeld, and Mel Weiss—waived their fees. Lieff Cabraser, for the work of Morris Ratner and others in the firm, asked for $1.5 million, which they donated to Columbia University Law School to establish a human rights legal clinic, and $100,000, which they gave to Greta Beer, a Holocaust survivor in her seventies who, like Estelle Sapir, campaigned for the Swiss banks to recognize the dormant account claims but whose father's prewar account she could never locate. The *pro bono* lawyers, however, went on to earn their million and more dollars from the subsequently filed German and Austrian slave labor and French bank litigation.

Second, the Jewish organizations. The WJC and other Jewish organizations used their work on the Swiss campaign (and the subsequently filed claims) not only to build their prestige in the Jewish community but also as a fund-raising tool, headlining their involvement with Holocaust restitution to solicit funds from their members.

Last, the politicians. Getting on the Holocaust restitution bandwagon became a popular means of getting votes. Sometimes, it worked (as in the case of the Florida insurance commissioner—now U.S. senator—Bill Nelson) and sometimes it did not (as in the case of Senator Alfonse D'Amato's failed reelection campaign).

All this does not take away from the hard work performed by many sincere and dedicated individuals, found in all three groups, which forced the Swiss to confront their wartime past. However, examining what the nonsurvivors received from the Swiss campaign makes the survivors' benefits seem quite meager.

Finally, there were two major injustices in the Swiss bank settlement. First, the Swiss banks were fortunate that the litigation concluded before all the facts about their nefarious activities had been fully revealed. In March 2002, after five years and $13 million, the Swiss government's Bergier Commission issued its final report.[91] The report confirmed that the Swiss banks had failed to return money and other assets deposited with them by Holocaust victims and that this failure was deliberate: "It is possible to speak of a deliberate classification of assets as 'unclaimed' and accounts as 'dormant' insofar as banks failed to co-operate actively after the Holocaust in surrendering the accounts, deposits or safe-deposit boxes they held and to assist relatives of murdered customers or restitution organizations."[92] The Bergier Commission historians also found that the Swiss banks had conspired together to reject rightful claims. "In 1954, the legal representatives of the big banks coordinated their response to heirs [of account holders] so that the banks would have at their disposal a concerted mechanism for deflecting any kind of enquiry."[93] Some of these "coordinated response[s]" included outright deception about the existence of information in their possession. As the Bergier report explains, "Some banks found it quite in order to give false information."[94] For other banks, their "aim [was] to find as few unclaimed assets as possible."[95]

Moreover, the banks did not stop there. They also urged the Swiss government not to enact laws that would have forced them to reveal these accounts. "The banks and their Association lobbied against legislation that would have required publication of the names of so called 'heirless assets accounts,' legislation that if enacted and implemented would have obviated the ICEP investigation and the controversy over the last thirty years."[96] Without such disclosure laws, "the claims of surviving Holocaust victims were usually rejected under the pretext of bank secrecy."[97]

The Swiss banks profited from these activities. "The banks were able to use the amounts remaining in the accounts and to earn income from them."[98] More egregiously, when claimants sought information about their accounts, they were charged search fees, which often exceeded the value of the account. "Examples show that claimants had to pay 25 francs in the 1950s and as much as 250 francs in the 1960s. Twenty years later, a search would cost 750 francs. Because dormant accounts often contained small amounts, these fees frequently exceeded the value of the assets being sought."[99] The banks also charged "administrative fees and other costs" against the dormant accounts and unclaimed safe-deposit boxes. Through the use of such fees, the banks simply made the accounts vanish. "Due to the deduction of such fees, unclaimed accounts, deposits and safe-deposit boxes could also disappear within a few decades,"[100] especially if the amount deposited by the Holocaust victim was small. "It was the small unclaimed balances that most often disappeared."[101]

The Bergier Commission historians also found that after the war the Swiss banks destroyed or failed to maintain records relating to Holocaust-era accounts[102] and that this destruction continued even after December 1996, when Swiss law prohibited the destruction of bank records. The report likewise revealed why the Volcker Committee researchers sometimes could not find a Holocaust-era account, despite proof of the account's existence presented by a claimant. As the report explained,

> The disappearance of all traces of assets from the Nazi era created a kind of higher degree of dormancy; the "dormant account" itself became "dormant." In other words, not only did the banks not have any information on the customers concerned, but researchers were also no longer able to obtain documents on these accounts at the bank during the period in question. Often, therefore, investigations got nowhere, so that summary sources or sample cases are the only sources of information on what happened.[103]

If these findings had come out when the litigation against the banks was still continuing, their impact on the litigation would have been momentous. Undoubtedly, the class action lawyers would not have settled for $1.25 billion. The WJC representatives would have acquired a powerful tool in their publicity campaign against the banks. American government officials, including Stuart Eizenstat, Senator D'Amato, and Comptroller Hevesi, likewise would have used the report to put further pressure on the Swiss banks to settle for more. It is critical that the Bergier Commission's Final Report, unlike the U.S. government–sponsored Eizenstat studies, was a study of a historical body created by the Swiss government itself. Not even the Volcker Committee's Final Report, issued under the auspices of the private Swiss banks, had such a distinguished pedigree. To use legal parlance, the Bergier Commission's Final Report was the "smoking gun" that the claimants' representatives were lacking when the litigation and the concomitant political campaign against the Swiss banks were at full throttle.

As it happened, the Bergier Commission's Final Report came out when the Swiss story and, for that matter, the entire Holocaust restitution saga had long finished being front-page news. The *New York Times* published a minor story on the report, and even that story's focus was on the findings of the Bergier Commission historians about the failings of the Swiss government to admit Jewish refugees during the war,[104] and not about the devastating findings about the Holocaust-era bank accounts.[105] Almost all other media either ignored the study or just briefly mentioned it.

Even if the lawyers now wanted to, it was no longer possible to have the $1.25 billion overturned after the Final Report came out. Under the release that the Swiss banks obtained, later-acquired facts could not be grounds for overturning the settlement.[106]

Timing, therefore, worked in favor of the Swiss banks. As the Bergier Commission's Final Report makes clear, for more than a half-century the Swiss banks had deliberately—and successfully—avoided returning money that did not belong to them. When the more complete truth was revealed about their reprehensible behavior with regard to the Holocaust-era accounts, the banks had already struck a favorable deal that immunized them from further liability.

The second injustice in the Swiss banks settlement involves the Swiss government–owned Swiss National Bank (SNB), the country's central bank (somewhat akin to the U.S. Federal Reserve). The settlement unfairly lets the government-owned SNB completely off the hook, even though as discussed earlier, it was the SNB, and not the private Swiss banks, that was the largest purchaser of gold stolen by the Nazis and therefore was the largest Swiss beneficiary of the Nazi regime. The Bergier Commission's Final Report also found that in 1941 the SNB granted Nazi Germany a credit line of 850 million Swiss francs. "With its willingness to grant Germany loans from public funds, Switzerland helped to bankroll the German war effort."[107]

As discussed earlier, soon after the interim Bergier Commission's report shone the spotlight on the SNB's extensive dealings with the Nazis, the plaintiffs' attorneys filed a lawsuit against the SNB.[108] The lawsuit detailed both the May 1998 findings of the Bergier Commission and the findings of the Eizenstat study issued one year earlier that the SNB had accepted gold from the Nazis that it knew to be stolen.

Less than two months later, the same lawyers who filed the SNB lawsuit and the WJC representatives who expressed outrage when the Bergier Commission's findings of the SNB's Nazi dealings were issued now agreed that in return for the $1.25 billion, they would end the litigation against the UBS and Credit Suisse, the two private banks paying the settlement amount, as well as the litigation against the SNB, which had contributed nothing to the settlement.

Immediately after the settlement, the Swiss government issued a statement in which it both distanced itself from the result and took pains to confirm that it would not be contributing any funds to the settlement:

> The Federal Council noted today that a settlement was finalized . . . between CS [Credit Suisse] Group, UBS AG, and the American plaintiffs. It hopes that this settlement calms the tense situations of recent months and promotes good economic relations. The precise content of the settlement is not yet known. The Federal Council has always stressed that negotiating such a settlement is a matter for the parties affected. Accordingly, it did not take part in these negotiations. For this reason, no obligation ensues for the Swiss Confederation from the settlement.[109]

Pascal Couchepin, the Swiss economics minister, flatly added, "There is no reason for the Swiss Government to pay anything."[110]

Most furious at the exclusion of SNB from the settlement were the Holocaust survivors in Israel, the largest group of survivors in the world. Moshe Sanbar, chair of the Center of Organizations of Holocaust Survivors in Israel and the former governor of the Bank of Israel, protested vehemently at this unfair result. His pleas were not heeded.[111]

To allay criticism of its failure to participate in the Swiss bank settlement, the Swiss president, Arnold Koller, proposed in March 1997 that Switzerland sell some of its $5 billion of gold reserves and use the proceeds to establish a so-called Solidarity Foundation to finance charitable projects, including aid to impoverished Holocaust survivors throughout the world. However, the sales of the Swiss gold reserves required approval through a referendum of Swiss voters. Five years later, the referendum still had not been held. In July 2002, President Kaspar Villiger announced that he was not going to live up to his predecessor's obligation. Even if the foundation is established, none of the funds would now be used to benefit Holocaust survivors. "The firm promises from former President Koller are no longer valid,"[112] President Villiger's spokesperson declared. It was not a big surprise. Stated Thomas Lyssy, vice president of the Federation of Jewish Communities in Switzerland, "For quite a while, we knew that Holocaust victims would not get a dollar out of the foundation."[113]

The Swiss politicians and bureaucrats were relieved. Without ever having to defend itself in court and without contributing anything to the Swiss bank settlement,[114] the Swiss government—the largest money launderer for the Nazis—had once again been able to escape responsibility for its acts.

"THE MOTHER OF ALL HOLOCAUST RESTITUTION SETTLEMENTS"

While acknowledging the drawbacks of the Swiss settlement—and conceding their significance—I still conclude that the accomplishments of the Swiss campaign outweigh its faults. The campaign was an unqualified triumph on the legal and political fronts, showing the enormous power of both the American system of justice and the American political process. Combining forces, the lawyers, Jewish activists, and both Jewish and non-Jewish politicians forced Switzerland and its most powerful industry to confront long-forgotten wrongdoings and make some recompense to right those wrongs. In 1995, when Switzerland's wartime past was first coming to light, no one would have imagined that the powerful Swiss banks would be forced to pay out more than a billion dollars for their wartime and postwar misdeeds or that the Swiss government would have to create historical commissions and task forces and to conduct studies to reevaluate events more than a half-century old.

Even more startling was the ability of the Swiss campaign to set the stage for the settlements achieved with Germany and its industries, Austria and its industries, French banks, European insurance companies, and also American corporations for their reprehensible wartime activities. Even the Holocaust's looted art claims (see chapter 5) can trace their results to the Swiss bank settlement. Explains WJC's Steinberg, "Until the Swiss bank scandal, frankly, museums were indifferent on this issue."[115] The Swiss campaign—judging by how it is already being emulated by other movements seeking redress for historical wrongs—will serve as a model for a long time to come.

While most survivors themselves may have won very little from the Swiss settlement and the culprits, for the most part, got off either easy or completely, the settlement was the first step in the Holocaust restitution campaign that followed.

When the Holocaust restitution campaign began in 1995, the focus was exclusively on the Swiss banks. Its goals then were limited: to find the money deposited in Swiss banks for safekeeping before the war primarily by European Jews and to return this money to their rightful heirs. Six years later, the results achieved were astounding. Not only did the litigation yield more than $1 billion in a settlement from the Swiss banks, but it also opened the floodgates for all the Holocaust restitution settlements to follow. Surely, if the campaign against the Swiss had failed, the Holocaust restitution movement would have gone nowhere. Success against the Swiss banks emboldened lawyers, politicians, and Jewish activists in the United States to take on other corporations and governments that had profited from the miseries of the Holocaust victims. In a very real sense, therefore, the Swiss banks settlement can be called "the mother of all Holocaust restitution settlements," yielding not only the $1.25 billion from the Swiss banks but also leading to an additional $7 billion being called for by other restitution claims.

Let me illustrate with one example, one that would have been totally unthinkable in 1995. The initial accusations that the Swiss banks failed to return money deposited with them for safekeeping by Holocaust victims led to inquiries about whether banks in other countries might also be holding such prewar and wartime dormant accounts. One surprising discovery was that Israel might be one of those countries.

In the 1930s, thousands of European Jews opened accounts at the Anglo-Palestine Bank in British Palestine. These accounts typically contained 1,000 British pounds (approximately $1,500), the amount required to receive an entry permit into British Mandate Palestine. As World War II unfolded, Great Britain classified these deposits as belonging to enemy aliens, since the European Jewish depositors came from Germany, Austria, and, eventually, the nations conquered by Nazi Germany. The fate of these deposits remained a mystery for more than a half-century until the onset of the campaign against the Swiss banks. In January 2000, Bank Leumi, Israel's largest bank and the Anglo-Palestine Bank's successor, admitted to holding approximately 13,000 dormant accounts, many of which were believed to have belonged to victims of Nazi persecution. Like the Swiss banks, Bank Leumi initially refuted the accusations that it might be holding such funds. This led to Bank Leumi's being accused of being no better than the Swiss banks.

Bank Leumi soon gave up the fight. Embarrassed into following the model adopted by the Swiss banks and other European corporations, it created a claims settlement process by which survivors and their heirs entitled to these funds would be eligible to receive them.[116] Soon it was discovered that other banks in Israel and some government institutions were holding assets belonging to Holocaust victims. In April 2001, the Israeli Knesset created a commission of inquiry to investigate the issue.

The Bank Leumi episode illustrates an important legacy of the Swiss campaign. Restitution claims made by Holocaust survivors—or, for that matter, any other historical claims for financial wrongs—can no longer be ignored by those accused of benefiting from those wrongs. Such accusations are now taken seriously.

The Swiss campaign also made other important contributions. In the face of the allegations against them, the Swiss banks and the Swiss government created, respectively, the Volcker Committee and the Bergier Commission to uncover the truth about Switzerland's financial shenanigans during World War II. The Swiss model is now the proto-type used by both European governments and private corporations when confronted with accusations about their wartime role (see chapter 7). After a half-century of silence, the full historical record is only now coming out about how German, Austrian, French, British, and even American companies profited from the Holocaust. The historical black hole of how commerce was conducted in Europe between 1933 and 1945 is finally being filled in.

Moreover, the Swiss campaign showed the enormous power that sanctions or, more precisely, the mere threat of sanctions can have in influencing the behavior of foreign corporations that do business in the United States. The regime of rolling sanctions instituted against the banks by New York City Comptroller Alan Hevesi's Executive Monitoring Committee was critical to getting the Swiss banks to the bargaining table. Hevesi's success also demonstrated that Eizenstat and the other federal officials, who were urging that talk of sanctions be dropped lest it lead to a trade war with Switzerland, were wrong. Sanctions and boycotts, and the threat of such, were not counterproductive to getting European multinationals to settle the wartime claims. Rather, the "one-two punch" of American lawyers first filing the class action lawsuits against the European defendants and American officials at the state and local levels then threatening to exclude the defendants from profitable U.S. deals unless they settled the suits was the perfect strategy to resolve the claims. This strategy was repeated and worked perfectly time and again, against succeeding claims made against German, Austrian, French, and Dutch defendants. To Eizenstat's displeasure, Hevesi became an important, if unwelcome, partner in the federal government's efforts to have the other European defendants follow the Swiss banks' example in resolving Holocaust-era claims. An announcement by Hevesi that his Executive Monitoring Committee would be holding a hearing to determine why a certain Holocaust-era claim was not being resolved would often be the only push needed to have a recalcitrant defendant come forward with a new proposal to conclude the matter.[117]

Finally, the Swiss bank litigation served to push back the time line for which wrongful acts can be adjudged by a U.S. court. Until this litigation, legal dogma held that activities that took place more than a half-century ago could not overcome the problem of the limitations period built into every civil action filed in the United States. The claims were just too old, it was believed, to be litigated now. In fact, before the Swiss bank litigation, civil suits filed regarding Holocaust-era events had already been dismissed by American courts as being time barred.

Here, there was no dismissal. Despite the claims stemming from events originating in the 1930s and 1940s, the Swiss banks were paying a significant sum to settle the claims. As a result of this victory, suits began to be filed against other corporate defendants for their activities during World War II. And not only against European companies. Japanese multinationals are now responding to American suits for their use of American POWs and foreign civilians as slaves during the war (see chapter 8).

THE LEGAL LEGACY

Perhaps the most enduring legacy of the Swiss bank litigation is its impact on American law. At first glance, it appears that the lawsuits filed against the Swiss banks could not be handled by U.S. courts because the activities in question occurred in Europe, not in the United States. Furthermore, the parties sued were foreign corporations, and many of the plaintiffs also were foreigners. And the acts originated more than a half-century ago. With such facts, the Swiss bank suits appeared to many people as one of those hopeless lawsuits filed more for publicity purposes than for any hope of success. The actual course of the litigation showed otherwise.

An important reason why the Swiss bank litigation was taken seriously by both the Swiss bank defendants and Judge Korman, despite these factors, was the victory achieved by the human rights bar over the last two decades in convincing American courts that human rights victims injured abroad can sue in the United States. That step began with *Filartiga v. Pena,* a landmark decision issued in 1980 by the Second Circuit Court of Appeals, in New York, which held that the perpetrator of state-sanctioned torture in Paraguay could be sued in the United States by the relatives of the deceased torture victim.[118] The court of appeals allowed the case to go forward, even though the torture was committed in Paraguay and all the parties in the litigation were Paraguayan. The decision was a ringing endorsement of the principle of universal jurisdiction, that certain human rights violations are so abhorrent to modern society that their perpetrators can be brought to justice anywhere in the world. The court found that "for purposes of civil liability, the torturer [today] has become like the pirate and slave trader before him[:] *hostis humani generis,* an enemy of all mankind."

For twenty years preceding the Swiss bank litigation, various human rights victims injured abroad came to the United States to sue, successfully, their perpetrators under the *hostis humani generis* principle. These lawsuits included a suit against former Philippine dictator Ferdinand Marcos, a suit against the indicted Serbian criminal Rodovan Karadzic, and various other lawsuits against foreign countries, corporations, and individuals for human rights violations committed abroad. For a foreign defendant to be sued, the courts require the defendants to be present in the United States, even momentarily.[119]

In 1985, the prestigious American Law Institute, which publishes summaries of American law in books known as restatements, recognized the *hostis humani* principle as being part of American law.[120] In 1992, Congress also came onboard by enacting the Torture Victim Protection Act (TVPA), extending the right of victims of foreign torture to sue in American courts to include American torture victims. (In an odd quirk of American law, until the TVPA was enacted, only foreigners could sue their *hostis humani generis* perpetrators; the TVPA now gives American nationals the same right to sue.)

By the time the Swiss bank cases were filed, American judges were familiar with the suits being presented to them involving acts committed on foreign soil against foreign defendants. Moreover, they were amenable to finding that U.S. courts had jurisdiction over such suits when the acts consisted of gross violations of human rights law committed by foreign defendants who were present in the United States. That was all that was needed for the lawyers representing the Holocaust survivors to fit their allegations into the existing *hostis humani generis* principle. According to the lawsuits, the Swiss banks, as active collaborators with one of the most despised regimes in the history of humankind, had committed gross violations of human rights law and had enriched themselves in the process. Moreover, the same Swiss banks were doing extensive business in New York, the locale where the suits were filed.

For the dormant account claims, the lawyers relied on a simple legal principle recognized by all legal systems of the world: unjust enrichment. Taken from both ancient Hebrew texts and Roman law, the rule of unjust enrichment requires judges to expunge from the wrongdoer those assets wrongly taken from, or not properly returned to, the victim. Here, the lawyers alleged, for more than fifty years the Swiss banks had kept money deposited with them that they were obliged to return to the depositors or their heirs. Instead, the lawsuits alleged, the banks had wrongfully kept the funds and invested them over the years to make millions.

The lawyers suing the Swiss banks, however, were not just the passive recipients of the two-decade precedent carried out largely by others. Rather, as a result of their settlement, they also extended *hostis humani generis* law to the United States.

A major practical problem faced by many of the *hostis humani generis* lawsuits was that upon receiving a multimillion-dollar judgment in the United States against the defendant perpetrators, the plaintiffs were then unable to collect on that judgment. The defendant did not possess any assets in the United States that could be executed upon to satisfy the judgment. Moreover, international law currently has no mechanism for collecting the funds obtained in a U.S. suit in a defendant's home country. For instance, more than twenty years after the end of the litigation, the successful plaintiffs victims in the *Filartiga* case still have only a paper judgment against the torturer defendant Pena. Similarly, two multimillion-dollar judgments against Rodovan Karadzic remain uncollected.

The plaintiffs and their lawyers in the *hostis humani generis* litigation have had to be satisfied with a moral victory. At least, the suffering of the foreign victims was recognized by an American court, the most prestigious in the world, and the actions of the perpetrator were condemned. The lawyers involved in the litigation had always hoped, however, that they could win a case in which the money judgment could also be collected.

The Swiss bank litigation turned out to be that case. The wealthy Swiss banks had plenty of assets in the United States to satisfy any judgment issued against them. Hence, another beneficial legacy of the $1.25 billion settlement with the Swiss, and this time, the *hostis humani generis* litigation yielded both a favorable result and an actual payment.

A final significant legacy of the Swiss bank litigation (and the other Holocaust-era restitution suits that followed) was to extend the *hostis humani generis* precedent to the corporate arena. The defendants in the Swiss bank litigation were not former dictators or foreign government officials now living in lonely exile in the United States or drop-in foreign dignitaries caught in the web of the American justice system while visiting the United States. Rather, these defendants were some of the most powerful corporations in the world. In direct contrast to the staid and honest image they developed over the years, the Swiss banks were being exposed as Hitler's secret bankers. (Later, German companies, also with sterling corporate images—names like Mercedes-Benz, BMV, VW, Siemens, and Allianz Insurance—faced similar accusations of having actively collaborated with the Nazis.) For the first time, therefore, the *Filartiga* precedent was being applied to hold corporations responsible for their activities.

The Swiss bank settlement and the subsequent corporate lawsuits it fostered are currently being used by legal advocacy groups seeking to turn multinationals into good global citizens. First to be sued have been the corporate oil giants.[121] Multinationals like ExxonMobil, Texaco, Royal Dutch/Shell, Chevron, and Unocal are now fighting suits in U.S. courts accusing them of engaging in human rights and environmental abuses in foreign countries. The suit against Unocal, for example, alleges that the oil company participated with its investment partner, the military dictatorship in Burma, in the enslavement and forced resettlement of the local population in the Burmese countryside where their joint venture project was being carried out.[122] The lawsuit against ExxonMobil is being pursued by Indonesian villagers in Aceh Province who contend that they have been victims of torture, kidnapping, rape, and murder of their relatives at the hands of the Indonesian military unit guarding ExxonMobil's natural gas field.[123] The Swiss bank litigation and the other Holocaust-era cases are being cited as precedents in these and other suits.

Already, Wall Street is starting to take notice, "watching and waiting—to see if Third World locals screwed by transnationals can obtain justice in [American] courts far from their villages."[124] According to Terry Collingsworth, executive director of the Washington, D.C.–based International Labor Rights Fund, the nongovernmental organization handling many of these lawsuits: "I've started getting calls from fund managers. They tell me that they cannot base stock recommendations on moral considerations. But if there is a chance a company could be damaged by a big award in a trial, its business practices overseas become quite relevant."[125] What is different in this latest round of international human rights law litigation is that these multinationals are being hauled into American courts not, like the Swiss banks, for their conduct years ago, but for activities stemming from ongoing investments today. The settlement with the Swiss banks for long-forgotten but then resurrected conduct remains a powerful warning to the world's corporate giants: your activities today may be judged many years in the future.

2

German Industry and Its Slaves

IN CONTRAST TO the recent disclosures about the abhorrent wartime acts of the Swiss, the heinous activities of Germany and its people during the war have been well known for a long time. However, while the massive killings of the Nazi regime are common knowledge, less well known is the extent of the complicity of German private industry with the Nazi regime. Between eight million and ten million people (with some estimates as high as twelve million) were forced to work as slaves during the Nazi era. "There was hardly a German company that did not use slave and forced labor during World War II," conceded Count Otto Graf Lambsdorff, the chief German government negotiator in the ensuing slave labor talks.[1] According to a report issued by the London-based Holocaust Educational Trust in 1999, at least one-half of the top twenty companies in Germany today used slave labor during the war.

Professor Neuborne, one of the lawyers now taking on the task of obtaining compensation for German slave labor, described in congressional testimony in 1999 the advantages obtained by German industry from their wartime slaves.

> Imagine the economic benefit to a wartime economy of being relieved from the obligation of paying wages to more than 50% of your labor force. The fruits of the unpaid slave and forced labor were realized in enormous wartime profits, most of which was paid out to large shareholders as dividends, much of it was reinvested in capital equipment that paved the way for [German] postwar corporate profitability.[2]

The use of slave labor permeated almost every segment of German society. Slaves were used not only by large and small German industrial concerns[3] but also by German schools and hospitals, where prisoners were used for menial labor; personal households, where captured civilians worked as cooks and maids; and even by German churches, which also utilized captive foreign labor during the war.[4]

A historical study published in August 1999 by the Auschwitz Museum in Poland, based on Nazi records discovered in newly opened Soviet archives, revealed the vast array of German companies that profited from what has been dubbed the "Holocaust bonanza." While an estimated 20,000 German companies throughout Germany used slave labor during wartime, the Auschwitz Museum study identified 400 German companies as the leading exploiters of slave labor from concentration camps. Of the 400 companies, 92 companies used slave labor from Buchenwald, 57 from Mauthausen, 52 from Dachau, and 51 from Auschwitz.

Miles Lerman, past chairman of the U.S. Holocaust Memorial Council and a Holocaust survivor himself, elaborated:

> It was not coincidental that IG Farben or any other industrial complex in Germany settled themselves around Auschwitz-Birkenau. They were getting labor for 10 cents a day. We are interested not in the dollars and cents but the fact that it was by design. They were trying to utilize and benefit from every aspect of the prisoners. First, their labor, then they were gassed for their hair, their gold teeth . . . even their bones were crushed and used as fertilizer.[5]

There were two kinds of Nazi slaves. First were those who were forced to work under conditions that were harsh but still allowed them to survive the war. Second were the prisoners who were taken from the concentration and death camps set up by the Nazis, who were worked to death, and who were replaced by a new batch upon their demise.[6] In *Less Than Slaves*, Benjamin Ferencz, one of the American prosecutors at Nuremberg, describes these two categories of slaves:

> The Jewish concentration camp workers were less than slaves. Slave-masters care for their human property and try to preserve it; it was the Nazi plan and intention that the Jews would be used up and then burned. The term "slave" is used in this [book] only because our vocabulary has no precise word to describe the lowly status of unpaid workers who are earmarked for destruction.[7]

In their lawsuits against German companies, the plaintiffs' lawyers began for the first time to distinguish between "slave laborers" and "forced laborers," defining the former as "concentration camp inmates earmarked for extermination" and the latter as "conquered civilian population and prisoners of war." [8] (As I will show, these terms were also used in the final settlement with the Germans to determine the amount of compensation.) Such a distinction, however, was not used by the Nazis, who used the term *zwangsarbeiter* (forced laborer) to describe all their involuntary workers. Moreover, the distinction between slave and forced laborers was also never adopted by the Nuremberg Tribunal. In this chapter, I refer to both as slave laborers, although a more accurate terminology would follow Ferencz's description of forced laborers as "slaves" and slave laborers as "less than slaves." Neither class of slave laborers was ever compensated for their labor.

Historians estimate that approximately 1.25 million of these former slave laborers are alive today. Since the 1950s, Germany has paid approximately $60 billion to some Jewish victims of Nazi persecution. Approximately 170,000 Jewish concentration camp survivors and their heirs throughout the world are receiving monthly pensions from Germany. The pensions are small, averaging $450 per month. After the fall of the Iron Curtain, the reunified Germany in the early 1990s paid an additional $980 million to reconciliation foundations in Poland, Russia, Belarus, Ukraine, and the Czech Republic, to be distributed to non-Jewish survivors in those countries. Again, the individual payments were meager, amounting to less than $500 for each non-Jewish survivor.

Payments for slave labor, however, to both Jewish and non-Jewish survivors, were specifically excluded from any reparations program. Former slave laborers found themselves in a "Catch-22" situation. The German government claimed that it was not obligated to make payments to them because the laborers worked during the war for private German industry. But German industry argued that any payments should come from government coffers, since the postwar German regime was the legal successor to the Third Reich. The German firms maintained that the Nazi regime forced them to use slave laborers to support the German wartime economy. According to Bernard Graef, head of Volkswagen's archives, "From a legal position the crimes of the Nazis were a state crime, and the issue of slave labour compensation must be addressed to the [German] government."[9] Neither government nor industry budged from its position that compensation was the other one's responsibility.

In October 1998, in response to lawsuits initiated on behalf of former slave laborers, Gerhard Schroeder, the newly elected chancellor of Germany, announced that he was reversing the policy of his predecessor, Helmut Kohl: his government would support the creation of a national foundation to compensate former slave laborers and others not covered under existing German reparation law.[10] Schroeder appointed his chief of staff, Bodo Hombach, to head a joint German government-industry group to work out the mechanics of such a fund. In July 1999, Hombach was replaced by Count Otto Graf Lambsdorff, a highly respected member of the opposition and a former economics minister. By that time, however, the plaintiffs' lawyers in the Swiss bank litigation, buoyed by the success of their $1.25 billion settlement, had already begun filing suits in American courts against various German—and even American—companies, seeking damages for their use of slave labor during World War II. According to Michael Hausfeld, now working on the lawsuits against the German companies,

> "The Swiss banks settlement dramatically changed the landscape of restitution on behalf of victims from all other sources. Among other companies "responsible for wrongly appropriating, inverting or outright stealing assets from the victims of the Holocaust," . . . there is a sense that if the Swiss banks were beaten, there really is no hope for them.[11]

Even announcements by some German companies in late 1998 that they would emulate the Swiss and set up historical commissions to investigate their role during the Nazi era and also voluntarily make payments to their former slave laborers still alive[12] did not dissuade the slave labor plaintiffs and their lawyers from continuing with their lawsuits. As reported in *The Economist* in 1998, "The list of firms now accused reads like a who's who of corporate Germany: it includes Siemens, BMW, Volkswagen, Daimler-Benz, MAN and Phillip Holzmann, as well as two Austrian groups, Voest and Steyr-Daimler-Puch. The number of targeted firms may soon reach 100."[13]

The American lawsuits continued to target corporations that brutalized and benefited from a vast slave labor force during World War II.

THE LITIGATION BEGINS

The first slave labor action in the United States was filed in March 1998 while the actions against the Swiss banks were still under way. Interestingly, the suit was filed not against a German company but against the American automotive giant Ford and its German subsidiary.

In a federal class action in Newark, New Jersey, the Ford Motor Company was accused of having "knowingly accepting substantial economic benefits" from the use of forced labor in Nazi Germany during World War II through its German subsidiary, Ford Werke A.G. According to the suit, Ford Werke was alleged to have "earned enormous profits from the aggressive use of forced labor under inhuman conditions."

The plaintiff, Elsa Iwanowa, originally from Russia and now living in Belgium, alleged that from 1942 to 1945, she performed unpaid "forced labor under inhuman conditions for Ford Werke A.G. at its Cologne plant." In October 1942, Iwanova, at age sixteen, was "abducted by Nazi troops and transported to Germany with approximately 2,000 other children [and] purchased along with 38 other children . . . by a representative of Ford Werke A.G. to work at the Cologne plant."

According to the complaint, Ford Werke, doing business in Germany since 1925 and headquartered in Cologne, was an aggressive bidder for laborers from occupied Europe dragooned into Germany by the Nazi war machine. "By 1942, 25% of the work force utilized by Ford Werke A.G. were unpaid, forced laborers," the complaint stated. Further, "by 1943, the percentage of unpaid, forced laborers at Ford Werke A.G. had grown to 50%, where it remained for the remainder of the war years." The complaint also alleged that "the use of unpaid, forced laborers by Ford Werke A.G. was immensely profitable" to the extent that "Ford Werke A.G.'s annual profits doubled by 1943." Following the war, Ford Werke A.G. continued to flourish, owing to its free labor supply during the war:

> Ford Werke A.G. continued to produce trucks at substantial profit at a time when much of Europe was devastated, benefiting from economic reserves and production capacity that had, in large part, been derived from the work of unpaid, forced laborers. By 1948, Henry Ford II was

able to arrive in Cologne to celebrate the 10,000th truck to roll off the postwar Ford (Cologne) assembly line.

The suit claimed that Ford Werke, unlike other subsidiaries of American-owned companies, was never nationalized or confiscated by the Nazis and that the parent company maintained a controlling 52 percent interest in the German subsidiary during the war years.

In a public response to the lawsuit, the Ford Motor Company countered that "the plant was under Nazi control during the war and that, although 'dividends were accumulated from German operations' on the parent company's behalf, Ford never received them."[14] A company spokesperson added: "It must be said that by anyone's measure this was one of the darkest periods of history mankind has known."[15]

In court, Ford filed two motions to dismiss, which were heard in March 1999, almost exactly one year after the lawsuit was filed. The district court took the extraordinary step of holding a full-day hearing on the motions and requested further documentation and briefing from the parties. When the district court scheduled an additional hearing in early August 1999, Ford brought in the "big guns": Warren Christopher, President Clinton's former secretary of state, appeared at the hearing as counsel for Ford. Christopher argued that the claims of the former slave laborers at Ford should be dismissed because payment to them would amount to war reparations, which can be negotiated only between governments.

Not long after the hearing and while the court was still considering Ford's motion, new historical evidence appeared that came back to haunt Ford. Newly released documents from the German wartime archives revealed that Ford Werke A.G. was one of fifty-one German companies to use Nazi victims from Auschwitz as slave laborers. In response, Ford again contended that the American parent company did not control Ford Werke A.G.'s operations in Nazi-occupied Europe.

Following the Ford lawsuit, fifty-six more lawsuits were filed against more than twenty different German and Austrian firms for their use of slave labor during World War II. The lawsuits were filed in California, Illinois, Indiana, New Jersey, and New York. The German chemical firm Degussa was sued for supplying the Zyklon B gas used in the gas chambers and for using the gold taken from victims of the Nazi regime. German pharmaceutical giants Bayer, Hoecht, and Schering were sued for conducting cruel medical experiments on Holocaust victims. The fashion designer Hugo Boss was sued for using slave labor during wartime to make the uniforms worn by the SS, the Hitler Youth, and the German Wehrmacht. A company spokesperson responded, "Although Hugo Boss AG is a completely different company, the management will not close its eyes to the past but rather deal with the issues in an open and forthright manner."[16]

The lawsuits were filed by not only Jewish survivors but also non-Jews from eastern Europe. Stated Jacek Turczynski, head of a Polish foundation working on behalf of 450,000 surviving former Polish slaves, "As long as there were no lawsuits, German companies refused to talk. Our lawsuit is intended to force German businesses to talk about our claims. . . . We hope that thanks to filing the lawsuit in the United States, America will become a spokesman for all victims."[17] Allyn Lite, a lawyer from New Jersey representing the Poles, explained how the class action lawsuit could be filed in the United States: "Poles can file lawsuits in the United States as long as companies have assets here."[18]

Both Mel Weiss and Burt Neuborne, seasoned attorneys, give credit to Deborah Sturman, at that time just two years out of law school, for convincing them to pursue slave labor litigation against German industry. When Sturman joined Weiss's law firm of Milberg Weiss, it was involved in the Swiss bank suits only as part of the Hausfeld team. As reported by the *Wall Street Journal*, which ran a story profiling Sturman,

> Ms. Sturman set out to persuade name partner Melvyn Weiss to file a slave-labor case on behalf of people who were forced by the Nazis to work for a variety of companies. 'There wasn't a day that she didn't come into my office and hawk [sic] me," says Mr. Weiss, who at first thought slave labor claims were too old to succeed. Ms. Sturman insisted that a case could be made.[19]

Sturman came up with the legal theory to justify why the cases were still ripe: the benchmark for filing such cases did not begin in 1945, at the end of World War II, as everyone assumed, but rather in 1989, the date of Germany's reunification. Until then, the suits could not be filed, Sturman pointed out, based on her careful study of the various postwar treaties between the Allies on the status of the two Germanys. With the 1989 date, the lawyers could make a strong argument that their slave labor suits being filed in 1997/98 were still timely. According to

Attorneys Melvyn Weiss and Deborah Sturman. *Courtesy of AP Photo / Herman J. Knippertz.*

Neuborne, "none of the more experienced lawyers realized they could bring a slave-labor lawsuit until [Sturman] explained why."[20]

THE PUBLICITY CAMPAIGN AGAINST GERMAN FIRMS

To exert maximum pressure on the German companies, the lawyers began an extensive publicity campaign. Concurrently with the filing of each new lawsuit, the lawyers held a press conference. On August 31, 1998, Volkswagen was sued twice on the same day, with one suit filed in a New Jersey federal court and the other in Brooklyn. Mel Weiss, one of the lawyers, stated at the press conference announcing his suit: "The ghost of the Third Reich will hang over every Volkswagen car unless the company takes action and provides justice to the thousands of its former slave laborers around the world."[21]

Ed Fagan resorted to more extravagant tactics. On a warm summer day in 1998, Fagan "led a group of Holocaust survivors on a parade through Frankfurt's financial district to shame German banks into a settlement."[22]

Later, when the Germans came to the negotiating table but delivered what the lawyers felt was an inadequate offer, the lawyers financed the publication of a series of full-page ads in the *New York Times*, each running one week apart, "naming and shaming" individual German companies. For Mercedes-Benz, underneath a logo of the company, the caption ran "Design. Performance. Slave Labor." For Ford, the ad read, "The Assembly Lines Ford Would Like to Forget," superimposed on a photograph of slave laborers working in striped uniforms and below that, a photograph of Henry Ford receiving Hitler's "Great Cross of the "German Eagle" in 1938.[23] The ad against Bayer featured a large aspirin with the tag "Bayer's Biggest Headache." The headline for all the ads was the same: "Justice. Compensation. Now."

The survivors were also encouraged to write letters to the companies, which they shared with the press. The *Toronto Star* reprinted one such letter, sent by a seventy-five-year-old survivor in Canada to Volkswagen's headquarters in Germany:

> My name is Philip Mendlowicz and I was a slave labourer in a concentration camp KZ Reichenbach from 1942 until 1945. I worked for your people 12 hours a day, six days a week. I walked three miles every day from the camp to the factory and from the factory to the camp, with no food or payment. I was making parts for the auto industry for the German army. I have no other proof; unfortunately, they did not give letters of reference in those days.
>
> Do you people think that I deserve some kind of payment from your company for my slave labour?[24]

In November 1998, *60 Minutes* ran a segment on the slave labor litigation. Reporter Leslie Stahl interviewed former slaves who had sued Volkswagen. The segment featured Professor Neuborne summing up the case for compensation: "Now at the end of the war, Volkswagen was in relatively good shape. And part of the miracle—part of the Volkswagen miracle—is attributable to the fact that the slaves and the forced laborers, under appalling conditions, made it possible for them to survive." Directly addressing the German companies, Professor Neuborne explained,

> Look, we don't want to criminally punish the people that were there. That was up to Nuremberg. That was the criminal aspect of this. What we want is for you to disgorge the money you made from this. You

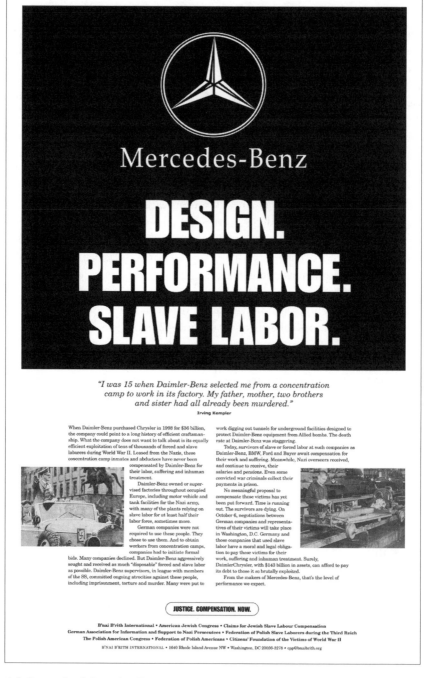
Ad directed at Mercedes-Benz. *Courtesy of Milberg Weiss Bershad Hyned & Lerach.*

earned enormous economic benefits by having people work for you for nothing—for nothing. . . . You've never conceded that you owe them any money, and it's time to pay up.[25]

In New York, Hevesi was holding regular meetings of his Executive Monitoring Committee and now threatening German firms, as he did earlier the Swiss banks, with sanctions if they did not settle soon. In California, to show public support for the litigation, Governor Gray Davis joined one such slave labor lawsuit, suing German firms in state court (in his private capacity as a California consumer) for unfair trade practices in failing to settle. Said Davis, "The lawsuit is frankly meant as a way of stepping up the heat on the discussions that are ongoing."[26]

THE GERMANS RESPOND

Like the Swiss banks, the German companies countered the lawsuits with a variety of substantive and procedural defenses. As procedural defenses, the German defendants listed the usual reasons cited by foreign defendants when they are sued in American courts. In fact, every procedural argument made by the German companies in their motions to dismiss can be found in the Swiss banks' earlier dismissal motions.[27]

For their substantive arguments, the German companies claimed that they were compelled by the Nazis to use slave labor. The response to the suits by the German industrial concern Siemens is typical and was echoed by the other companies using slave labor during World War II. According to Siemens, "During the course of World War II, German industry had no choice but to participate in the Nazi regime's 'wartime economic production program.'"[28] The absence of sufficient labor meant that "companies were compelled to turn to laborers provided by the government. Operating in a totalitarian wartime economy, Siemens was also mandated to accept these conditions."[29] In essence, Siemens threw the responsibility back on the German government. The phrase "wartime economic production program" is the euphemism used by German companies when referring to their use of slave labor.[30]

Hoping to stop the litigation in its tracks, the German government and industry took another tack. Following up on his postelection promise back in October 1998, Chancellor Schroeder proceeded with plans for a national foundation to compensate Germany's former slave labor-ers. On February 16, 1999, he called a press conference with twelve Ger-man companies to announce the establishment of a DM 3 billion ($1.7 billion) fund called the German Economy Foundation Initiative.[31] A month later, Joschka Fischer, Schroeder's foreign minister, met with Jewish leaders in New York. Commenting on the German Fund pro-posal, he simply said: "German companies should learn their lesson from the experience of Swiss banks and should not wait until the pres-sure of public opinion has grown so strong that they are forced to face up to their responsibility."[32]

To the distress of the German government and industry, the Ger-man Fund proposal did nothing to stop the lawsuits. In fact, on the very day that the fund was being announced in Germany, a new federal class action lawsuit was filed in the United States against Bayer, one of the fund companies, alleging that it had participated in medical experi-ments at Auschwitz conducted by the infamous Dr. Josef Mengele.

At the press conference announcing the fund, Schroeder made it clear that it was being created as a means of shortening the lawsuits filed against German industry in the United States. The fund, he said, was being established "to counter lawsuits, particularly class action suits, and to remove the basis of the campaign being led against Ger-man industry and our country."[33] Such an admission explicitly demon-strated the strength of American law. Until the lawsuits were filed in the United States, both German industry and the German government had been able to avoid dealing with the issue for more than a half-century.

According to the Schroeder plan, the slave labor fund was to be fi-nanced entirely by German industry, with first twelve and then sixteen prominent German companies originally agreeing to participate.[34] Pay-ments to the slave laborers would begin on September 1, 1999, the six-tieth anniversary of Germany's attack on Poland, marking the start of World War II.

German government and industry leaders then began negotiating with various Jewish organizations and plaintiffs' attorneys in the United States on the details of the fund. The first meeting was held at the State Department and chaired by Stuart Eizenstat. Still holding the position of undersecretary of state, Eizenstat now turned his attention to the German campaign, in which he took a much more active role than he had in the Swiss settlement. Eizenstat and Count Lambsdorff, the German government representative, skillfully guided the negotiations

U.S. Undersecretary of Treasury Stuart Eizenstat and Count Otto Lambsdorff, American and German government negotiators at the German slave labor talks. *Courtesy of AP Photo / Herman J. Knippertz.*

through various fits and starts until a breakthrough was achieved.[35] As Lambsdorff optimistically put it in mid-1999, following one negotiating session when the talks appeared to be faltering, "We are doomed to succeed. Fate demands it."[36] Added Eizenstat, "We dare not fail. There's just too much at stake."[37]

In November 2001, I appeared at a symposium at Fordham Law School where Eizenstat and Lambsdorff were also speakers. Eizenstat by then had left the government, while Lambsdorff, as vice chair, was still heavily involved with the German foundation. The two men came from different backgrounds and were also of different generations: Lambsdorff, a seventy-two-year-old courtly German count, had lived through World War II and bore his generation's responsibility for the wartime deeds of the German people; and Eizenstat, a "boomer baby" southern Jew whose family had not experienced the horrors of the Holocaust but who now was given the task of resolving this deeply emotional issue. It was clear that both men had a great deal of respect for each other. One of Lambsdorff's favorite lines was to say that the two of them had worked so closely together that "we are often taken for twins, despite our obvious physical differences."[38] Eizenstat explained that it also helped that they had met years earlier, during Eizenstat's appointment in the Carter administration, and came away from that experience as friends.

One brilliant tactical move by Eizenstat and Lambsdorff was to bring all interested parties, as Lambsdorff put it, under one "big tent" to hammer out the issues. In addition to the trial lawyers, German industry heads, and American Jewish leaders, representatives of the state of Israel, and the governments of Belarus, the Czech Republic, Poland, Russia, and Ukraine were invited to the talks. While having so many representatives made the talks unwieldy at times, it allowed all parties to be present when important disputes were discussed. Once an agreement on an issue was reached in the "big tent," Lambsdorff and Eisenstat knew that the issue had been settled. Thirteen such "big tent" meetings were held, as well as many other smaller side sessions, all chaired by the two government representatives, between early 1999 and the signing of the final accords in July 2000.

Along with the claimants' representatives, Eizenstat was heartened that the Germans, unlike the Swiss, were ready to bargain not long after the first lawsuit was filed. As with the Swiss banks, however, the major obstacle was money. The plaintiffs' attorneys representing the uncompensated slave laborers and American Jewish leaders unanimously felt that the amount of DM 3 billion German marks ($1.7 billion) offered by the Germans was woefully inadequate.

In June 1999, negotiations almost broke down when the German companies scheduled a news conference in Berlin on the eve of the second negotiating session to be held in Germany, to announce some specifics about the fund, which they now named "Remembrance, Responsibility and the Future" (*Erinnerung, Verantwortung und Zukunft*). While this announcement was hailed by some as "the first comprehensive proposal raised on slave labor issues by German firms since lawsuits on these matters were first filed,"[39] the claimants' representatives and Jewish leaders severely criticized this unilateral move by the Germans.

The German announcement, made during intense negotiations, resembled the tactic of the Swiss banks in July 1998, when, in the midst of their negotiations with the same representatives of the Holocaust victims, the banks publicly announced their "final offer" of $600 million, an offer that they later had to abandon.

Responding to the German unilateral move, Hausfeld commented:

We were led to believe . . . that we were engaging in a process where there would be working groups and a confidential exchange of information and ideas, leading each side to assess the viability of a workable solution. . . . Instead they unilaterally announce a program that is totally unacceptable in tone and terms.[40]

American Jewish leaders also "expressed dismay about the German plan." Eizenstat, the consummate diplomat, told representatives of the German companies "that their move had not been helpful to the process and that aspects of the [fund] proposal were unacceptable."[41] Mel Weiss, the class action lawyer, put it more bluntly, "Who are they kidding—$1.7 billion?"[42]

In response to the companies' offer, the lawyers countered with a settlement figure of $20 billion. The lawyers claimed that even this figure was modest and would come nowhere close to either extracting from German industry the present value of the profits it had earned on the backs of the slave laborers or paying the wages and a half-century's accrued interest due to the former involuntary workers. The lawyers pointed to "the $20,000 figure awarded by the United States to the thousands of Japanese-Americans placed in detention camps during WWII as the closest analogy." They recommended that each former German slave receive $30,000, which "translated into a $3,000 principal payment to each slave laborer, and an interest component for 50 years delay in payment of $27,000."[43]

Another guide was the settlement in 1998 between Germany and the United States to pay those few Americans of Jewish descent who had been trapped in Nazi-occupied Europe and were sent to concentration camps. In that payout, each such still-living survivor—approximately 230 in all—received between $30,000 to $250,000, depending on the hardships suffered. These payments grew out of the settlement in 1995 of a lawsuit brought by the American survivor Hugo Princz, a U.S. citizen who had the misfortune of being in Nazi-occupied Europe during the war. Princz sued the German government for compensation and lost on the grounds that Germany was immune to litigation on the grounds of sovereign immunity. But under pressure from the U.S. government, Germany settled with him and ten others for $2.1 million. The 1998 settlement included other American citizens in a similar situation to Princz.

Hearing the $20 billion counteroffer, the Germans blanched. The lawyers had a simple response: "The dollar figures are so high because the crime was so vast."[44]

By September 1, 1999, the original deadline set by Schroeder, the talks were at an impasse, and the parties adjourned without a settlement. After meeting with the leaders of the sixteen German companies proposing the fund, Schroeder labeled the financial demands of the American lawyers "completely unrealistic."[45]

Still the parties did not give up. Failing to meet the September 1 deadline, Germany then set for itself a "millennium deadline," hoping to reach a comprehensive settlement before the close of the twentieth century.

THE HOLOCAUST RESTITUTION MOVEMENT SUFFERS ITS FIRST LEGAL DEFEAT

Two weeks after Schroeder's pessimistic assessment, the claimants and their attorneys were hit by a legal bombshell. On September 13, 1999, two federal judges sitting in New Jersey issued separate rulings summarily dismissing five slave labor lawsuits filed in the United States. Judge Joseph Greeneway Jr. dismissed the lawsuit against Ford and its German subsidiary Ford Werke.[46] Judge Dickinson R. Debevoise dismissed four separate lawsuits filed against German companies Degussa and Siemens.[47]

The rulings marked the first significant loss in the modern era of Holocaust restitution litigation. Before the Swiss bank settlement, legal wisdom held that American courts could not be used to resolve Holocaust-era claims. Failed litigation had created this view. Beginning in 1943, approximately one dozen lawsuits had been filed in American courts over property losses and other damages arising from the Holocaust,[48] and almost all of them were dismissed. Then the $1.25 billion settlement in 1998 with the Swiss banks appeared to turn the tide. True, Judge Korman never ruled on the legal arguments made by both sides in the Swiss bank litigation. Nevertheless, it was believed that if the claimants' arguments had no merit, either Korman would have summarily dismissed the suits, or the Swiss banks' lawyers never would have come to the bargaining table; they would have simply awaited the expected dismissal ruling from Judge Korman. In the slave labor litigation, however, the two New Jersey federal judges did what Judge Korman declined to do: they examined the legal arguments made by both sides and ruled that the slave labor lawsuits—and by implication every other Holocaust-era restitution suit—could not be adjudicated in the United States.

In their rulings, neither judge held that the cases were without merit. In fact, both opinions are rife with factual and legal findings in favor of the plaintiffs. Indeed, in the Degussa/Siemens case, Judge Debevoise found that the allegations of knowledge and culpability were true:

> Plaintiffs' factual allegations . . . are totally consistent with the history of the Nazi era and with the record developed during the postwar trials in Nuremberg. In brief, Degussa's and Siemens's executives were fully aware of the widespread use of slave labor and of the inhumane conditions in which the victims lived and worked. The two corporations were aware that this program was utilized not only to advance the German war effort, but also as part of the Nazi goal of exterminating the entire Jewish community in Germany, in the territories of its allies and in the conquered lands. Degussa was aware of the uses to which the Zyklon B it manufactured would be used in the concentration camps and was aware that the gold it refined was seized from the Jewish people at their places of residence, when they arrived at the concentration camps and from their bodies before and after they had been killed.
>
> Knowing this, Degussa and Siemens voluntarily participated and profited from the use of slave labor and, in the case of Degussa, in the manufacture and sale of Zyklon B and the refining of the stolen gold.[49]

Furthermore, the court unequivocally stated: "There can be little doubt that the acts in which the defendant corporations are alleged to have engaged were and are proscribed by customary international law."[50]

Judge Greeneway, likewise, found that Ford's "use of unpaid, forced labor during World War II violated clearly established norms of customary international law."[51] According to the court, Elsa Iwanowa's charge that "'she was literally purchased, along with 38 other children . . . by a representative of [Ford Werke]' . . . [suffices] to support an allegation that [Ford and Ford Werke] participated in slave trading."[52]

Despite these positive findings in favor of the plaintiffs, the two judges still found it necessary to dismiss the suits. Judge Greeneway examined the various treaties signed between postwar Germany and the Allied powers. These treaties, he held, contemplated that all wartime claims would be pursued only through government-to-government negotiations and not through private litigation.

Judge Debevoise also reviewed the various postwar treaties between defeated Germany and the Allied powers and came to the same conclusion:

> The critical issue is whether in light of post World War II diplomatic history, the plaintiff victims, and representatives of victims of the Nazi regime, can bring an action in this Court against private German companies which participated in and profited from the atrocities committed against plaintiffs and those they seek to represent.[53]

He answered this question in the negative. In his view, the question of restitution was a political question that the court declined to adjudicate: "To state the ultimate conclusion . . . the questions whether the reparation agreements made adequate provision for the victims of Nazi oppression and whether Germany has adequately implemented the reparations agreements are political questions which a court must decline to determine."[54]

Judge Debevoise expressed a personal desire to help the plaintiffs (and others like them): "Every human instinct yearns to remediate in some way the immeasurable wrongs inflicted upon so many people by Nazi Germany so many years ago, wrongs in which corporate Germany unquestionably participated." He concluded, however, that he did "not have the power to engage in such remediation."[55]

In sum, both judges adopted Warren Christopher's argument, which he made in the Ford case, that these cases were seeking reparations and reparations remained the province of government-to-government negotiations and were outside the purview of the courts.

At the time, I analyzed both decisions in a law review article to show why they were wrongly decided.[56] Contrary to the two judges' legal conclusions, the slave labor cases did not seek reparation payments from Germany. In fact, the German state was not even a defendant in any of the slave labor suits. Rather, these were private lawsuits between private parties, in which former laborers of German companies sought compensation from these companies for unpaid wages and other damages stemming from the use of the plaintiffs and others like them as slaves. The various treaties cited by the judges, therefore, were not relevant to these suits.

California State Senator Tom Hayden put the result in more dramatic terms: "While an American citizen can sue a corporation for millions for making a faulty toaster, a Holocaust survivor will not be able to sue a corporation for being the slave of a regime that put humans in ovens."[57]

The two court decisions hurt the movement both figuratively and financially. Had the judges not dismissed the lawsuits but waited, like Judge Korman, for the parties to reach a settlement, the eventual settlement amount could have been higher, and more money would have been available to the survivors.

THE DM 10 BILLION SETTLEMENT

On September 14, 1999, one day after the New Jersey rulings, Eizenstat testified before the U.S. House Banking Committee and took the opportunity to chide all the parties for their intransigence. Focusing on German industry, Eizenstat remarked,

> I hope the German industry realizes just how far the U.S. government has gone in the interests of an equitable settlement. We have devoted the better part of the year, and considerable staff resources, to creating a framework for productive negotiation. . . . It is now time that they make a proposal to settle the suits in a fashion consistent with their moral responsibility.[58]

Turning to the plaintiffs' class action lawyers, Eizenstat likewise noted,

> I hope that plaintiffs' attorneys are aware that the initial monetary demands they have put forward in this negotiation are not considered realistic by German industry and German government and make it more difficult for that government to muster public support for helping fund a reasonable solution. They will need to show flexibility if these cases are to be settled within the lifetimes of the survivors they represent.[59]

On October 7, the Germans doubled their offer from $1.7 billion to $3.3 billion. "The companies already involved will not put more on the table. That is for sure," said one of the lawyers representing the German companies to the *New York Times*.[60] Countered the plaintiffs' lawyer Bob Swift, "We are not going to accept peanuts but want to negotiate something fair and credible. We have a moral imperative to do it because of the age of the survivors."[61] The November "big tent" meeting was going to be canceled. There was nothing to discuss.

Yet a month later, on December 19, 1999, the parties settled for DM 10 billion (at that time, approximately $5.2 billion). How was this achieved? Again, the litigation played an important part. The dismissals of the five lawsuits appeared to significantly shift the strong offensive posture of Holocaust claimants and their lawyers, who one year earlier had achieved an important milestone with the $1.25 billion Swiss settlement. Suddenly, the plaintiffs' bar was faced with the prospect that other courts might follow the precedent of the two New Jersey judges and likewise dismiss other pending Holocaust lawsuits. Equally significant, even if the two decisions were to be overturned on appeal, aging Holocaust survivors might not be alive when the dismissals were reversed and the lawsuits were allowed to go forward. Ford, Degussa, Siemens, and (by association) the other companies being sued had achieved a significant strategic victory with these dismissals.

The now-chastened lawyers and Jewish representatives scaled down their demands. To their credit, the German government and representatives of German industries did not walk away from the bargaining table upon obtaining their legal victory. Even if they were now less fearful of American litigation, practical considerations led the Germans to press for a global settlement akin to the settlement achieved by the Swiss banks.

First, like the Swiss, the German companies were still under the threat of sanctions imposed by state and local governments. Beginning in July 1999, Alan Hevesi, comptroller of New York City and the architect of the sanctions that forced the Swiss banks to settle, continued to threaten that state and local governments would impose sanctions on German firms if the slave labor claims were not settled. In Congress, Senators Charles Schumer and Robert Torricelli introduced legislation that would have overturned the court rulings and allowed survivors to sue companies in U.S. courts.

More important, those German multinationals doing a lot of business in the United States wanted to avoid the negative publicity that fresh allegations, unearthed from new historical research, might bring them. Sensitive to their image, the German companies badly desired to put their Nazi past behind them. As an editorial in the *Wall Street Journal* explained:

> German companies are racing to follow the Swiss banks in paying up because they want their brand names to be acceptable globally. Deutsche Bank is in the process of buying Bankers Trust [of New York]; Volkswagen has launched a new Beetle; Daimler Chrysler doesn't want Jeeps and Lebarons to become "Nazi" cars in the eyes of the public.[62]

Finally, the plaintiffs' lawyers had filed appeals of the dismissals and were pressing the U.S. Department of Justice to enter the litigation, arguing that the two judges misinterpreted the treaties. According to some of the plaintiffs' lawyers, the Department of Justice had been ready to file such a memorandum before the two judges, entering the litigation on the side of the plaintiffs, but was told by Eizenstat to hold off lest it upset negotiations with German industry and the German government.

THE BERLIN DEAL

Following the September 1999 court rulings, the parties worked furiously to reach a settlement before the start of 2000, trying to meet the so-called millennium deadline. For the next three months, they shuttled between United States and Germany, bringing together all the parties necessary to effectuate the deal under the symbolic "big tent," which moved between the two continents.

On December 19, 1999, a deal was struck in Berlin. The December millennium settlement was a classic compromise, similar to the result achieved in the Swiss bank settlement negotiations. In October 1999, the German government and participating industries doubled their February 1999 initial offer of DM 3 billion ($1.7 billion), to be funded exclusively by German industry, to DM 6 billion ($3.3 billion), with the German government now agreeing to put up a portion of the funds.[63] In November 1999, the figure was then raised to DM 7 billion ($3.5 billion) when the German government threw in an additional DM 1 billion. The German government then began soliciting other German corporations to join the effort and pledge to make contributions. When it became clear that additional pledges were not forthcoming, the German government sweetened its offer to match the contribution of German industry. Thereupon, the claimants' representatives, including the same class action attorneys who had earlier negotiated the deal with the Swiss banks, lowered their demand and accepted the German offer.[64]

As the settlement stood, the Germans would pay 10 billion marks, valued at that time at $5.2 billion,[65] into the German Fund, with half the money coming from the German government and half from German industry. Last-minute compromises shrank the deal to less than what it appeared to be. Even though the settlement was billed as slave labor claims, the slave labor claimants had to share the DM 10 billion with other claims against Germany. By contributing to the settlement fund, German banks inserted themselves into the deal, so that any claims against them for expropriating bank accounts and other assets of Jewish account holders also had to paid out of the DM 10 billion. The German insurance companies, likewise, became participants, and insurance claims against German companies arising from the Nazi era also came out of this DM 10 billion. In total, DM 1 billion was allocated for nonslave labor claims, clumped under the category of "payments to persons who suffered property loss."[66] The Germans also allocated DM 700 million for Holocaust education and other humanitarian projects that did not directly benefit the survivors.

The survivors did not learn how much they each would receive until March 2000, more than three months after the original DM 10 billion deal was struck in Berlin. As with the Swiss settlement, the actual division of the settlement was not agreed upon in December 1999. During the interim, the parties under the "big tent" engaged in long and often bitter negotiations on how to divide up the limited DM 10 billion pie among more than one million claimants, often pitting the government officials of eastern Europe and the representatives of the non-Jewish claimants against the representatives of the Jewish organizations and Israel. The non-Jewish representatives wanted a greater share to be allocated to the forced labor class, while the Jewish delegates favored the slave labor and looted property claimants, among whom almost all the beneficiaries would be Jewish survivors.[67] For instance, Israel

Singer, leading the negotiations for the World Jewish Congress (WJC), explained that the fund should be for Holocaust victims, not all war victims. Without defining who was a "Holocaust victim" and who merely a "war victim," Singer earlier stated on German radio, "One should not try to make every victim a Holocaust victim."[68] As reported in the *New York Times*, "Talks in recent weeks were marked by heated disagreements—between Poland and negotiators for Jewish victims, between the German government, and all the claimants and between Central European states. 'Frankly, people were getting very tired of the sight of each other,' said one person involved in the talks."[69]

Under the March 2000 agreement, those slave laborers who were held in a concentration camp received a maximum payment of DM 15,000 (approximately $7,500). The maximum payout for former slaves not held in a concentration camp was one-third of that amount, DM 5,000 (approximately $2,500). Almost all the Jewish survivors were in concentration camps during the war and so could qualify for the greater payment. In contrast, most, but not all, the non-Jewish survivors were not in concentration camps and so would receive the smaller amount. If a survivor—Jewish or non-Jewish—was not in a concentration camp but held in "another place of confinement" under "inhumane prison conditions, insufficient nutrition, and lack of medical care," the survivor could still qualify for the DM 15,000 payment.[70]

Unlike the Swiss bank settlement, every victim was eligible for compensation, without regard to national origin or religion (see chapter 1). As Eizenstat explained, "No racial, ethnic or religious group will get favorable treatment. A slave or forced laborer is a victim of the Holocaust, whether he or she is Czech, Pole, Jew, Romani or another nationality or religion."[71] Of course, the broad eligibility diluted the amounts of the individual settlements, which was the very reason why the Swiss banks settlement was limited to the favored VTNPs.

The country-by-country allocations were as follows: $862 million for survivors in Ukraine, $417.5 million for Russia, $347 million for Belarus, $211 million for the Czech Republic, and $906 million for survivors in Poland. The Claims Conference, the Jewish organization distributing pension funds to Holocaust survivors under the original accord with West Germany, earlier received the same amount as Poland did, to be divided among Jewish survivors worldwide, except those living in the former Soviet Union. Another $400 million was allocated for division among other countries.

On December 20, 1999, President Clinton issued a statement praising the settlement. The deal, he stated, "satisfies the requirements of those representing the victims. We close the twentieth century with an extraordinary achievement that will bring an added measure of material and moral justice to the victims of this century's most terrible crime. It will help us start a new millennium on higher ground."

The final agreement, known collectively as the Berlin Accords, was concluded during formal ceremonies held on July 17, 2000, with President Clinton and Chancellor Schroeder in attendance. The Berlin Accords consisted of three documents: (1) a Joint Statement of Principles executed by all parties; (2) the Executive Agreement between Germany and the United States, obligating the executive branch to seek dismissal from American courts all present and future litigation against any German entity arising out of World War II;[72] and (3) German legislation establishing the joint public-private German Fund Foundation,[73] which the German parliament promptly enacted the next month, on August 12, 2000.

One of the most moving events of the day came after the formal ceremonies at the Bellevue Castle residence of German President Johannes Rau. Speaking before an audience that included many survivors, Rau, on behalf of the German nation, solemnly begged for forgiveness and declared that the victims' "sorrow will be acknowledged as sorrow and the injustice that was done to them will be called injustice." Earlier, on a visit to Israel, Rau addressed the Israeli Knesset and made a similar, emotional apology:

> With the people of Israel watching, I bow in humility before those murdered, before those who don't have graves where I could ask them for forgiveness for what Germans have done, for myself and my generation, for the sake of our children and grandchildren, whose future I would like to see alongside the children of Israel.

For many survivors, these words of contrition meant much more than any money they would ever receive from the Germans.

Testifying in Congress in early 2000, Count Lambsdorff predicted that the first payments would reach the recipients "within the course of this year."[74] As the Swiss bank settlement showed, making payment predictions for Holocaust restitution claims is always risky. It was not until mid-2001 when the first payments began to trickle in, with most survivors not getting their checks until mid-2002. Before the money could flow, two more hurdles had to be overcome.

THE REQUIREMENT OF "LEGAL PEACE"

German industries would never admit that they bore any legal responsibility to their former slave laborers. At most, they conceded some vague notions of historic or moral responsibility.[75] Nevertheless, the Germans acknowledged from the outset that a major incentive for paying the slave laborers was to get rid of the bothersome American litigation. Chancellor Schroeder explicitly acknowledged back in February 1999, when the German Foundation was first announced, that the Germany was doing this "to counter lawsuits, particularly class action lawsuits, and to remove the basis of the campaign being led against German industry and our country."[76] German industries, in a Web site charting the progress of the settlement fund, stated: "For the Foundation to be established and for the funds to be made available, it is an indispensable prerequisite that the [German] enterprises have full and lasting legal certainty, in other words, that they are safe from legal action in the future."[77] Of course, "safe from legal action" meant immunity from class action lawsuits in the United States. The Germans were not afraid of being sued anywhere in the world, even in Germany, for their wartime activities, except in the United States.

The Germans came up with a legal term signifying that they no longer would be subject to litigation in American courts arising from Nazi-era events: legal peace. "Legal peace" meant (1) the full and complete dismissal of all then-pending Holocaust-era lawsuits against German defendants[78] and (2) protection from future litigation. Until German industries and the German government, to their satisfaction, obtained this "legal peace," they were not going to part with any of their money, regardless of the moral compulsion they felt to compensate the former, now elderly, slave laborers. Manfred Gentz, chairman of the German industry fund and chief financial officer of Daimler-Chrysler, explained, "It would be a catastrophe if we gave away 10 billion marks and then in three or four years the individual cases came back. We have to prevent that."[79] The Germans left no wiggle room for this condition:

"Legal peace" would be established, and the money would begin to flow only when the German Bundestag, parliament, so declared.[80] Until then, everything remained on hold.

Satisfying the two "legal peace" conditions imposed by the Germans proved harder than anticipated. The first difficulty was finding a way to protect German companies from future litigation. To their surprise, the Germans learned that the U.S. executive branch did not have the legal right to simply outlaw such future lawsuits. Formal ceremonies scheduled in June 2000 were put off because Eizenstat and the plaintiffs' lawyers could not come up with a legal solution to satisfy the German firms. Lambsdorff explained, "We have to avoid lawsuits that can be made in the future. One cannot assure 100 percent legal protection . . . but on the other hand, within the legal system statements can be made which 97 percent of the courts would accept."[81] What the Germans finally accepted as a " 97 percent guarantee" was something quite unusual, never used before in American foreign relations law. As part of the Berlin Accords in July 2000, President Clinton and Chancellor Schroeder signed an executive agreement committing the United States to file a court document—called a "Statement of Interest"—in any future Holocaust-related litigation against German defendants that would (1) inform the court handling the litigation that the foreign policy interests of the United States called for the recognition of the German Foundation as the exclusive forum for the resolution of disputes over the Holocaust-era conduct of German industry and (2) urge the dismissal of the lawsuit "on any legal ground."[82]

The other condition for "legal peace"—the dismissal of all pending lawsuits—appeared to be a simple matter. All the parties agreed that the fifty-plus existing suits should be dismissed, and the plaintiffs' lawyers were ready to file motions with the respective courts seeking dismissal. The U.S. government, if necessary, would file separate legal papers likewise urging prompt dismissal.

The implementation of this simple legal step, however, proved even more elusive. In fact, it almost destroyed the settlement. Credit, or blame, is due to a noteworthy feature of the American legal system: judges in the United States are independent and do not take "marching orders" from the other branches of the government. While American courts are quite sensitive to foreign policy concerns and usually defer to the executive branch's wishes when told that a certain case affects U.S. foreign policy, both the U.S. Supreme Court as well as federal and even state courts have at times rejected outcomes suggested by the executive branch when they felt it would produce unjust results.

This is precisely what happened here. On December 5, 2000, federal judge William Bassler, sitting in New Jersey, before whom all slave labor cases were consolidated, complied with the motions and promptly dismissed the slave labor cases before him to assist in the rapid effectuation of the DM 10 billion settlement.[83] On December 14, 2000, federal judge Michael Mukasey, sitting in New York, likewise dismissed the pending lawsuits against German insurance companies (see chapter 3). Professor Neuborne was hoping that "the money [would] start flowing by Christmas [2000]."[84] Then, the parties hit a major snag; one federal judge refused to play the game.

The origins of this problem go back to June 1998 when the Swiss bank litigation was still under way. That month, lawyers Fagan and Swift opened a new front in the Holocaust restitution movement by filing suit against Deutsche Bank and Dresdner Bank, the two largest banks in Germany and some of the largest in the world. During World War II, both banks maintained close business relationships with the Nazi war machine and appear to have profited handsomely from such dealings. A historical commission hired by Deutsche Bank issued a report in February 1999, finding that it had financed the building of Auschwitz. Earlier, in July 1998, the commission confirmed that Deutsche Bank had profited from gold plundered from Holocaust victims. During the war, Deutsche Bank purchased more than 4.4 tons of gold from the Reichsbank, the German central bank. Included in the purchases was "744 kilograms [1,637 pounds of] dental gold taken from Jews' teeth, wedding bands and personal jewelry."[85] A historical report by the Dresdner Bank found that in Nazi-occupied lands, "the saying went, 'Right after the first German bank comes Dr. Rasche from the Dresdner Bank.'"[86]

Following Fagan and Swift's suit, Hausfeld and others filed six other federal class action lawsuits against both German and Austrian banks for their involvement in wartime plundering and profiteering. In March 1999, the seven actions were consolidated in federal court in Manhattan before one judge, Shirley Wohl Kram, and entitled *In re Austrian and German Bank Holocaust Litigation.*

In March 1999, the Austrian banks reached a separate settlement with Fagan and Swift, agreeing to pay $40 million. This was equivalent to only $4 million in pre–World War II dollars, an amount far below what the Austrian banks actually stole from their Jewish victims.

Like Judge Korman in the Swiss bank litigation, Judge Kram held a "fairness hearing" in November 1999 to determine whether the settlement with the Austrian banks should be approved. Numerous claimants filed objections to the settlement, urging that it be rejected as being too low.

To obtain approval from Judge Kram, the lawyers explained that in addition to the $40 million, the Austrian banks were assigning to the Austrian Holocaust victims any claims the Austrian banks had against German banks for plunder and mismanagement arising from their forced takeover after Nazi Germany's annexation of Austria in 1938. The Austrian banks represented that these assigned claims were worth approximately $300 million,[87] thereby adding substantial value to the Austrian bank settlement. Upon conclusion of the assignment, it was contemplated, the Austrian Holocaust victims would step into the shoes of the Austrian banks and demand from the German banks this $300 million as damages for the German banks' plunder of the Austrian banks. Moreover, the Austrian banks would share with the plaintiffs' lawyers wartime documents detailing the dealings of the German banks in wartime Austria. Fagan, urging approval of the settlement, justified the low amount by explaining that this "will provide us with documents that will open the way to the main vein of gold . . . pointing to Germany's Deutsche Bank and Dresdner Bank."[88] On January 10, 2000, Judge Kram approved the Austrian bank settlement.[89] (The first set of payments to the Austrian bank claimants went out two years later, in August 2002.)

Unfortunately, Fagan's "main vein of gold" proved to be a bust. No valuable documents were found in the Austrian banks' archives. Moreover, the assignment to the Austrian Holocaust victims of the Austrian banks' claims against the German banks proved to be worthless, extinguishing a postwar agreement between Austria and Germany. This important fact was never revealed to Judge Kram. When the parties—including the same attorneys who had earlier convinced her to approve the settlement—appeared before Judge Kram a year later seeking dismissal of the case against the German banks, she was furious. Feeling misled by their earlier representations and realizing now that the Austrian bank claimants would not be getting additional funds from the Germans, Judge Kram, on March 7, 2001, denied dismissal.[90] Even after the U.S. government counsel filed briefs urging her to reconsider and claiming that her actions were greatly damaging millions of elderly survivors worldwide,[91] Judge Kram, asserting her judicial independence, held firm. She refused to dismiss the action against the German banks unless additional funds would be forthcoming to the Austrian bank claimants.

This was a major snag. According to Professor Neuborne, "We have hit a stone wall. If something doesn't change, the foundation will disintegrate."[92] The Germans were aghast, not believing that one American judge could hold up the entire process. They urged that the case be taken away from Judge Kram and assigned to another judge. Count Lambsdorff did not mince his words: "We must employ all means to wipe out Judge Kram's decision so that the fund payments can begin as soon as possible."[93] The German lawyers went so far as to accuse her of having an ulterior motive for not dismissing the suits. "Michael Kohler, a lawyer for the companies in the fund, said her decision was motivated by the fear that the Austrian pay-outs [she fashioned] would now look insufficient in comparison" to the much-higher German settlement.[94]

Eventually, the parties had no choice but to appeal to the Second Circuit Court of Appeals. Everyone was nervous. The German parliament was leaving for its summer recess in July, and it needed to declare "legal peace" before its adjournment. The parties asked for an expedited appeal. In a highly unusual move, Judge Kram hired as special counsel David Boies, Gore's lead attorney during the Gore/Bush election controversy, to appear before the appeals court to explain her actions.

The pressure on all sides, especially by the U.S. government, proved too much for the appeals court. On May 18, 2001, three days after hearing oral arguments, the Second Circuit issued an extraordinary document, a writ of mandamus. The writ directed Judge Kram to immediately dismiss the action. In issuing the writ, the appeals court realized that a normal appeals rule could not work in this case. "Further delay in these judicial proceedings is to be avoided. Survivors of the Holocaust are elderly, [and some petitioners] estimate that more that 1,000 potential beneficiaries of the German foundation die each month."[95] Neuborne praised the ruling enthusiastically: "This is everything we could have possibly asked for. And for the court to act this fast is astonishing."[96] Judge Kram now had no choice but to dismiss the action. Three days later, on May 30, 2001, the German parliament enacted a resolution determining that "legal peace" had finally been achieved in the United States.

The German parliament was wrong. The Germans did not achieve "legal peace" with this ruling. More legal battles loomed on the horizon, as lawyers for the claimants had to resort to additional lawsuits to get the German companies to comply with the settlement agreement.

THE GERMAN COMPANIES ARE RELUCTANT TO PAY

In addition to the delay in obtaining "legal peace," another major factor in slowing down the journey to distribution was the reluctance of the German companies to pay their share of the contribution. When the deal was announced in December 1999, the Germans promised DM 10 billion without actually having the funds in hand. The sixteen companies creating the fund did not want to be the sole contributors of the DM 5 billion share due from private industry. Since more than 20,000 German companies used slave labor during wartime and many of these companies were still in existence, fairness dictated that these companies also contribute to the German Fund. The German government encouraged this effort and, in fact, began a public relations campaign urging all German companies, whether in existence during the war or created afterward, to join the fund.[97] The German public also was encouraged to participate, in an effort to show that the entire German nation had come together to be part of the final German mea culpa for wrongs committed during the World War II.

Unfortunately, the effort did not yield the expected results. While public opinion polls showed that the German public was overwhelmingly in favor of the settlement and that contributions had come from many diverse segments of German society, including schoolchildren, German companies did not join the payment fervor. As the London-based daily *Independent* put it, "German industry was slow to raise its half of the kitty . . . and there were times when it seemed to be looking for excuses not to pay up."[98]

The German government tried to sweeten the pot by making the contributions tax deductible. (As a result, the German government, which initially was not even going to be a contributor to this German industry initiative, ended up footing about three-quarters of the final bill.) The founding companies began a newspaper-advertising blitz in the latter half of 2000 under the slogan "We will join," urging all German companies, large and small, to contribute to the fund. Germany's finance minister even went on national television seeking contributions.[99] Israeli President Moshe Katsav, on a visit to Germany, made a similar appeal: "I expect German industry to put aside petty legal considerations. The issue here is not courts and anonymous decisions but people. . . . I'm calling on German industry to help people while there is still time and make your promised payments."[100] Polish Prime Minister Jerzy Buzek also urged Germany to find a way to release the money without waiting for all the technical matters to be resolved. Buzek pointed out that " a victim dies every 11 minutes."[101] The president of the German parliament, Wolfgang Thierse, in a meeting with American Jewish rabbis, expressed his "deepest shame" that the government-industry fund had so far failed to deliver the promised compensation."[102]

What finally worked was humiliation. With the German public becoming increasingly disturbed, the recalcitrant German companies were "shamed into generosity by growing outrage among the German public."[103] On the day in May 2001 when the German parliament passed a law clearing the last obstacle for payment, German industry so far had contributed only about two-thirds of the money pledged. It was not until October 5, 2001, almost five months later, that the entire portion of German industry's contribution to the fund had been collected. Not wanting to wait any longer, the Germans, without still having the entire fund in place, began making payments to the survivors from the money already collected in June 2001.[104]

THE PAYMENTS BEGIN TO BE MADE

After many false starts, the payments to the slave laborers finally started going out in June 2001. The London *Independent* called it "the last great postwar compensation deal."[105] To reach that stage, on May 30, 2001, the German parliament passed a law—with only a few members voting against it—declaring that "legal peace" had been achieved. With "legal peace" now existing between the U.S. class action lawyers and Germany, the parliament finally authorized the release of the funds to the survivors.

Urging the German legislators to vote for the law, Chancellor Schroeder repeated the "rough justice" mantra that "compensation in the truest sense of the word is hardly possible" but pled with the legis-lators to close "the last great chapter of our historical responsibility." The German Fund, he maintained, "sends a signal that Germany is fully conscious of the terrible crimes of its past, and will remain so."[106] Count Lambsdorff echoed the theme: "We have tried to draw a financial line under the darkest chapter of our history. But we cannot and must never draw a moral line."[107] He concluded, "Only if we recognize that can there be a way out of the dark past into a bright future."[108]

The *New York Times* reported an unfortunate undercurrent amid all these mea culpa statements: "The word blackmail was often used in pri-vate by Germans, reflecting a broad sense that the country had already done a lot to try to compensate for its crimes and was being subjected to further humiliation by a new generation of sharp American lawyers."[109]

A week later, in June 2001, the checks started to go out. The first to receive payments were the neediest survivors, those living in eastern Europe or in the former Soviet Union. Checks then began going out to survivors in the United States and Israel. Even then, things did not go smoothly. In some instances, the husband received payment, but the wife waited months to receive a check, even though both applied at the same time and were interned in the same concentration camp during the war.

At the outset, claimants did not receive the entire DM 15,000. Rather, the first set of payments paid out only DM 10,000 (equivalent at the time to $4,650). This led to more confusion and disappointment, since the sur-vivors had been told, and the media had widely reported, at the time of the settlement and thereafter that the amount would be DM 15,000 (about $7,500) for slave labor claimants. To add to the muddle, the VTNP survivors in the Swiss bank settlement also began receiving at the same time a check for $1,000 (later increased to $1,450) from the slave labor portion of the Swiss bank settlement (see chapter 1). Many believed that the $1,000 came from the Germans, since both the German and Swiss funds were processed through the Claims Conference, with only the fine print on the check indicating the source of the funds.

Additional Holocaust restitution settlements also either began to pay out or had a claims filing deadline coming up at approximately the same time. By the end of 2001, Holocaust survivors had to track Holo-caust restitution settlements from Austria, Belgium, the Czech Repub-lic, France, Netherlands, Romania, and the ICHEIC (International Commission on Holocaust Era Insurance Claims) insurance claims process, each with its own filing deadline and eligibility requirements. It was no wonder that in publicizing the various settlements to Jewish survivors, the Claims Conference advised, referring to the claim forms that came with each settlement, "When in Doubt, Fill It Out."

Nevertheless, once the German restitution process began, the funds flowed quite quickly. By June 2002, one year after the payments first started to go out, more than DM 2.6 billion ($1.3 billion) had been distributed to claimants worldwide, of which more than $300 million was paid to Jewish survivors through the Claims Conference.[110]

The Germans did not want to have any legal responsibility for distributing the funds or assume the administrative task of directly distributing the money, which went to individuals in forty-nine countries, from Argentina to Zimbabwe.[111] Rather, they contracted with seven non-German organizations for this task, labeled "partner organizations" of the German Fund. For the Jewish survivors around the world eligible for payments under the German Fund, other than those in some eastern European countries and Russia,[112] the Claims Conference, having worked since the 1950s with Germany on distributing German reparations, was the logical choice. It both processed the claims, deciding who would be eligible for payment, and then funneled the payments from the German Fund to the Jewish survivors. For the non-Jewish survivors, a nongovernmental organization (NGO) from Switzerland, the International Organization for Migration (IOM), won the largest distribution contract. It had no prior experience in this field, having worked mainly on international migration issues. However, it took on the job confidently and, after some initial start-up delays, expeditiously processed the claims for the non-Jewish beneficiaries of the German Fund.[113]

In fact, the IOM was saddled with the much larger task, since 80 percent of the beneficiaries of the German settlement were former non-Jewish slaves. Some of them were eligible to receive the larger slave labor payment, owing to their harsh treatment by the Nazis, and others, because of a less severe work regime, were eligible only for the smaller forced labor payout. There now were two organizations making distributions, one to Jews and the other to non-Jews, and their work could be compared for efficiency. This sense of competition between the two organizations helped make the process of distributing the German Fund money more effective.

In sum, DM 8.1 billion was allocated to compensate former slaves, the primary purpose of the fund; DM 1 billion was allocated for property losses, which included (1) payments to persons who suffered property losses at the hands of the Nazis but who, for technical reasons, could not collect under existing German indemnification programs and (2) payments for unpaid Holocaust insurance policies issued by German insurance companies. The remainder was set aside for various social and humanitarian projects to help needy survivors and for Holocaust education, designated as "projects of the 'Remembrance and Future Fund.'"[114]

THE LAWYERS ARE PAID

The issue of attorneys' fees for Holocaust restitution litigation is a sensitive one, often provoking heated discussions. Even before any of the attorneys received fees, many survivors and American Jewish organizations began to assert that the class action attorneys should be taking all the Holocaust restitution cases *pro bono,* lest the lawyers profit from the miseries of the Holocaust. The moral debate acquired practical significance with the DM 10 billion settlement, since the German slave labor litigation was the first category of Holocaust restitution suits in which the attorneys collected fees for their work. For many of them, it was a welcome relief. They had been working on these cases for more than five years without being paid, spending not only their time but also paying all their expenses for the cases, which now totaled tens of thousands of dollars.

The lawyers all took on the cases on a contingency basis, that wonderful invention of American law that opens the American courthouse to those who cannot afford to hire a lawyer to prosecute their case. Under the contingency fee system, the lawyer is paid only if the case is resolved successfully, with the lawyer taking a percentage of the award recovered. In class action litigation, such fees must also be approved by the court. While the Swiss banks' class action cases settled first, Judge Korman declined to approve any attorneys' fees until a significant portion of the claimants had received payment from the Swiss settlement. But in the German settlement, the lawyers were paid first.[115]

The same attorneys who prosecuted the Swiss bank cases also represented the claimants in the German litigation. In the Swiss settlement, most of the attorneys did not seek fees (see chapter 1). Not so for this litigation. Here, all the lawyers applied to be paid for their work.

Why didn't these lawyers also prosecute these cases *pro bono*? The most common answer given by the lawyers was that they could not afford to continue prosecuting Holocaust restitution suits without compensation. The litigation was becoming quite expensive; the German companies, like the Swiss banks, had hired top-notch counsel to defend them. As in the Swiss bank litigation, the defense attorneys filed many motions to have the cases dismissed. The prosecuting lawyers insisted that to be able to devote their time and that of their associates, paralegals, historians, and other experts to these suits, they needed to be paid. From the attorneys' perspective, the survivors were getting a "two-for-one bargain": the attorneys prosecuted both the Swiss bank and German suits but were charging only for the latter litigation.

The lawyers made sure that once the deal had been completed, it would include a provision for their fees. The German Foundation Law passed by the Bundestag in July 2000 specified that payments should be made to "attorneys and counsel whose activity on behalf of persons entitled to payments . . . contributed to the establishment of the Foundation or otherwise were favorable to its creation, particularly by taking part in the multilateral negotiations that preceded the establishment of the Foundation or by filing complaints on behalf of claimants." The Foundation Law further specified that the fees should be determined by arbitration.

The process of resolving the fee issue was taken care of soon after the German parliament completed the agreement. In accordance with the German Foundation Law, two American arbitrators were chosen, lawyer Kenneth R. Feinberg, who later gained fame as the special master in the 9/11 Disaster Fund, and Nicholas D. Katzenbach, President Lyndon Johnson's attorney general. The attorneys seeking fees submitted to the arbitrators documentation of the work they did. In the documentation, they also explained what they had contributed to the prosecution and resolution of the cases.

In June 2001, the fee awards were issued. Fifty-one lawyers were awarded fees, totaling $59.9 million. While the amount may appear large, it is only about 1.2 percent of the total $5 billion settlement. As a comparison, in typical class action settlements, fee awards generally range between 15 and 22 percent of the total settlement amount, which in this case would have been at least $750 million.

Nine of the lawyers, as the Israeli daily *Ha'aretz* reported, were awarded fees above $1 million.[116] Mel Weiss received the highest fee, $7.3 million. *Ha'aretz* chose to point out that "this sum is equal to the amount to be distributed to 1,000 survivors, each of whom spent several years at forced labor."[117] Hausfeld was awarded $5.8 million for his work. Swift received $4.3 million, and Fagan collected $4.4 million. The arbitrators gave Professor Neuborne a $4.3 million award. These amounts included reimbursement to the attorneys of the costs they had been advancing on these cases since their filing in 1997.

In class action litigation, the successful plaintiffs' attorneys are awarded either an hourly rate multiplied by the amount of hours expended (called a *lodestar amount*) and, very often, a bonus to reflect the lawyers' contribution to bringing about the settlement. Neither Feinberg nor Katzenbach, citing the confidentiality of the process, would disclose whether any of the lawyers had received such bonuses. Professor Neuborne revealed, however, that his lodestar amount had been doubled by the arbitrators. Fagan stated that "his $4.4 million was almost exactly the straight lodestar amount he asked for."[118] Eizenstat called the fee awards "very reasonable and modest in light of the enormous amount of work put in by the lawyers."[119]

Soon after, Paul Spiegel, a leader of Germany's Jewish community, issued a public appeal to the lawyers, urging them to donate their fees to the German Fund, to help increase the payments to the survivors.[120] According to Spiegel, "I am convinced that the lawyers have a legal right to their money, but not a moral right. I am not saying that the lawyers are greedy. It is just immoral when the highest payments to survivors are about $7,000 and the lawyers are getting millions."[121] The lawyers were not interested. Michael Witti, a German lawyer who was working with Fagan and Swift and who was awarded about $4 million for his work, publicly responded to Spiegel's proposal. Witti explained that the fees would enable him to continue representing survivors for other wartime claims, such as helping recover confiscated property in eastern Europe. The fees are needed, Witti elaborated, "so I can hire experts, so I can travel and have office staff. And this money gives me the support for this."[122] He concluded: "If you are not [fiscally] responsible, you run away and take commercial cases. But I have an obligation to do human rights cases."[123] Morris Ratner, the American lawyer whose firm donated their fees from the Swiss and Austrian bank settlements but took fees in the German settlement, made a similar point:

I think the question of "why the lawyers did not take the German cases pro bono" is the wrong question. The question is, how do we incentivize [sic] competent counsel to invest years of work, and hundreds of thousands of dollars, in worthy, high risk, human rights cases? I don't think the answer is vilifying them for getting some very modest fees (compared to what we would have earned in a routine business case).[124]

As an example, in the aftermath of the Holocaust restitution litigation, Lieff Cabraser (Ratner's firm), as well as Hausfeld, Weiss, Swift, and others involved in the Holocaust suits, accepted as clients the aging former slaves of Japan's industrial wartime policy. To date, these lawyers have been working on these cases for more than three years without receiving any fees and spending tens of thousands of dollars in litigation expenses. If these suits against Japan and Japanese private industry do not succeed (so far they have not—see chapter 8), the money earned by the lawyers from the German slave labor settlement in reality will provide the funding to litigate these latter human rights suits.

Diane Leigh Davison, a Baltimore class action lawyer working on the cases, had a more straightforward explanation of why she was charging her Holocaust survivor clients. "You don't say to a surgeon, 'Don't take your fee.'"[125]

The lawyers also pointed out that without their intervention, the Germans would not have settled. One example: After the settlement, some survivors in Britain made noises about filing their own separate lawsuits in European courts.[126] It was all a bluff. No English lawyer was willing to take such a case. Only the lawyers in America were bold enough to take on the Germans.

THE DEAL ALMOST UNRAVELS

The Swiss bank settlement came close to falling apart on various occasions during the postsettlement process. Each time, however, Judge Korman was able to steer the parties forward.

At the insistence of the German side, the German settlement was created outside American court jurisdiction. At one point after the settlement, Arthur Miller, a well-known Harvard Law School professor who had been working with the plaintiffs' side, suggested that all the

German cases be consolidated and transferred to Judge Korman, who would then oversee the settlement's implementation, as he had with the Swiss bank deal. The Germans rejected this suggestion outright. "Any effort to bring the [German] foundation under a U.S. court will not work and will be resisted," said a source close to the German side who declined to be named.[127]

Without a Judge Korman, however, there was no arbiter to keep the parties in line. Moreover, the glue that held together the original negotiations, the Eisenstat/Lambsdorff team of government representatives, was no longer in place. After January 2001, with President Clinton out of office, Eizenstat left the government. Without the two respected government officials working together, the deal began unraveling even as the fund's money was being distributed. The main culprits were the German companies.

The German companies first demanded that they receive credit for any money that the claimants had received previously from Germany. The claimants' representatives balked. This settlement was all "new money" and had no relation to payments made under previous German government compensation programs. Eizenstat agreed; giving German companies credits for past payouts was not part of the deal. In February 2000, the Germans gave in, and Eizenstat was able to announce, "All parties now agree there will be no offsets."[128]

The second point of contention was accrued interest, which the companies held onto while the German captains of industry were haggling over the final conditions of the settlement and the attainment of "legal peace" in the United States. The German companies agreed to hand over only DM 100 million, the minimum amount stated in the settlement documents. The claimants' representatives refused. It had taken eighteen months until the deal was made, and the companies, they argued, were obligated to contribute to the foundation the interest accrued on their entire DM 5 million share since December 19, 1999, when the deal was brokered. Otherwise, the deal arranged on December 19, 1999, was not worth DM 10 billion but some discounted amount in the future when the German industry's share would be paid.

Third, the German companies claimed that the money contributed by the general populace should be credited to the German industry's DM 5 billion share. The claimants balked again. German industry was obliged to pay the full DM 5 billion. Any funds received from the German public, they argued, including contributions made by German churches, charities, and schoolchildren, should be added to the DM 10 billion total, to help raise the individual payouts to each survivor. The public contributions were not meant to be deducted from industry's obligation.

Fourth, the three founding German banks in the settlement—Deutsche Bank, Commerzbank, and Dresdner Bank—were accused of engaging in financial shenanigans while transferring the funds to the victims. The money paid out to the victims first had to be converted from German marks into the local currencies of the countries where the victims resided and then transferred to those countries. The three banks, all with offices throughout the world, agreed to carry out this task. One of the first was the transfer of more than DM 1.3 billion into Poland and the conversion of these German marks into Polish zlotys. It turned out that the banks, in making the "marks into zlotys" exchange, earned a quick profit for themselves. From the time that the banks received the marks to the time of the actual conversion, the value of the zloty plummeted, and so the banks earned an extra 10 percent in the exchange. Of the course, the banks' profit also meant 10 percent fewer zlotys going to Polish victims. The claimants' representatives argued that the banks had a duty to avoid such speculative dealings with Holocaust funds, considered "sacred money," and urged them to relinquish this profit.

The final disputed point involved the German insurance companies' participation in the German settlement. As the settlement was first envisioned, insurance claims were not part of the deal. Instead, this was a settlement of the slave labor and related claims; the failure of the German, and other European, insurers to honor policies was a separate matter to be handled through the International Commission on Holocaust Era Insurance Claims (ICHEIC), a nongovernmental body created in 1998 (see chapter 3). During the German negotiations, Allianz, the German insurer giant which was a founding member of both ICHEIC and the German Fund, lobbied for the insurance claims against the German insurers to be taken out of ICHEIC and placed within the German settlement. The claimants' representatives protested, and the matter was never resolved when the deal was negotiated in late December 1999.

As the parties began to discuss how the fund should be distributed, Allianz again insisted that the DM 10 billion include claims against German insurance companies. As support, Allianz pointed to a letter written by President Clinton to Chancellor Schroeder shortly before the talks were concluded in December, stating that the German Fund should be the exclusive forum for all claims against German companies. Count Lambsdorff supported Allianz. "We had assumed from the outset that [insurance] claims would be fully included in the 10 billion marks. We made that very clear in Berlin."[129] But Eizenstat disagreed. "We thought that the claims part of insurance would be covered outside the 10 billion marks, in the ICHEIC process."[130]

Eizenstat eventually gave in and convinced the claimants' representatives to do the same. The claims against the German insurers would be paid out of the DM 10 billion. After the German insurance companies conceded this point, it was widely believed that Allianz, like the other German companies, would be making a proportionate contribution to the fund, which amounted to DM 550 million. Not so. When it came time to make the payment, in 2001, Allianz paid less than the other companies, claiming that the German Foundation should give it credit for all the money it had been contributing since 1998 to help run ICHEIC. Allianz claimed a credit of DM 130 million, or about 20 percent of its obligation to the German Foundation. Worse, Allianz did even not notify the parties, or even the foundation's board, that it had unilaterally deducted 20 percent from its contribution. Rather, Allianz misled everyone by announcing publicly that all of its payments to the German Foundation had been completed, without disclosing that a portion had been withheld.

The plaintiffs' attorneys, American Jewish leaders, Israeli government representatives, state insurance regulators, and even Lawrence Eagleburger, head of ICHEIC, were outraged. Not only had Allianz obtained immunity from the ongoing insurance litigation by inserting itself into the German Fund, but now the company was refusing to make its full contribution to the fund by claiming that all of its previous voluntary payments to ICHEIC should be deducted from the sum it owed to the fund. By the end of 2001, Neuborne, as the representative of the claimants on the German Foundation, had had enough. In November 2001, he filed suit against the original founding German companies to enforce the settlement agreement.[131] A few days earlier, Hausfeld filed his own separate lawsuit against the U.S. government, seeking a court order declaring the deal dead and barring the U.S. government from filing further Statements of Interest in cases in which the Germans would be sued.[132] "Legal peace" had ended, and "legal war" broke out again.

In his suit, filed in the same federal court in Brooklyn that had handled the Swiss bank litigation, Neuborne made the same accusations against the German companies that he had made earlier against the Swiss banks after the Swiss settlement: the defendants were not living up to their part of the bargain. The German companies, to say the least, were not happy. According to Wolfgang Gibowski, the spokesperson for the German companies after the preliminary settlement, in response to an earlier round of lawsuits filed against the companies, "We do not expect to be free from all lawsuits in the future. That would be heaven, and we are living on earth. What we do expect is that some of the same people who signed the agreement don't file additional lawsuits. That seems to us to be misuse."[133]

Nevertheless, the litigation tactic worked, at least for a while. The German companies quickly gave in on some of the disputed items. At Lambsdorff's urging, both Neuborne and Hausfeld voluntarily dismissed their lawsuits a month later, with a promise that the unresolved points would also be settled soon.[134] If not, they were ready to reopen the litigation. As Neuborne explained, "That might be the only thing that would shake the [German] companies loose."[135]

While Allianz eventually agreed to drop its demand for a credit on its obligation to the German Foundation for its previous contributions to ICHEIC, the other disputed points could not be resolved. Therefore, seven months later, in June 2002, Neuborne had to file another lawsuit to further shake the companies loose.[136] In this suit, Neuborne was back in court still seeking to make the German companies pay the full amount of accrued interest on their delayed DM 5 billion contribution to the settlement. The amount was not small: at least DM 100 million (approximately $50 million) was at stake, all of which would go to survivors. As of November 2002, "legal peace" still had not been restored.

SUMMING UP THE SETTLEMENT

In retrospect, there were many similarities, but also significant differences, between the Swiss and the German settlements. First, both settlements were "global" in nature. In return for the DM 10 billion payout, all claims against the German state and any German entity were forever extinguished. Unlike the Swiss bank settlement, however, the German payers were not limited to private industry. Rather, the German government was the prime mover behind the settlement and contributed one-half the DM 10 billion. In fact, the German government's contribution was even greater: to encourage German industry to participate, the companies contributing to the German Fund could write off the contribution on their taxes. This was in stark contrast to the Swiss settlement scenario, in which the Swiss government refused either to participate in the settlement discussions or to advance any funds. At every turn, the German government seemed more eager to resolve the claims than were the private companies actually being sued.

Second, while the total settlement amounts in the German case appear to be large, the individual payouts in both settlements were quite small. The slave labor recipients in the Swiss bank settlement received approximately $1,500; in the German settlement, the payouts to the slave laborers ranged from $2,500 to $7,500. The German settlement, however, did not limit the class of beneficiaries to certain ethnic or other groups persecuted by the Nazis. Rather, any survivor who was forced to work for the Nazis received compensation.

Third, both the Swiss and German settlements were driven by the desire of the European entities to put an end to the bothersome American litigation. The previous chapter described how the Swiss were forced into the settlement by the "one-two punch" of the American class action lawsuit coupled with the threat of American sanctions. The Germans settled for the same reasons. While the German government and companies officially claimed that they were motivated by morality, and not by pressure of American litigation, their acts belied this claim. As a condition for payments of any funds, the Germans insisted that all class action litigation against German companies had to cease and that they be assured of protection from any such lawsuits in the future. To prove the point, they withheld payment to the aging survivors until such a guarantee was fully in place.

Finally, while both settlements came in response to the class action litigation, the German settlement was reached outside the American court system. Rather, the settlement was crafted by the same plaintiffs' lawyers who reached the $1.25 billion agreement with the Swiss banks, but without a federal judge acting as an arbiter. Instead of a Judge Korman pressuring the parties to settle, the German negotiations benefited from the large role played by the Clinton and Schroeder administrations.

Not having to comply with American class action litigation rules proved to be a large timesaver. As a result, the German payments went out at almost the same time as the first payouts from the Swiss bank settlement, even though the latter settlement had been reached sixteen months earlier. However, without a federal judge overseeing the settlement process, there was no neutral party to turn to for resolution of the problems that inevitably arose after the settlement agreement was signed. When disputes arose in the postsettlement stage and the plaintiffs' claimants accused the Germans of breaching the agreement, they were forced to file a new lawsuit to enforce it.

Noting these differences, let us turn to the reactions of the survivors themselves to the German settlement.

WHAT DO SURVIVORS THINK OF THE SETTLEMENT?

Contrary to popular belief and even numerous media reports, the German settlement did not primarily benefit Jewish victims of Nazi Germany. Rather, approximately 80 percent of the beneficiaries of the German Fund were non-Jews, mostly survivors living in Russia and the Slavic countries of eastern Europe. Approximately one million still-living former Slav slave laborers have received, or will receive, DM 5,000 (approximately $2,500) from the German Fund. Approximately 250,000 still-living other survivors, mostly Jews, are entitled to DM 15,000 (approximately $7,500).[137]

I have rarely met a survivor, Jewish or non-Jewish, satisfied with these amounts. As one survivor explained, "I think the whole thing is a terrible scandal, that one has to wait fifty years to be paid. And naturally there is no relation [between the compensation and] what we had to suffer."[137] Noah Flug, an Auschwitz survivor who heads an umbrella group of Holocaust survivors in Israel and who participated in the slave labor negotiations, pointed out that "two-thirds of the people who could have been eligible for money already have died."[139]

Most survivors have grudgingly accepted the fact that this is the best that could now, and at last, be achieved. With the survivor population dying at the rate of 10 percent per year, any more moves to extract a larger payout from the Germans, even if successful, would only cause further delays and reduce the number of survivors who could obtain some measure of justice during their lifetime. As Flug put it, "I have a lot of mixed feelings about this agreement, because I cannot understand why it took so long. But as the saying goes, better late than never."[140] Flug was echoing a common refrain of the survivors.

Abraham Katz, a seventy-eight-year-old retired machinist living with his wife in Salt Lake City and barely getting by on Social Security and a small pension, speaks of the settlement as follows:

> It doesn't seem like much, just $7,000 if I get it. But if someone should get this, I believe it should be a person like me. I lost my entire family—my mother, Miry, my father, Locyer, and my two sisters. I went through such hell, I was deprived of my youth and suffered so over the years. And while it doesn't sound like much, it would help tremendously at this stage of my life.[141]

Gideon Taylor, a young Jewish Irish lawyer who is now running the daily affairs of the Claims Conference and who was involved in the negotiations, commented, "We don't speak of justice, we speak of a measure of justice. We don't speak of making whole, but of symbolic payments by companies that had never really acknowledged responsibility and are now doing so at last."[142]

The most vocal opposition to the settlement came from some Jewish survivor groups in the United States and Great Britain. These survivors spoke of the paltry sum they would be receiving. To them, DM 15,000 ($7,500) amounts to an insult, considering both the horrendous hardships they endured as slave laborers and the benefits gained by German private industry from their work. As the Los Angeles–based survivor Si Frumkin, who was forced to work for a German firm building an aircraft factory near Dachau, said, "I worked there for a year, seven days a week. Even taking into account the minimum wage in Germany at that time, plus interest, that company owes me around $80,000. I can't even begin to think what else they owe for my father, who died working there."[143] Frumkin said he was disgusted at "the idea that I am supposed to be satisfied with [the settlement]."[144] As for the actions of the executive branch in brokering the settlement, Frumkin adds, "It makes me sick that our government is going to go to court to stop any private proceedings against those companies. That is not what our government was elected to do."[145] Ted Deutch of Los Angeles, whose brother was murdered by the guards of the German company where they were slaves, remarks, "I am devastated. If there is justice, this is injustice."[146] Toni Klar of Camp Hill, Pennsylvania, who at age sixteen was shipped to Bergen-Belsen and applied for the funds, said,

"They will never be able to compensate us. I will never forget, and I will never forgive."[147]

The blustery language of the American lawyers did not help keep in check the expectations of the survivors in the United States. At the time of the court filings in 1998 and early 1999, the lawyers asserted in their lawsuits that they were seeking "at least $75,000 for each of the surviving victims."[148] Attorney Deborah Sturman, referring to criticism of the lawyers' $20 billion demand, explained, "Twenty billion doesn't sound too high and it's going to be more."[149] Ed Fagan concurred. "This case won't be settled for $10 billion or 10 billion marks."[150] When the Germans first announced the fund in February 1999, Mel Weiss blasted it as "nothing but an obvious attempt to cheapen the impact for [German industry]. Taking some crumbs from each of these companies will make [the fund] look bigger. They are doing nothing but creating an illusion."[151] Eight months later, in December 1999, Weiss and the other lawyers were encouraging the survivors to accept the illusion.[152]

In California, one of the major supporters of the slave laborers' claims was the California state senator Tom Hayden. In 1998, Hayden sponsored a state law specifically authorizing former World War II slaves to bring legal actions in California against their former corporate masters. Following the settlement, Hayden published an editorial in the *Los Angeles Times*, whose title expressed the views of many Holocaust survivors: : "Ex-slave Laborers Deserve Far Better; Rich Firms Get Good Press with Token Payments, but What about the Victims?"[153] Hayden pointedly asked, "Why is this agreement being hailed by the Clinton administration as a historic settlement when, in any other context, it would be dismissed as a slap on the wrist of the bully?"[154] Hayden also responded to the mantra that the DM 10 billion settlement was necessary lest more survivors die without receiving compensation:

> The repeated argument of U.S. negotiators is that World War II slave laborers are aging and infirm and deserve closure before they all die. That is true, but it is being politically manipulated to force an inadequate settlement. The United States did not make survivor compensation a priority until legislators and lawyers representing survivors began taking action. . . . For 50 years, the Cold War interests of the American government, which defined Germany as a key anti-Soviet ally, took precedence. Even today, the NATO alliance, including

Germany's involvement in the "humanitarian" bombing of Yugoslavia earlier this year, is more strategic to State Department types than achieving full compensation for victims of slavery almost 60 years ago.[155]

Responding to the survivors' complaints, all Lambsdorff could say was, "Believe me, I wish we had greater funds available for distribution. But 10 billion marks is what we got and what was agreed upon by all the participating parties after long and arduous negotiations."[156]

Defending the settlement, Eizenstat pointed out the German Foundation will "without question, provide benefits to more victims, and will do so faster and with less uncertainty than would litigation, with its attendant delays and legal hurdles."[157] Eizenstat made a valid point. Proceeding with the litigation was risky. The Holocaust slave labor lawsuits, as shown, were not going well. Two federal judges had already dismissed five of the cases, and other judges might follow this precedent with the remaining suits. Even if the dismissals were overturned on appeal, this could take at least one year, and by that time more survivors would have died. If a trial on the merits were eventually held and the slave laborers received a favorable verdict, the German companies could appeal that result. This would produce more delays and an even smaller pool of beneficiaries.[158] As Hausfeld somberly concluded, the settlement "is not enough if you judge what should have been done, [but] it is clear that this is the best achievable result."[159]

In the United States, a commentary from the *Pittsburgh-Post Gazette* sums up the mixed emotions about the actual settlement and its symbolic value:

> Nobody can pretend that the paltry sum of $7500 per slave laborer, or any dollar amount for that matter, could ever right the heinous historical crimes involved. But, however unsatisfactory, damages are accorded an important role, a symbolic one, in our jurisprudence as a means of assigning, and accepting responsibility. For those aged . . . surviving slave laborers, the amount of the checks will surely not be as significant as their symbolic meaning, as a statement from the world and from the German people that what was done to these workers was wrong and has not been forgotten.[160]

In Israel, the *Jerusalem Post* questioned even the symbolic value of the settlement:

> The agreement . . . on how to allocate the DM 10 billion German "slave labor" fund is not a victory for justice. It reflects the triumph of practicality. The war has been over for 55 years. The surviving Nazi victims are old and dying. The longer victims' advocates held out for benefits, the fewer survivors there would be to collect them. . . . In closing this deal, Germany's industrial giants are getting off incredibly lightly. . . . Among the unsettling elements of the deal is that, when stripped to its core, the slave-labor agreement cannot be called a humanitarian gesture, because it comes with a price. In exchange for this deal, German companies expect to receive "legal peace" from any lawsuits in the United States.
>
> Justice should have come a half-century ago, when hundreds of thousands of survivors would have been able to use the payments—however symbolic—to rebuild their lives, not ease their pain at twilight.[161]

Among those who were pleased to receive the funds were survivors in the former Soviet Union and eastern Europe, both Jewish and non-Jewish, to whom the amounts were not merely symbolic. Known as "double victims" for having suffered terrible hardships first under Nazism and then Communism, they received the payments at an opportune time. Just as these survivors were getting older and ready to retire, Communism collapsed. In its aftermath came the end of the social safety net created under Communism, which included free medical care and subsidized prices for food and housing. The elderly survivors were now left to fend for themselves on their meager, and now greatly devalued, pensions. A payment of even a few thousand dollars would go a long way for them. My mother's elderly cousin in Odessa, to whom our family regularly sends monthly packages of food and medicine, was ecstatic to receive the funds, as she had been surviving on a monthly pension of $100.

Tragically, for many of these survivors, the payment from the slave labor fund would be the only payment they would ever receive for the suffering they endured during World War II. Unlike the survivors living in the United States, Western Europe, and Israel, who had been receiving monthly payments from West Germany since the 1950s, most of the survivors living behind the Iron Curtain had been cut out of the West German postwar reparations system.[162]

THE AUSTRIANS ALSO SETTLE

The Austrians also agreed to compensate their former slave laborers. As in the German slave labor agreement, Eizenstat was closely involved in the negotiations. Eizenstat's Austrian counterpart in the slave labor negotiations, taking Lambsdorff's role, was Maria Schaumeyer, the respected former head of the Austrian National Bank. Schaumeyer was appointed in February 2000, just days after the inauguration of Wolfgang Schuessel as the Austrian chancellor, and was given the title of "special representative for the settlement of slave and forced labour related issues." Schuessel moved quickly to appoint Schaumeyer to the post and gave her a mandate to expeditiously resolve the slave labor issue. In fact, Schuessel raised the issue of slave labor compensation in his inaugural address.[163] As with the Germans, it appears that politics had a lot to do with his move. In Austria's case, however, it was a means of helping neutralize the international outcry from Schuessel's decision to allow the far-right Freedom Party to join his government as a junior partner.

In October 2000, Eizenstat and Schaumeyer worked out an agreement with which the WJC and the class action lawyers concurred. The final settlement was in many respects similar to the German slave labor deal, and it in fact used that settlement as a model. The Austrian government and its industry agreed to create a foundation under Austrian law to compensate the former slave laborers, and they capped the total payouts at 6 billion Austrian shillings ($410 million). The Austrians named their slave labor foundation the Austrian Fund for Reconciliation, Peace and Cooperation. Called the Austrian Reconciliation Fund for short, it came into existence in November 2000, after the foundation law was passed unanimously by the Austrian parliament. The Austrian fund would begin to make payments only after all the lawsuits against Austrian firms were dismissed and "legal peace" between Austria and the United States was established. As the Austrian slave labor Web site explains,

Deputy Secretary Eizenstat assured Dr. Schaumeyer that Austria would be treated equally with Germany and that Austria could obtain a similar Executive Agreement with the United States which would oblige the U.S. Administration in all future potential law suits concerning slave and forced labour to submit a Statement of Interest to the courts, declaring that . . . the Austrian Reconciliation Fund would be seen as the only forum and remedy for such claims.[164]

Nevertheless, Austria, like Germany, labeled these payouts as being made completely "on a voluntary basis."[165] Payments to the former victims were also made through the same partner organizations used by the German Foundation: the Claims Conference for the former Jewish slaves of Austrian industry and the local bodies in Poland, Russia, Belarus, Ukraine, and the Czech Republic, which were by then receiving funds from the German Foundation and which now were given the additional role of likewise distributing payments to the former non-Jewish Austrian slaves still alive in their countries.

An Austrian historical commission estimated that approximately one million Jewish and non-Jewish slaves from eastern Europe toiled in Austria during the war and that about 150,000 are still alive today. (One exception: inmates at Dachau and Mauthausen, located in Austria, are being paid from the German Foundation, since they are covered by German law.) As with the German settlement, the claimants were divided into two categories: non-Jews, primarily eastern European Slavs, who were dragooned into Austria to work for Austrian industry; and Jews, who survived the Reich's "death-through-work" program in Nazi Austria. Each forced laborer is entitled to receive between 20,000 and 35,000 Austrian shillings (approximately $1,500 to $2,500); each slave laborer is paid 105,000 Austrian shillings (approximately $ 7,500). These amounts are roughly equivalent to the payouts made by Germany, the only difference being the different fluctuating currency values between the Austrian shilling and the German mark (and, now, the European Union's euro). Forced laborer mothers whose children were taken away from them and placed in the *kinderheim* in Austria, where the children perished from mistreatment, are entitled to an extra 5,000 Austrian shillings (approximately $350) for the death of their child. Applicants could apply until November 2002, and currently all payouts are expected to be made by November 2003, within one year of the close of the application process.

In January 2001, just days before the end of the Clinton administration and Eizenstat's return to private life, Eizenstat and the Austrians worked out a final agreement on the nonlabor restitution issues.[166] In this second agreement, Austria agreed to compensate its former Jewish citizens persecuted in Austria after the Nazis came to power and, as their first official act, stripped Austria's 200,000 Jews of their citizenship. Two types of outstanding nonlabor claims were resolved by this agreement: Austria agreed to settle claims for the seizure of Jewish property and to pay pensions to all survivors from Austria, including child survivors. Each of the approximately 20,000 still-living survivors originally from Austria is entitled to receive $7,000. As of November 2002, no payments had yet been made to these survivors because of the ongoing litigation of the nonlabor claims.

The nonslave labor settlement has been criticized as inadequate and as having been put together hurriedly to close another set of claims before Clinton left office. Others blame it on "Holocaust fatigue" by the time it came to settle with the Austrians. Eizenstat, the WJC, and the class action lawyers no longer had the stamina to take on Austria with the same vigor they applied to the Swiss and German negotiations. According to Dr. Ariel Muzicant, president of the Austrian Jewish Community, "Our own historians estimate the total amount of property seized from Austria's Jews at roughly $14 billion, of which 60 percent was never returned and never compensated."[167]

In February 2001, a month after Eizenstat put together the second Austrian deal, a suit was filed in federal court in Los Angeles by some of the nonlabor claimants against Austria seeking to void the deal. As of November 2002, this lawsuit was still pending. Austria, like Germany before it, is presently withholding payments on this portion of the settlement because of this pending litigation. For the slave labor claims, all lawsuits against Austrian firms were dismissed by the class action lawyers, and so the first payments to the laborers went out in early 2002. More than 20,000 former slaves have already received their one-time payout.

The Austrian government's actions to compensate former slave laborers and to settle other wartime claims could not have come without the precedent set by Germany. The events that followed the filing of earlier Holocaust-era claims in U.S. courts compelled the Austrian government and Austrian industry to settle. However, various issues are yet to be resolved, not the least being the Holocaust looted art found in Austria (see chapter 5).

Austria has perpetuated the myth that it was Hitler's first victim and not his first ally. Unfortunately, the myth still prevails, despite the financial settlements. As Anton Pelinka, a professor of politics at Innsbruck University in Austria, stated in the aftermath of the settlements, in Austria, "the problem has been ignored since 1945, and the next generation will have to . . . come to terms with Austria's past."[168]

3

Reclaiming Prewar Insurance Policies

BEFORE WORLD WAR II, insurance policies and annuities were popular investment vehicles for Jews in prewar Europe; in fact, an insurance policy came to be known as "a poor man's Swiss bank account."[1]

A report in 1999 from the then Washington State Insurance Commissioner Deborah Senn (the Senn Report) explains the role of insurance for the Jewish merchant class in prewar Europe:

> In addition to affording protection against loss or injury to life and property, insurance was widely perceived by Jews as a sound means of saving and investment, an issue of heightened concern to a vulnerable minority group. Jewish family breadwinners were more likely to be self-employed business owners and professionals who purchased insurance directly from agents, rather than through group or workplace plans. The anecdotal evidence is that Jewish families were more likely to purchase larger-than-average policies.[2]

An insurance trade journal examining the Holocaust-era insurance issue explains further:

> In the time between the two world wars, life insurance policies and annuities were popular investments. Then, investors had no US bull market, zero-coupon bonds or an abundance of other financial opportunities. During that time, Jewish families bought policies worth an estimated $2 billion to $2.5 billion in today's dollars, about ten times higher than the prewar value.[3]

A number of other experts estimated the figure to be much higher, closer to $10 billion in today's dollars.

The Senn Report testifies to the popularity of insurance in prewar Europe. For example, in 1939 each household in Germany held, on average, two insurance policies, a situation not much different from that today. By 1938, 1.5 million Czechoslovaks were covered by life insurance of some kind.

One common policy was known as a "dowry policy," to be paid when a girl reached adulthood and used to cover her dowry when she married. (A corollary for boys was an education insurance policy.) Erna Gans, a Holocaust survivor from Poland, describes the practice: "When I was born, my father bought an insurance policy in my name. And at 21, I was supposed to get 5,000 gold dollars to be used for my dowry."[4] Ms. Gans's father bought the dowry policy at her birth from the Italian insurer Reunione Adriatica, now owned by the German insurer Allianz. At the time of her death in April 1999, her claim had still not been paid.

Gans's statement contains an important point: because of the unstable economic climate in prewar Europe, especially in eastern and central Europe, payment on the policies was often designated in U.S. dollars or some other western European currency. The Senn Report explains that the foreign insurance carriers doing business in this region were able to attract business from the Jewish merchant class by guaranteeing that claims would be paid either in the local currency or, "at the policyholder's option, in gold or U.S. dollars anywhere in the world."[5] Another example is Solomon Heitner, a Holocaust survivor now living in California, who holds an insurance policy that his grandfather bought in 1931 from Reunione Adriatica. The policy, issued in Poland, states, "We are responsible for all the obligations with all our assets in Poland or outside."[6]

Many Jews in prewar Europe also worked in the insurance industry, holding positions at all levels. Franz Kafka, though a law graduate, held the post of senior secretary at the Workers' Accident Insurance Institute in Prague. Some of the current claimants to Holocaust-era insurance come from Jewish families long involved in the insurance business in prewar Europe.

There is one critical qualifier to this scenario: it does not apply to the millions of Jews living in prewar Soviet Union. The contrast in my parents' situation—my father was from Poland, and my mother was from the Soviet Union—illustrates this point. Before the war, my father lived in Warsaw, and his family operated a tavern. We have no idea, however, whether my tavern-owner grandparents bought insurance policies from any of the western European insurance companies widely operating in prewar Warsaw. My father is no longer alive, and by the time

Holocaust-era insurance became an issue, he could no longer tell us whether his parents held insurance. So far, our last name has not appeared on any of the recently released Holocaust-era insurance lists. My mother, however, comes from a small village in Ukraine. After the Bolshevik Revolution in 1917, private enterprise was abolished, and most of the significant private property was nationalized. For this reason, we are certain that my mother has no insurance claim.

Like the Swiss banks, the insurance companies that sold insurance to the local Jewish populace either are still in existence today or are successor companies to the insurers who sold the prewar policies to Jews throughout eastern and central Europe. Many of these European insurance companies significantly expanded after the war, not only in the insurance market, but also in related businesses. In effect, they have become gigantic multinational insurance and financial services conglomerates. As with all multinationals, a major chunk of their profits are generated from operations in the United States, either directly or through subsidiaries. A few examples will suffice.

The second largest insurance company in the world is Allianz A.G. of Germany. In 1996, when Holocaust-era insurance claims first came under scrutiny, Allianz collected $6.2 billion in premiums in the United States. Unknown to most Americans, Allianz owns more than thirty U.S. subsidiaries, including its most famous one, the Fireman's Fund Insurance Companies. The power of Allianz was described by the *Wall Street Journal* in 1999: "Not much happens in corporate Germany without input from the country's largest insurer, Allianz AG."[7]

The Zurich Insurance Group from Switzerland, another company involved in the prewar European insurance market, also has a strong presence in the United States today. In 1996, Zurich collected $5.8 billion in premiums in the United States. Zurich owns thirty-three U.S.-based subsidiaries, including Zurich Kemper Insurance, Fidelity and Deposit Insurance, the Maryland Companies, and the American insurance stalwart, Farmers Group Insurance.

Another Swiss insurance company that participated in the prewar European insurance market is the Winterthur Group, owned by the Swiss bank Credit Suisse. In 1996, Winterthur collected $1.4 billion in premiums in the United States. Its U.S. operations include Unigard Insurance, Southern Guaranty Insurance, Vanguard Insurance, and five other subsidiaries.

The European insurance company with the most notoriety in regard to Holocaust-era insurance is Assicurazioni Generali S.p.A, commonly known as Generali. It is the largest insurance company in Italy, with more than $40 billion in assets. Generali operates in 45 countries, owns close to 120 insurance companies and 60 financial and real estate companies worldwide, and has a workforce of almost 57,000. Its corporate motto is "Insurance without Borders." In 1999, Generali collected approximately $700 million in premiums in the United States, which it earned through various U.S.-based subsidiaries, the most famous being INA Insurance.

Generali was founded in 1831 by a group of Jewish merchants in Trieste, Italy. Its chairman until recently was a Holocaust survivor of Auschwitz. "Except for the period from 1938 until the end of World War II, Jews were always leaders in the company, and continue so today," the *Jerusalem Post* reported.[8] Generali also owns Migdal Insurance, Israel's largest insurance company, which it purchased in 1997. The corporate logo of Generali is the "Lion of Judah," a symbol well known to the Jewish people. Known for these reasons as a "Jewish company" in prewar Europe, its agents saturated the major Jewish population centers. Generali was the leading foreign insurance company in Poland, Czechoslovakia, and Hungary; the company had offices selling policies directly to consumers in those three countries and also in Bulgaria, Yugoslavia, and Greece. According to another *Jerusalem Post* story, Generali sold "the most life insurance and annuity policies in Eastern Europe during the 1920's, 1930's and 1940's, frequently to Jews."[9] Some published reports estimated that Generali wrote up to 80 percent of the Jewish policies in prewar Europe, but the company disputes this figure.[10] The Senn Report estimates that Generali had a market share of between one-fourth to one-third of policies sold in prewar Poland, Czechoslovakia, and Hungary.[11]

THE NAZIS' CONFISCATION OF INSURANCE BENEFITS

The Nazis' persecution of Jews in Germany included the confiscation of insurance policies from its Jewish citizens. "After April 1938, German Jews were required to report to Nazi authorities all their property and personal valuables, including insurance policies," the Senn Report explains. "These comprehensive property declarations enabled the [Nazi] regime to seize the assets of German Jews. After the 1938 *Anschluss*—the annexation of Austria—this technique was used to seize assets of Jews in that country as well."[12]

A striking example of the theft of insurance proceeds by the Nazis, and the German insurers' collusion in such theft, occurred in November 1938 in the aftermath of Kristallnacht, the state-sponsored pogrom in which synagogues were burned and Jewish homes and businesses were destroyed all over Germany. Even though many of the Jewish merchants whose shops and other properties were damaged or looted by the Nazis during the campaign held casualty insurance to cover their losses (estimated at $270 million in today's currency, according to a Nazi-era German document uncovered in 2001),[13] the Nazis ordered the insurance companies to pay all such claims to the state rather than to the injured parties. In a deal made with the insurers, the companies were allowed to expunge the claims of their Jewish policyholders by paying only a fraction of the claims' value to the German state.[14]

This confiscation was later "expanded to include denial of life insurance, health insurance, and pension benefits for [Germany's] Jews."[15] The German insurance companies made arrangements with the Nazis that allowed them to pay less on the claims to the German government in lieu of paying the Jewish claimants. In a "sweetheart deal," the insurers were allowed to keep for themselves a transaction fee of anywhere from 15 to 25 percent for such payouts. Once the policy was paid to the Nazis instead of the Jewish policyholder, the policy was considered to be extinguished, the file on it closed, and the required customary reserves backing the full face value of the policy no longer in place.

The German insurers, like other German companies, supported Hitler and his regime. Indeed, Allianz's CEO, Kurt Schmidt, became Hitler's minister of economy in 1933. Documents unearthed in Poland in 1997 revealed that during the war, Allianz insured a number of concentration camps, including Auschwitz and Dachau, for damage caused by "careless or malicious actions on the part of prisoners."[16]

A 1999 article in *Best's Review*, a leading insurance journal, describing Allianz's recent emergence as world insurance giant, also recounted its wartime history:

> As Allianz strives to maintain market leadership in a rapidly changing industry, it looks to its sometimes-painful past. The company has reserved a portion of its Munich headquarters complex as the Allianz

Center for Corporate History, remembering nearly 110 years that are full of growth and innovation, but also recalling embarrassing ties to the Nazi era. . . . A forthright attitude can't quite hide the discomfort of the subject when it is broached during an interview at the head-quarters. Official remarks float between directness and euphemisms, at times referring explicitly to the Nazis, at others speaking "of the years from 1933 to 1945." As to Schmidt, especially awkward are the ties of the one former Allianz chairman to the early years of Adolf Hitler's regime. Kurt Schmidt left Allianz in 1933 to become second minister for economic affairs in the Nazi government. In what the company casts as a kind of blessing in disguise, Schmidt suffered a heart attack in 1934, from which he never recovered. He stepped down in 1935 for health reasons, avoiding the peril of a public break with Hitler on ideological grounds. The picture of Schmidt that has been as-sembled [by Allianz] reveals an ambivalent figure who saw real op-portunities to do good from an economic perspective. Schmidt was part of SS Chief Heinrich Himmler's circle of friends, but he also had a French wife and English relatives and never embraced all of Hitler's policies, especially his racial ideology, according to the company.[17]

As for the revelation about insuring Auschwitz, Allianz took pains to explain the nuances behind accusations that it insured concentration camps. In fact, the company says, it participated with other insurers in covering industrial companies that happened to have facilities in the camps. The government self-insured its own property.[18]

In June 1997, Allianz hired Professor Gerald D. Feldman, director of the Center of German and European Studies at the University of California at Berkeley, to research its wartime history. As Feldman pointed out, Allianz continued to whitewash its wartime history until hiring himself and his researchers to conduct their study:

The immediate reasons for their decision to promote such a study at that time were very clear. On the one hand, Allianz—along with a number of other German and European insurance companies—was charged in class actions in U.S. courts with failure to properly dis-charge their obligations toward Jewish policyholders. Allianz thus had the problem of explaining what had happened to the policies of its Jewish customers. On the other hand, Allianz found itself confronted with press reports [citing to a June 1997 story in the German weekly

Der Spiegel] about insuring SS-owned factories in the concentration camps, among them factories in Auschwitz. The revelations inevitably lent new importance and significance to what had previously been known but unappreciated or neglected.[19]

As Feldman indicates, until the class action lawsuits were filed and an exposé in the popular media prompted a new look into Allianz's shady past, the insurance giant was content to let its wartime history be forgotten. When Allianz celebrated its centenary in 1990, he writes, "neither General Director Wolfgang Schieren nor the invited speaker on the occasion, the prominent journalist and Hitler biographer Joachim Fest, gave even a suggestion that Allianz might in any way have been implicated in the Third Reich."[20]

Professor Feldman issued his report in 2001. In remarkable detail, his study shows the close collusion of not only Allianz, but the entire German insurance industry, with the Nazi regime. In defense of Allianz and the other German insurers, Feldman noted: "The individuals running Allianz and the insurance industry were compelled to conduct their business in the context of a regime that powerfully influenced relations in ways that to a substantial degree did not conform to any 'economic logic' previously known to them."[21] The way that Allianz and the other German insurers adapted to the "Nazi way of doing business"— and the degree of compulsion they actually faced—was beyond the scope of his study.

One would think that Allianz, possessing such a checkered wartime history and at the same time making such an aggressive push into the U.S. market, would deal promptly and fairly with Holocaust-era insurance claims. Even if such claims lacked full documentation, it would be in Allianz's best interest, purely for public relations purposes, to bend over backward to close out the remaining insurance claims that focused attention on its wartime past. Curiously, Allianz has not chosen this route. In a misstep equal to the banal statements made by some Swiss officials when confronted with claims for their wartime activities (see chapter 1), Herbert Hansmeyer, a the managing director in charge of Allianz's Western Hemisphere operations, described the company's moves in finally dealing with such claims as "an act of appeasement."[22] Putting salt on the wound still felt by Holocaust survivors, Hansmeyer added: "I cannot become very emotional about insurance claims that are 60 years old."[23]

Faced with claims on its prewar policies, Allianz has often asserted that the policies either had lapsed or were paid out. "Practically all claims have been paid out in the 1950's and 1960's in [West German government] compensation proceedings,"[24] Joerg Allgaeurer of Allianz asserted. Danny Kadden, Deborah Senn's chief adviser on Holocaust insurance issues and now an advocate for survivors, strongly disagreed: "We have very good reason to believe a significant number, if not most, of the policies sold by German companies to victims of the Holocaust remain unpaid to the rightful owners of the policies today."[25]

The case of Ralph Meyerstein, now eighty-one and living in Maryland, exemplifies Allianz's typically cavalier response to claimants. At age eighteen, shortly after Hitler came to power, Ralph was sent away by his parents from Germany to London. While there, he received a letter from his mother, dated August 4, 1939, which he still possesses, telling him that "Allianz ist in Ordnung" ("Allianz is in order"). He believes the message meant that the two policies his father purchased in the 1920s were being kept up-to-date. The last communication Meyerstein received from his parents was a letter dated November 9, 1941. The Nazis deported them to the East, he later learned, where they perished.

After the war, Allianz confirmed the existence of the two policies that Meyerstein's father had purchased but failed to pay on them. Meyerstein was "told that the policies must have been cashed in or lapsed because his father's name did not appear on a record of those holding Allianz insurance policies as of December 1941."[26] In 1961, he received from the West German government restitution of approximately $800, which he claims was for lost or stolen property of his parents and did not include payment on the Allianz policies. Nevertheless, in August 2002, after Meyerstein filed a claim with Allianz, the company denied the claim, citing the West German government's restitution payment as the reason.

EUROPEAN INSURERS AND SURVIVORS' POSTWAR CLAIMS

With the conquest of Europe by Nazi Germany, the insurance companies in the occupied countries became subject to Nazi laws. Many of the local companies' assets were simply taken over by the Nazis, and their insurance portfolios were transferred to German companies that were favored by the Nazi regime. As a result, the German insurers obtained substantial benefits from the Nazi conquest of Europe. A wartime OSS report concluded,

> Axis monopoly of the European insurance business has proved immensely profitable to those concerned in it, several German companies having, according to recent reports, doubled and in some cases quadrupled their incomes. The importance of the role played by the insurance business in the Nazi economy is indicated by the statement that it was "the handmaiden of German industrial expansion in occupied countries."[27]

The wartime role of the German insurers reverberates in the world economy to the present day. German insurers were poised for tremendous growth as soon as the war was over and obtained a head start over their European competitors, making them the leading insurance companies in the world. According to a report in the *Wall Street Journal*,

> Allianz picked up the core of its stock holdings after World War II. At a time when German companies were desperate for capital, Allianz was one of the few sources of cash to rebuild the bombed-out country. As German corporations regained momentum and became global players, Allianz continued to invest and maintain its influence in boardrooms.[28]

Some insurers opposed the Nazis. According to Generali, it resisted Nazification of its offices in occupied Europe, helped its Jewish employees escape to safety, and generally lost assets as a result of the Nazi occupation.

While European insurers, both German and non-German, have been accused of profiting from the Holocaust by doing business with the Nazis, the main accusation against them is similar to that made against the Swiss banks. Like the Swiss banks, European insurers such as AXA, Allianz, Generali, Winterthur, and Zurich Insurance Group were accused of not honoring policies bought from them by Holocaust victims in prewar Europe.

The claim made by the Stern family, the most famous of the Holocaust-era insurance claims cases, is in many ways representative. The claim stems from the activities of Moshe "Mor" Stern, a wealthy Jewish merchant who died in the Holocaust. Before the war, Mor had a successful wine-and-spirits production business in Uzghorod, Hungary. He and his wife, Regina, had six sons and one daughter. In 1944, the entire Stern family, except for one son, was transported to Auschwitz. Mor, Regina, and three sons perished there.

In June 1945, soon after the war ended, Adolf Stern, Mor's oldest son who survived the Buchenwald concentration camp, made his way to Generali's offices in Prague seeking payment on the family's insurance policies. Adolf was twenty-eight years old at the time.

In his lawsuit filed fifty years later, in April 1998, Adolf, now eighty-two and retired in Florida, described what happened next:

> The Assicurazioni Generali officials were less than kind. They stated that I would have to produce a death certificate and copies of the relevant insurance policies before they would process the claims. I explained that Hitler did not pass out death certificates and that all family insurance documentation was confiscated by the Third Reich. They declined my request to retrieve from Generali's own files the insurance and annuity policies sold to my family. The officials said that Generali could not help me and they had me forcibly removed from the premises by a security guard. I was humiliated.[29]

Adolf and his other surviving siblings claimed that before the war Mor took out substantial life insurance and annuity policies and a dowry policy for his daughter, Edith, through the Prague office of Generali. According to the Sterns, Mor bought the policies between 1929 and 1939 and prepaid the premiums on the policies through 1944. Unfortunately, the surviving children had no documentation, all of which was lost during the war.

For the next fifty years, Adolf and his other siblings, and subsequently their children, repeatedly petitioned Generali to make payment on Mor's policies. They were rebuffed each time.

In a letter dated August 31, 1972, to Edith, who was now living in Israel, Generali stated that it had found no documentation of any life insurance policy on Mor Stern: "Referring to your letter of the 19th of August, 1972, we wish to inform you that in the local records of our former Czechoslovakian stock we have not traced any assurance offered on the life of Mr. Mor Stern."[30] By the 1990s, Mor's grandchildren were now pursuing the claims. In a letter dated October 11, 1996, to Martin Stern, one of the grandchildren living in Israel, Generali again denied that it had any records of any policies issued to Mor Stern:

> Assicurazioni Generali has no direct knowledge of the incidents described in the letter of Mr. Stern (to which the new items relate). Assicurazioni Generali made efforts to find records relating to the insurance policy of the late Mr. Morris Stern, allegedly issued in Prague in 1929/30. Unfortunately, no such records were found, as the documents and details relating to specific policies were normally kept in the Prague Branch Office.[31]

In December 1996, there was a breakthrough. As Martin, the grandson, pursued his search, a Generali clerk found and faxed to him a copy of one of the annuity policies. Policy no. 115285 was issued to Mor Stern on April 23, 1929, payable upon Mor's death to his surviving heirs or payable to him in 1949 if he was still alive. The initial premium on the policy had a payout value of at least 400,000 Czech koruna, equivalent at that time to approximately $15,000. Mor had paid the original policy until 1939. Adolf had paid an additional five years' worth of premiums, making the policy current until 1944. Records of the policy were found at an archive warehouse at Generali's headquarters in Trieste. The archive contained "water copies," akin to carbon copies, of the policies, listing the basic information about each policy written.

Confronted now with the policies, Generali resorted to another argument. Because its Prague office was nationalized after the war by the Communist government of Czechoslovakia, Generali claimed that it was no longer obligated to pay on the policy. The Sterns, they suggested, would have to turn to the new post-Communist Czech government for relief.

In hearings before the U.S. House of Representatives' Banking Committee, held in 1998, Scott Vayer, Generali's in-house American counsel, explained the company's legal position:

> The question with respect to Generali, then, is more pointed—why were policies that were issued in Eastern and Central Europe not paid? The short answer is that Generali's businesses, as well as those of other insurers in those countries, were nationalized, expropriated, or liquidated by the governments that came into power in those countries

Kiplinger photo of Mor Stern, policy, and Jewish star—collage. *Courtesy of Larry Sultan and Lisa Stern.*

after the war. The assets and property that backed insurance throughout Central and Eastern Europe were confiscated. The Communist regimes that swept across Central and Eastern Europe and seized control in Czechoslovakia, Hungary, Poland and other countries became the successors to our insurance business. They became legally and morally obligated to the Holocaust victims and their families who were the beneficiaries of policies issued by Generali before the war, when it had control of its business and assets. And if, for whatever reason, their claims may or may not have been made before, it is to the governments and successor entities in those countries that the families of the victims should be looking, morally and legally, for recompense.[32]

THE LITIGATION BEGINS

Despite some criticism of the outcomes achieved in the Swiss bank and German slave labor litigation, the litigation is generally viewed as successful, even if the results were mixed. Not so, though, for the litigation of the Holocaust-era insurance claims. Other than some initial legal victories, the whole litigation enterprise can be seen as a failure. For the most part, the same can be said for the entire effort in the Holocaust-era insurance claims: a lot of money was spent with little to show for it.

At the outset, the litigation strategy appeared promising. It began not much differently than the other Holocaust-era suits. On March 30, 1997, Edward Fagan and Robert Swift, who in October 1996 had filed the first Holocaust-era lawsuit, against the Swiss banks, opened a new front in the Holocaust restitution movement by filing a class action against Generali and fifteen other European insurance companies for failing to pay on their Holocaust-era insurance policies. The suit sought $1 billion from each insurance defendant. For this suit, Fagan added to his legal team the New York law firm of Anderson, Kill & Olick, which specializes in insurance claims litigation. The lawsuit was brought in federal court in Manhattan by Martha Drucker Cornell, a Holocaust survivor living in Queens, New York, and twenty-eight other plaintiffs, all Jewish survivors.[33]

At the end of the next year, on December 30, 1998, Hausfeld and Weiss filed their own class action lawsuit, on behalf of another group of Jewish survivors, likewise listing Generali as the lead defendant and naming twenty-three other defendant insurance companies.[34] A total of twenty-five European insurance companies now faced litigation in the United States arising from their Holocaust-era activities.

The two suits were consolidated before the federal chief judge, Michael Mukasey, in Manhattan, who would now be asked to play the role of Chief Judge Korman in the Swiss bank litigation. As they did with the other Holocaust lawsuits, the defendant insurers responded to the lawsuits with several motions to dismiss. The arguments were substantially the same as those raised in the Swiss bank and German slave labor litigation. It appeared that the attorneys for both sides involved in all these suits could now just do a "cookie cutter" job on their briefs, essentially duplicating the claims and counterclaims made in the dismissal motions filed in the other suits.

In what has now become an informal term in this litigation area, Judge Mukasey "Kormanized" the motions; like Judge Korman, he held onto the motions to dismiss without issuing a ruling on them, in order to give the parties a chance to settle the matter outside court. In a critical difference, however, Judge Mukasey, unlike Judge Korman, was unwilling to act as a mediator in search of a settlement. As a result, the suits languished in his court for years without any end in sight, and elderly Holocaust survivors became increasingly bitter that they could not get their day in court.

Between the filings of the two federal class action lawsuits, the Stern family, still unable to get Generali to recognize their claims, filed their own lawsuit in California. Since the federal cases were not moving, the *Stern* lawsuit became the most prominent case in the Holocaust-era insurance struggle.

THE SUCCESSFUL *STERN V. GENERALI* ACTION

The lawyers in the Stern lawsuit used a strategy completely different from that of the lawyers on the East Coast in the Holocaust restitution movement. First, the Stern lawsuit was not a class action. Rather, the Stern family made a legal claim on behalf of themselves only, seeking to obtain payment from only one insurance company, Generali, for money allegedly owed to the heirs of Mor Stern. Second, unlike the plaintiffs' lawyers on the East Coast who went into federal court, the Stern lawyers filed their lawsuit in California state court. Finally, the Stern lawyers recruited California politicians to assist them in the litigation by having California enact legislation dealing specifically with Holocaust-era insurance claims. This last innovation was soon duplicated by both other states and Congress.[35]

The strategy was successful. While the federal class action lawsuits

Plaintiff Adolph Stern and
his attorney Lisa Stern.
*Courtesy of the Miami Herald /
Carl Juste.*

in Manhattan became mired in legal delays, and Judge Mukasey eventually dismissed most of them, the Stern action in California—and other individual state lawsuits filed by the same legal team—succeeded in forcing settlements from Generali.

One member of the Stern family filing the claim against Generali was Mor's grandson, Alan Stern, a London-born businessman in his forties who had settled in Los Angeles after coming to the United States. His American-born wife, Lisa Stern, who describes herself as "a nice Jewish American girl from Orange County," is a lawyer who played a pivotal role in the ensuing litigation.

The extended Stern family, residing in Florida, London, Jerusalem, and Los Angeles, turned to Lisa Stern, the lawyer in the family, for help with their claim. But Lisa Stern did not want to take on Generali by herself, so for help, she turned to one of the best lawyers in California, William Shernoff. In his forty years of practice, Shernoff had taken on some of the biggest insurance companies in the United States, suing them for failing to honor obligations to their policyholders or other victims. Shernoff also is Jewish. The Holocaust-era insurance cases were thus dream cases for him, an important legacy with which to cap his distinguished legal career. He therefore gladly accepted the Stern case and other similar insurance cases Lisa Stern brought to him.

Shernoff and Stern filed their first lawsuit, *Stern v. Assicurazioni Generali S.p.A.*, on February 5, 1998. The suit sought $10 million in compensatory damages and $125 million in punitive damages. The lawsuit, filed in Los Angeles Superior Court by the children and grandchildren of Mor Stern, listed Adolf Stern as the lead plaintiff. On April 2, 1998, Shernoff and Stern filed three more individual lawsuits against Generali on behalf of other Holocaust heirs with similar claims for failing to pay on Holocaust-era policies. In all, the Shernoff/Stern team filed a dozen individual insurance actions in California, suing both Generali and other European insurers.

Their flagship case, however, remained the well-publicized *Stern* action. The *Los Angeles Times* published a long feature on the case,[36] and other stories appeared in both local and national law journals.[37] Even the popular television program *Law and Order,* in one of its "taken from the headlines" scripts, featured an episode loosely based on the *Stern* case (the insurance company in the episode was called Federali Insurance).

In response, Generali filed a motion to dismiss the lawsuit, in which it conceded the existence of policy no. 115285. According to Generali, the document faxed to Martin Stern was not the original policy, which was written in Hungarian, but a "German-language summary of the Policy that Generali found in its files and transmitted to the Sterns in 1996." Generali explained that the summary was an "abstract reflecting certain terms and conditions" of the policy.[38] Generali also noted in its motion papers that it had now searched for other policies belonging to Mor Stern, which had yielded another policy, policy no. 115438, issued on May 10, 1929. Generali believed that this policy was a replacement policy for policy no. 115285.[39]

Nevertheless, Generali argued that the suit should be dismissed on procedural grounds. Specifically, Generali maintained that California courts lacked personal jurisdiction over the company. According to Generali, it had conducted only minimal business in California, not enough for it to be sued there. Moreover, Generali pointed to a "forum-selection" clause in policy nos. 115438 and 115285, stating that all disputes regarding the policies must be settled in Prague.

In filing its dismissal motion, Generali faced a major obstacle. In May 1998, after this lawsuit was filed, California enacted the Holocaust Victim Insurance Act (HVIA). The HVIA specifically gave California jurisdiction over Holocaust-era insurance cases, nullified any forum-selection clauses in a Holocaust-era policy, and extended until 2010 the statute of limitations for filing Holocaust-era insurance suits.[40] California law had now denied Generali one of its most important arguments.

Credit for this astute move belongs to Shernoff and Stern. Shortly after filing their lawsuits, the two lawyers talked to sympathetic state legislators about the purported injustices being perpetrated on Holocaust victims. The legislators took action by introducing the HVIA, and both chambers of the California legislature, controlled by the Democratic Party, unanimously passed the bill. It was designated as an urgency measure, thereby making it effective upon the governor's signature. California's governor, Pete Wilson, a Republican, immediately signed the bill into law.[41]

Generali had been outmaneuvered. Confronted with the HVIA, Generali now argued that the act was unconstitutional.

The case was heard by Judge Florence-Marie Cooper.[42] On January 15, 1999, she denied Generali's dismissal motion. In so doing, she sidestepped the HVIA's constitutionality by holding that even without the statute, she would have allowed the case to proceed.

As Judge Cooper noted, even though Generali's sales of insurance in California "represent[ed] only 1% of its world-wide business, it has sold insurance resulting in millions of dollars in premiums paid by California residents—$27 million in [premiums from California] in 1997 alone."[43] She also found that Generali had been selling insurance in California since 1958, at one time had an office and owned a subsidiary in California, and, most significantly, had both sued and been sued in California in the past.

Moreover, Judge Cooper refused to recognize the forum-selection clause. As she explained, "When such clauses are part of a preprinted form, designed by the insurer and imposed on the insured, they are not binding."[44]

Generali was also caught in a lie. A sworn declaration filed by an executive of Generali in support of the motion claimed that it "cannot locate any records of ever having filed a lawsuit in the California state courts."[45] In fact, as Shernoff pointed out to Judge Cooper at the dismissal hearing, Generali had brought "at least 24 lawsuits . . . in California in recent years."[46] Judge Cooper found that the declaration, "if not dishonest, was at least disingenuous and clearly designed to mislead the court on the critical issue of whether defendant had substantial contacts with California, and had subjected itself to the jurisdiction of California courts."[47] Judge Cooper fined Generali $14,126.06, the amount that Shernoff allegedly had spent "in order to disprove the misleading statement in defendant's declaration."[48]

In November 1999, the *Stern* case settled. While the terms remain confidential, the *New York Times*, citing "people knowledgeable about the deal," reported the settlement to be $1.25 million.[49] Although this was substantially less than the $10 million in insurance claims and $125 million in punitive damages that the Sterns had sought, it nevertheless holds the record of being the highest settlement for any Holocaust-era insurance claim. No other payout even comes close.

In February 2000, Stern and Shernoff settled four more cases on behalf of elderly Holocaust survivors living in California. Three of the four cases quickly settled after the California judge presiding over these cases ordered the president of Generali to come from Italy to California to help effectuate the settlement.

The litigation strategy appeared to be working beautifully. It seemed that that Generali and the other European insurers would soon fold and settle the remaining lawsuits against them. Unfortunately, that did not happen. The post-*Stern* settlements in fact became the last settlements for Holocaust-era insurance litigation. Stern and Shernoff could not reach any more agreements, and in New York, Judge Mukasey soon dismissed almost all the suits against the other insurers.

In March and August 2000, respectively, Judge Mukasey granted the motion of two insurance defendants, France's UAP-Vie and Austria's Der Anker Allgemeine Versicherungs A.G., to dismiss them as defendants for lack of personal jurisdiction.[50] Unlike Judge Cooper in the *Stern* litigation in California, Judge Mukasey held that these two insurers did not have a sufficient business presence in New York for him to have personal jurisdiction over them with regard to these suits. Later that year, in December 2000, he dismissed eighteen German insurers as defendants because of the German slave labor settlement. That settlement (see chapter 2) stipulated that all "German" companies would henceforth be immune from Holocaust-related litigation in the United States. Judge Mukasey interpreted the term "German" to include all insurance companies operating within the borders of the Third Reich, including Austrian insurance companies.[51] In July 2002, he dismissed two more of the defendants from the insurance class action litigation, the Swiss insurers Basler Lieben and Winterthur, on the ground that he did not have jurisdiction over them because they did not do enough business in New York.[52]

Out of the original twenty-five named in the class action lawsuits, only two European insurance companies—Generali and

Zurich—remained as defendants. Litigation against the two companies continues.

COUNTERATTACK: THE EUROPEAN INSURERS STRIKE BACK

The European insurers were successful not only in fending off the class action lawsuits filed against them; they also took the additional step of filing their own lawsuits in American courts. With such suits, the insurers were able to prevent various states from enforcing statutes that would have compelled them to reveal the names of their prewar policyholders.

California was the first state to enact such a statute, as a companion piece to the HVIA legislation. The law, the California Holocaust Victim Insurance Relief Act, known popularly as the California Holocaust Registry Law,[53] was passed unanimously by the California legislature and came into force on October 10, 1999. It requires all insurance companies licensed in California to provide lists of all the policies they or an affiliated company issued for persons living in Europe between 1920 and 1945, from which the California Department of Insurance can create an open and accessible registry of all policyholders. The law gave the insurance companies 180 days from enactment, or until April 7, 2000, to provide such lists. In December 1999, Chuck Quackenbush, then California's insurance commissioner, began holding hearings to determine whether the insurers would comply with the law and issued subpoenas to eight European insurance companies doing business in California to appear in court.

The California insurance commissioner's style was reminiscent of that of former U.S. Senator Alfonse D'Amato, who four years earlier at the Senate Banking Committee hearings grilled the Swiss banks over their failure to recognize the claims of dormant prewar bank accounts. At the hearings, held over two days in Los Angeles and San Francisco and widely publicized, Quackenbush threatened to expel from California any insurance company failing to provide full policyholder lists in accordance with the Registry Law. "If there is no compliance by April 6, we will be throwing these companies out of California,"[54] Quackenbush declared in a prehearing statement. Calling the recalcitrant European insurance carriers "a bunch of thieves,"[55] he noted the consequences of forcing the companies out of the important California market. "Once they leave California, they have to leave the U.S. market," he observed.[56] At the hearing in San Francisco, Quackenbush warned Christopher Carnicelli, the head of Generali's operations in the United States, "I will lower the hammer on you if are not going to comply with our law."[57]

Quackenbush's bravado came to naught, and Carnicelli had the last laugh. Instead of complying with the law, the insurance companies adopted the strategy used until now by the claimants' lawyers, namely, litigation. Backed by the American Insurance Association, the insurance industry's trade group, the companies filed four separate lawsuits on the eve of compliance that sought to prevent California from enforcing the law. The insurers contended that the Registry Law was an impermissible attempt by California to regulate transactions that took place wholly outside the state—in Europe—and more than fifty years ago. As such, the insurers argued, the California Registry law violated the U.S. Constitution, since it unduly interfered with the exclusive power of the federal government to regulate foreign affairs and foreign commerce. In response, California argued that the law did not attempt to interfere with the powers of the federal government; rather, it was part of the states' traditional function to regulate insurance carriers licensed to do business in the state.

The insurance companies' litigation strategy prevailed. In June 2000, the U.S. federal district judge William B. Schubb in Sacramento issued an injunction blocking enforcement of the California statute. Judge Schubb agreed with the insurance companies' argument that the Registry Law was unconstitutional. On appeal, the Ninth Circuit reversed this part of his decision.[58] It disagreed with Judge Schubb's ruling that the Registry Law intruded into the foreign affairs and foreign commerce powers of the federal government, since the state law did not target companies of any specific country, but only a certain type of transaction. It was, however, a hollow victory. At the end of its long opinion rejecting every ground raised by the insurance companies and accepted by Judge Schubb, the Ninth Circuit nevertheless held that it would leave in place the injunction issued by Judge Schubb, on the ground that the Registry Law might violate the due process clause of the Constitution. The Ninth Circuit remanded the cases back to Judge Schubb to examine the impact of the Registry Law on the due process clause, something Judge Schubb had not considered in his initial decision.

On remand, Judge Schubb ruled again in favor of the insurance companies, finding that the Registry Law did indeed violate due process because it denied the insurance companies a meaningful hearing before the revocation of their licenses by the California Insurance Commissioner for failure to comply with the law.[59]

In July 2002, the Ninth Circuit reversed Judge Schubb again, holding that the due process rights of the European insurers would not be violated by their forced compliance with the Registry Law.[60] The California Department of Insurance is now seeking to enforce the California Registry Law, to date without success, despite its victory before the Ninth Circuit. As of November 2002, the European insurers still had not produced their prewar policyholder lists.

The insurance companies also succeeded in blocking a similar disclosure law in Florida, enacted in 1998 and supported by the former Florida insurance commissioner (now U.S. senator) Bill Nelson. In the end, the federal district judge in Florida held that because the statute allowed the Florida insurance commissioner to enforce "transactions entered in Germany between German companies having no connection with Florida," it amounted to an unconstitutional overreaching of Florida's jurisdiction.[61]

The European insurance companies, unlike the Swiss banks and German companies that were sued for uncompensated slave labor, were able to neutralize the sting of the class action lawsuits against them. Even more significant, the insurers successfully used the American litigation process to hamstring the efforts of state insurance commissioners to force the insurers to reveal their Holocaust-era policyholder lists.

While the European insurers were able to disable the litigation process launched against them, the lawsuits, along with political pressure, did force some of the insurers to join a nonadversarial mechanism that had been set up earlier, when the first suits were filed, to resolve the insurance claims. ICHEIC, the International Commission on Holocaust Era Insurance Claims, now became the last great hope for the settlement of these claims. Unfortunately, it also proved to be a bitter disappointment for the survivors and their heirs.

Suppose Your Family Had a Holocaust Era Insurance Policy and You Just Didn't Know About It?

If you are a Holocaust survivor or the heir of a Holocaust victim, you may have a legitimate unpaid Holocaust era life, education or dowry insurance claim and the opportunity exists for you to receive payment. You can now file claims through a new Claims Resolution Process set up by the **International Commission on Holocaust Era Insurance Claims**.

The Commission consists of representatives of United States insurance regulators, five European insurance companies and their subsidiaries, the State of Israel, worldwide Jewish and Holocaust survivor organizations and European regulators as Observers.

The unique Claims Resolution Process provides individuals with a central source for information on, investigation into, and payment of those outstanding policies, without any charge to the claimants.

For more information, mail in the request to the right, or visit the website www.icheic.org

or call 1-800-957-3203

Yes, I'd like to learn more about
The Holocaust Era Insurance
Claims Process

Name _____

Address _____
_____

City _____

State _____ Zip Code _____

Country_____

Preferred Language_____

Mail to:
International Commission
PO Box 1163
Wall Street Station
New York, NY 10268
USA   US-ENG-ORGK

ICHEIC outreach ad. *Courtesy of the Cohen Group.*

THE CREATION OF ICHEIC

Soon after the first class action lawsuit was filed against them in March 1997, the European insurance companies began to follow the game plan invented by the Swiss banks during their earlier struggle with the Holocaust-era claims. The insurance companies realized that a useful tactic that the Swiss had employed in the litigation filed against them was the creation of a commission headed by a prominent American diplomat. Such a commission, they saw, could propose a settlement less costly than the compromises or judgments reached in U.S. courts. It would also allow them to argue in court that the lawsuits against them should be dismissed, or at least put in abeyance, because of the existence of an alternative to the court process. As we have seen, the Swiss banks created and funded the so-called International Committee of Eminent Persons (ICEP), headed by Paul Volcker, the distinguished former head of the Federal Reserve Board. The European insurance companies' version of the Volcker-style ICEP was the International Commission on Holocaust-era Insurance Claims (ICHEIC, pronounced "Eye-check"). To head it, they recruited another eminent American, the former secretary of state (under the first Bush administration) and long-time diplomat, Lawrence Eagleburger.

As in the Swiss bank scenario, state officials had a powerful tool they could use to pressure the insurance companies to come to the bargaining table. Insurance is regulated state-by-state, and the individual state insurance commissioners could threaten the European insurance companies with expulsion from their states if the companies refused to negotiate the settlement. As explained by the former Florida insurance commissioner Bill Nelson, "Many of these European insurance companies now have operations in the United States. That's our hook."[62]

Unfortunately, the hook did not work, the litigation became tied up in the courts, and ICHEIC—originally seen as an alternative means of settlement—has been a colossal failure for the claimants and, as a result, a colossal success for the European insurers. Using the ICHEIC process, the European insurers have been able to delay the payment of most Holocaust insurance claims, to make minimal settlements on some claims, and to avoid revealing the names of possible claim holders. Most important, unlike the Swiss bank cases, the existence of the nonadversarial body has been a powerful tool in the hands of the European insurance defendants to tie up the litigation against them. Whereas ICEP did not stop the litigation against the Swiss banks, ICHEIC has effectively prevented the elderly Holocaust insurance claimants from getting their day in court.

It did not start off that way. The origins of ICHEIC go back to 1997 and the involvement of the state insurance commissioners in the Holocaust restitution issue. The commissioners first became aware of the problem after the publicity generated by the filing of the Cornell action in March 1997. In September 1997, the National Association of Insurance Commissioners (NAIC), composed of the insurance regulators in all fifty states, created the so-called Working Group on Holocaust and Insurance Issues. Deborah Senn, the insurance commissioner of the state of Washington who read a news article about the litigation and raised the issue before the other commissioners, was appointed chair of the twenty-one-state working group. It appeared that Senn would do for Holocaust insurance claims what Alan Hevesi, New York City's comptroller, did for the Swiss bank claims. Senn began holding hearings in various U.S. cities, inviting Holocaust survivors to testify how they had been cheated by the European insurers of the proceeds rightfully owed to them. Six such hearings were held between September 1997 and February 1998. Senn also invited these companies to come and explain their reasons for nonpayment of prewar policies to Jews. When they refused to do so, or if they did appear but explained away their nonpayment, Senn and the other state insurance commissioners began threatening to revoke the licenses of the European insurers for failing to honor these claims.

Unfortunately, Senn was not allowed to finish her job. In April 1998, in a kind of coup, NAIC dissolved the working group and removed Senn from her leading role on this issue. The working group was replaced by another body, the nine-member Holocaust Task Force, chaired by Glenn Pomeroy, the insurance commissioner from North Dakota and the president of NAIC. That same month, the insurance commissioners from California, New York, and Florida, which together contain the largest concentration of Holocaust survivors in the United States, directly approached four of the European insurers sued (Allianz of Germany, AXA of France, Generali of Italy, and Zurich of Switzerland) and signed a nonbinding memorandum of intent (MOI) aiming to resolve the insurance claims. The World Jewish Congress (WJC), now heavily involved in Holocaust restitution through the Swiss bank cases, also signed the MOI. The WJC's secretary-general, Rabbi Israel Singer (who also served as vice president of the Claims Conference and in 2002 became its head), convinced the WJC likewise to come on board. One of the MOI's goals was the creation of an international commission to settle the Holocaust-era insurance claims outside the litigation arena.

On August 24, 1998, two weeks after the Swiss banks settled, the preliminary MOI led to the signing of a more formal memorandum of understanding (MOU) and the creation of the commission. In October 1998, the sixty-eight-year-old Eagleburger was appointed chairman of ICHEIC,[63] marking the formal start of the commission.

Six European insurance companies originally agreed to participate in the commission: France's AXA, Germany's Allianz, Italy's Generali, and Swiss insurers Winterthur Lieben (owned by Credit Suisse Bank), Zurich Insurance Group, and Basler Lieben (also known as Baloise Life). For the last four years, Eagleburger has tried to convince other European insurers sued to join the commission, all without success. Indeed, his sole achievement was getting the Association of Insurers in the Netherlands to join the ICHEIC process in 2000.

At various times there was speculation that various other European insurance companies would be joining the commission. Specifically, Prudential Insurance in the United Kingdom (no relation to Prudential Insurance in the United States) and two Austrian insurers, Der Anker Allgemeine Versicherungs and UNIQA Personenversicherung, were named. But nothing happened. Seeing ICHEIC's poor progress, these insurers understandably decided not to join the commission. In December 1999, Dutch insurers Aegon, ING, and Fortis entered into a separate $4.2 million settlement with California, to be used to distribute cash grants to needy survivors in the state. A month earlier, the Dutch insurance companies and Dutch Jewish organizations agreed on a $21 million settlement and established the Sjoa Foundation, an organization in Holland investigating and resolving unpaid insurance policy claims by Holocaust-era victims submitted by persons around the world. In November 2000, after political pressure from the United States, the Dutch Insurance Association signed a memorandum of association with ICHEIC on behalf of the Dutch insurance companies. In so doing, the association agreed to apply ICHEIC valuation standards to evaluation claims against Dutch insurance companies.

Ironically, these separate settlements made ICHEIC even less effective, since the five insurers who created it represented only a portion of the prewar European insurance market. As a result, ICHEIC's original goal—to create a comprehensive claims resolution tribunal for all Holocaust-era claims, akin to the Swiss bank claims resolution tribunals or the "big tent" settlement achieved with the Germans—was never realized.

In return for joining ICHEIC, the NAIC promised the participating insurers a "safe harbor," meaning no threats, sanctions, boycotts, or other regulatory pressures of the kind experienced by the Swiss banks. If at any time a participating insurer was found not to be cooperating in good faith with the ICHEIC process, the "safe harbor" could be removed.

It is no surprise that all the six insurance companies that agreed to join ICHEIC sold insurance in the United States and that one of the six companies, Switzerland's Basler Lieben, withdrew from the commission soon after it stopped selling insurance and closed shop in the United States. In its January 1999 withdrawal letter to Eagleburger, Basler Lieben was now able to express what the remaining insurance companies were afraid to state openly: the insurance companies cared little about the fate of the survivors and the morality or legality of their insurance claims. They joined this commission because they were being forced to do so. The resignation letter from Bruno Dallo, Basler Lieben's general counsel, bluntly stated:

> No longer with U.S. affiliates, and no longer subject to regulatory sanctions—that is absent the duress that forced Basler Lieben to sign the MOU in the first place—[Basler Lieben] cannot put itself at the risk of "consensus" achieved by others, including [insurance] carriers who still function within the Commission, in fear of regulatory sanctions, public reprisals and onerous legislative requirements.[64]

From its inception through its troubled history, the insurers' commitment to ICHEIC as a settlement process remained low.

ICHEIC BEGINS ITS WORK

In November 1998, the European insurers made their initial contribution to ICHEIC, a $5 million preliminary start-up fund for the commission to hire staff and open offices in London and Washington. The companies also pledged to contribute $90 million to a humanitarian fund but later reneged on that promise.

Why have two offices and why a second office in London, one of the most expensive cities in the world, which of course, increased the ICHEIC's administrative costs? Again, the fear of American litigation was a factor. The European insurers insisted that all claims processed by ICHEIC must be done outside the United States, lest their work be scrutinized by U.S. courts and lead to more lawsuits. For further protection, ICHEIC was chartered under Swiss law. But this tactic did not work. In 2001, Shernoff and Stern filed another lawsuit, *Haberfeld v. Generali*, alleging that the Italian insurer was using ICHEIC as a vehicle to delay paying valid claims to Holocaust survivors. The suit was transferred to Judge Mukasey, who, as with all the other Holocaust insurance lawsuits that had come before him, put the suit on hold. In September 2002, after a year of futile efforts, Judge Mukasey finally allowed the ninety-year-old Felicia Haberfeld to continue with her litigation.

ICHEIC was ready to begin its work. The commission was composed of six members representing the insurers and the European insurance regulators; six representing the U.S. insurance regulators (three seats always being held by the regulators from California, New York, and Florida) and various Jewish groups (including representatives of the WJC, the Claims Conference, and the State of Israel, which was invited to participate in the negotiations. The members would operate by "consensus," meaning that their decisions had to be unanimous. In the event of a deadlock, Eagleburger, as the thirteenth member, would have the tie-breaking vote. It was a good plan in theory but one that often led to delays. Eagleburger often pressured one side or other (most often the insurers) to go along with some proposal rather than using his vote to break the deadlock. With a chairman and funding in place, ICHEIC began holding monthly meetings, shifting from Washington, D.C., to London and even to Jerusalem. Initial indications did not look promising. The *Financial Times* reported in April 1999 that "the commission is in deadlock after four months of talks. Little progress has been made on issues including the valuation of policies, the allowances to be made for inflation and the problem of dealing with claims against companies nationalized by East European communist governments after the war."[65]

Not for the first time and after a few months of operation, ICHEIC was ready to fall apart. Commented Elan Steinberg of the WJC, sitting on the ICHEIC board, "The meeting on May 6 [1999, in London] is a crit-

Attorneys William M. Shernoff and Lisa Stern announcing at a press conference, at the Simon Wiesenthal Center in Los Angeles, a new lawsuit against the Italian insurance company Assicurazioni Generali. *Courtesy of Lisa Stern and William M. Shernoff.*

ical moment. At that point, we will be able to see whether this experiment will work or not. Flesh and blood claimants will have to know that there's an independent process by which their claims can be fairly determined."[66]

At this point, the state insurance commissioners and other state government officials started to apply political pressure, with California leading the way. On the eve of the May meeting, California's governor, Gray Davis, and its insurance commissioner, Chuck Quackenbush, held a bipartisan press conference at the Simon Wiesenthal Center in Los Angeles, issuing stern warnings to the European insurers. Davis, a Democrat, announced, "We come to send a message [to the insurance companies]. You can pay now or we guarantee you will pay more later." Added Quackenbush, then the highest-ranking Republican office-holder in California,[67] "There is a limit to our patience. When they feel the heat, they will see the light." With a special budget allocation from the California legislature for this work, the California Department of Insurance began running full-page ads, even in the London newspapers where the commission was meeting, chastising the insurance companies. Under the headline "Time Is Running Out," one ad began:

> For sixty years, insurance companies have profited by not paying on insurance policies issued to Jews and others who were murdered by the Nazis during the Holocaust. The average age of a survivor is 80 years old. Meanwhile, the average Californian only lives to age 74. Every year, thousands of survivors pass away. If these people are to achieve any measure of justice from the companies that took advantage of them, it must occur now.

A second ad was even more explicit:

THE INSURANCE COMPANIES

> After the Holocaust, they broke their promises. *They lied.* They said, "Give us a little money each week and if something bad happens to you we'll take care of your family." Well something had happened. Something really bad, and the insurance companies didn't live up to their end of the bargain. And they still haven't.

Both ads concluded with the following tag line: "It's about *restitution,* it's about *justice* and it's about *time. Haven't they been waiting long enough?*"

The pressure worked. At the May 1999 meeting in London, the commission achieved what appeared to be a significant breakthrough when the five participating insurers agreed to abandon their two most potent arguments: (1) that they need not pay because the local offices that had written the policies had been nationalized by the postwar Communist governments and (2) that the value of the unpaid prewar-issued policies was now negligible. Earlier, Eagleburger had announced that if the May meeting was successful, he hoped that ICHEIC's payment of claims to survivors would start shortly thereafter.[68] Unfortunately, no final agreements were reached at the June 1999 meeting in Jerusalem. So Eagleburger then set his own deadline: at the time of the next meeting in Washington, D.C., all outstanding issues would have to be settled. But the July 1999 meeting also ended without an agreement. As a result, Eagleburger announced his first directive (Eagleburger calls his directives "decision memoranda"): the European insurers would

According to defenders of the ICHEIC process, the enormous gap between the money spent on expenses and the actual payouts will eventually be closed when the mechanisms set up in place through these initial outlays begin to yield significant results. Elan Steinberg of the WJC predicted: "By the end of this five-year process . . . ICHEIC will have spent some $80 million, but it will also have paid policy beneficiaries $500 million in reparations."[79] This seems highly unlikely.

Eagleburger acknowledged his salary—which he stated is $360,000—and defended it in an April 11, 2002, letter to Representative Henry Waxman, a ranking minority member of the House Reform Committee that held hearings on ICHEIC's efficacy. In his letter, Eagleburger noted that "my ICHEIC responsibilities have been sufficiently demanding that I have given up membership on several boards and foregone speaking engagements, etc., with a total cost to me of over $600,000 per year."[80]

In Israel, the daily newspaper *Ha'aretz* outlined what it called the "essential picture":

> The [ICHEIC] claims process has so far poured millions of dollars into the pockets of various service providers—public relations agencies, accounting firms hired to audit the insurance company reports, the lawyers handling the class action suits that prompted the companies settle, and many others. The policy beneficiaries and Holocaust survivors, on the other hand, are . . . yet to receive any money at all.[81]

While the last portion is hyperbole—a few survivors or heirs did receive some benefits—and the statement about the lawyers is misleading—since, as shown, the lawyers were excluded from ICHEIC—the overall picture painted by *Ha'aretz* was, and continues to be, fundamentally correct.

Most egregious was the fact that after receiving a claim, the ICHEIC insurers still repeatedly failed to follow the Relaxed Standards of Proof and other agreed-upon guidelines established by ICHEIC. The companies continued to reject claims on such specious grounds as

1. They never issued a policy, even though the claimant gave them a copy of the policy.
2. The policy was paid out, but the company never provided proof of such payment.

3. The policy was paid out, but payment was made to the Nazis.
4. The policy was issued by a local office that was nationalized by a Communist government after the war.
5. The claimant, a Holocaust survivor, received compensation from West Germany, which included payment for unpaid insurance.

Under ICHEIC's rules, none of these was a valid reason for rejecting a claim:

1. Regarding the first reason, in a July 2, 1999, agreement, the ICHEIC companies pledged that once a claimant documented the existence of a policy, the burden of proof would shift to the company to show why the claim should not be paid.
2. Regarding the second reason, if a company claimed that it had paid on the policy, it had to show proof of such payment, the standard claims procedure in the American insurance market.
3. Regarding the third reason, the German insurers in effect argued that because the Gestapo ordered them to confiscate Jewish policies and make payment to the German state, they had been relieved of any legal liability. In a September 17, 2001, directive, Eagleburger specifically excluded this reason for failing to pay a claim under ICHEIC. Earlier, in a directive dated September 29, 2000, Eagleburger stated, "Valid claims on confiscated policies should be compensated in full like any other valid claims." Nevertheless, the insurers still insist that this is a proper legal argument and have denied claims on this ground. Moreover, the insurers require those claimants with whom they settle to recognize, as a condition of the settlement, that the insurers have no legal liability to pay the claims of such confiscated policies.
4. Regarding the fourth reason, as discussed earlier in a directive dated July 6, 2000, Eagleburger specifically excluded this reason for failing to pay a claim.
5. Regarding the final reason, this argument, made by Allianz and other German insurers, is specious. The postwar payments received by survivors coming out of the death camps were not for lost insurance but were meant as token compensation for their suffering and the deaths of their loved ones, in many instances, entire families. German industry also tried to take credit for these postwar payments to reduce the $7,500 lump-sum pay-

ment to Jewish survivors who applied for compensation under the German slave labor fund (see chapter 2). The German effort failed. Jewish recipients of the West German postwar payment program did not have their slave labor settlement reduced because of previous payments, and the same logic should govern Holocaust-era insurance claims.

Even when a company accepted a claim, it often made what is known in the insurance industry parlance as a "low-ball offer," by either reducing the original value of the policy without giving reasons for doing so or failing to apply the agreed-upon ICHEIC valuation guidelines to determine the current worth of the policy.

Unfortunately, because ICHEIC is a private commission, there is no outside monitor to review its work. ICHEIC also has no monitoring system to review the companies' offers and rejections. Without oversight, the ICHEIC insurers are free to decide how, or even whether, they will follow the ICHEIC guidelines for each claim presented to them. As a result, after three years of operation and more than $40 million in expenses, only about 1 percent of the claims sent to the commission have been paid. The individual California lawsuits filed by Shernoff and Stern yielded higher individual settlements for their clients than did the individual settlements reached through the so-called nonadversarial ICHEIC process. As Shernoff explained in a letter to Judge Mukasey, "Of the five cases [we] settled, Generali paid a minimum of 10 times the ICHEIC valuation of the contract benefit, and as much as 290 times the ICHEIC valuation."[82]

Earlier, Shernoff, who filed a new lawsuit against Generali concurrently with the negative press reports about the ICHEIC process, commented, "It's amazing what is going on. Insurance companies have not really treated these people fairly for 50 years, yet they are calling the shots [at ICHEIC] and trying to bypass a judicial system. That's just dead wrong."[83]

Another major problem was Eagleburger's inability to get the ICHEIC insurers to publish the names of their Holocaust-era policyholders. As in the case of the unpaid Swiss bank accounts, the publication of names of Holocaust-era insurance policyholders is indispensable to identify potential claimants. Just as the U.S. ambassador to Switzerland, Madeline Kunin, was startled to find her mother's name on the Swiss banks' first dormant accounts list published in 1997, so unexpected discoveries might be made if the European insurers also published lists of their prewar policyholders. Already one such surprising find occurred in April 2000, after ICHEIC posted on its first list on the Internet—a very limited list of names provided by the participating insurers and also based on Austrian archives containing asset declarations filed by Jews in Nazi Austria: a policy turned up belonging to the father of former Jerusalem mayor Teddy Kollek, who was born in Austria.

Without the disclosure of complete policyholder lists, as Israel's Bobby Brown explained, "many survivors and their heirs will have no knowledge as to whether their relatives and their heirs purchased any insurance, whether they are eligible to make a claim, or against what company such a claim should be made."[84] Deborah Senn clarified this:

> Survivors emerged from camps and hiding places with nothing in their hands. For many families, only child survivors remained at war's end, and they lacked knowledge of family assets. Today, many families with rightful insurance claims are simply unaware of the existence of a policy. Most potential claimants have no documentation. If comprehensive policyholder lists are not published, families will not know they have a claim.[85]

The lists, therefore, drive the entire claims process.

For this reason, the MOU resolution that established ICHEIC called for the "publication of the names of Holocaust victims who held unpaid insurance policies." Unfortunately, by February 2002, more than three years into ICHEIC's existence and at the end of the two-year claims period, the five ICHEIC insurers had published approximately 9,200 names out of the millions that they possess, some of which may be the names of unpaid policyholders. The individual breakdowns were as follows: 8,740 names by Generali; 318 names by Allianz and 17 names by its Italian subsidiary Reunione Adriatica; 191 names by AXA; 20 names by Zurich Insurance Group; and 4 names by Winterthur.

Even the 9,200 figure is misleading. Although approximately 54,000 names are listed on ICHEIC's Web site, fewer than one-quarter of those names have come from ICHEIC's insurance companies. Rather, the Vienna State Archives submitted approximately 9,000 names and 15,000 policies, based on assets declaration forms forcibly filed by Jews in Nazi Austria; the Dutch-created Sjoa Foundation for Holocaust-era insurance restitution lists approximately 800 names, which are included in

ICHEIC's list; and the rest come from ICHEIC-funded research in German and Austrian archives.

This is a disgrace. Allianz alone is said to have records of between 1.5 million and 2 million prewar policy files. AXA apparently has computerized files containing 570,000 prewar and wartime policyholder names. The Swiss insurers likewise possess, but have refused to share with ICHEIC, its prewar and wartime files. Winterthur located approximately 65,000 files for policies in force in 1940, and Zurich identified 22,000 policies sold in Nazi-occupied Europe.

While Generali may seem to be the "good guy" among the ICHEIC insurers, with the longest list of published names and the largest amount of paid claims, the reality is quite different. As discussed earlier, Generali, the "Jewish insurance company" with its Lion of Judah symbol, sold the most insurance policies to the Jews of prewar Europe. But the experience of Adolf Stern, related earlier, illustrates the typical fashion in which Generali resisted payment on these policies after the war. In fact, the very first lawsuit in the United States for nonpayment of a Holocaust-era policy was filed against Generali in 1942, even as the war was raging. Max Buxbaum, a Czechoslovak linen merchant, purchased eight life insurance policies from Generali. The policies were payable at any of the locations where Generali conducted business, with the policy providing for payment to be made by "dollar check New York." Generali refused payment on the ground that additional requirements had been imposed by the German Reich government on the collection of life insurance policies by Jews. The Buxbaums, a Jewish family, did not meet those requirements. A New York state judge ruled for the plaintiffs, ordering Generali to make payment on the polices on the basis of standard contract principles.[86]

Fifty-five years later, Generali contended that it could not pay because after the war the records of policies it wrote in prewar eastern Europe either had been destroyed or were in the possession of the nationalized companies in eastern Europe set up after the takeover of their local offices by the postwar Communist regimes. For example, when first confronted with accusations that it was failing to honor valid Holocaust-era policies, Generali went into "damage control" mode. In 1997, it published an ad in various newspapers around the world, including Jewish newspapers, announcing the establishment of a $12 million humanitarian fund in Israel "in honor of Generali policyholders who perished in the Holocaust." In the ad, Generali asserted,

During and after the dark years of World War II, Generali faced expropriations of its properties and the properties of its insureds [*sic*]. The racial laws of the Nazi and fascist era and the state action of Soviet-dominated regimes in Central and Eastern Europe severely damaged Generali's ability to do business there. The cold-war Communist regimes in Eastern Europe nationalized and expropriated all major businesses, seizing all of Generali's insurance businesses there, including its offices, 184 buildings and 14 companies controlled by Generali. As a result, Generali today has very little information and few records regarding policies issued by its former branches in Central and Eastern Europe.

The last sentence is patently false. In fact, as described earlier, Generali was discovered to have kept partial backup records of its prewar policies, known as "water copies," at its archive warehouse in Trieste. Faced with this disclosure, Generali revealed that it had found almost 340,000 names, representing 585,000 unpaid prewar insurance policies. But the company soon backed away from this figure and maintained that the true number of unpaid policies was about 100,000. In the Swiss bank restitution, the banks allowed ICHEIP to conduct an independent audit of its prewar dormant accounts. Generali (and, for that matter, the other European insurers that have issued lists of its prewar policyholders) have refused to do the same. As discussed earlier, the European insurers even filed suits to block state laws obligating them to reveal their Holocaust-era insurance lists. As a result, no independent auditor has verified that Generali's list of names, or even its process of creating the list, is credible.

In June 1999, Generali put the names on a CD-ROM disk and turned it over to ICHEIC, on the condition that the names not be made public. Instead, at about the same time, Generali agreed to give the Yad Vashem Holocaust Center in Israel the disk in order to match Generali's list with Yad Vashem's list of Jews who perished in the Holocaust. Even though Generali agreed to make this list public, it is obvious that such a stripped-down list would have significant omissions. Yad Vashem itself admits that even its list of Holocaust victims is incomplete (containing only 3.6 million names out of the 6 million victims), and so it is likely that many of the policyholders' names on the Generali list will never be made public because there is no match. Moreover, the process matches Generali's policyholders' names only with deceased victims. Policies owned by survivors will not be revealed. Finally, Generali conceded that the list on its disk does not include policies sold by its subsidiaries and affiliates in eastern and central Europe, as well as countries such as Greece where it operated through branch offices. According to some estimates, this would exclude up to one-half the prewar policies for which Generali is responsible.

Even with all these qualifications, the issuance of the list was held up for three years because of a payment dispute between the private company subcontracted by Yad Vashem to process the two lists and ICHEIC. In early 2002, a list of 8,740 names was finally made public (and appears now on ICHEIC's Web site). However, this also proved to be a disappointment. For a name on the Generali list to be made public, the name, address, and birth date had to match perfectly the information on the Yad Vashem list. If the spelling of the first or last name was not identical, or the birth date or place of birth was not exactly the same, the name was omitted. For instance, consider all the other possible variations of the spelling of "Eizenstat"—Eisenstaedt and Eizenstädt being other spellings of this name appearing on the Swiss banks' dormant accounts list (see chapter 1) and so on—and the inequity of this becomes obvious. Birth dates could also be a day or so off or misidentified, a very likely event in prewar eastern Europe, or could include typos, and the same was true for places of birth. As a result, potential claimants, Holocaust survivors, and other relatives of those who perished in the Holocaust do not know whether to make a claim with Generali. Israeli parliamentarian Michael Kleiner spoke out on how he would advise Eagleburger to solve the problem (advice that Eagleburger did not take, and Generali refused to follow):

> I told him if he really wants a breakthrough . . . he must force an immediate release on the Internet of the 100,000 names presented by Generali in May [1999]. People are not coming forward because they don't have evidence; they don't know if they have a policy. They are neither approaching the Israeli committee nor the American committee [of ICHEIC].[87]

Deborah Senn would have gone even further. "Why not publish all 340,000 names," she argues, since Generali also put those names on a separate CD-ROM, which it has refused to share with anyone. As she explained, "I believe they are turning down clearly valid claims. To be on the Yad Vashem list, a person has to be dead. But what about those who survived? I have a survivor in my state [of Washington] who was the policyholder and her name has not appeared on Generali's list."[88] Senn was right. The sifting process is not only costly and time-consuming but also unnecessary. The most practical and fairest solution is to have Generali and the other European insurers simply publish their complete lists without first running them through Yad Vashem.

Even though he is not directly involved in the insurance claims process, Eizenstat likewise noted the importance of publishing lists of prewar insurance policies. Speaking at the German Foundation's signing ceremony in July 2000 for the Berlin Accords, Eizenstat, who finally yielded to the German insurers' demands that they be included in the German slave labor settlement (see chapter 2), urged the German insurers to make their lists public:

> It is critically important that all German insurance companies cooperate with the process established by the International Commission on Holocaust Era Insurance Claims, or ICHEIC. This includes publishing lists of unpaid insurance policies and subjecting themselves to audit. Unless German insurance companies make these lists available through ICHEIC, potential claimants cannot know their eligibility, and the insurance companies will have failed to assume their moral responsibility.[89]

His advice fell on deaf ears. At first, the German insurers were going to join ICHEIC as part of the German settlement, but later they backed off this commitment. The only German insurer initially willing to disclose names was Allianz, which agreed in October 2000 to follow Generali's lead and submit to Yad Vashem a partial list of names (147,000 out of 1.5 million names of prewar policyholders) for cross-checking. Finally, in September 2002, as part of their agreement to make full payment to ICHEIC from the German Foundation (see chapter 2), Allianz and the other German insurance companies agreed to publish lists of likely prewar Jewish policyholders. Under the deal, names of Jews who lived in Germany from 1933 to 1938 (taken from the 1938 census conducted by Nazi Germany and other archival materials) will be matched to a database of prewar German insurance policies. The electronic database is said to contain information about more than five million prewar and wartime policies. It remains unclear, however, how many of these policies will be made public. Successful claimants are also supposed to receive at least eight times the face value of the policies discovered through this process. Based on past experience, however, there is no guarantee that the companies will honor this commitment rather than, as before, using a technicality to decrease their payments to individual claimants or even to disqualify a worthy claim entirely. As Stuart Eizenstat diplomatically explained, "Given the complexities of insurance, continued vigilance will be necessary."[90] As of this writing, therefore, publication and eventual payments to survivors or heirs based on this September 2002 agreement seem a long time away.

The European insurers also claim that they are prevented from releasing names of prewar policyholders because of privacy laws in their home countries. In fact, this is not a real obstacle. The Swiss banks got around their strict secrecy laws by obtaining special permission from the Swiss government to publish names of prewar and wartime dormant account holders. The Dutch insurers did the same.[91] The German insurance companies' deal worked out with ICHEIC in September 2002, which included a promise to publish policyholders' names, demonstrates that privacy laws are not a real obstacle.

Moreover, the issue of how to deal with European privacy laws is not new. With the internationalization of commerce, American courts handling international business disputes have been confronting these laws over the last five decades when litigants try to obtain information (known in legal parlance as *discovery*) from business entities located in Europe. In so doing, American courts have formulated special remedies to obtain such information in the course of the lawsuit without running afoul of the European privacy rules. These special rules could be easily adopted to the Holocaust insurance claims.

A final point on the European insurers' contention that the privacy laws in their own countries prevent them from releasing information about prewar policies. As the Bergier Commission's report demonstrated, the Swiss banks made exactly this argument more than fifty-five years ago to prevent the heirs of those who deposited money with them—and then perished in the Holocaust—to claim such funds. The same type of pernicious conduct committed by the Swiss banks a half-century earlier that allowed them to keep money belonging to the survivors of the Holocaust or their rightful heirs—namely, their reliance on strict legality, their failure to cooperate with government officials, and their creative establishment of various roadblocks to deny the claimants their funds—is now being committed by the European insurance companies. The banks were able to get away with this until the 1990s, when both the Volcker Committee Report and the final Bergier Commission Report exposed their conduct. The European insurance companies are committing the same egregious acts today. It should not take another fifty years to expose it.

The insurance companies' final concern is that the costs of researching and compiling such lists would be high. Allianz, for instance, claims that it would take 270 people an entire year to comb through its two million prewar files, some handwritten in old-fashioned Gothic German, to find unpaid claims.[92] This argument is also specious. No one is asking the European insurance companies to search through its old archives for unpaid policies to Jewish policyholders. Rather, at most, the insurers are being asked to collate their archival policies into lists of policyholders and make the lists public. True, that may require some expense, but the insurers are some of the largest multinationals in the world and can well afford it. A portion of the millions already spent on ICHEIC's administrative expenses, for example, could have been used for this purpose.

Deborah Senn stated the obvious reason why the insurers do not want to make public a list of Holocaust-era policyholders: "It serves the purposes of the insurers to resist publication of names which would inevitably expand the number of claimants. In short, if you suppress the names, you suppress the claims."[93] Commenting on the behavior of the ICHEIC companies, the WJC's Elan Steinberg did not mince his words: "From a moral point of view, it's revolting. From a business point of view, it's stupid. It's going to end up costing them so much more than it would have if they did this the right way."[94]

Steinberg, however, missed an essential point. Cost may not be the most important consideration for the insurance companies dealing with Holocaust-era claims. Rather, it is more important for the insurers to demonstrate that the entire movement was bogus from the outset, that in fact almost no significant claims for unpaid policies from Holocaust era ever existed. The European insurers, like the Swiss banks before them, do not want to "take a public relations hit" from an end result establishing that Holocaust survivors and heirs were deprived for more than sixty years of money rightfully due to them. As discussed in chapter 1, the liability of the Swiss banks was capped at $1.25 billion, and yet the banks strongly resisted the full publication of prewar- and wartime-era accounts, as this would show the full extent of their failure to return money deposited with them for safekeeping. Similarly, Allianz and Generali have been able to cap the extent of their financial liability, Allianz by inserting itself into the German slave labor settlement (see chapter 2) and Generali through a November 2000 settlement with ICHEIC for $100 million. Therefore, no matter how many claims are approved, or their amounts, both insurers already know their maximum payout. Nevertheless, both insurers have been reluctant to recognize the claims presented to them. A spokesperson for Allianz, defending the German company's record of rejecting every fast-track claim, explained that the rejections show "what the companies were saying all along: They will not pay for a claim that is not valid against them, even with lowest common denominator of proof."[95] For Allianz and the other insurers, if payment is made on a claim, it is preferable that it be through a separate humanitarian fund established within ICHEIC because such a payment would in effect say that the claim was invalid from the outset.

Danny Kadden, Senn's former adviser on Holocaust insurance issues, summed it up this way: "They want to be able to say they paid voluntarily out of the goodness of their hearts a fraction of the value of the policies, not the full amount because they were obligated."[96]

THE U.S. CONGRESS STEPS IN

Embarrassed by the public disclosure of these failures by ICHEIC, Eagleburger promised to do better. In November 2001, the House Government Reform Committee, concerned with the spate of negative press reports about ICHEIC and its work, held a daylong hearing on the issue.[97] During a bitter exchange between Eagleburger and Representative Henry Waxman of California, the ranking minority member of the committee, Waxman accused ICHEIC of not properly managing its finances. He also pointed out that there is no oversight over the insurance companies to see if they are, in fact, applying the ICHEIC's relaxed standards in reviewing the claims and whether the standards are being applied uniformly by each of the five companies. In his overall evaluation, Waxman concluded: "ICHEIC is simply not working well."[98]

Referring to the litany of problems and the testimony of survivors concerning the difficulties they encountered with the ICHEIC process, Waxman commented, "I think you're a little disdainful of us and of the people who spoke here today."[99] Eagleburger shot back, "That's the dumbest thing I've heard. Don't you tell me that I'm disdainful of these people who suffered so much."[100] Eagleburger acknowledged, however, that the task has "taken too long and it's cost too much."[101] In response to questions on how well the ICHEIC insurers were applying the relaxed standards of proof in evaluating the claims, Eagleburger forthrightly acknowledged, "I can't be sure with what enthusiasm these companies do so."[102] As a remedy, he promised to set up an ICHEIC "policing force" to improve the companies' performance.

Again, months went by without progress. By early 2002, ICHEIC had run up $40 million in expenses and, of the now 81,000 claims received, made offers on about 1,000, still only about 1.5 percent of the claims received.[103] Moreover, of the 1,000 offers made by the ICHEIC insurers, many were for small sums, nowhere close to the valuation figure established by Eagleburger in his July 1999 directive. According to the *New York Times*, citing several ICHEIC members, some of the insurers' offers were as low as $500, which survivor groups labeled "insulting."[104] For this reason, as of August 2002, the claimants had accepted fewer than half the offers made by the ICHEIC insurers (totaling $20 million, of which $14 million came from Generali). Moreover, many are being accepted because the elderly claimants no longer have the will to continue to fight the insurance companies. In their defense, the companies point out that the number of offers is small because the claimants often fail to provide sufficient data to have a claim honored. Of the approximately 80,000 claim forms received by ICHEIC, only about 9,600— a little more than 10 percent—identify a particular ICHEIC insurer as the issuer of the prewar policy. The rest contain only sparse information or are more an inquiry than a claim for payment. Without more information, the companies argue, they cannot honor the claims, even under ICHEIC's relaxed standards of proof.

The lack of documentation, however, is a problem of the insurance companies' own making. Since the insurers have resisted publishing the names of their prewar policyholders, the claimants filing claims with ICHEIC cannot provide more detailed information. In effect, the insurers are withholding information that would make the claims process more effective and are relying on the predictable consequences that follow as an excuse for their poor performance.

The situation of Holocaust survivor Barbara Rodbell, of Chapel Hill, North Carolina, is a typical example. Rodbell, now seventy-six, fled with her family from Berlin at age nine and eventually went into hiding in Amsterdam. After the war, she was left an orphan and penniless. Like most survivors, the only relics of her pre-Holocaust life are "letters, photographs—much less financial records to support her claims . . . 'I can't prove or disprove, that's the terrible thing.'"[105] Her parents, who would have had the financial particulars of their prewar life, perished in the Holocaust. All she knows is that her father was a successful lawyer in Berlin and would have had insurance. Allianz and the other German insurance companies have refused, however, to provide names of their prewar policyholders, thereby withholding critical information that Rodbell could use to support her claim. Renee Fink, also a Holocaust survivor living in North Carolina, concurs: "This is such a double-whammy. It's infuriating—we have no proof."[106]

Israel Arbeiter, a survivor from Poland now living in Massachusetts, recalls an insurance agent calling on his parents weekly to collect money for insurance policy premiums. Like Rodbell, he does not know the name of the company the agent represented. "It's mind-boggling why they don't want to release the names of people they have. . . . It looks to me like they are waiting until we all die and they won't have to pay. It's a crime what they are doing."[107]

Another survivor, Si Frumkin, explained why the circumstances of his family in prewar Lithuania would have made it "inconceivable that a man like my Papa—an educated, sophisticated, cosmopolitan businessman [who owned an auto dealership]—would not have a life insurance policy."[108] Yet Frumkin, who as a teenager saw his father perish in a concentration camp, admitted that "I am convinced that he did, but I cannot prove it." Frumkin asked, "Why aren't the names publicized on TV and the Internet and the newspapers, like the lists from the Swiss banks were? And why aren't the [insurance] companies penalized for not revealing their own lists?"[109] In exasperation, Frumkin labeled ICHEIC, composed of the five ICHEIC insurers, as "more fittingly the Gang of Five or GNOF" (pronounced "goniff" in Yiddish, meaning "thief"), and the entire process "a scam."[110]

Finally, there is the secrecy with which ICHEIC operates. Its negotiation sessions are not open to the public, which is understandable. As the Swiss banks and German slave labor talks showed, secrecy and confidentiality are necessary in order for the negotiating parties to make progress. But ICHEIC's reticence to reveal information extends to almost every other aspect of its work. Its expenditures are tightly guarded and, most often, are revealed only through embarrassing leaks. Such vital data as how many claims have been received, how many have been processed by each ICHEIC insurer, how many offers have been made by each insurer and for what amounts, and, most important, how much has been paid out by each insurer also are kept secret. In contrast, the Swiss banks' Claims Resolution Tribunal posts on its Web site (www.crt-ii.org) detailed information about its payouts. In a similar pursuit of transparency, the official Web site for the Swiss bank settlement (www.swissbankclaims.com) posts all documents generated in the course of the settlement. The French bank settlement's Dray Commission (see chapter 4) does the same (www.civs.gouv.fr). The ICHEIC Web site (www.icheic.org), in comparison, has almost no such material. Also, Eagleburger's directives ("decision memoranda") are marked privileged and confidential and not published. Even the MOU, the original document establishing ICHEIC, was briefly posted on the ICHEIC Web site in 1999 but has now been removed.[111]

Above all, the lists of prewar and wartime policyholders held by the ICHEIC insurers are kept secret. Most of these lists have not been turned over to ICHEIC, and not all those that have is the commission allowed to make public. Instead, the data must first be sifted through the incomplete and often inaccurate Yad Vashem database of Holocaust victims, or other archival databases, and only then are those names appearing on both lists made public. Therefore, the decision about what names will eventually be revealed is completely arbitrary. Attorney Sam Dubbin, who represents a coalition of Holocaust-survivor groups in South Florida (the area with the third largest concentration of survivors in the United States), summed up for then Attorney General Janet Reno the end results of this deliberately eliminatory process:

> Let me put this in perspective: There were at least 10 million Jews in Europe before WWII. Six million perished; four million survived. If the ICHEIC is limited to disclosing only the names companies selected which then match with one of the 3.6 million names [of Holocaust victims out of 6 million] on file at Yad Vashem, at best only 36% of all possible policy names will "match" and thus be disclosed. That is, *under the ICHEIC system* [of disclosing only those names on insurance prewar policy lists that match the name of a Holocaust victim on

file at Yad Vashem] *64% of the Jewish policyholders will not even be identified.*[112]

Dubbin reiterated the problem inherent in the selective publication of names based on computerized matches and described how the wide variations in the spelling and transliteration of names and towns could result in a computer's failing to make a proper match:

> There is so much variance in the spellings of various European cities and towns, as well as the names of the victims and policy holders. My own clients have seen substantial confusion (giving the companies the benefit of the doubt) in the attempt to match names and policies. This is another reason any settlement must require the companies to make full and total disclosures, including all available policy files and information, such as names of agents, and not be allowed to engage in a selective, unaccountable disclosure process of their own design.

The ICHEIC insurers insist, however, that the business of the commission be done in secret. ICHEIC is not an American entity but a body created under Swiss law. No insurance data are sent to the United States. Rather, all claims, including appeals, are processed through the ICHEIC office in London. All this is done in order to avoid the scrutiny of American laws promoting transparency and public access.

EAGLEBURGER'S TEMPORARY RESIGNATION

An editorial in the *Financial Times* in January 2002, described ICHEIC as having "descended from an unedifying spectacle into disarray"[113] and the ICHEIC claims process as "rotten."[114] This harshly critical opinion, unusual for a conservative, business-oriented newspaper, was prompted by one of the most embarrassing episodes in ICHEIC's sorry history.

On January 23, during a stormy ICHEIC meeting in Washington, D.C., Eagleburger, in frustration, resigned in the middle of a negotiating session. As reported by the *Baltimore Sun*, quoting one of the participants, " Someone called out, Mr. Chairman, and he said, 'You don't have a chairman anymore.'"[115]

The next day Eagleburger took back his resignation after the

ICHEIC insurers agreed to establish a monitoring committee to review the rejected claims. They also gave Eagleburger written assurances that they would abide by his directives ("decision memoranda"). "We sat down and talked straight with each other . . . [which] set a new atmosphere,"[116] explained Eagleburger. In effect, the "working by consensus" method enshrined in the ICHEIC's founding documents has been abandoned. Eagleburger gets to rule by decree, and the ICHEIC insurers have promised to abide by his decisions. Unfortunately, Eagleburger has talked tough before without any substantive results. More than two years earlier, in August 1999, Eagleburger made a pronouncement similar to his January 2000 ultimatum, telling the ICHEIC insurers, "Tough, you either abide by my decision or you walk."[117] The insurers did neither.

Representative Henry Waxman, ICHEIC's most severe congressional critic, saw the expanded authority given to Eagleburger as "the last chance to fulfill the long-standing commitment to victims of the Holocaust who have insurance coverage."[118] Unfortunately, this latest ultimatum was only one more in the sequence of "last chances" and "going-to-the-brink" scenarios faced by ICHEIC during its three-year existence.

As Nat Shapo, Illinois's commissioner of insurance and now chair of the National Association of Insurance Commissioners (NAIC) Holocaust Task Force, explained, "It's just a preposterous, ridiculous situation where the way we resolve problems is for the chairman to quit and then be talked back into staying."[119] Shapo also expressed frustration about the atmosphere of distrust at ICHEIC and accused its insurers of "continu[ing] to scuttle the discussions."[120] He noted that ICHEIC, which he and his fellow insurance commissioners were instrumental in creating, "is dangerously close to becoming a frivolous exercise."[121]

Shapo also pulled out the threat of American litigation as a means to have the companies comply. The NAIC commissioners are "nearly at a point . . . of revoking the safe harbor standing [of the ICHEIC insurers]. We are looking at a critical period over the next few months over whether this can be resolved. If it can't, it's unlikely the safe harbors and the legal peace in the U.S. courts can be sustained."[122] Even Eizenstat, now out of government, weighed in on the issue, not-so-subtly warning the insurance companies about the impending perils of litigation. Resolve the outstanding issues, Eizenstat urged the companies, in order "to avoid reopening insurance cases which have already been dismissed."[123] Later that month, Eagleburger issued his first postresignation directive: the claims application process, which began two years earlier, will be extended for another six months, from February 15 to September 30, 2002. "The deadline must be extended in order to allow adequate time to collect lists [of insurance policyholders] from the companies, process them through Yad Vashem in Jerusalem and publish the names on our Web site with adequate time for the public to review the lists," explained Eagleburger.[124] In September 2002, the deadline was extended a second time, to March 30, 2003.

Eagleburger also consented to an outside audit of ICHEIC's claims process. The audit, conducted by a group of experts labeled the Executive Monitoring Group (EMG) and headed by British Lord Archer of Sandwell, was completed in May 2002. It confirmed what had been suspected all along. As reported by the *Financial Times*,

> Lord Archer uncovered "systematic faults" including the rejection [by the ICHEIC insurers] of 280 claims from families whose policy documents had somehow survived the Holocaust. In most of those cases, the companies' excuse was that they had simply failed to find the victim's name in their own records. . . . Lord Archer's broadside has revealed the extent of the disarray at the heart of it all. All Eagleburger could do was to call an emergency meeting . . . urging all parties to remember that "what's left of [the commission's] reputation is at stake."[125]

In a June 2002 memo to the ICHEIC companies following the audit, Eagleburger warned, "The problems identified in the EMG's report are deeply disturbing. If the failures in the companies' claims processing are as numerous and as serious as appears from the Group's report, the integrity of the ICHEIC process would be put in jeopardy."[126] He also added this admonishment:

> There can be no adequate explanation for the length of time it is taking companies to process claims. At the outset, we committed ourselves to an expeditious resolution of claims. The EMG's finding is that we are not even remotely living up to this goal. . . . These delays in processing claims mean justice is being denied to our claimants, most of them old and infirm. This is a major threat to our credibility.[127]

Eagleburger's memo to the ICHEIC insurers ended with a not-so-veiled threat:

> A final note. There is substantial history to demonstrate that declarations from here [meaning from Eagleburger's Washington, D.C., offices] that an action or actions must be taken do not necessarily result in any meaningful outcome. That condition cannot continue. For example, either there will be real and meaningful reduction in the time taken to process a claim or there will have to be public consequences.[128]

It all had been said by Eagleburger before, from his January 2000 admonition to the ICHEIC insurers of "tough, you either abide by my decision or you walk" to the June 2000 declaration that "the kabuki dance is over."

In September 2002, Eagleburger announced a significant victory when, after bitter negotiations, Allianz agreed to drop its demand that its obligation to the German Foundation be offset by its contributions since 1998 to help run ICHEIC (see chapter 2). Allianz's wholly unjustified demand for an offset on its promised obligation delayed for more than a year the Holocaust restitution obligations of all the German insurance companies. Eagleburger, however, was willing to accede to Allianz's demand. The other claimants' representatives on ICHEIC likewise were willing to work out a compromise, giving Allianz partial credit as the price for moving the process forward. The sole holdout was Nat Shapo, Illiniois's insurance director and the head of the NAIC Holocaust Task Force. His only ally on the ICHEIC board was Moshe Sanbar, the Holocaust survivor from Israel appointed to represent survivors' interests. When Shapo threatened to resign from ICHEIC and to take regulatory action against Allianz in his state, Sanbar announced that he would follow Shapo. The State Department supported Eagleburger's compromise and pressured Shapo to drop his demand. But Shapo held firm. On September 18, 2002, as Shapo was about to take action, Allianz, to everyone's surprise, gave in. The German Foundation representative announced at an ICHEIC meeting that Allianz had reconsidered its position and was dropping its claim for reimbursement. Commenting on the wasted time and Allianz's last-minute turnaround, Shapo explained:

This was a terribly disappointing episode. The German insurance companies were, in my view, asking for reimbursements that they had no right to under the controlling agreements. I couldn't accept that the regulators and the Jewish side (with the exception of Moshe Sanbar) were willing to go along with the Chairman's plan to give the companies $15 million of the survivors' money. I thought that this exposed ICHEIC's fundamental weakness as a body—if the companies could violate categorical pledges with no consequence, how could claimants expect that, when push came to shove, anyone would stand up for them on the commitments in the new agreement, which included mandates on issues like lists, audits, and claims monitoring? It was a very ugly situation, but I thought the survivors needed to know that someone was going to say what they mean and mean what they say when it came to the promises that had been made to them."[129]

As of November 2002, ICHEIC was still in existence but seemed to be on its last legs. In July 2002, Neal Sher, its chief of staff, resigned. At about the same time, the *Baltimore Sun* published another exposé, revealing, among other matters, that "Sher's first-class or business–class airfare to Rome, Berlin and other cities often totaled $5,000 or more per trip."[130] It followed up its story with an editorial that suggested:

ICHEIC is in need of immediate and deep reform. It must be run with much greater transparency, stop wasting money on lavish expenses that could go to claims or Jewish causes, force insurers to publish lists of policyholders, and allow a greater role on its board for Holocaust survivors and heirs."[131]

The editorial is correct, except on the last point. As I discuss next, ICHEIC did not need more survivors and heirs on its board. Instead, it needed more lawyers.

WHY DID THE INSURANCE RESTITUTION FOUNDER?

The restitution movements launched against the Swiss banks, German industry, and other European companies achieved "rough justice" settlements that, while not perfect, could still be labeled successful. For these claims, the American lawyers, Jewish groups, and politicians were able to get the upper hand in the negotiations with their European adversaries through a skillful combination of litigation, political pressure, and diplomacy.

Not so with the Holocaust insurance restitution. The five insurance companies that joined ICHEIC were able to outmaneuver the representatives of the Jewish organizations and the state insurance commissioners on the ICHEIC board. Moreover, the European insurers were able to drag out the claims settlement process, avoided for the most part publishing lists of possible dormant Holocaust-era insurance policies, and entered into settlements that did not accurately reflect the amounts they owed. Allianz was able to insert itself into the German slave labor settlement, where it never belonged (see chapter 2), and thereby limit its liability as well as the liability of its Italian subsidiary, Reunione Adriatica, which wrote a significant number of policies in prewar eastern Europe. Following Allianz's lead, the other German insurers were included in the "big tent" settlement with Germany, limiting their liability to a ceiling of only DM 300 million (approximately $150 million), likewise an arbitrary amount with no relationship to the amount owed by the German insurers. After all the dust settled, the actual payouts made by the European insurers, both inside and outside ICHEIC, represented only a small fraction of the companies' true liability for their Holocaust-era policies.

Why were the insurance companies able to outwit the claimants' representatives? The answer has a great deal to do with the makeup of the ICHEIC board. As discussed earlier, the Holocaust claimants' interests were represented in ICHEIC through (1) the WJC and organizations closely affiliated with it, (2) the State of Israel, and (3) the state insurance commissioners of the NAIC. Missing, however, were the plaintiffs' lawyers, who were specifically kept out of the ICHEIC process by the WJC and the NAIC on the ground that it was a nonadversarial body.

In August 1998, when ICHEIC was created, Elan Steinberg of the WJC explained in not-so-polite language that the lawyers were being shut out because they were in it [only] for the money" and thereby could not represent the best interests of the survivors. "Maybe the lawyers are upset because we have said that we will tell the court that we think this money should not go to lawyers,"[132] Steinberg said.

Eizenstat, without making any accusations against the lawyers, likewise supported the view that ICHEIC could produce better results than litigation could. "Litigation would take years, if not decades to be completed."[133] Of course, he was wrong. The Swiss banks, German slave labor settlement, and the other Holocaust lawsuits, discussed in later chapters, did not take decades to complete. All settled within a few years. Eizenstat also added, "We believe the commission is the best vehicle for resolving Holocaust Era Insurance Claims because it brings together many of the interested parties in a cooperative, non-confrontational process."[134] Note the word *many*; unlike in the "big tent" meetings that Eizenstat was conducting in order to settle the German claims, in which *all* interested parties were participating, here the lawyers were missing. Curious, since Eizenstat claims credit for getting the lawyers involved in the slave labor negotiations. In his own words: "I insisted [that the plaintiffs' attorneys] had to be involved, because they held the keys to the dismissal of the cases. If they didn't agree to the terms of the settlement, we couldn't negotiate for them, and in the end if they weren't satisfied they wouldn't dismiss their cases."[135] Similarly, for the French bank claims, Eizenstat also insisted that he would not participate in the negotiations with the French government and the French banks without having the attorneys present who filed the suits (see chapter 4). Unfortunately, when trying to resolve the Holocaust insurance claims, Eizenstat failed to follow his own advice. Rather than demanding that the class action attorneys also be included in the insurance negotiations, since they likewise held the keys to dismissing the insurance cases, Eizenstat went along with the end run by the WJC and the NAIC to keep the lawyers out of ICHEIC from the start.

The WJC and the NAIC—and Eizenstat—failed to realize that the aggressive lawyers with their heavy hammer of litigation were critical to getting the European defendants, including the insurance companies, to settle all the Holocaust restitution claims, including insurance claims.

The lawyers, who had been instrumental in settling the Swiss bank claims and were now heavily involved in the German negotiations, were incensed. Fagan blasted the NAIC for "putting politics ahead of claimants' rights. [ICHEIC] does not allow survivor claimants to have parity or a voice in the process. The [memorandum of understanding] document [setting up ICHEIC] doesn't promise money, it doesn't promise time frames, its doesn't promise survivors a say. But it does make a lot of insurance commissioners big-time political stars."[136]

Linda Gerstel, an insurance law specialist that Fagan brought on board, expressed a similar sentiment. Gerstel labeled ICHEIC "a bureaucratic-laden process that repeats a lot of the mistakes of the Volcker Commission." According to Gerstel, "had the lawyers been allowed input into the ICHEIC process, there would have been more transparency and accountability." The lawyers "were particularly needed [since] the ICHEIC membership had insurance commissioners at the same table as the insurance companies, a process akin to having the fox guarding the henhouse." As she pointed out, in many states, insurance "commissioners have an interest in regulating insurance in a mild-mannered way, since they depend on the insurance companies' continued business and since many commissioners come from the ranks of insurance companies themselves."[137]

In March 2000, in my article "Nuremberg in America," I stated that "time will tell whether keeping the lawyers out was a wise move." We now know that it was a big mistake. The WJC's Rabbi Singer and Elan Steinberg, Israeli government officials, and the NAIC commissioners simply were no match for the insurance executives on the ICHEIC board and their insurance lawyers advising them in the background. Without Burt Neuborne, Mel Weiss, Michael Hausfeld, Bob Swift, and the other experienced class action lawyers and insurance law specialists like Shernoff and Gerstel, who are used to facing off large multinationals, including insurance companies, and extracting the largest possible settlements from them, the ICHEIC negotiations simply bogged down in a quagmire of technical details.

Most to blame for keeping the lawyers out are the WJC representatives and the NAIC commissioners. By insisting that the lawyers be excluded from ICHEIC and thereby breaking up the successful team of lawyers, state government officials, and Jewish representatives used in the Swiss bank and German slave labor settlements, they doomed ICHEIC to failure. As Steinberg exclaimed in frustration, two years after keeping the lawyers out of ICHEIC: "I have found my experience on the international commission dispiriting. It's been a struggle every step of the way."[138]

Dr. Avi Becker, who succeeded Singer in 2002 as head of the WJC's day-to-day operations, put on a strong defense of his predecessor's decisions in June 2000. Focusing on the almost total failure of the WJC negotiators to get the ICHEIC insurers to release the names of prewar policyholders, Becker asserted that "the problem of releasing names is a difficult one with regard to all the organizations with which we are negotiating, including the Swiss banks, with which an agreement has already been signed."[139] Becker, of course, was right. The Swiss banks have been less than forthcoming, to put it mildly, in releasing names of prewar bank depositors, even though the banks' liability was capped at the $1.25 billion settlement figure. Nevertheless, the lists of prewar depositors released by the Swiss banks have been much more extensive than the lists released by the ICHEIC insurers. While I cannot be sure, I believe that having the lawyers on the ICHEIC negotiating team and putting additional pressure on the insurers through the litigation process would have forced the insurers to release additional lists of prewar insurance policyholders. Becker also noted that compromises needed to be made, lest opportunities for settlements be lost:

> We have to realize that the more time passes, the international situation that enabled us to achieve agreements is gradually disappearing, and therefore agreements have to be reached. Jewish leadership is also distinguished by its ability to make difficult decisions, and of course, it is easiest to stand on the sidelines and criticize.[140]

What about Eagleburger's efforts? No one can dispute his commitment and passion, or the difficult assignment he accepted when agreeing to serve as chairman of ICHEIC. In November 2001, following the intense grilling by the members of the House Government Reform Committee, Eagleburger labeled his job "a monumental pain in the neck."[141] At a May 2002 dinner in his honor held by the Jewish charity B'nai Zion, Eagleburger further explained that throughout his long diplomatic career, he had negotiated with lots of "'nasty people, including Russians and Cubans. Nobody comes close to matching European insurance companies."[142]

In October 2000, in an exchange of letters with congressional critics, Eagleburger provided his most spirited defense of ICHEIC. Calling some of the accusations made by members of Congress against ICHEIC "both personally insulting and nonsense," he explained: "What too many critics fail to understand is that what the ICHEIC had to do has never been done before." He enumerated the various obstacles the commission faced:

1. "We have been winding our way through an extremely complicated field, relying on documentation, if it exists at all, that is some fifty to sixty years old."
2. "We have had to arrive at agreements on how to value policies written in some twelve currencies, several of which no longer exist or bear no relationship to their historic value."
3. "We have had to reach an agreement on what level of relaxed standards of proof [is] appropriate (given the dearth of documentation to establish a claim)."
4. "We have had to reach agreement on the publication of lists of potential claimants when European privacy laws often stand in the way of our broadcasting those names."
5. "We have had to reach agreement on how to inform potential claimants that they now have an opportunity to make a claim (something they never had before). We have had to put in place a system for receiving claims and routing them to the appropriate company or companies."[143]

All fair comments. However, the claimants and their representatives in Swiss, German, French, Austrian, and other Holocaust restitution settlements faced problems not unlike these and were able to overcome them. For example, the CRT I and CRT II tribunals for settling Swiss bank claims (see chapter 1) and the Drai Commission tribunal in France established to process restitution by French banks (see chapter 4) are good examples of relatively effective tribunals for resolving financial claims from the Holocaust era. The results achieved by these bodies demonstrate even more starkly ICHEIC's failure as a claims resolution tribunal.

In hindsight, since ICHEIC did not follow the "big tent" model of the Swiss and German negotiations and did not permit all the relevant parties, especially the lawyers, to participate in the negotiations, it would have been better not to have established ICHEIC at all. Shernoff was right when he labeled ICHEIC as nothing more than a device used by the insurance companies "to supplant the public judicial process with ICHEIC's secret process that is answerable to no one."[144] Instead of giving the insurers "safe harbor" from litigation and political pressure as an inducement for joining the unworkable commission, the litigation strategy should have been allowed to proceed forward at full steam.

Holocaust survivor Israel Arbeiter of Newton, Massachusetts, expressed a common sentiment of the survivors: "This is outrageous, to spend $40 million to collect that small an amount. If they can't do the job, they should get out of the way and let somebody else do it, not sit back in their offices and get high salaries."[145] That somebody else was the class action lawyers. As the Swiss, German, French, and Austrian settlements show, the adversarial "class action litigation coupled with political pressure" yielded higher, speedier, and more just results than those achieved by the nonadversarial process attempted through ICHEIC.

In February 2000, at the launch of ICHEIC's two-year claims process, Eagleburger solemnly announced:

> This commission was established to establish a just process . . . that will expeditiously address the issue of unpaid policies issued to victims of the Holocaust. . . . We are guided by the principle that we want to be able to say that we have done everything possible to reach all potential claimants and pay Holocaust-related insurance claims in a fair and expeditious manner.[146]

To date, ICHEIC has not even come close to fulfilling its mandate.

Lest readers think that ICHEIC has never helped resolve a claim, let me end with a rare example of an ICHEIC success story. While the claim technically was handled outside the ICHEIC's claims resolution process and the claimant himself does not give ICHEIC credit for its resolution, the ICHEIC standards were critical to resolving the claim.

The claim was made by Steven Pridham, formerly known as Siegmund Feinberg. Mr. Pridham was born in 1923 to well-to-do parents in what was then Memel, Lithuania. His father, Abraham Feinberg, owned a textile factory in Memel and a rubber products factory in Kaunas. The Feinbergs sent Siegmund to England in 1937, where he attended Kings College in Tauton. In the summer, Siegmund would return to Memel. The city and its surrounding areas were known as Memelland, Lithuanian territory that had been part of Germany before World War I.

When Hitler came to power and began calling for the return of "lost" German territories to the Reich, Abraham Feinberg became increasingly concerned for his family's safety and sent his wife, Feige, to England in September 1938. Shortly thereafter, Abraham himself moved to Kaunas, located in that part of Lithuania not initially claimed by Hitler. In March 1939, the German army occupied Memel. In August or September 1939, either shortly before or after World War II broke out, Abraham joined his wife in London but died of stomach cancer a few months after his arrival.

Due to the combination of Abraham's prescience and fate, the immediate Feinberg family escaped Nazi persecution. Siegmund and his mother Feige spent the war years in England. In 1947, the twenty-four-year-old Siegmund Feinberg anglicized his name to Steven Pridham. Later, Pridham immigrated to Israel and in 1978 came to the United States. A U.S. citizen since 1997, Pridham resides in Minneapolis.

Pridham had been aware for more than fifty years that before the war his father purchased life insurance from Allianz, but unfortunately, Pridham had no documentation. He does remember that his mother wrote to Allianz from England in 1940, seeking benefits upon his father's death but that no benefits were paid to her. In 1999, when the issue of Holocaust-era insurance was being resurrected along with other wartime restitution claims, Pridham contacted Allianz. His handwritten queries to Allianz in Germany yielded a series of peculiar responses. In a letter dated March 24, 2000, Allianz informed Pridham that it had no records of Abraham's ever purchasing insurance from the company, but a few days after the letter arrived, an Allianz representative called from Germany to explain that the company had made a mistake. Allianz had located documents in its archives confirming that Pridham's father had indeed purchased two Allianz life insurance policies before the war.

In a letter dated November 23, 2000, Allianz denied Pridham's claim. According to the denial letter, Allianz had confirmed that upon being informed in 1940 by Feige Feinberg from London that Abraham had died, sometime in 1941 it had made payment on the policies to the Nazi state. The letter explained:

> Our intent is—in accordance with the guidelines of the International Commission—to compensate life insurance policies for which no payment was made from the insurance company. This, however, does not apply to your inquiry as we definitely know that under the [policy] numbers entered in the [Allianz] central register[,] no benefits remained with Allianz [on the policies].

For Allianz, cold logic prevailed. In essence, they were telling Pridham: We are obligated to pay out only on policies on which we made "no payment." Since, in your case, we made a payment—not to your family but to the Nazis—our obligation to pay benefits has been fully discharged.

Pridham did not give up. He contacted the ICHEIC appeals office for help, but it could not make progress on the matter. A breakthrough finally occurred through the media. In May 2001, *Forbes* magazine published an article detailing the saga of Holocaust-era insurance. The story prominently featured Pridham's claim and Allianz's denial of the claim.

The *Forbes* article came to the attention of Kevin Murphy, deputy commissioner of the Minnesota Department of Commerce, the state agency in charge of licensing and regulating insurance companies in Minnesota. Murphy called Pridham and invited him for a visit. He was interested in the matter because Pridham was a resident of Minnesota. By that time, the agency already had taken an active interest in Holocaust-era insurance claims. It had helped enact a law, signed by Governor Jesse Ventura in May 2000, aimed to pressure European insurance companies doing business in Minnesota to cooperate with ICHEIC. Like the laws passed earlier in California and Washington, this law gave authority to the Minnesota Department of Commerce to strip the licenses from insurers if their parent companies failed to pay out on the Holocaust-era insurance claims.

Luck again came into the picture: Allianz just happened to have its North American headquarters in Minnesota. Deputy Commissioner Murphy decided to circumvent both the ICHEIC process and the Allianz personnel dealing with the matter in Germany and contacted the Allianz offices in Minneapolis directly. In his letter of July 13, 2001, to Margery Hughes, president of Allianz of North America, Murphy explained that after reviewing Pridham's claims, the Commerce Department had found that the claims had "merit and that a favorable resolution of same should be made by Allianz forthwith." He also made known the fact that the Minnesota Commerce Department had taken an interest in the Pridham matter ("About a month ago, Mr. and Mrs. Steven Pridham visited the Minnesota Department of Commerce at *my* invitation"—italics added) and that the media were publicizing the claim (Murphy enclosed a copy of the *Forbes* article).

The tactic worked. Two weeks later, Allianz of Germany wrote Pridham, this time agreeing to recognize his claims. The offer of payment, however, was small. Allianz offered to pay Pridham only DM 14,918.96, or approximately $7,500.

In reaching this figure, Allianz turned to a mathematical trick often used by European companies when dealing with Holocaust-era insurance claims. In the ruins of World War II, most currencies in postwar Europe were greatly devalued.[147] When faced with insurance policies that they must honor, the ICHEIC insurers have relied on these devaluations to reduce their payment offers on the prewar policies. In Pridham's case, the two policies issued to Abraham were denominated in U.S. dollars, for a total of $3,804. (As explained earlier, in prewar eastern Europe it was not unusual to purchase a policy from a reliable foreign insurance company, rather than a local carrier, and to designate the policy in a more stable foreign currency than the less stable, local currency. Abraham Feinberg had bought the insurance policies in prewar Lithuania from a German insurer and had the policies denominated in American dollars.) In its calculations, Allianz first converted these dollar-denominated policies into Nazi Reichmarks and then into postwar West German deutsche marks. As a result, even after taking into account the ICHEIC multiplier of 8 to find the present value of a prewar policy, Allianz's calculations showed that almost seventy years later, these two policies, issued in dollars and valued at almost $4,000, were worth less than twice that amount.

In September 2001, the Commerce Department put Pridham in contact with Steve Hunegs, a private attorney with a firm in Minneapolis. A long-time activist in the local Jewish community, Hunegs had been working with the Commerce Department in getting Minnesota's Holocaust insurance law passed.

Both Hunegs and Murphy were dissatisfied with Allianz's decision. Again, however, rather than replying to the offer from Allianz in Germany, they continued to deal directly with Allianz in Minneapolis. Their contact was Suzanne Peppin, Allianz's chief legal officer in the United States. Face-to-face meetings followed, with the Commerce Department making known that it would vigorously pursue this matter and Hunegs questioning why a dollar-denominated policy was being converted into German currency. To her credit, Peppin also wanted the matter resolved and asked for a reevaluation from Allianz in Germany. Here came another stroke of luck for Pridham. It turned out that the

Nazi law mandating the conversion of insurance policies written in foreign currencies into Nazi Reichmarks was not applicable in Kaunas, where Abraham had taken temporary refuge after fleeing Memel, since Kaunas was not part of Memelland. As a result, Abraham's life insurance policies written in U.S. dollars would not have been converted into Reichmarks.

This one detail made all the difference. On September 25, 2001, Allianz made a new offer to Pridham. This time the offer came from Peppin and was in U.S. dollars. Taking into account the interest on the total $3,804 face values of the original policies denominated in U.S. dollars and using the ICHEIC multiplier of 28.7 for such dollar-denominated policies maturing in 1939 (at Abraham's death), Allianz had now agreed to settle for $115,472.44, fifteen times more than its previous offer. In January 2002, sixty-two years after his father's death, the seventy-eight-year-old Pridham received from Allianz the insurance benefits on the prewar life insurance policies purchased by his father.

Pridham's settlement of $115,000 is the highest publicly known payout on any policy paid out by a European insurer without resort to litigation. While ICHEIC was not directly involved in the negotiations leading to the settlement and Pridham maintains that "I don't think they had any role [in the settlement],"[148] Allianz applied the ICHEIC rules to settle the matter. The process was not smooth; it took time and required a great deal of perseverance. Pridham also needed the aid of government regulators and a private attorney. However, at least for one heir to a Holocaust-era insurance policy, a fair settlement was achieved without resorting to litigation and, more or less, through the ICHEIC process.

4

Confronting the French Banks

THE LITIGATION AGAINST the French banks for their activities during World War II received less attention in the United States than did the litigation against the other European actors. When the Swiss banks were sued in late 1996 and early 1997, they were the sole defendants and received the full spotlight of public interest. By the time the litigation against the French banks began at the end of 1997, the Holocaust restitution movement was in full swing. As a result, the claims against the Swiss banks, German industry, European insurance companies, and even European and American museums for Nazi-looted art often overshadowed the litigation against the French. When a global settlement was reached with the French banks in January 2001, much less attention was paid to it than the other Holocaust restitution settlements; the French settlement was viewed as a "cleanup" deal, addressing claims that necessarily needed to be concluded now that the seemingly more important claims against the Swiss and the Germans had been resolved.

The importance of the French litigation in the Holocaust restitution story, however, cannot be underestimated, for both the legal precedents it established and its role in forcing a reluctant French nation to confront a less-than-noble part of its wartime past. In France, the litigation and its aftermath became critical ingredients of the recent movement to restore historical memory of the role played by the French in persecuting the Jews during the war. In the United States, the litigation was consequential because the lawyers who filed suit against the French banks accomplished what no other plaintiffs' lawyers in the Holocaust restitution movement had been able to do: they convinced the federal judge presiding over the case to deny a motion by the foreign defendants to dismiss a class action lawsuit filed for Holocaust-era events, that is, for activities occurring more than a half-century ago on foreign soil. This landmark decision "not to dismiss" was a "home run" for the American litigators and led to the rapid conclusion of the litigation, with the French banks agreeing to a deal.

THE JEWS IN VICHY AND OCCUPIED FRANCE

Nazi Germany conquered France in June 1940, but the Nazis allowed a portion of southern France to remain unoccupied, albeit ruled by a government beholden to the Germans. That part of unoccupied France, about two-fifths of its territory, was governed by Marshal Henri-Philippe Pétain, France's military hero from World War I. Known as Vichy France, for the town where the vassal state had its seat of government, the rump French state existed until France was liberated in 1944.

France's Jewish population numbered approximately 330,000 at the time of the Nazi invasion in 1940, or less than 1 percent of the population. About 160,000 Jews, mostly in Paris, were trapped in the Nazi-occupied zone. Many of them were refugees who had sought safety in France after earlier Nazi takeovers of their former homelands. As with the Jewish population of other nations coming under Hitler's rule, their persecution soon followed the German conquest. The persecution was not limited to Jews in the Nazi-occupied zone; rather, Jews living under the Vichy government—most of whom had fled from the Nazi-occupied zone after the invasion—likewise became subject to discrimination and maltreatment in accordance with decrees by the Vichy government. In fact, French officials in both the occupied and unoccupied (Vichy) zones of France willingly took on the job of persecuting their Jewish population, at times acting more harshly than the Nazi officials ruling occupied France. The most dramatic example was the deportation of Jews from Drancy, the most infamous of the concentration camps in occupied France, where the French officials herded the Jews. Even though the Nazi officials demanded only the roundup of Jewish adults in Drancy, located outside Paris, the French officials went beyond the German orders to include 4,000 Jewish children, who were then shipped off to Auschwitz for extermination. Eventually, an estimated 76,000 Jews were deported from France "to the East," including about 6,000 children, one-third of them under the age of six. Of those deported, only 2,500, or about 3 percent, survived the death camps.[1]

Besides stripping Jews of their civil rights, the Nazi conquest also led to discriminatory economic measures against the Jews in France. The German military government in occupied France ordered measures against Jews in September 1940 and the "Aryanization" of their property in April 1941. These measures were implemented by the French bureaucracy. The puppet regime in Vichy adopted statutes based on German measures to expropriate Jewish property in March and June 1941. As in other countries controlled or conquered by the Nazis, the measures authorized the theft of Jewish property in France by both Nazi and French government bodies and private institutions. One of those private institutions was the banks, whose long-forgotten activities during wartime came under renewed scrutiny in the United States in the aftermath of the litigation against the Swiss banks.

Soon after the Nazi conquest of France, French banks in both occupied and Vichy France began to ferret out and confiscate the accounts of their Jewish account holders. Approximately 80,000 such accounts, representing some 56,400 depositors aged fifteen or older, were identified and then "Aryanized" by more than one hundred banks operating in wartime France. In addition, approximately 6,000 safe-deposit boxes were frozen. It is important to keep in mind that like the calculations of other Jewish assets stolen during the war, these figures are only estimates, based on information reported by the French banks to the French government's study mission for Jewish looted assets.[2] The actual figures may be much higher, since no one has verified the banks' calculations, and the French banks' wartime records, like those of the Swiss banks, are incomplete. Moreover, these figures represent only those accounts taken away from Jews in the occupied zone and do not include any accounts confiscated in Vichy France.

Aryanization, the term used to designate the cleansing of the French economy of Jewish influence, of course, was nothing more than the legalized and not-so-legalized looting of Jewish property. Like the victims of the Swiss banks, the victims of the French banks' theft have remained uncompensated for the most part for the last sixty years.

When confronted with their wartime actions against their Jewish account holders, the French banks maintained that they were complying with either Nazi law or Vichy law. Moreover, they claimed, they were forced to do so: the anti-Jewish laws promulgated by the Nazis in occupied France or by the Vichy government mandated that they find the assets of their Jewish customers and seize them. But according to Professor Richard Weisberg's testimony before the House Committee on Banking and Financial Services, "These banks not only followed the law, they made the law. They were enormously influential on questions such as who should become an Aryan administrator and what fees should an individual be allowed in administering Jewish property."[3]

In fact, compulsion was not the reason for the banks' behavior. Historians examining the banks' activities during this period have shown that the banks readily complied with these anti-Jewish laws and earned substantial profits as a result.[4] One indication is that the French banks began seizing and freezing the bank accounts of their Jewish depositors even *before* the relevant laws and regulations requiring them to do so were in place. According to Professor Weisberg, "The banking industry [in wartime France] was one of the few that *anticipated* the promulgation of laws by instituting anti-Jewish policies before any law required it."[5] To cite just one example: on October 18, 1940, the German authorities issued an ordinance, paragraph 4 of which allowed a party to annul any agreement dealing with Jewish property, individual or corporate. The ordinance was silent on the subject of bank accounts held by Jews. Nevertheless, the following month, Crédit Lyonnais issued this directive:

> On the basis of this order (of 18 October 1940), assets held by Israelites, which have not been frozen, may be governed by special measures and this must lead us to exercise caution in our relations with them.
>
> We do not believe that withdrawals of clean French securities or capital will be affected by paragraph 4 of the order, but it should be ensured that accounts do not show debit balances if we have not received a regular security before 23 May 1940. However, other operations: discounts, advances, security sales, appointments of representatives, etc. should be examined very carefully before being implemented.[6]

Three months later, Crédit Lyonnais's internal regulations for its Jewish customers became even more severe:

> As far as cash is concerned, Israelite assets are in principle not restricted. However, large sums should not be withdrawn. . . . Other operations . . . must in principle be refused if they involve significant amounts and may therefore constitute flight of fortune unless, of course, they are justified by authorization from the German authorities.[7]

This was how Crédit Lyonnais was operating even before the Nazis issued, on May 28, 1941, the very first ordinance specifically dealing with bank accounts and other assets of clients considered to be Jewish.

As with the other corporate actors discussed in this study, the French banks' motive for their actions seems to be pure greed, an opportunity to earn extra profits.

After the war, France was eager to hide its complicity with the Nazis in persecuting the Jews. Led by General Charles de Gaulle, the wartime French hero and later president of postwar France, the French government began a consistent policy of covering up its history of collaboration as a way of restoring French honor and glory; historical denial and obfuscation became the norm. The story of the French banks was no exception. With the collusion of the French government, the banks hid their wartime activities from their Jewish customers. In doing so, the major French banks engaged in what one legal expert described as a "post-war falsification of their activities from 1940 to 1944. . . . The banks apparently destroyed evidence in order to exculpate themselves."[8]

J'ACCUSE: THE LITIGATION BEGINS

In December 1997, the first lawsuit was filed against the French banks. Unlike the other Holocaust restitution suits, this new litigation was not initiated by Ed Fagan and his legal compatriots. Rather, the French banks were sued by a team of New York lawyers headed by Roy Carlin and Kenneth McCallion. Carlin and McCallion recruited Richard Weisberg, a professor at Cardozo Law School and a former professor of French literature at the University of Chicago, who had written a monumental study of the misuse of law in Vichy France. McCallion also brought on board Harriet Tamen, a solo practitioner in New York who had previously worked as an in-house counsel for Crédit Lyonnais. Professor Vivian Curran of the University of Pittsburgh Law School, who had followed Weisberg's footsteps in researching and writing about the French legal system during the war, also joined the team as an adviser, as did Professor Malvina Halberstam, Weisberg's colleague at Cardozo.

The lawsuit, *Bodner v. Banque Paribas*, was brought by sixteen elderly Holocaust survivors. The plaintiffs, all American citizens at the time the lawsuit was filed, were either former French nationals or refugees living in France during the Nazi occupation. The lead plaintiff, Fernande Bodner, was an elderly survivor living in Brooklyn who lost her father after he was deported from France. Ms. Bodner was saved by French Catholics who hid her. Like Estelle Sapir in the Swiss bank litigation, Ms. Bodner's father had told her before he was deported about his accounts in the Paris branch of Banque Paribas.

All the plaintiffs were Jewish, and their class action lawsuit was brought on behalf of "the Jewish victims and survivors of the Nazi Holocaust in France, their heirs and beneficiaries."[9] Limiting the class to Jewish victims made the case less complicated, especially upon settlement. Unlike the Swiss bank litigation, in which the plaintiffs' lawyers had to create a special category entitled "Victims or Targets of Nazi Persecution" (see chapter 1) and allow some non-Jewish victims to recover while keeping others out, in the French bank litigation it was clear from the outset that the lawsuit was for only the Jewish victims of the French banks' wartime activities. Six large French banks were sued: Banque Paribas, Crédit Lyonnais, Société Generale, Crédit Commercial de France, Crédit Agricole Indosuez, Natexis, and also Britain's Barclays Bank, which maintained a branch in Paris during the occupation.

A year later, McCallion, Tamen, and Carlin filed a second suit against the French banks. For this lawsuit, they asked Michael Hausfeld and Melvyn Weiss and their team of lawyers to join forces. As in the other Holocaust restitution suits filed by Hausfeld and Weiss, the younger lawyers, Deborah Sturman from Milberg Weiss and Morris Ratner from Lieff Cabraser, would do the lion's share of their firms' work on the case. The expanded team's combined class action lawsuit, _Benisti v. Banque Paribas_,[10] was filed on behalf of eighteen other Holocaust survivors or heirs of victims. In contrast to the _Bodner_ class action, all these plaintiffs in _Benisti_ were aliens, elderly Jews who had survived the Holocaust but lived in other countries. The alleged basis for jurisdiction of this suit was the Alien Torts Claims Act, the _hostis humani generis_ federal statute discussed in chapter 1, which allowed aliens to bring civil suits in American courts for gross violations of international human rights law.

As in _Bodner_, the named plaintiffs in _Benisti_ sought to represent only Jewish victims. The defendants in this suit were the same six French banks named in the _Bodner_ action. This lawsuit, however, added one additional French bank, the Banque Nationale de Paris, as well as two American banks, Chase Manhattan and J. P. Morgan. Like the British bank Barclays, these American financial institutions had branches in Nazi-occupied Paris and were also accused of stealing Jewish accounts.

Bodner and *Benisti* were filed in the same federal courthouse in Brooklyn where the Swiss bank actions were litigated and settled. Both cases were assigned to Judge Sterling Johnson Jr., whose chambers are a few doors down from Judge Korman's.

Three months later, in March 1999, Ratner and Sturman pulled another trick from their Swiss bank litigation experience. They opened a Western front in the litigation against the French banks by filing a lawsuit against the banks in California, in state court in San Francisco,[11] where Lieff Cabraser had its head office. Morris Ratner was the lawyer in charge of this case. Whereas the federal lawsuits were class actions, the California state suit was a quasi class action, filed under a peculiar California law allowing plaintiffs to sue both individually and on behalf of the general public for unfair business activities conducted in California. The suit maintained that the failure by the French banks that did business in California to return money belonging to the victims who were California residents amounted to an unfair business practice triggering the California statute.

The French banks hired well-known national law firms to defend them, which soon filed several motions to dismiss the suits in both New York and San Francisco. The arguments raised in the motions were now becoming boilerplate, with the banks repeating the same legal arguments first made by the Swiss banks and then by other European defendants in the subsequently filed Holocaust-era suits.

The French banks contended that either the American courts lacked jurisdiction over them or that the courts were not the proper forum in which to bring such suits; that the claims were not properly alleged; that the claims were too late; and that the plaintiffs lacked standing to sue. Finally, like the Swiss banks earlier, the French banks vigorously argued that because the wartime role of the French banks was now being examined in France, the American judges should defer to those proceedings and put these lawsuits "on hold"—in legal parlance, abstain from deciding the suits.

FRENCH FACT-FINDING:
THE MATTÉOLI AND DRAI COMMISSIONS

In the Swiss bank suits as the accusations grew and became louder, the Swiss bankers responded by forming the private fact-finding International Committee of Eminent Persons (ICEP), headed by Paul Volcker. Later, when the Swiss government was faced with attacks on the wartime behavior of Swiss public institutions, it created a historical committee, the Bergier Commission, to uncover and report the true history of wartime Switzerland (see chapter 1).

The private French banks did not follow the example of their Swiss banking compatriots. There was no parallel Volcker Committee for the French banks. But the French government did follow the example of the Swiss authorities. In March 1997, French Prime Minister Alain Juppé created through a decree the "Prime Minister's Office Study Mission into the Looting of Jewish Assets in France," essentially a French version of the Bergier Commission. The study mission was popularly known as the "Mattéoli Commission," named after its chairperson, a former cabinet minister and Resistance fighter Jean Mattéoli. Its task was to study, as the decree carefully worded it, "the various forms of spoliation visited upon the Jews of France during World War II" and the postwar efforts to remedy such spoliation. The phrase "visited upon the Jews " suggests some kind of a plague or act of God, rather than actions by real people toward French Jewish citizens and Jewish residents of France. Nevertheless, despite the disembodied phraseology, the French nation was finally ready to examine the various forms of robbery committed on its Jewish populace sixty years earlier.

The Mattéoli Commission published two interim reports, in December 1997 and February 1999, and one final report in April 2000, after which it closed up shop. The mandate of the nine-member commission was limited to determining what had been taken from the Jews in France during wartime. As described by one of its members, French historian Claire Andrieu, "the Mattéoli Commission is deeply convinced that truth is the first step towards justice. Our doctrine is: Facts first."[12] And the facts that the commission discovered after, in its own words, "spend[ing] three years searching in the dark shadows"[13] were unsettling. As Jean Mattéoli explained in his foreword to the final report:

The extent of the despoilment and the ramifications without number were the first factors to surprise us. By accumulating the status of persons and that of property, by combining professional prohibitions and the confiscation of all types of movable and immovable property, the Nazi authorities and the Vichy government bound Jews in an inextricable lattice of crimes against human rights.[14]

The commission found that every segment of the French economy, except for agriculture, fishing, mining, and forestry, in which few Jews were involved, had engaged in the thievery:

"Aryan" companies participated in the despoilment or profited from it (and particularly the professions, as competition was eliminated) either because of "temporary administrators" who were appointed to "Jewish" companies themselves stemmed from "aryanised activities" or because of the expulsion of Jewish executives and shareholders.[15]

The Mattéoli Commission report also confirmed the banks' abhorrent policies. "The rapidity with which the spoliation measures were applied, both by the Ministry of Finance and by the organizations representing the banking profession and by the banks themselves, leave[s] little room for questions."[16] Taking special note of the American banks' activities, the report observed that they could have resisted the Nazi's Aryanization policies but chose not to.

The Mattéoli Commission also examined what restitution was made after the war. In his foreword to the final report, Mattéoli commented, "The second surprise, a fortunate one, was to note the extent and diversity of restitution means."[17] Nevertheless, despite the immediate postwar efforts at restitution, Mattéoli noted that the "victims did not always receive all their property nor enjoy all the compensation to which they were entitled. Others who succeeded in having the statutes concerning their case applied suffered from the length and complexity of the formalities in question."[18]

In its final remarks, the Mattéoli Commission also admitted that its findings, based on events that began more than sixty years ago, were necessarily incomplete.

We should not labour under any illusion however. Even if all the archives were available, if no file had been lost, it would be a vain attempt to trace, almost two-thirds of a century after the events, what actually happened down to the finest detail. We must resign ourselves to the fact that many points will remain imperfectly explained.[19]

The point is fairly made and equally applicable to every other historical commission discussed throughout this book, whether examining the wartime activities of a nation, an entire industry, or even a particular company.

Before disbanding, the Mattéoli Commission recommended restitution in all cases in which it had not yet been made. The eighth recommendation of the Mattéoli Commission's final report states: "In cases where property, the existence of which in 1940 is established, has been the subject of spoliation but not yet been returned or compensated, compensation is a right irrespective of any statutes of limitations which may be in effect."[20] To do so, the commission urged the establishment of a successor governmental commission to consider making payments to the victims of the spoliation. In the words of Jean Mattéoli, the commission "proposed the creation of a body that would examine individual claims from victims of anti-Semitic legislation passed during the Occupation."[21]

Lionel Jospin, who became prime minister in June 1997 after the parliamentary election victory of the socialists (and who, in 2002, lost the run-off spot for the French presidency to right-wing extremist Jean-Marie Le Pen) followed Mattéoli's recommendation. On September 10, 1999, Jospin announced the creation of a post–Mattéoli Commission to oversee compensation payments to individual victims, the so-called Commission for the Compensation of Victims of Spoliation Resulting from Anti-Semitic Legislation in Force during the Occupation, otherwise known as the Drai Commission, after its chair, the noted French jurist Pierre Drai. Like the Mattéoli Commission, it consisted of nine members and staff. As noted at that time by Henri Hadjenberg, then head of the Jewish community in France, "This marks the first time a state, other than Germany, recognizes the principle of individual reparation. . . . It's something we have been waiting for, for years."[22] France was making significant progress. Nevertheless, the litigation with the French banks remained unresolved.

POLITICAL PRESSURE IN THE UNITED STATES

Just four days after Jospin's announcement establishing the Drai Commission, the French banks came under fire in the United States. On September 14, 1999, the U.S. House of Representatives Banking Committee, chaired by Republican Congressman Jim Leach, held its second in a series of hearings on Holocaust restitution. Leach had now taken over the role played three years earlier by the later-defeated Senator Alfonse D'Amato during the Senate Banking Committee's hearing on Holocaust restitution. At these latest hearings, the actions of the French banks, like the actions of the Swiss banks earlier, came under scrutiny of the U.S. Congress.

One of those testifying was Professor Claire Andrieu, a history professor at the Sorbonne who had served on the Mattéoli Commission dealing with bank issues. In defense of the banks' wartime actions, Professor Andrieu contended that the French banks stole from the Jews by means of the anti-Jewish laws, that is, the occupying Germans created a temptation for the banks to steal—a temptation, which Professor Andrieu neglected to mention, the banks could have resisted but did not. She also made a point of adding that it was not only the French banks that stole from the Jews but also American banks with branches in France. This fact was calculated to make the French banks' actions seem less heinous.

The timing of the Leach hearings was seen as sending a message to the banks: settle the litigation or be subject to the same scrutiny and pressure as applied earlier to the Swiss banks. Not coincidentally, the hearings were held while two of the defendant French banks, Société Generale and Banque Paribas, were awaiting approval from bank regulators for a merger in the United States.

At this point, Alan Hevesi, the comptroller of New York City, also chose to enter the fray. Hevesi's Executive Monitoring Committee added the issue of the French banks to its September 1999 meeting agenda, an action widely regarded as "a way to pressure French banks to settle the lawsuits."[23]

The political pressure proved to be a significant element in moving the French banks to strive for a speedy end to the litigation. To their credit, the French banks realized that if they were to avoid the trauma experienced one year earlier by the Swiss banks at the hands of federal and local politicians—and not jeopardize their ability to do business in the United States—they had to remove the issue from the American political arena.

THE FRENCH GOVERNMENT INTERVENES

The French government came to the aid of the banks in the American litigation by filing an *amicus* brief supporting dismissal. In its *amicus* brief filed with Judge Johnson in Brooklyn's federal court, France asserted that the litigation in the United States against these private French banks "infringe[s] upon [France's] sovereign duty to take responsibility for, and interferes with its current efforts to address, the wrongs committed against residents of France within its borders."[24]

Surprisingly, the organized Jewish community in France, the third largest in the world after those in Israel and the United States, also weighed in against the litigation in the United States and the concomitant pressure by American-based Jewish organizations against the banks. It was basically a turf war, with the local Jewish community in France siding with the French government, and the World Jewish Congress (WJC) wanting to keep the focus of the struggle in the United States. What most upset the French Jews was the claim by the WJC and its related organization, the World Jewish Restitution Organization (WJRO), that the suit represented the interests of the victims and heirs from Vichy France and Nazi activities during the war. That is, the local Jewish organizations in France wanted the WJC to stay out of what they regarded as their issue. But the WJC argued that not all the victims of the French banks' misfeasance were French nationals but included many Jewish refugees who had fled to France after the Nazis conquered their countries. According to Elan Steinberg, then executive director of the WJC, "The most salient fact to understand here is that while the Holocaust in France took the lives of 75,000 Jews, 70 percent were non-French Jews [i.e., refugees from Poland, Austria, Germany, Belgium, and other European countries]. It is indeed a French Jewish issue, and the French Jewish community must be involved, but it is also undeniably a world Jewish issue."[25] Professor Adolphe Steg, deputy chairman of the Mattéoli Commission and a leading member of the French Jewish community, countered:

Even for the foreign Jews who have suffered in France and left France for other countries, who would better represent them than [the French Jews] who have lived exactly the same experience in France? . . . The French Jewish community, which is composed of many thousands of survivors, are the best representatives of these Jews.[26]

In response to the French government's intervention in the litigation, Comptroller Alan Hevesi filed his own *amicus* brief, urging rejection of the dismissal motions.[27] Hevesi directly addressed France's assertion to be the sole arbiter of the claims:

At first, [France's] argument has some superficial appeal. However, France's real sovereign interest in taking responsibility for and addressing the events of the Holocaust is in exploring its own responsibility for the persecution of French Jews and other minorities and its own provision of restitution for the acts of the French government and/or its citizens. Its purported interest in these cases, which are private claims against private parties, amounts to a demand to be the sole arbiter of all claims asserted by any French Holocaust victim against any private defendant, and does not rise to a level demanding deference from this Court.

In regard to the American interest in this litigation, Hevesi noted the following on the basis of claims by Holocaust survivors now living outside France:

Indeed, this country, this State and this City all have an enormous countervailing interest in providing a forum in which U.S. citizens and Holocaust survivors living elsewhere can reclaim property misappropriated by French banks doing business here, which overshadows whatever interest French government has in forcing the plaintiffs to forgo litigating their claims. None of the legal theories advanced by the French Republic—*forum non conveniens*, international comity, or the Act of State Doctrine—requires this Court to decline to exercise jurisdiction over these actions.[28]

Later in the brief, Hevesi expounded further on the theme of private claims against private institutions having little to do with the issue of French sovereignty:

There is no doubt about the cultural importance to the French people of coming to terms with their history, but the simple fact that these private lawsuits against private entities accrued in occupied France does not mean they violate French sovereignty. Whether the misappropriation occurred with the explicit or tacit approval of the French government, or whether the Vichy government was itself legitimate, simply is irrelevant to the disposition of the U.S. litigation, which comprises straightforward commercial claims against the French banks.[29]

Hevesi also added what turned out to be a productive suggestion: "If the French government determines that the plaintiffs are entitled to additional restitution from the public institutions that persecuted and participated in the theft of their property, it may freely provide for it notwithstanding any U.S. litigation against the private wrongdoers."[30] The French government, in fact, followed up on this suggestion by creating a government fund for those who were made orphans as a result of the persecution of Jews in France.

The Clinton administration abstained from direct involvement, keenly aware of the work being done by Eizenstat and other government officials and also the interjection of France and the New York City comptroller into the proceedings. The full court press from the Holocaust restitution campaign—class action litigation coupled with political pressure—was now being applied against the French banks.

THE SETTLEMENTS BY BARCLAYS BANK AND J. P. MORGAN

As explained earlier, the lawsuits filed against the French banks also named as defendants the British bank Barclays and two American banks, Chase Manhattan Bank and J. P. Morgan. These three non-French banks had branches in France at the time of the German occupation.

Soon after the lawsuits were filed, Barclays conducted an internal study to determine whether and how many of its Jewish customers in their twelve branches in France at the time of the occupation had their assets "Aryanized" after the Nazi takeover. The study found that as best as it could determine, the Barclays office in wartime France had 343 Jewish customers and that approximately 95 percent of them survived the war and were presumed to have participated in the postwar restitution process. Following the study, Barclays broke ranks with the other banks and decided to enter into a separate settlement with the plaintiffs and in July 1999 agreed on a settlement of $3.6 million.

The plaintiffs' attorneys agreed that the present Barclays Bank management assumed the role of the "good guys" when compared with that of the other defendants in the Holocaust litigation movement. Presented with adverse facts about some of the bank's actions in wartime France, Barclays squarely confronted the problem and tried to resolve it. According to a Barclays representative: "We are a bit different from the Swiss and French banks. We have sought not to have a drawn out legal battle."[31]

While the $3.6 million settlement with Barclays is not huge, especially compared with the other settlements reached later in the Holocaust restitution litigation, its timing was important. The deal was reached after the August 1998 Swiss bank settlement and so became the second successful resolution of a Holocaust-era class action lawsuit. The settlement therefore provided a critical psychological boost to the lawyers and other activists working in the Holocaust restitution movement.

After this second victory in the Holocaust restitution litigation came a big defeat: the September 1999 issuance of the two German slave labor decisions by the federal judges in New Jersey, dismissing the class action lawsuits for wartime slave labor (see chapter 2).

Each of the two American banks sued for their wartime activities in France took a different strategy: J. P. Morgan, like Barclays, also decided to settle quickly, but Chase Manhattan Bank joined the other French banks in filing a motion with Judge Johnson urging the dismissal of the litigation.

Chase Manhattan Bank was one of five American banks with branches in Paris when the Nazis conquered France, after which it closed two of its branches and the Nazis shut down a third. One branch in Paris, however, remained open. Carlos Niedermann, the manager of that branch, wrote to his superiors in the United States, mentioning his good relations with the Nazis. Niedermann urged that the Paris branch continue doing business by detailing the potential financial opportunities provided by Nazi rule. Thereafter, German accounts were opened in the Chase branch, and Niedermann approved loans to finance German industry assisting the Nazi war machine. Niedermann was not just a rogue employee acting in secrecy and isolation. A report issued by the U.S. Federal Reserve in April 1945 after it investigated Chase's Paris branch concluded that Chase's New York headquarters was well aware of the activities taking place in the Paris branch but did nothing to stop them. A report by the U.S. Treasury Department likewise concluded that the U.S. Chase knew of Niedermann's activities, at least until late 1942, well after the United States declared war on Germany in December 1941.

J. P. Morgan was the other American bank to continue operating in Paris after the Nazi occupation. To endear itself to the Nazis and the Vichy officials, the local office boasted of its anti-Semitic hiring policies and the fact that none of J. P. Morgan's partners was a Jew. The Nazis gave the bank its seal of approval by designating it "an international Aryan organization."

In the litigation against the two American banks more than a half-century later, both maintained that they had lost control of the branches' operations after the occupation and so could do nothing to prohibit their activities in Paris. Chase also claimed that its Paris branch had scaled back its involvement with the Nazis, and in any case, its own internal probe revealed that only three accounts of Jewish customers had been looted and only eleven safe-deposit boxes had been stolen.

In 1999, the American media began publicizing the suits, highlighting the specific allegations against the American banks. The TV news program *Dateline NBC* aired a segment on the subject; CBS News and CNN likewise ran stories publicizing the wartime findings of the U.S. government agencies concerning these banks.

Following the stories, J. P. Morgan decided, like Barclays, also to break ranks with the other defendant banks and enter into a separate settlement with the plaintiffs. Like Barclays, J. P. Morgan announced that it would not be joining the French banks' motion to dismiss filed with Judge Johnson. The settlement with J. P. Morgan was concluded in September 2000 and, because it had fewer Jewish accounts, for an amount less than Barclays, $2.75 million.

Under the settlement rules for class action litigation, Judge Johnson (like Judge Korman in the Swiss bank settlement) was required to hold a fairness hearing to approve the two agreements. A joint hearing for both deals was held in October 2001, and since no objections were filed, Judge Johnson approved both settlements.

Claimants with documentation of accounts in the French branches of the two banks had until September 30, 2002, to file claims. It appears that money will be left over after all the claims, even those with minimal documentation, are paid. The two settlements, however, took into account such a contingency, providing that if any money were left undistributed after all the claims were paid, then the money would be "donate[d] to one or more non-profit charitable institution(s) . . . to be used for purposes of advancing research and knowledge concerning the Holocaust, including research to assist Holocaust survivors and their heirs."[32] The Barclays Bank management insisted that the money for these activities be spent in France.

Interestingly, J. P. Morgan and Chase Manhattan merged in 2002 to become J. P. Morgan Chase & Co. But the Chase Manhattan part of the new entity was specifically excluded from participating in the J. P. Morgan Bank settlement and instead became a party in the Drai Commission's settlement in January 2001. The new J. P. Morgan Chase conglomerate, therefore, is a party in both settlements.

JUDGE JOHNSON'S LANDMARK DECISION

The French banks' motion to dismiss still lay before Judge Johnson, along with numerous briefs supporting and refuting it. From a legal standpoint, his ruling would be critical to the entire Holocaust restitution movement.

European defendants and their lawyers who entered into Holocaust-era settlements minimize the role played by U.S. litigation in obtaining the settlements, arguing that none of the lawsuits resulted in court rulings in the plaintiffs' favor. Judge Korman, they point out, never ruled on the Swiss banks' motion to dismiss; although Judge Debevoise and Greeneway did issue rulings in the German slave labor litigation, they were in favor of the German companies and held that the Holocaust-era claims should be dismissed. The plaintiffs' lawyers countered that *if* Judge Korman had ruled on the Swiss banks' motion—a decision he delayed making in order to give the parties time to come to the bargaining table—he probably would have denied the motion. For the German slave labor cases, the plaintiffs' lawyers argued that both judges simply made incorrect rulings, which they appealed and expected to have overturned on appeal.[33] They also pointed out that the lawyers in the U.S. Department of Justice who examined the slave labor cases presented Eizenstat with a legal memorandum concluding that the cases should not have been dismissed.

One need not speculate about how a case might have turned out to show that the defense lawyers' and their clients' proposition—that all court decisions had favored the defense—is simply wrong. The plaintiffs' lawyers, in fact, obtained significant legal rulings in their favor, and those rulings forced the European defendants to settle shortly thereafter. In chapter 2, I described how Judge Cooper ruled in favor of the *Stern* plaintiffs and against Generali's motion to dismiss, upholding the bringing of the Holocaust-era insurance lawsuit in California state court. The French bank litigation represents another instance of the plaintiffs' lawyers' scoring a solid and unambiguous victory in the Holocaust restitution litigation campaign.[34] Moreover, whereas *Stern* was a state court lawsuit dealing with an individual action, the *Bodner* and *Benisti* French bank actions were class actions litigated in federal court.

On August 31, 2000, Judge Sterling Johnson, presiding over the French banks' class action litigation, denied the banks' motion to dismiss the lawsuits by holding that U.S. federal courts have jurisdiction over such litigation. In effect, Judge Johnson did what his Brooklyn federal courthouse colleague, Judge Korman, never had to do: he examined the arguments made earlier by the Swiss banks and now being made by the French banks and found them wanting. He found no reason that these cases—against the French banks and, by analogy, the Swiss banks—for events stemming from the Holocaust could not be litigated in the United States.

Readers interested in the technicalities of the law and international litigation in U.S. courts would benefit from reading the entire text of Judge Johnson's decision, in which he explains his reasons for finding jurisdiction and allowing the cases to proceed to trial.[35] In a superbly crafted ten-page legal opinion, he considers each argument raised by the French banks and, in a methodical and straightforward fashion, shows how each is not a ground to have the cases dismissed. His opinion also shows that he understood the relationship between the relevant U.S. law and the facts of the case, demonstrating how this law allows a lawsuit that is (1) brought for claims stemming from the Holocaust era, (2) taking place in Europe, (3) filed by foreigners as well as Americans, and (4) for a violation of international law to be heard by a judge in the United States.

Judge Johnson, an African American jurist, probably knew little about Holocaust restitution when the case started but a lot about ethnic discrimination of the kind suffered by Jews in wartime France. By the time he held oral arguments in the case and issued his opinion, he had become an expert on the subject of the Holocaust. His expertise also extends into international human rights law as incorporated into U.S. law. Following the Second Circuit decision in *Filartiga* and its progeny, he recognized that the lawsuits against the French banks fall within existing American *hostis humani generis* and international law precedents adopted by federal courts over the last twenty years (see chapter 1).

The tone of Judge Johnson's opinion makes clear that these cases ended up before a judge *not* sympathetic to the French banks' arguments. Moreover, Judge Johnson concluded his opinion by stating that he was now ready to grant the plaintiffs the most dreaded of tools to use against the French banks: legal discovery.[36] This unique and, to foreign litigants, strange mechanism of American litigation forces parties to disclose to their opponents not only all documents and records relevant to the lawsuit but also anything that may lead to the discovery of such relevant documents and records. For this case, it meant that the French banks would be forced to divulge their lists of wartime accounts as well as open their wartime archives for inspection by the plaintiffs' lawyers. In effect, the plaintiffs' lawyers would now be allowed to rummage through the French banks' private files anywhere in the world, including France, to find any undisclosed "dirty laundry" and expose it to the world. No other Holocaust-era lawsuit had been able to reach that stage of litigation.

In a last-ditch effort to prevent this disastrous scenario, the banks' defense lawyers filed a motion to delay discovery with the magistrate judge who was assisting Judge Johnson on the case. On December 21, 2000, when the magistrate judge refused to grant such a delay—and instead opted to follow Judge Johnson's dictate to have the parties "immediately" begin a "thorough" discovery[37]—the French banks ran out of legal maneuvers to sabotage or delay the effects of full-blown American class action litigation. It was time to settle the cases and as quickly as possible. Under the guidance of Stuart Eizenstat, who was more than willing to add one more settlement of a Holocaust-era claim to his credit before leaving government, the French banks' litigation settled within a month.

THE UNITED STATES–FRANCE ACCORD OF JANUARY 2001

The French banks were now ready to settle but wanted what every other European defendant wanted in the Holocaust restitution litigation: a complete end to the irksome lawsuits in the United States involving claims arising from events during World War II. This meant not only the dismissal of current litigation but also immunity from future lawsuits. In the Swiss bank litigation, this was achieved through the traditional two-step process for concluding class actions in the United States: first, the signing of a formal written settlement agreement between the parties, and second, the approval of the settlement by the judge presiding over the action through a "fairness hearing," as in the Swiss bank settlement.

As we saw in the slave labor claims negotiations, the Germans came up with a better method for concluding litigation over Holocaust-era claims; they called it "legal peace." Legal peace meant not only that the lawsuits would be dismissed and the settlement independently approved by a judge; it also required that the U.S. government step in as a third-party guarantor of the deal. If any lawsuit were filed in the future against any German company involving World War II claims, the U.S. executive branch would use its best efforts to block such litigation. The United States' guarantee for the German companies came through the "Berlin Accords," the diplomatic agreements signed by Germany and the United States in Berlin in July 2000.

The French banks wanted the same. The way in which the Swiss banks settled was no longer good enough. Transforming the settlement of the private dispute between former slaves of German companies and their masters into a diplomatic accord did make some sense, since three-quarters of the funds to the German slave labor settlement came from the German government. For the French bank settlement, however, as in the Swiss bank settlement, all the money was coming from private French banks.[38] Nevertheless, the French banks sought what the German companies had obtained from the U.S. government: not only dismissal with prejudice of all the litigation but also legal peace guaranteed by the U.S. executive branch and spelled out in a diplomatic agreement between the French and U.S. governments. President Bill Clinton was ready to oblige, in one of his last official acts, in which Eizenstat and the French ambassador, Jacques Andréani, had played the critical role of interlocutors between the private litigants in getting them to settle the lawsuits.

Time was running short. On January 20, 2001, President-elect George W. Bush would be taking over, and a deal needed to be put together soon by Eizenstat and Andréani. On January 18, 2001, in the closing days of the Clinton administration, with less than forty-eight hours left, Eizenstat brought the parties to the State Department for a final meeting, put them in separate rooms, and began shuttling between the two rooms in the hopes of working out a deal. The rapid-fire diplomacy worked, and the parties settled on the very same day. The negotiated deal was spelled out in the Agreement between the Government of the United States of America and the Government of France concerning Payments for Certain Losses Suffered during World War II.[39]

Eizenstat and the plaintiffs' lawyers and Jewish representatives had learned their lessons well. In many ways, French legal peace is a significant improvement over German legal peace, and it also incorporates some of the beneficial terms of the Swiss banks' court-approved settlement.

THE DRAI COMMISSION'S SETTLEMENT

Under the settlement, the French banks agreed to pay through the Drai Commission all claims of Jewish victims or their heirs whose accounts or other assets were stolen from them by banks operating in France during the occupation.

Like the ICHEIC insurance claims process (see chapter 3), the banks agreed to consider the claims using "relaxed standards of proof."[40] There is one important, but critical, difference in how the relaxed-proof standards were applied by the ICHEIC insurers and in the French bank settlement. The ICHEIC insurance companies themselves processed the claims and decided whether the information submitted met the relaxed standards of proof and, if so, how much to award the claimant. This procedure proved to be a disaster (see chapter 3). Since the ICHEIC insurers responsible for paying out the money also were deciding whether to honor the claim and for how much, they naturally leaned toward paying as few claims as possible and for as little as possible. Worst of all, little could be done to force the European insurers to pay the claims.

In the French settlement, the French banks do not process the claims. Rather, the claims are processed exclusively and independently by the Drai Commission. The banks have no choice but to accept the awards issued by the Drai Commission and to pay them. During the claims examination stage, the Drai Commission examiners can, however, consult with the bank from which funds are sought and seek its opinion in evaluating the claim. The lawyers even were able to have the French government become a third-party guarantor for these payouts. Article 1, section 4, of the United States–France Agreement states that "France agrees to ensure that the Banks will promptly pay, in full, all claims approved by the [Drai] Commission." Failure to do so means that the French government can be sued in an American court along with the French banks.

In that sense, the French bank claims process is similar to the Swiss bank settlement process, with the Drai Commission playing the role of the Zurich-based Claims Resolution Tribunal-II (CRT-II), making all the claims settlement decisions without interference from the Swiss banks. It also is an improvement on CRT-II, since it puts the full faith and credit of the Republic of France behind the private French banks' promise to pay such claims.

There also are major differences in the mode of operation of the Swiss CRT-II and the French Drai Commission. First, the CRT-II, though located in Zurich, was created and exists under the supervision of a U.S. court—Judge Korman—and is run by two Americans, Michael Bradfield and Paul Volcker, chosen by Judge Korman. The Drai Commission is a French administrative body created by the prime minister, over whom neither Judge Johnson nor any other American person or entity has any authority. Of course, since the Drai arbitrators are French civil servants and do not work for the French banks, they are more likely to make independent decisions about the bank claims submitted. Moreover, the plaintiffs' representatives were able to use a portion of the settlement funds to employ an overseer, who works in the commission office in Paris to make sure that the claims process is fair, consistent, and expeditious. Eric Freedman, a British lecturer at the University of Orléans's law and humanities faculties in Paris, is the designated plaintiffs' representative for the commission. This became an important component of the deal. As Rabbi Abraham Cooper, associate dean of the Simon Wiesenthal Center, explained to me, the center was insisting that a full-time plaintiff's representative be placed in the

Drai Commission's offices to oversee implementation of the settlement.

> By having Eric Freedman there, working for us every day, we are making sure that every claim submitted to the Drai Commission is properly evaluated and considered. This innovation of the French bank settlement—having an "insider" following through on the deal originally put together—can serve as a model for the implementation stage of other Holocaust restitution agreements or, for that matter, for other settlements of historical wrongs. I wish ICHEIC [the International Commission on Holocaust-Era Insurance Claims—see chapter 3] had a claimants' representative placed in each of the five European insurance companies processing Holocaust-era insurance claims. It would have made ICHEIC a much more effective entity.

Second, diverting from the CRT-II, lists of dormant accounts held by the French banks are not published. As part of its investigatory work, the Mattéoli Commission obtained from the French banks a list of some 63,000 accounts held by Jews during World War II. The information was collated, computerized, placed on a disk, and delivered to the Drai Commission to fulfill its compensation mandate. Neither the two French governmental commissions nor the French banks, however, despite hints that they would do so, have published this list. Thus, unlike the Swiss bank settlement, in which the Swiss banks allowed the publication of at least a partial list of probable dormant accounts belonging to Holocaust victims, a similar list compiled by the French banks remains secret. A Holocaust survivor or heir believing that he or she is entitled to restitution from a French bank must apply to the Drai Commission, which then checks the claim against the French banks' dormant accounts list.

As discussed in the previous chapters with respect to other Holocaust restitution settlements, such secrecy and lack of transparency are untenable. The French banks' list should have been made public, not least because every time a list of dormant wartime assets is published, surprises appear. For example, the publication of the Swiss banks' list led to the discovery that Madeline Albright, the former U.S. secretary of state, and Madeline Kunin, the U.S. ambassador to Switzerland, were heirs to Holocaust victim dormant accounts. The partial publication of the ICHEIC insurance lists revealed that Teddy Kollek, the former mayor of Jerusalem, was the beneficiary of a Holocaust-era insurance policy. Similar unexpected beneficiaries might appear if the French banks' list also was made public. As it is, persons who may be potential beneficiaries will never know this. As the French banks' distribution process is set up, a claimant is basically told, "You apply, tell us all the facts you have supporting your claim for restitution of dormant account funds, and we will then tell you whether your name appears on our secret list."

The French banks, supported by the French government, argue that the publication of such lists is unlawful under French law, enacted to protect the privacy of the very persons who want the list published. At the congressional hearings on the French bank issues, Representative Jim Leach rightly called this rationale both Kafkaesque and a "Catch-22." Moreover, just as the Mattéoli Commission was able to obtain special governmental exemptions to research wartime files containing private information protected by the very same French laws, so the Drai Commission could have obtained a special exemption to be allowed to publish the list.

In addition, the French banks generated the list of dormant accounts of their former wartime Jewish customers themselves, without any outside supervision. Therefore, there is no way to verify whether the French banks' list of 63,000 dormant accounts is correct or complete. In the Swiss banks' search, it was the independent Volcker Committee that compiled the list, not the Swiss banks. As the WJC's Elan Steinberg noted, "This is not accountability. It [is] as if the Swiss banks, without the independent oversight of the Volcker Commission, were allowed to unilaterally determine which were relevant accounts."[41]

A final difference between the Swiss and French bank settlements and, for that matter, the German slave labor settlement is that the French bank settlement does not set a monetary cap on the total amount of money that can be paid, whereas the Swiss bank settlement is capped at $1.25 billion, with $800 million allocated to the bank claimants. The Germans also agreed to pay a set amount—$5 billion—and no more. The French banks theoretically have unlimited liability, since they agreed to pay all awards issued by the Drai Commission. To cover the awards, the French banks deposited $50 million in an interest-bearing escrow account and have agreed that they "shall replenish the account as necessary to ensure that the amount in the account does not drop below $25 million, regardless of payment of the Awards."[42]

In agreeing to a "no limit" settlement, the banks are betting that the total amount of the payments awarded by the Drai Commission to French Holocaust survivors or victims' heirs, based on the 63,000 dormant accounts discovered by the French banks, will not exceed $50 million, or some amount close to it. According to the plaintiffs' attorney Harriet Tamen,

> The banks felt perfectly safe in agreeing to this because, for a claimant to receive any money from this Fund, the victim must have specific proof as to the existence of the account and the amount on deposit. Since few Holocaust victims kept bank records in the concentration camps, the number of victims eligible for restitution from this fund is likely to be very limited. Furthermore, any unclaimed funds in this account go back to the banks.[43]

One other reason that the banks may prove to be correct is that the current value multiplier for any unclaimed funds found by the Drai Commission for a claimant is low: 1.8 times the amount of money on deposit in the account at the time of the occupation. (Compare that with the ICHEIC's multiplier of approximately 7.5 for the face value of unpaid policies from the Holocaust era.) This means, for instance, that if a survivor or heir is found to be eligible for compensation from (1) an unpaid wartime insurance policy held by the French insurer AXA with the face value of 1,000 French francs (Fr 1,000) and (2) an unpaid wartime bank account of the same amount with Crédit Lyonnais, the claimant will receive Fr 7,500 (approximately $1,000) for the wartime insurance policy, but only Fr 1,700 (approximately $220) for the wartime bank account. This is patently unfair.

The French banks also agreed to give the Drai Commission another $22.5 million to pay the so-called soft claims, those applications whose claims for a wartime bank account cannot be verified or located. The money will be distributed through a special fund set up for this purpose. Like the German "Remembrance, Responsibility and the Future" public foundation created to pay each former slave laborer a fixed amount of either DM 15,000 or DM 5,000 ($7,500 or $2,500), each "soft claim" claimant will receive a fixed sum of $1,500. A second distribution, up to another $1,500, will be made if any money is left over after the initial payout. If money still remains after the two distributions, it will be transferred to a French public foundation to be used for both

Holocaust and general human rights education and remembrance projects. Unlike the Germans, who insisted that a fixed portion of the settlement money be allocated to Holocaust education and remembrance, the French did not insist on this provision. However, the French banks "seeded" the foundation with a contribution of Euro 100 million.

Another innovative feature of the French bank settlement mandates that any "hard claim" claimant receives as much as a "soft claim" claimant does. For instance, if the Drai Commission investigators locate a dormant account worth less than $1,500, the claimant will receive the money from the revolving $50 million "hard claims" fund and the balance, up to $1,500, from the special fund. (If a second distribution is made from the special fund, these claimants also will receive such a distribution.) Therefore, each person filing a claim with the Drai Commission will receive at least $1,500.

The requirements for receiving the funds are quite lenient. All a claimant needs to do is to submit an affidavit attesting that he or she "believe[s] that my family had one or more bank accounts in a bank located in France during the Second World War [and that] restitution has never been made for one or more bank accounts (or other bank-related assets, such as the contents of safe deposit boxes) to myself or other members of my family." He or she also must submit proof of residency in France at the time. In effect, any Jewish survivor from France or, for that matter, any person in the world with a family member who lived in France at the time or during the German occupation, is eligible to receive $1,500 from the special fund.

Another curious feature of the French bank settlement is that as it is structured, it creates a conflict between the interests of the French government and those of the private French banks.

The French banks, naturally, want to keep the number of "hard claimants" and total payouts as small as possible, not only to limit their financial exposure, but also for public relations purposes. Like the Swiss banks, when all the money has been paid out, the French banks want to be able say, "See, we told you so. As it turned out, in fact there were few unpaid wartime accounts." Therefore, the more "soft claims" and the fewer "hard claims" there are, the better it will be for the banks.

The French government, however, does not care about the extent of the "hard claims" payouts, since they are coming from private banks, and the banks must replenish the "hard claims" fund if it falls below $25 million. If a claimant can prove that a French bank is holding a wartime account of a Jewish depositor, the French government is committed to make the bank pay out those funds. The government, however, is not too eager to pay the "soft claim" claimants because any money left over will go to a French public foundation. Moreover, the payouts are supposed to be made even to claimants without any documentation. To the French government, this seems unfair. For this reason, the French government, which committed itself to publicizing the settlement in the United States–France Agreement, has been slow to publicize the special fund and the liberal requirements for receiving money from the special fund. According to Professor Weisberg, applicants whose hard claims have been denied by the Drai Commission for lack of documentation, or applicants for other funds from the French government related to the Holocaust, such as the orphans' fund,[44] often are not told that they can receive a minimum of $1,500 from the special fund merely by filing an affidavit claiming that they believe a family member may have held a bank account in a French bank during the war.

In summary, the total payout made by the French banks to end this litigation amounted to approximately $172.5 million: $50 million to the Drai Commission to pay the "hard claims," $22.5 million to cover the "soft claims," and Euro 100 million (approximately $100 million) for administrative expenses and Holocaust humanitarian projects. Of course, the "no cap" provision for the "hard claims" means that the maximum payout may exceed that amount, but probably not by much.

THE AFTERMATH AND THE LEGACY OF THE SETTLEMENT

According to the preamble of the United States–France Agreement, the amount of the French bank settlement represents "full disgorgement by the French government, the Banks, and other private and public institutions of any unjust enrichment based on assets left with such institutions and never restituted [sic] to their former owners, as well as a substantial contribution in recognition of the suffering of Holocaust victims in France." The French banks, likewise, can argue that in effect, they are making a full disgorgement, since they promised to pay out all dormant account claims, even if they rose above the $175 million that they initially allocated. However, as pointed out earlier, the banks have not allowed (1) the publication of their list of wartime dormant accounts and

(2) outside auditors to search their wartime archives to confirm the accuracy of the list. As a result, a full accounting of what the French banks truly owe will never be made. By insisting on these two conditions, the banks essentially limited their liability to a ceiling figure of $175 million.

As with the other Holocaust restitution settlements, it can well be disputed whether $175 million comes anywhere close to a "full disgorgement . . . of any unjust enrichment" by the banks of their theft of Jewish assets during the occupation and whether the Euro 100 million is really a "substantial" humanitarian contribution in light of the suffering by the Jews in wartime France. Again, however, the reality is that aging Holocaust survivors could not wait much longer. The Holocaust restitution movement was also running out of steam, with the curtain soon falling on the Clinton White House and Eizenstat's departure from the government. The plaintiffs' representatives, therefore, had no choice but to take the deal put together by Eizenstat and Andréani.

How well is the agreement being implemented? According to the plaintiffs' attorney Morris Ratner:

> There have been implementation problems in all the [non-court-supervised] agreements, stemming from the absence of a court supervising the process. The French case is just part of the pattern. . . . In each instance: the US government is out of the picture. The Jewish groups aren't sufficiently critical of the details, and the lawyers, by the design of the Executive Agreement, have no role. The upshot? There's a mechanism in place for aggressive and sophisticated property victims to get paid in France. But one has to be aggressive and sophisticated.[45]

Harriet Tamen, Ratner's fellow counsel for the claimants, is less positive:

> The Drai Commission moves with all deliberate slowness to research and award claims. Although at the rapporteur level, there is effort and good will, at the level of the Commission itself, there are obstacles and lack of trust. Recommendations for payment made by the rapporteurs are being arbitrarily reduced, information is not forthcoming; various provisions of the settlement agreement are being ignored; and implementation issues not covered are being unilaterally decided in ways that only minimize payments to victims.[46]

As with the other Holocaust restitution deals worked out during the Clinton years, the legacy of the French bank settlement goes well beyond money.

In the United States, the French bank decision issued by Judge Johnson should make an important contribution to the body of U.S. law now beginning to recognize the legal culpability of foreign corporate actors for human rights violations committed abroad, even if the violations are based on events taking place in another era. I hope that multinational corporations, both domestic or foreign, doing business abroad hear Judge Johnson's message: violate international human rights of individuals today, anywhere in the world, and you may find yourself legally liable for such violations in a U.S. court many years from now.

After World War II, the French refused to confront their shameful history of collaboration with the Nazi regime. Historians who wanted to study the wartime history of occupied France and Vichy France were discouraged from doing so, and publishers declined to publish their studies in France. Graduate students who wanted to do scholarly research in the area could not get faculty advisers. As Professor Vivian Curran pointed out, "Eminent [historians] . . . refused to be advisors to graduate students interested in writing their doctoral dissertation in the area of Vichy. Since professorships are government positions in France, the government could prevent Vichy scholars from access to university teaching."[47] The failure to examine in postwar France the French banks' shameful conduct during the occupation was "yet another instance of suppression and attempted erasure.[48]

A major step in the recognition of France's participation in the Holocaust was taken in July 1995 when French President Jacques Chirac apologized to the Jews for France's wartime role. Yet as Professor Weisberg told me, there still is doubt whether this reevaluation will stick or whether France will revert to its long-standing habit of whitewashing its wartime history.[49] Already there are signs of such neo-revisionism. In the first part of 2002, France experienced its worst wave of anti-Semitism since World War II, with synagogues being bombed, Jewish cemeteries desecrated, and overtly observant Jews attacked. The first round of the presidential election in April 2002 elevated Jean-Marie Le Pen, an extreme rightist who labeled the Holocaust gas chambers a mere detail of World War II, to the second-place finisher and qualifier for the May 2002 run-off against the incumbent Jacques Chirac. In an election rally on the eve of his run-off with Le Pen, Chirac specifically tied him to France's Vichy past. Chirac's overwhelming victory over Le Pen, and Le Pen's party's failure to win even a single seat in the follow-up congressional elections helped minimize France's recent ignominy. Nevertheless, it is a painful lesson that the Holocaust and the reprehensible role played by the French people toward one of its minorities must be constantly recalled in France lest it be repeated. The Holocaust restitution litigation against the French banks served as an important reminder.

THE BELGIANS ALSO SETTLE

In July 2002, more than two years after the French banks' agreement, the Belgian banks followed their French colleagues' example and settled their outstanding wartime claims. Under an agreement reached between the Belgian Banks Association (known as the ABB) and representatives of the Jewish community in Belgium, the banks agreed to pay Euro 55.5 million. A week earlier, the Belgian government, its central bank, and Belgian insurance companies signed a separate agreement to pay out Euro 55.8 million.

Two distinguishing features mark the Belgian agreement. First, litigation in the United States was not required to resolve the claims. No Belgian company was ever sued in the United States for its wartime activities. Second, this was completely a home-grown agreement. Not the WJC, the Simon Wiesenthal Center, or any other American Jewish group—or, for that matter, the Bush administration—was involved in the negotiations. The local Jewish community in Belgium did it all on its own.

The Holocaust restitution model created in America could now be taken up by Belgian Jews and followed by them to achieve the same results that previously could only be accomplished by American involvement. Jewish communities in other European nations are likely to follow the Belgian example.

5

Litigating Holocaust Looted Art

BETWEEN 1933 AND 1945, the Germans stole approximately 600,000 pieces of art from both museums and private collections throughout Europe, including paintings, sculpture, objects d'art, and tapestries.[1] When rare books, stamps, coins, and fine furniture are added, the figure goes into the millions. It took 29,984 railroad cars, according to records from the Nuremberg trials, to transport all the stolen art to Germany. The value of the art plundered during the Holocaust exceeded the total value of all the art in the United States in 1945: $2.5 billion at 1945 prices or $20.5 billion today.[2] The Nazi art confiscation program was the greatest displacement of art in human history. As explained by one heir of a Holocaust victim who was killed and whose art was stolen: "You ask, did they kill? Yes, they killed. They killed for art, when it suited them. So killing Jews and confiscating art somehow went together."[3]

Hitler, an unsuccessful art student, was obsessed with art. According to Professor Jonathan Petropoulos, a historian at Claremont McKenna College in California and a leading expert on Nazi-looted art, in addition to stealing, Hitler "spent more on art then anybody in the history of the world,"[4] freely using state funds for this purpose. One of Hitler's grand plans was to build a Führermuseum in Linz, Austria, where many of his favorite paintings among the looted art would eventually be displayed. Professor Petropoulos estimates that "the Germans have today 1,532 paintings (1,076 of which hang in museums and the remainder in government offices and embassies) that came from the collections of Hitler, Hermann Goering, Martin Bormann, and other Nazi leaders, and were deemed not to have come from victims' collections."[5]

After Hitler's rise to power and throughout the war years, there was a brisk market for works stolen by the Germans, as they did not keep all of what they stole. Much of what they considered "degenerate art" (modern art not favored by Hitler, works of Jewish artists, and art

however, that they did not take sufficient heed and a number of works with problematic provenance entered both public and private collections in this country. There is compelling evidence that museums, which were dependent on contributions from donors, as a rule did not ask questions about the origins of the objects they received.[14]

Thomas Kline, an art law attorney representing some of the Holocaust looted art claimants, put it more bluntly when describing the policies of the U.S. art world until caught in the dragnet of the Holocaust restitution movement:

> Countless objects found their way into the art market and onto our shores [after the war]. Once here, the further movement of this art was facilitated by the "ask-me-no-questions-and-I'll-tell-you-no-lies" method of operation in the art market. For decades, the art market has opposed regulation and scrutiny, and has argued that imposing a reasonable duty of reasonable diligence on art dealers would cripple the art business. It has continued to operate on the basis of a wink and a nod, and as a direct result, stolen art has moved freely into major private collections and our most prestigious museums, where claimants find it today.[15]

Commenting on American museums' reluctance, at least until recently, to discover and publicize the origin of its collections, the Israeli daily *Ha'aretz* observed, "It is difficult to say which item is easier to locate and return: a [Holocaust-era dormant] Swiss bank account or a [Holocaust looted] painting hanging on the wall of an American museum."[16]

Professor Petropoulos confirmed that American museums are not the only culprits. He noted that an overlooked problem is Holocaust looted artworks currently in the hands of American private collectors who, until the recent scandals and lawsuits, likewise eagerly participated in the "no questions asked" policy. Petropoulos agreed with Ronald Lauder, chairman of the board of New York's Museum of Modern Art and head of the Commission for Art Recovery (CAR), that "a sizeable number of victims' works [are today] in private collections."[17]

Professor Petropoulos also raised an additional point about private collections: "Holocaust assets are not only about works by Michelangelo and Matisse. Obviously many of the less valuable objects were never properly restituted and are now in private hands."[18] To illustrate, Petropoulos referred to an article in the *New Yorker* by Israeli author Aharon Appelfeld, recounting a visit to his ancestral village in the Ukraine where he was born and from where his parents were taken and murdered. No Jews reside there today. Going inside the villagers' homes, Appelfeld was astonished to find property belonging to his family's former Jewish neighbors: books, furniture, folk art. Appelfeld observed, "Today I know that many of my mother's jewels are to be found in the village houses, and certainly quite a few gifts that my father brought from [his trips to] Vienna or Prague. Everything was stolen and now lives in captivity."[19] From this example, Petropoulos concluded: "In short, victims' assets are still in private hands; many are still in Europe, and the evidence indicates that some ultimately came to the United States."[20]

According to one estimate, about 2,000 Holocaust looted artworks around the world have been returned since 1998, most from museums and public galleries.[21] The efforts to restore art plundered during the Holocaust to its rightful owners, who today most often are heirs of the Jewish person or family from whom the Nazis stole the art, have been an important component of the Holocaust restitution campaign. As the following discussion reveals, these efforts began at the same time as the demands were being made on the Swiss banks to right the wrongs for their wartime and postwar behavior. The various Holocaust art restitution success stories and sometimes failures also came at the same time the other restitution claims were being settled.

This was not pure coincidence. As claimants, Jewish organizations, federal and state government officials, and other activists began in the late 1990s to look at the still-lingering wrongs committed by European corporate actors during World War II, they realized that the issue of missing Nazi-stolen art likewise needed to be addressed. Like the other property restitution claims, Holocaust art also was property stolen from Jews that had not been properly returned to its owners or their heirs after the war.

As with the other Holocaust restitution claims, especially the claims on the Swiss banks, books published in the late 1990s about the subject helped expose the extent of the problem. Especially important were Hector Feliciano's *The Lost Museum*, first published in France in 1996 and then in the United States in 1997,[22] and Lynn Nicholas's *The Rape of Europa*, published in 1994.[23] In his book, Feliciano, a Puerto Rico–born journalist living in Paris, described how many of the artworks stolen by the Nazis had turned up in French museums, with the museums simply turning a blind eye to their checkered provenance, never bothering to determine whether the prewar owners or any of their heirs were still alive. The book caused a sensation in France and led to a fresh look at the problem of Nazi-stolen artworks, not only in France, but around the world. Nicholas's earlier work also was critical, disclosing the location of many of the missing pieces. The Holocaust art cases helped drive the entire Holocaust restitution movement. Discoveries that valuable artworks hanging in public museums or in the private collections of prominent persons had been stolen by the Nazis make good stories and so were widely reported by the media. They covered these claims as part of the bigger Holocaust restitution picture, which kept the Holocaust restitution movement in the public eye.

The Holocaust art success stories—a claimant obtaining the return of a Holocaust artwork, through either litigation or mediation[24]—emboldened the entire Holocaust restitution movement and helped those working on nonart Holocaust issues to continue their work. For example, the first Holocaust looted art lawsuit during the restitution campaign, *Goodman v. Searle,* was settled in August 1998, the same month that the first Holocaust corporate restitution was settled with the Swiss banks. Like the Swiss bank settlement, the *Goodman* art settlement came at a critical time, driving home the message that Holocaust restitution claims could succeed.

At the same time, the corporate Holocaust restitution suits helped push along the Holocaust looted art claims. According to Anna Kisluk, director of New York's Art Loss Register, "for a long time, people thought they couldn't do anything. In the wake of the gold issue and the Swiss bank accounts, [though,] many people are coming forward."[25] In 2002, Monica Dugot of New York State's Holocaust Claims Processing Office could look back at all the Holocaust restitution cases and come to the same conclusion: "Holocaust asset class action lawsuits [against European corporations] have helped to educate and to focus the discussion, in part by creating a climate that encourages constructive thinking and resourcefulness. This climate has had a ripple effect, not only here but also in Europe."[26]

I stress all this because the recovery of Nazi-stolen art has sometimes been viewed as not part of the Holocaust restitution movement. Part of the reason is that many of the people involved in the other

Holocaust restitution claims did not participate in the Holocaust art restitution. Hausfeld, Weiss, Fagan, Swift and the Lieff Cabaraser firm did not take on the Holocaust art cases.[27] Moreover, although the Swiss and German global settlements applied to every other wartime restitution claim, they specifically excluded claims for Holocaust looted art. These initial global settlements became the models for later settlements. As a result, as Monica Dugot pointed out, "Looted art has been carved out of every Holocaust-asset settlement to date and art claims have been handled on an ad hoc basis—there has been no systematic remedial process."[28] Nevertheless, many of the persons working on corporate restitution claims also played a critical role in the Holocaust looted art cases. These included various Clinton administration officials (although Eizenstat's work with stolen art was only tangential, others in the State Department spent much time on the issue. J. D. Bindenagel, for instance, who began his Holocaust restitution work at the State Department by focusing on Holocaust looted art later was appointed as the State Department's special envoy on Holocaust issues) and the World Jewish Congress (WJC), including Singer and Steinberg. Holocaust art restitution, therefore, is part and parcel of what I have labeled as the modern Holocaust restitution movement.

According to experts, the present effort to return the looted art is more complex than the issues of other Holocaust-era restitution claims. First because so much art and other cultural objects were looted and then misplaced, returning them to their proper owners is a nearly impossible job.[29] It was very difficult immediately after the war and has become even more difficult more than a half-century later, with both the art and the victims or their heirs dispersed worldwide. Monica Dugot of the New York State's Holocaust Claims Processing Office, working for the last four years matching owners with the looted art, explained:

> I speak from experience when I tell you that restituting a painting is not a simple task. Holocaust-era provenance research is time-consuming. Often this is due to the paucity of published and accessible provenance information. It is very labor-intensive. The information needed to resolve a case is usually in more than one place. Pre-war collections have not survived in their entirety—they have been dispersed and consequently items can surface anywhere—presenting considerable logistical challenges and making it a global issue.[30]

There is also the misconception that because of the German reputation for efficiency and record keeping, every Nazi-stolen artwork must have been marked and categorized, with a paper trail for each work. While true in many cases, it is as equally not true for thousands of other artworks, cultural objects, and heirlooms—especially those not of museum quality. Professor Petropoulos cited a passage from an interview conducted in 1948 by the American authorities with Dr. von Crannach-Sichart, the former director of a prominent Munich auction house used by the Nazis to "fence" stolen artworks:

> During the course of the year 1941, a shipment of the Gestapo Prague arrived by truck with the order to sell the contents by auction. They mostly were paintings by old and modern painters, some graphic maps and some Persian rugs. Not a single object of international value or higher quality was among these items. They rather had a generally medium rank, so that it was not worthwhile to have a special auction for them. . . . We were not told from where the objects originated. There were no further orders. The objects were sold during the following auction. Because of the above-mentioned reason we are no more able to state to which owner they went.[31]

A second reason for the complexity of the problem is that a large-scale return of such World War II–looted art "could disrupt the art market, especially for French Impressionist paintings, which were a favorite target of Nazi looters."[32]

Last, unlike the claims of Nazi-stolen gold, dormant Swiss accounts, or the use of slave labor, when the perpetrators knew—or at least should have suspected—that they were engaging in wrongful activities, many (though not all) of the present owners of Nazi-looted art bought it in good faith, without any knowledge or suspicion of their controversial heritage. Rabbi Marvin Hier, dean of the Wiesenthal Center, expressed sympathy for such innocent, good-faith purchasers. According to Hier, "In no way should these people be faulted. They were misled themselves. It is not the same as the Swiss bankers who knew in advance that it was Nazi gold they were acquiring."[33]

While Rabbi Hier may present a strong moral defense for the truly innocent possessor of Holocaust looted art, his argument would not win in an American courtroom. According to Howard Spiegler, a partner in the New York law firm of Herrick, Feinstein, specializing in art law (and counsel for the plaintiffs in the *Schiele* case discussed later):

> Underlying any claim for the recovery of Nazi-looted art in the United States is a single, fundamental rule that is at the core of all cultural property cases: no one, not even a good faith purchaser, can obtain good title to stolen property. This simple rule is accepted and applied as a fundamental tenet of property law in the United States.[34]

The rule is based on an ancient English legal maxim, stated in Latin: *Nemo dat quod— non habeat* [You cannot give what you do not have].[35] Civil-law countries, however, do not follow this maxim. Rather, continental Europe is much more protective of the innocent buyer and adheres to the legal rule that a good-faith purchaser may acquire a legitimate title to stolen goods. For instance, in Switzerland a good-faith purchaser can obtain clear title to stolen property after five years. For this reason, as well as others, the United States—as for all other Holocaust restitution claims—remains the forum of choice for claimants seeking the return of Holocaust looted art.

The practical consequences of this legal rule in the United States are monumental. As Stanford University law professor and art law expert John Henry Merriman explains, Because "the law is clear that the [original] owner is entitled to recover the work from a good-faith purchaser . . . [c]ollectors can wake up one morning to the threat of forfeiting objects they acquired in good faith."[36]

Interestingly, such good-faith purchasers are often pitted against claimants who may not even be the original owners from whom the artworks were stolen but are the surviving—sometimes distant—relatives or heirs of the victims. In the case of art stolen by the Nazis from German collector Max Silberberg, the only surviving heir is his daughter-in-law, who, at age eighty-five and living modestly all her life, now possesses artworks worth millions. Another example is the claim of *Dead City III*, a Nazi-looted painting by Egon Schiele. The claimants to the painting are the widows of the sons of the victim's cousin, not even the blood relatives of the victim from whom the Nazis stole the painting and who perished in the Holocaust.

Because of the problem's complexity, at least five different organizations have been working on the issue. Since their efforts often overlap, these organizations have both worked together and also stumbled into each other.

In the United States, the WJC formed the Commission for Art Recovery (CAR), whose mission is to "identify and locate art stolen by the Nazis and their collaborators" and "register claims for the victims of Nazi art theft."[37] CAR is chaired by Ronald Lauder, an art collector, philanthropist, heir to the Lauder cosmetics fortune, former U.S. ambassador to Austria, and chairman of New York's Museum of Modern Art (MoMA). Because of his two positions as chairman of MoMA and head of CAR, Lauder was pulled in opposite directions in the *Schiele* case. While CAR is concerned about restoring Nazi-stolen art to its former owners, MoMA was trying to return the Schiele paintings to Austria.

A second organization in the United States involved with the issue is the Holocaust Art Restitution Project (HARP), formerly affiliated with the B'nai B'rith Klutznick National Jewish Museum in Washington, D.C.[38] As I will show, HARP was critical to the restitution of one important work in the United States and has been involved behind the scenes in the restitution of a number of other artworks both in the United States and abroad.

A third body in the United States that is actively involved in the restitution of Holocaust looted art is the Holocaust Claims Processing Office (HCPO) of the New York State Department of Banking.[39] The HCPO, established in 1997 as a division of the New York State Banking Department, does not limit its work to helping Holocaust claimants with banking issues or even to assisting only New York residents. Its deputy director, Monica Dugot, also has played an important role in the Holocaust looted art debate, and the office has been instrumental in the restitution of numerous looted artworks.

In Europe, the Commission for Looted Art in Europe (and using the acronym ECLA), founded in March 1999 in London by the European Council of Jewish Communities and the Conference of European Rabbis, is trying to trace Nazi-stolen art.[40] Its director, Anne Webber, has been an important player in the field of recovering Nazi-stolen art in Europe.

Finally, the Art Loss Register (ALR), also based in London and founded in 1991 by auction houses to help retrieve all stolen art, not just that from the Holocaust, has also become actively involved in searching

for art lost during the Holocaust and returning it to its rightful owners.[41] ALR claims to have compiled the world's largest commercial database, nearly 100,000 items of stolen and missing art, antiques, and valuables. Although ALR is a commercial enterprise, it helps claimants
searching for Holocaust looted art by listing their claims on its database
free of charge.

LITIGATION OF HOLOCAUST LOOTED ART
IN THE UNITED STATES

Even though American legal rules involving stolen art may appear to be
clear, the actual litigation of Holocaust art claims is, on the whole, complex, time-consuming, and expensive. As eloquently explained by one
commentator:

> Why bother with recovering it at all? Plundering is, after all, the hand-
> maiden of war. And the world's museums are filled with objects lifted
> during conflicts from the Romans on. But this is no Elgin Marbles con-
> troversy. The Nazis weren't simply out to enrich themselves. Their
> looting was part of the Final Solution. They wanted to eradicate a race
> by extinguishing its culture as well as its people. This gives these
> works of art a unique resonance, the more so since some of them were
> used as barter for safe passage out of Germany or Austria for family
> members. The objects are symbols of a terrible crime; recovering them
> is an equally symbolic form of justice.[42]

As for the other Holocaust restitution claims, litigation in American
courts proved to be the engine driving the claims forward. But unlike
the other Holocaust restitution categories, there were no major class actions dealing with Nazi-stolen art. Rather, Holocaust looted art litigation has been confined to fewer than a handful of lawsuits, with each
applying to a specific artwork.

Edgar Hilaire Germaine Degas, French painter, 1834–1917. *Landscape with Smokestacks*, 1890, pastel over monotype, on textured cream woven paper, edge-mounted on board, 31.7 x 41.6 cm. *Purchased from the collection of Fritz and Louise Gutmann; gift of Daniel C. Searle, 1998.915, image © The Art Institute of Chicago.*

GOODMAN V. SEARLE
(DEGAS'S *LANDSCAPE WITH SMOKESTACKS*)

August 1998 proved to be an important date for Holocaust restitution litigation. It marked the settlement of the Swiss bank class action litigation and also the settlement of the first Holocaust looted art case since the onset of the Holocaust restitution movement.[43]

The case was concluded using the classic American litigation model, already seen in the Holocaust suits discussed earlier. The defendant tried to get the case thrown out of court (or at least delay the start of trial), was unable to do so, and, when trial became imminent, the case settled.

Before the settlement, the case attained some notoriety, similar to that of the *Stern v. Generali insurance* case (see chapter 3). In July 1998, *60*

Minutes, an American television news program, ran a segment on the case. The next month, PBS, the American public television network, featured an entire documentary on the litigation, entitled "Making a Killing."

The case involved the artwork *Landscape with Smokestacks,* an 1890 pastel by Edouard Degas, which made its way to the United States from Europe. Before the war, the painting belonged to Friedrich and Louise Gutmann, a prominent German family of Jewish descent that had converted to Christianity and moved to Holland. Friedrich Gutmann, the family patriarch, purchased the Degas in 1932. Gutmann was raised in a prestigious banking family and founded his own bank in Holland after World War I. He assembled an impressive art collection over the years, including works by Botticelli, Gainsborough, Holbein, and three modern art pieces, of which the Degas pastel was one.

In April 1939, anticipating the oncoming war, Gutmann sent the painting to an art dealer in Paris for safekeeping. The dealer placed the painting, along with other artworks belonging to the Gutmann family, in storage in Paris to protect them from seizure by the Germans.

In 1943, Friedrich and Louise Gutmann attempted to escape from Nazi-occupied Holland to Italy, where their daughter Lili was living. They were arrested by the Nazis and sent to concentration camps, where they perished. Before their deaths, Friedrich and Louise relinquished many of their valuable possessions to the Nazis under a "forced sale."

After the war, the Gutmann children, Lili and her brother Bernard, attempted to locate their parents' possessions, including the artworks sent to Paris. They were unsuccessful. Bernard moved to England after the war, where his two sons, Simon and Nick, were born. He began a new life and anglicized his last name to Goodman.

In the 1970s, both Simon and Nick Goodman moved to Southern California, where they now reside. The Goodman grandchildren continued the mission started by their survivor relatives. Earlier, Bernard and Lili instituted restitution proceedings in West Germany, seeking compensation for their parents' stolen possessions. In 1961, during the proceedings, the West German government informed them that its own efforts to find the Degas and other Gutmann art had proved fruitless and that "further investigations hold no prospect of success." The Gutmann art collection was not in West Germany. As a result, the West Germans then paid 50 percent of the Degas's value to Lili and Bernard.

What happened to the artwork once Friedrich shipped it to Paris, no one knew. The trail had gone cold.

Unable to locate the Degas, the Goodman family came to believe that if it still existed, it most likely was in the Soviet Union, where it may have been taken by victorious Soviet forces. At best, they hoped, the pastel was buried somewhere in a basement of a Soviet museum or a storage depot.

After the fall of the Soviet Union in 1991, Bernard and Lili and the Goodman grandsons hoped that their family's art collection would turn up once the post–Soviet Russian government revealed what art loot it had been holding since 1945.

In 1994, Bernard died. Shortly thereafter came a bombshell. Simon, living in Los Angeles, was leafing through art books at the UCLA Art Library where, to his amazement, he discovered a photo of the Degas pastel. The book listed the artwork as being in the private collection of Daniel Searle, a Chicago pharmaceutical tycoon. The Goodman brothers then learned that Searle had bought the pastel for $850,000 in 1987 from a private art dealer in Manhattan.

On December 5, 1995, the Gutmann heirs wrote to Searle demanding the return of the *Degas*. Searle refused, claiming that the artwork rightfully belonged to him. Simon, Nick, and their aunt Lili, now in her mid-seventies, then filed suit in federal court in Manhattan, basing their jurisdiction on the fact that Searle had bought the Degas there. Searle's attorneys successfully petitioned to have the suit moved to federal court in Chicago. There, Searle's attorneys filed a motion of summary judgment.

A summary judgment motion is a pretrial legal maneuver in which the moving party seeks to convince the presiding judge that the case should be decided without a trial. When, as here, the motion is made by the defense, the defendant argues that the judge should simply issue a judgment for the defendant, thereby dismissing the plaintiff's lawsuit. The grounds for dismissal are that both the undisputed facts and the law governing the case are so completely in favor of the defendant that it would be a waste of time for the case to be heard by a jury. If the judge grants the motion, the case is over, and a summary, or speedy, judgment is entered for the defendant. In support of the motion, Searle's attorneys claimed that the facts clearly showed that the Degas was never even stolen by the Nazis but, rather, was one of Friedrich Gutmann's artworks sold before his deportation when he began experiencing financial difficulties during the war. The Gutmann heirs disputed this allegation. They admitted that Friedrich had indeed sold some artworks from his collection to stay alive but that all such sales were well documented. In this case, no bill of sale or other proof of the Degas pastel's being sold could be found.

The Gutmann heirs also argued that Searle either was, or should have been, aware of the Degas's checkered pedigree, or provenance. According to the provenance that Searle obtained, "when he purchased the [Degas] from Emile Wolf in 1987, the [Degas] had passed through the hands of Hans Wendland—a card-carrying Nazi who[m] the U.S. government interrogated and concluded was instrumental in the trade of art looted by the Nazis in France—and Wendland's brother-in-law, Hans Fankhauser."[44]

Searle, however, claimed that when he purchased the pastel, he relied on the expertise of the curators from the Art Institute of Chicago, a museum at which he is a trustee, who assured him that the artwork had a clean provenance. The plaintiffs' attorneys, however, took pretrial depositions from the two curators who reviewed the provenance of the Degas for Searle in 1987. Apparently, the curators missed evidence pointing to flaws in the pastel's ownership records, including the fact that it was once owned by the notorious Wendland, known as the most successful wartime fence for art looted by the Nazis.

Searle made another argument in his summary judgment motion. He asserted that the Gutmann heirs had waited too long to bring their lawsuit, and as a result, the suit was "time barred," regardless of the merits of their other claims. As with every other Holocaust restitution lawsuit discussed in this book, the time limitations defense is a powerful argument favoring the defendant, including a party being sued to recover an artwork stolen by the Nazis more than a half-century ago. In fact, the same defense was raised in an earlier Holocaust art restitution suit brought in New York in the 1960s. *Menzel v. List*[45] involved a Chagall painting. The original owners found the Chagall, which had been stolen from them by the Nazis in 1941 in Belgium, almost twenty years later in New York. The defendant, a private party, had purchased the painting in 1955 from a reputable New York art dealer. Faced with a lawsuit to return the painting, the defendant argued that the limitations period for filing the suit had expired. The original owners should have sued, the defendant asserted, within three years of his acquisition of the Chagall, the limitations period in New York for bringing suit for stolen property. The New York intermediate appellate court rejected this argument, instead holding that the limitations period for bringing suits for stolen art begins to run only after the plaintiff has made a demand to return the painting and the defendant refuses the demand. The plaintiff then has three years from the date of refusal to file his lawsuit. As a result, the court held that the plaintiff's lawsuit was timely. Examining the merits of the case, the court found that since the Chagall was stolen property, even though the defendant was an innocent purchaser, he had never acquired good title for the artwork. As a result, the defendant was ordered to turn over the painting to its original owners. *Menzel v. List* is now one of the leading art cases in New York, if not in the United States. Its "demand and refusal" rule was subsequently recognized by the New York Court of Appeals, the highest court in New York.

The Goodman plaintiffs wanted to rely on the New York rule to defeat Searle's time-bar argument. The problem, however, was that this case was being heard in federal court in Chicago, and Illinois's rule was different from New York's. Under Illinois law, the limitations period in a stolen art case is stricter than in New York. Like most American jurisdictions, Illinois follows the so-called discovery rule for suits for the return of stolen objects. Under the discovery rule, the time period for filing the suit also does not necessarily begin when the object is stolen but when plaintiff first discovers that the defendant holds the object. Unlike the "demand and refusal" jurisdictions, the "discovery" jurisdictions add another requirement: the former owners or heirs must show that they conducted a reasonably diligent search for the stolen art during the time the artwork was missing. Failing to do so leads to an automatic dismissal of the suit. If Searle could show that the plaintiffs would have discovered the existence of the artwork in the United States through a diligent search but did not do so, the lawsuit would be dismissed, regardless of the merits of their claims.

In support, Searle argued that the Gutmann heirs "reasonably should have known of the location of the landscape long before Searle bought it."[46] Searle pointed out that (1) in 1968 and 1974 books were published that included information about the Degas and its location and (2) the Degas was exhibited earlier at three college museums in the United States (the Fogg Museum at Harvard University in 1965, the Rhode Island School of Design in 1968, and the Finch College Museum in 1974).

Attempting to avoid having their case thrown out of court on this procedural ground, the plaintiffs first claimed that New York law applied and that the federal judge in Chicago hearing this case, under complex legal choice-of-law rules, was bound to apply the New York law. As support, plaintiffs argued that even though the Degas was located in Chicago when the suit was filed and defendant Searle resided there, the plaintiffs did not reside in Chicago, and the action involved ownership of a stolen artwork purchased by Searle on the New York art market. The plaintiffs argued that their action met the New York statute of limitations, since they brought their lawsuit within three years of Searle's refusal to return the Degas to them. If the judge chose to apply Illinois law, the plaintiffs argued that they had diligently searched for the painting for more than fifty years. As support, the plaintiffs explained that Bernard and Lili

> reported their losses immediately after the war to the Allied Forces and to government officials in France, Germany and Holland . . . [and] to the international police organization known as Interpol at Scotland Yard. They consulted art experts; presented photographs of the paintings on television; and listed the [Degas] in a stolen art registry maintained by the International Foundation for Art Research ("IFAR") as soon as they learned of IFAR's existence.[47]

Despite taking all these actions, they still could not locate the artwork.

On July 18, 1998, the federal judge presiding over the case denied Searle's summary judgment motion, but he allowed Searle to raise these arguments again at trial. This was shaping up to be a difficult legal battle, with both sides having credible arguments in their favor. The lawyers were getting ready for trial, scheduled for September 9, 1998. The plaintiffs were worried. They had already spent almost three years in litigation, paid more than $100,000 for lawyers' fees, and would have to pay another $100,000 by the time the trial would be over. Even if they won, it would not mean that they would then get the pastel; Searle could appeal and tie up the dispute for another three years. It was time to see whether a settlement could be worked out.

Nick Goodman then made a bold move. Rather than requesting the plaintiffs' lawyers to work out a settlement with Searle's attorneys, he called Searle himself, asking whether a deal could be worked out. Searle was amenable. A month before trial, on August 7, 1998, the parties reached a compromise and ended their dispute.

Under what the *Jerusalem Post* hailed as a "Solomonic" settlement,[48] Searle and the Gutmann heirs agreed to share ownership of the *Degas*. Searle donated his one-half interest to the Art Institute of Chicago, and the museum agreed to buy the plaintiffs' half-interest. The institute agreed to install a plaque next to the pastel identifying it as a "purchase from the collection of Friedrich and Louise Gutmann and a gift of Daniel C. Searle."

Even this deal took some time to put together. The Degas had to be appraised, to determine how much Searle had to pay to the Gutmann heirs for their one-half ownership of the artwork. In late fall 1999, almost one year after the compromise was announced, the settlement was completed.[49] According to Nick Goodman, after paying the costs of litigation, the Gutmann heirs were "at least able to break even. Overall, I'm pleased with the result. The painting was brought back to the family, it is now hanging in a beautiful museum, and, most importantly, we significantly raised public awareness of this issue."[50] In June 1999, the Art Institute began publicly displaying *Landscape with Smokestacks*, and Nick Goodman flew to Chicago to view it himself.

Almost three years later, the Gutmann heirs scored another success. In April 2002, the Dutch government agreed to return to them 233 works of art, including paintings, antique furniture, tableware, and cutlery, that Friedrich and Louise Gutmann were forced to sell to the Nazis in Holland before their deportation. After the war, the Gutmann objects were returned to Holland, where they became state property. In 2002, the Dutch government created a special commission to investigate claims made by relatives for the return of Nazi-stolen art located in Holland. The return of the Gutmann collection was the Dutch government's first extensive restitution of such art.

Unlike the Degas, there were no masterpieces or artworks of prominent artists among the returned objects. Indeed, most of the objects were not even on display but had been kept in storage in various museums throughout the country. Nick Goodman estimates that the returned objects are valued at hundreds of thousands of dollars. More important, however, was the sentimental value of the objects to the Gutmann heirs, especially Lili, who was still alive when they were returned.

ROSENBERG V. THE SEATTLE ART MUSEUM
(MATISSE'S ODALISQUE)

In June 1999, the second modern-day Holocaust looted art case to reach litigation—and the first against an American museum—also settled. *Rosenberg v. The Seattle Art Museum* was filed in July 1998 in a Seattle federal court. The case involved the painting *Odalisque*, a 1928 work by Henri Matisse.

Before the war, the painting belonged to Paul Rosenberg, one of the most prominent and wealthy art dealers in prewar France. Rosenberg acquired the *Odalisque* in 1929, one year after it was painted by Matisse, and the painting became part of Rosenberg's personal art collection.

Because Rosenberg was Jewish, he fled France for the United States in 1941, one year after the Nazi occupation. The Nazis then seized more than four hundred of his paintings, which included some of the greatest works of modern art in prewar Europe. After the war, Rosenberg returned to Paris and, by the time he died in the late 1950s, managed to recover most of his stolen art. The *Odalisque*, however, was not one of them.

As with the stolen Degas, the legal journey leading to the return of the *Odalisque* came about through pure serendipity. As mentioned earlier, Hector Feliciano's *Lost Museum,* a book describing the numerous artworks stolen by the Nazis and found in France, led to a reexamination of the problem of artworks stolen by the Nazis. Feliciano described many of the missing art works and included a long discussion of the *Odalisque.* In 1997, *The Lost Museum* was published in the United States. Shortly after the book's English-language publication, a grandson of Prentice Bloedel, a Canadian timber magnate, was at a party in Seattle and happened to be flipping through the pages of Feliciano's book, lying on the party host's coffee table. He spotted a photograph of the *Odalisque* and recognized it as a painting that had been hanging for many years at his grandparents' country home. A year earlier, the Bloedel family had donated the painting to the Seattle Art Museum, commonly known by its acronym SAM. The Bloedels then contacted Feliciano. He, in turn, informed Paul Rosenberg's heirs, Elaine Rosenberg and Micheline Sinclair, daughter-in-law and daughter, respectively, of Paul Rosenberg. Paul Rosenberg and his wife and their other child, a son, were now deceased. The daughter Micheline Sinclair resides in France, and the daughter-in-law Elaine Rosenberg lives in New York City.

According to a study conducted by HARP, the *Odalisque* found its way from Paris to Seattle through a most circuitous, fifty-year-long route. In early 1940, Paul Rosenberg, anticipating war, placed the painting for safekeeping in a bank vault outside Paris. In 1941, after the Nazi invasion of France, the Einsatzstab Reichsleiter Rosenberg (known as the ERR), a Nazi party agency headed by Nazi ideologue Alfred Rosenberg (definitely no relation) and co-opted by Reichsmarschall Hermann Goering (both of whom were prosecuted and convicted as war criminals at the Nuremberg Tribunal), seized the painting from the bank vault. During its looting spree, the ERR was responsible for stealing approximately 21,000 artworks, mainly from France. The ERR shipped the *Odalisque* back to Paris and in 1942 traded it and another painting (by Gauguin) from Paul Rosenberg's collection, which it considered "degenerate art," for a painting from the Renaissance period. Nazi records show that the trade was made with a shady German art dealer. The dealer, interrogated by the Allies after the war, claimed that he shipped the painting along with others to a warehouse in Germany but that the shipment had never arrived.

It appears that the dealer was lying, since in early 1954 the painting turned up at the Galerie Drouant-David, a now-defunct art gallery in Paris. Soon after, the *Odalisque* crossed the Atlantic Ocean when the Paris gallery sold the painting to Knoedler & Co., a renowned art gallery in New York City. How the Paris art gallery obtained the *Odalisque* is unknown, and the whereabouts of the painting between 1941 and 1954, when it was acquired by the Galerie Drouant-David of Paris, remains a mystery.

In November 1954, Knoedler & Co. sold the painting to the Bloedel family, living in Washington State. The Bloedels paid $18,000 for the painting and hung it in the living room of their country estate on Bainbridge Island, Washington. In 1991, they donated it, in part, to SAM. In 1996, upon the death of Prentice Bloedel, his wife donated the remainder to the museum. By that time, the *Odalisque* was valued at approximately $2 million.

In August 1997, the Rosenberg heirs contacted SAM, informing it of their ownership claim on the *Odalisque*. Through their attorneys, the museum and the two women then attempted to settle the matter. In the mean time, with the media publicizing the discovery of a Nazi-stolen painting hanging in Seattle's principal museum, the museum removed the *Odalisque* from the public display.

In July 1998, Elaine Rosenberg and Micheline Sinclair brought suit for the recovery of the painting. In June 1999, while the litigation was ongoing, SAM agreed to return the painting to the Rosenberg family. The museum was prompted to do so when during the litigation, it contacted HARP, the Holocaust Art Restitution Project, to determine the provenance of the *Odalisque.* It was not easy. Two HARP researchers spent more than a year sifting through old exhibition catalogs and documents before piecing together the painting's circuitous journey. As reported by the *Seattle Times*, "Tracing looted art is not the sort of thing you can do on the Internet. . . . The report was several months late."[51]

After obtaining the HARP study, the Seattle Art Museum's board of directors unanimously approved the return of the painting to the Rosenberg family. The HARP report, according to Mimi Gates, the museum's director,

> answered several crucial questions about the history of the painting. . . . [It] prove[d] the painting is the one taken by the Nazis from the vault where Rosenberg hid his collection. The report also makes clear that Rosenberg, who died in 1959 after moving his art business to New York, never again saw the painting or had the chance to bring it back into his collection. This is a pivotal point, since it apparently proves Rosenberg never sold the painting to anyone.[52]

According to another director, "it took time to determine the ownership of this particular 'Odalisque' because Matisse made several paintings named 'Odalisque.'"[53] Concluded Gates, "Now that we've had thorough research, and now that the HARP report is completed, this is the right thing to do."[54] Ronald Lauder, head of CAR, praised the museum's actions. "This is the first time an American museum has returned art work like this. This is very important."[55]

In an ironic footnote to the dispute, the painting was soon sold twice and disappeared from view. A few months after receiving the painting from the museum, the Rosenberg heirs sold it to casino mogul Steve Wynn, who put it on display at his Bellagio Hotel and Casino in Las Vegas where it had a larger but a different kind of audience from those who viewed it at the Seattle Art Museum. Not long after, Wynn sold the Bellagio and separately the *Odalisque* "through a dealer for $11 million to a company with a post-office box in the Grand Cayman Islands. . . . The last word was that it had been shipped to Switzerland."[56]

Earlier, in April 1999, the Rosenberg heirs received another piece of good news when a French museum agreed, without litigation, to return to them a Monet masterpiece, *Nympheas, 1904*, one of Monet's forty-eight water lily paintings. The painting is estimated to be worth approximately $7.5 million. Taken from Paul Rosenberg's chateau in 1940 and kept by Nazi Foreign Minister Joachim von Ribbentrop during the war, the painting turned up on loan at a Monet exhibition in November 1998 at Boston's Museum of Fine Arts (MFA). The Rosenberg heirs first spotted the painting at the MFA exhibition. The painting was returned to France after leaving Boston amid controversy. Unlike the *Schiele* case (see later discussion), the Rosenberg heirs did not attempt to hold the painting in the United States, and the French museum voluntarily returned it. The Rosenbergs also sold the *Nympheas* after its recovery, purportedly for between $20 million to $25 million.

Thereafter, another interesting piece of litigation ensued. In May 2001, Hector Feliciano sued Elaine Rosenberg and the other Rosenberg heirs in New York state court in Manhattan for $6.8 million, claiming that he was entitled to a "finder's fee" for helping the Rosenberg family recover both the Nazi-looted Matisse and the Monet. Feliciano claims that before he arrived on the scene, the Rosenberg family "had stopped systematically looking for the stolen Rosenberg art"[57] and that his efforts resulted in the Rosenbergs' recovering $39 million worth of paintings, including these two paintings. Feliciano's $6.8 million demand was based on a 17.5-percent "finder's fee," which he claimed was standard in the art industry. Feliciano asserted that he had an oral contract with Elaine Rosenberg that he would be "rewarded for his work."[58]

Elaine Rosenberg and the other heirs are denying Feliciano's claim. They assert, along with a variety of legal defenses (for example, the claim of an oral contract is legally defective under New York law), that Feliciano performed his work searching for Rosenberg stolen art not for them but as part of his own research efforts in writing *The Lost Museum*. The book revolves around his search for the lost art of five Jewish families, one of whom was the Rosenbergs. In the book's acknowledgments, Feliciano states that it would have been "inconceivable" for him to write *The Lost Museum* without Elaine Rosenberg's assistance. He thanks her "for her friendship, ideas, hospitality and for the unlimited access to the Paul Rosenberg archives she offered me."[59] Hector Feliciano and Elaine Rosenberg, formerly close friends, are now bitter rivals.

THE MOMA SCHIELE LITIGATION (SCHIELE'S *PORTRAIT OF WALLY* AND *DEAD CITY III*)

Without a doubt, the most famous and influential Holocaust looted art case was the litigation over the Schiele paintings on loan from Austria to New York's Museum of Modern Art (MoMA). The legal dispute went all the way to New York State's highest court and is now winding its way through the federal court system. After five years, there still is no end in sight. Comments Hector Feliciano, "I believe it is a pity, because of all the time, energy and money wasted on this, by all sides. It should be solved in a quicker manner."[60] The litigation has created a bombshell in the art world, transforming the way in which art is traded and lent both in the United States and around the world. The full consequences of the litigation are still to be determined.

What makes the litigation unique is that it is the only Holocaust restitution case to be adjudicated through the U.S. criminal law system. All other Holocaust restitution cases were decided as private legal disputes between private individuals or entities without resort to criminal law. Here, because the government is seeking forfeiture, a civil remedy under criminal law, the major legal actors include government prosecutors.

Frightening to museums worldwide is that it all started as an apparently ordinary transaction. From October 1997 to January 1998, MoMA held an exhibition of artwork by the Austrian modernist painter Egon Schiele. The exhibition, entitled "Egon Schiele: The Leopold Collection, Vienna," contained 150 works of art on loan from the Leopold Museum in Austria. The exhibition had been on a worldwide tour for three years and was next scheduled to go to Barcelona. Among the Schiele works were two of his paintings, *Dead City III* (*Dead City*) and *Portrait of Wally* (*Wally*). The exhibition was brought to MoMA through an agreement with the government-financed Leopold Foundation in Austria.

The Leopold Foundation has interesting origins. Dr. Rudolph

Leopold, a retired Austrian ophthalmologist, is an avid collector of Schiele's works and eventually acquired the largest collection of Schiele art in the world. In 1994, in order to pay back taxes, Leopold sold the collection to the Austrian government, which established a foundation and museum in his name and appointed him as the museum's director for life.

The Schiele exhibition was a great success for MoMA. As the exhibition was winding down, the heirs of two Holocaust victims contacted MoMA with a most unexpected accusation. *Dead City* and *Wally* had been stolen by the Nazis. Two separate letters addressed to Glen D. Lowry, director of MoMA, and received on December 31, 1997, five days before the exhibition was to close, informed him that *Wally* had been stolen from Lea Bondi Jaray (Bondi), an Austrian Jewish art dealer who fled Austria in 1938. *Dead City* had been stolen from Fritz Grunbaum, also an Austrian Jew, who did not survive the war.

Leopold acquired *Dead City* in 1954. Earlier it had been in the United States, exhibited in New York at the Guggenheim Museum. It then had left New York without any problems. According to the Grunbaum heirs (and to the complaint filed by the government authorities seeking forfeiture of the painting), the painting belonged to Fritz Grunbaum, who was arrested following the Anschluss, the annexation of Austria by Nazi Germany in March 1938, and who later perished at Dachau. The heirs claimed that *Dead City* was stolen by the Nazis or their collaborators after Grunbaum's arrest and eventually came into Leopold's possession.

Leopold's possession of *Wally* has a more twisted history. According to the Bondi heirs (and to the complaint filed by the government authorities seeking forfeiture of the painting), in April 1938, a month after the Anschluss, Lea Bondi was forced to sell her gallery to a non-Jew under Austria's "Aryanization" laws. The purchaser, Friedrich Welz, an Austrian Nazi and Salzburg's most famous art dealer, then forced her also to give him the *Wally*, hanging in Bondi's apartment. As described by the federal judge presiding over the case, based on allegations in the plaintiffs' lawsuit:

> [After obtaining Bondi's gallery, and d]uring a subsequent visit to Bondi's apartment, Welz saw Wally hanging on the wall and insisted that his Aryanization of the gallery entitled him to it. Bondi responded that Wally was part of her private collection and had nothing to do

with the gallery, but "Welz continued to pressure [her] for the painting until [Bondi's] husband finally told her that, as they wanted to leave Austria, perhaps as soon as the next day, she should not resist Welz, because 'you know what he [Welz] can do.'" Bondi then surrendered the painting to Welz and fled to London.[61]

After the war, the U.S. Army arrested Welz as a suspected war criminal and seized all his possessions, including his art. At that point, according to the Bondi heirs, the U.S. Army authorities sorting out Welz's possessions made a mistake. The authorities confused *Portrait of Wally*, which depicted Schiele's mistress, Valerie (Wally) Neuzil, with a Schiele drawing entitled *Portrait of His Wife*. The latter belonged to Dr. Heinrich Rieger, an Austrian Jewish dentist who collected Schiele's works. During the war, Rieger perished in the Holocaust, and his art also was "Aryanized" by Welz. After the war, Rieger's children, using postwar Austrian restitution laws, sued Welz seeking the return of Dr. Rieger's art collection. The Restitution Commission granted the children ownership of the collection, including *Portrait of His Wife*. The Rieger heirs then sold some of the art to the Austrian National Gallery, housed at the Belvedere Palace in Vienna (and known for that reason also as the Belvedere Gallery). The Austrian government authorities, who had obtained custody of *Wally* from the U.S. Army as a result of its confusion between Schiele's wife and mistress, sent the portrait of Schiele's mistress, rather than of his wife, to the Belvedere Gallery to effectuate the Rieger sale.

The Austrian government and the Belvedere Gallery were aware of both the mixup and Bondi's claim to the painting. In fact, Dr. Karl Garzarolli, then director of the Belvedere Gallery, noted in the gallery records that the artwork it received in the Rieger sale was *Wally*. The postwar Austrian government and its museums, however, were not eager to return Holocaust looted art to its Jewish owners, instead hoping to keep as much of it as possible. Bondi, who recovered her art gallery under the Austrian postwar restitution laws, did not receive *Wally*. Instead, the painting of Schiele's mistress became part of the gallery's permanent collection.

In 1953 and living in London, Bondi met Leopold, the avid Schiele collector from Vienna, who came to visit her to help him locate Schiele pieces that he could purchase. Bondi allegedly made Leopold aware of her claim to the painting hanging in the Belvedere Gallery, and Leopold agreed to help Bondi get it back in return for her assistance in his search for additional Schiele art. Instead, in 1954 Leopold traded to the Belvedere Gallery another Schiele in his possession for *Wally*. Three years later Bondi learned that Leopold now had *Wally* when she saw a catalog for an exhibition that listed Leopold as the owner of the painting. Until her death in London in 1969, Bondi tried without success to get the painting back from Leopold.

The heirs pursuing the paintings for both the Bondi and Grunbaum families now live in the United States and Canada. New Jersey resident Henry Bondi, Lea's nephew, laid claim to *Wally* on behalf of about forty Bondi heirs around the world. Two sisters, Rita and Kathleen Reif, of New York and Canada, respectively, and the cousins of Fritz Grunbaum, claimed *Dead City* as the sole heirs of Fritz Grunbaum.

Leopold disputed both families' allegations. As his attorney, Steve Harnick, explained, "My client rejects these claims [by the Bondi and Reif heirs] entirely. He's a good-faith purchaser, and we believe he has rightful ownership of the paintings under all applicable laws."[62]

In their letters to MoMA, the Bondi and Grunbaum heirs asked the museum to hold onto the paintings, allowing them to remain in New York pending determination of their true ownership.

MoMA replied that it would deny these requests. Although the museum expressed sympathy for the claims, Lowry insisted that MoMA's loan agreement with the Austrian government required the museum, upon conclusion of its exhibition, to ship the paintings back to Europe, where they would next be shown in Barcelona.

In most stolen property cases, the party who seeks the return of alleged stolen property and who knows that the property may be taken out of the jurisdiction at any time petitions the court through emergency proceedings to issue an injunction keeping the property within the jurisdiction until the ownership dispute is decided through an ordinary civil action. This traditional route, however, was unavailable to the Bondi and Grunbaum heirs. For claims involving stolen art, New York law, specifically section 12.03 of the New York Arts and Cultural Affairs Law (ACAL), known as the antiseizure law, bars parties seeking recovery of stolen artwork to seek such emergency relief. But the law did not prohibit the claimants from filing a civil suit in New York against the Leopold Foundation seeking a determination that the two paintings rightfully belonged to them.

While available in theory, however, such a civil suit would have faced serious practical difficulties. Even if a New York judge ruled for the heirs, there was no effective way to enforce the judgment. With the paintings back in Austria, the Leopold Foundation could have thumbed its nose at the American judgment. As every international law specialist practicing in the United States knows, enforcing an American judgment abroad is a difficult and usually impossible proposition. Governments of foreign countries and their courts can recognize or ignore the U.S. civil judgments at their discretion. (For criminal proceedings, countries enter into bilateral extradition treaties, but no such parallel treaties exist in the civil arena.)

Having been prevented from getting relief through the civil courts, the heirs then tried another route and contacted the New York district attorney's office. This move could not guarantee them success. Robert Morgenthau, Manhattan's district attorney, could have sat on their request, and the paintings would have left New York the next morning. Instead, Morgenthau sprang into action. Hours before the paintings were to be returned to the Austrian government, he was able to stop their departure from New York by impaneling a state criminal grand jury. On Morgenthau's recommendation, the grand jury issued a subpoena ordering MoMA to appear as a witness before it and to produce the two paintings, thereby effectively preventing their departure.

The *Portrait of Wally* has been held captive in the United States since 1998, with the media reporting each step of the legal drama.

After being served with the subpoenas, MoMA filed legal proceedings in New York state court to quash them. Much to Austria's displeasure, MoMA and Morgenthau then agreed that the paintings would remain in the United States, in the custody of MoMA, pending the resolution of this dispute.

In its application to quash the criminal subpoena that kept the two paintings from leaving New York, MoMA relied on ACAL 12.03, New York's antiseizure law. The law provides that art loans from out-of-state lenders made to not-for-profit institutions in New York are exempt from seizure.[63] MoMA argued that the language of the law is clear, prohibiting any type of legal procedure or maneuver that would result in the seizure or attachment of a work of fine art that is in New York State on loan to a museum for an exhibition in the state. MoMA also pointed to the purpose of the law to support its argument, what lawyers call the law's legislative history. The law was passed to encourage the lending of art from out of state to exhibitions held in New York State. If the owners of out-state artworks worry that their works might be seized after being lent for an exhibit in New York, they are less likely to make the loan.

Morgenthau's argument was also straightforward. ACAL section 12.03 applies only to civil proceedings. Nothing in the law prohibits criminal authorities from stepping in and holding an artwork found in New York for which it has strong evidence that it is stolen, until such time that the authorities determine whether the work in fact is stolen. Legal precedent was on Morgenthau's side. The law had never been used to stop criminal prosecutors; all previous cases applying the law had been civil suits.

In May 1998, the New York Supreme Court judge presiding over the case ruled in favor of MoMA. The trial judge held that while Morgenthau had every right to conduct a criminal investigation to determine whether the two paintings were stolen property, he had no right to ask the grand jury to order the seizure of the paintings while their legal status was being investigated. But the Manhattan district attorney did not give up. He filed an appeal.

In March 1999, the Appellate Division of the New York Supreme Court, the intermediate appellate court, reversed the decision.[64] Contrary to the ruling of the trial judge, the appellate court held that ACAL, section 12.03, was not intended to affect criminal proceedings such as the one being conducted by Morgenthau. Focusing on the language of the law, the appellate court held that a subpoena to appear before a grand jury and produce evidence did not constitute "seizure," and therefore issuing a subpoena to MoMA did not violate section 12.03 prohibiting "a seizure . . . upon any work of art."[65] In so deciding, the appellate court ignored the pleas of MoMA and a dozen New York museums, including the Jewish Museum, that they would be unable to borrow out-of-state art if lenders believed that their loaned art could be seized in criminal proceedings once it entered New York.

It was now MoMA's turn to appeal. The New York Court of Appeals, the highest court in New York State, does not accept an appeal of every case. Here, however, there were important legal questions to resolve, and of course, the case had become notorious. The court accepted the appeal.

In September 1999, it issued its ruling. In a six-to-one decision, the Court of Appeals reversed the appellate court below and upheld the decision of the trial judge.[66] It held that the antiseizure law permits no exceptions and applies to any legal proceedings that would result in keeping the paintings in New York beyond the agreed-upon loan period. In this case, the court held, because the criminal subpoena issued by the grand jury had led to an indefinite detention of the paintings in New York, it amounted to a seizure of the artworks.

The decision did not sit well with the state legislators. In May 2000, the New York state legislature unanimously enacted an amendment to ACAL, section 12.03, announcing that the law prohibited seizure only in civil, and not in criminal, proceedings. The amendment was passed despite strong opposition from New York museums, which urged its defeat. When it reached the desk of New York Governor George Pataki, the *New York Times* published an editorial urging him to "firmly reject" the change. On May 25, 2000, Pataki signed the legislation into law.

The amendment, however, was of no practical significance to the Schiele works. Since the New York Court of Appeals had ruled that the grand jury subpoena was void, *Dead City* and *Wally* were now free to leave New York State. *Dead City* was shipped back to Vienna, where it is now safely ensconced at the Leopold Museum.[67] *Wally*, however, still is being held hostage in New York, stored for safekeeping, first by MoMA and now by the U.S. Customs Service, until final resolution of the case.

The next round of litigation brought more high legal drama. As soon as the New York Court of Appeals dealt Morgenthau the final blow, Mary Jo White, then the federal U.S. attorney in Manhattan, immediately took up the legal baton from the state district attorney. Within hours of the New York court decision voiding the state subpoena, White obtained an emergency court warrant allowing the U.S. Customs Service in New York to seize *Wally*. The federal warrant was issued on the ground that the painting was stolen property knowingly imported into the United States in violation of the U.S. National Stolen Property Act.[68] Various federal statutes then authorized federal authorities to confiscate any property brought into the United States valued at more than $5,000 and known to be stolen.[69] Any stolen property is covered, not just art, and the seizure is usually made by the U.S. Customs Service. Contemporaneously with the warrant application, White filed a civil suit in federal court in Manhattan seeking permanent forfeiture of the painting from the Leopold Foundation. Like the warrant, the civil forfeiture action asserted that in violation of the National Stolen Property Act, the foundation had transported *Wally* into the United States knowing that it was property stolen by Welz. In the same action, the Lea Bondi heirs and the Leopold Museum filed competing claims for the painting.

By coincidence, the case was randomly assigned to a federal judge already quite familiar with the world of Holocaust restitution: Chief Judge Michael Mukasey, who was handling the class action Holocaust insurance litigation (see chapter 3).

As in the other Holocaust restitution suits, the briefs filed by the parties (U.S. government, the Bondi heirs, MoMA, the Leopold Foundation, and the Republic of Austria) were voluminous, equal to those filed before Judge Edward Korman in the Swiss banks' class actions. The parties presented Judge Mukasey with complex legal contentions based on foreign law (art and property law of Austria), international law (the Austrian State Treaty of 1955 ending the occupation of Austria by the Allies and creating the current Austrian state), and a panoply of procedural arguments. The American Association of Museums and the Association of Art Museum Directors, as well as nine major museums, likewise intervened in the federal litigation. These parties submitted *amicus* briefs urging Judge Mukasey to dismiss the U.S. government's forfeiture suit. Their arguments were similar to those they presented before the New York legislature, contending that if the federal government succeeded in its forfeiture action, it would result in a major upheaval of the art world. Amid all this legal excitement, another party intervened in the suit, claiming to be the grandson of Lea Bondi's husband and the proper owner of the painting.

In July 2000, Judge Mukasey issued his decision in what is now known as *Portrait of Wally I*.[70] In his ruling, the judge dismissed the U.S. government's forfeiture case. He found that the case could not proceed, since under federal law, *Wally* was not stolen property when it was brought into the United States for the MoMA exhibit. According to the court's reasoning, even if the painting had been stolen when it was taken from Lea Bondi, it ceased to be stolen property when it was recovered by the U.S. Army from Welz. As a result, the legal predicate that would trigger the National Stolen Property Act—that is, the property at issue must be "stolen"—was missing.

The U.S. attorney, like the New York district attorney, lost the case. Unless White were able to convince an appellate court to reverse Judge

Mukasey's ruling, *Wally* would soon be joining *Dead City* at the Leopold Museum in Vienna.

Before appealing, White tried another legal maneuver. She asked Judge Mukasey to reconsider his decision and allow her to reargue the case to convince him that he had made a mistake. As an alternative, White asked Judge Mukasey to reopen the case, take away his final judgment dismissing the action, and allow the U.S. government to file a new complaint in the case, in effect to start the forfeiture proceedings anew. The strategy for the last request was to file another complaint that would now make the government's allegations fit the requirements of the National Stolen Property Act as interpreted by Judge Mukasey, that is, to make *Wally* "stolen property." It was a lot to ask, and the chance that Judge Mukasey would grant these requests was slim. Judges almost never take back their final judgments, and especially when, as here, they have deliberated over the case and issued an opinion considering the various arguments presented by both sides. The request to file a new complaint also was unlikely to be granted. The U.S. government had already had "three bites at the apple" to file a proper complaint in this civil forfeiture action. Previously, the government had filed its original complaint, then an amended complaint, and then a second amended complaint. Now it was asking permission to file a third amended complaint, its fourth original pleading.

In December 2000, Judge Mukasey issued *Portrait of Wally II*.[71] The motion for reargument was denied. Surprisingly, however, he allowed the U.S. government to file a fourth complaint in the case. In explaining his unusual decision Judge Mukasey noted that "this is not [an] ordinary case. . . . This case involves substantial issues of public policy relating to property stolen during World War II. . . . There are more interests potentially at stake here than those of the immediate parties pursing this lawsuit."[72] The next month, the U.S. government filed its third amended complaint.

In April 2002, twenty-one months after his first decision and more than a year after the U.S. government filed its new complaint, Judge Mukasey issued *Portrait of Wally III*.[73] Reversing his ruling of almost two years earlier, the judge now held that *Wally* was indeed "stolen property" under federal law. In so deciding, the judge examined again the legal consequence of the painting being recovered by U.S. armed forces after the war in light of the new allegations made by the U.S. government in its third amended complaint.

In his original decision in 2000, Judge Mukasey held that when the U.S. Army recovered the painting from Welz, it did so on behalf of its true owner, who happened to be Bondi.

> In this case, the United States' Forces were charged with recovering stolen items and acting on behalf of the items' true owners. . . . Accordingly, when they recovered the painting they did so as agents of Lea Bondi—even though they did not know her name, or that the painting was hers.[74]

As a result, the painting lost its status as "stolen" because agents of Bondi, the U.S. Army, recovered the painting for her. In the 2002 decision, Judge Mukasey now agreed with the U.S. government's position that the U.S. Army could not have been Lea Bondi's "agent" when it took possession of the painting from Welz. To reach this opposing legal conclusion, Judge Mukasey gave a different factual twist to the immediate postwar events in Austria. Relying on the amended allegations in the government's latest complaint, the occupying U.S. Army in Austria was "collecting all property" of suspected war criminals like Welz, whether stolen or not. Since it was seizing all properties of suspected war criminals, the U.S. Army "did not even know that *Wally* was stolen." Rather, *Wally* had now "merely passed through the hands of government officials who were unaware that the property was stolen and who were under no legally enforceable duty to act on [Lea Bondi's] behalf." The army's "lack of knowledge" of *Wally*'s status and its "lack of duty" to return the painting to Lea Bondi precluded the army from being Bondi's agent. According to Judge Mukasey, "I therefore rescind my prior ruling that Wally could not be considered stolen."[75]

Judge Mukasey's contradictory legal conclusions about whether or not the U.S. Army was an "agent" of Lea Bondi when it recovered the painting show all this to have been an empty exercise. His modified opinion in *Portrait of Wally III* that the army was not Lea's "agent" was nothing more than a way of backtracking from his original error in *Portrait of Wally I* in trying to decide this case by futilely determining whether the painting was technically "stolen property" under federal law. If the painting belonged to Bondi and was never returned to her, it is stolen property. The U.S. Army's temporary holding of the painting is irrelevant.[76]

In this latest opinion, Judge Mukasey also dismissed the jurisdictional arguments made by the Leopold Foundation, MoMA, and Austria, which filed *amicus* briefs. In another defeat for Austria, Judge Mukasey denied the defendants' motion to dismiss the Bondi heirs from the lawsuit. Last, he dismissed the separate claim by the grandson of Bondi's husband to the painting.

It was a stunning reversal. Contrary to his decision in 2000, the U.S. government and the Bondi heirs had now won a decisive victory in the case. Moreover, unlike the litigation over the Klimt paintings in the *Altmann* case (discussed later), the other Holocaust looted art suit in which Austria is embroiled, Judge Mukasey's order in this case was not legally appealable, since Austria was not a named party in the lawsuit. Austria's Leopold Foundation (and dragging with it the hapless MoMA) was now being forced to go to trial to determine which competing claimant was the rightful owner of *Wally*. Once decided, the painting will be turned over to its proper owner. Howard Spiegler, partner in Herrick Feinstein, the Manhattan art law firm representing the Bondi heirs, was extremely pleased. "The family of Lea Bondi Jaray is very gratified that the case will now proceed to discovery and trial," he told the *Art Newspaper*.[77] Next, once the parties have exchanged documents and replied to interrogatories through discovery, is to take the deposition of Dr. Leopold, still alive and living in Vienna.

Museum directors and others involved in the art business are extremely critical of the entire effort mounted by the state and federal authorities to keep paintings in the United States until their ownership is determined and to resolve their ownership by an American court. In their view, the litigation has made foreign museums and collectors wary of lending artworks to American cultural establishments. "It is always difficult to persuade individuals and institutions to lend art, and this is just another factor that will discourage them," stated Stephen W. Clark, associate general counsel for MoMA. He added, "No one is going to say they are not going to lend because we have overreaching prosecutors. They are just going to say the works are not available."[78]

Spiegler disagreed, pointing out that American federal law also has an antiseizure statute providing immunity from seizure for lent "objects of cultural significance."[79] MoMA, however, did not apply for immunity under the law and therefore could not avail itself of federal protection when Morgenthau and then White came to seize the paintings.

While the federal antiseizure law has long been on the books, until the *Schiele* controversy it was used mainly for major exhibitions traveling throughout the United States. Now, applications are more common, even for loans of artworks to a single museum. However, the U.S. State Department's Office of the Legal Advisor, which reviews the applications, has begun to require detailed provenance information about the foreign about-to-be loaned artworks before granting immunity. Some museums argue that despite the possible increase in the monetary value of the foreign collection that its exhibition in a major American museum might bring, a foreign lender still may be unwilling to lend the artwork because it would not want to subject it to strict U.S. government scrutiny. Better to keep a low profile and keep the art out of the United States, they may figure, rather than raise problems about its ownership. Regardless of what ultimately happens to *Wally,* the Schiele saga has important consequences. Seeing what happened to MoMA, museums across United States, not just in New York, are paying much closer attention to the provenance of artworks that they seek to borrow from abroad for temporary exhibitions. Likewise, foreign lenders are closely examining the provenance of objects that they are asked to lend, lest the object be seized while on loan to a museum or some other cultural institution in the United States. As mentioned earlier, museums and other public institutions are now more likely to seek federal immunity from seizure and to subject the work to federal scrutiny before bringing a lent artwork into the United States. As a result of *Schiele*, stolen art is less likely now to enter the United States.

The *Schiele* litigation has also reverberated beyond the issue of artworks being lent to American museums from abroad. Its widespread notoriety has been an important factor in the international art world's becoming more vigilant about checking the provenance of all artworks. As the London-based *New Statesman* explained,

> Top auction houses now take a dubious view of everything on offer. "Innocent until proven guilty" may be a cliché of the Anglo-Saxon way of life but, over the last five years, the very opposite attitude has proved effective in the art world. . . . This change in attitude is fuelled by . . . the publicity given to "Holocaust art," the vast number of paintings and other objects now swilling around in the market that were once owned by Jews who were deliberately dispossessed by the Nazis. . . . No one quite knows how many Nazi-looted artworks are out there, waiting to be discovered, but it is sufficient a headache for most of the

important art fairs, such as Maastricht and the Grosvenor House in London, to insist that all dealers showing with them run their exhibits through the Art Loss Register's database of Nazi-looted objects. Sotheby's has three lawyers working on the matter.[80]

The Schiele litigation also resulted in the passage of new state legislation. As already mentioned, New York amended its antiseizure law to allow criminal authorities to seize lent artworks in New York that they suspect of being stolen. Taking a cue from New York, other states have passed similar laws, specifically Texas, Rhode Island, and Vermont.

Finally, the Schiele controversy forced the Austrian government to confront the problem of Nazi-stolen art and led to the exposure of the widespread possession by Austrian museums and galleries today of such art. This is turn, led to the *Altmann v. Austria* litigation discussed later.

WARIN V. WILDENSTEIN & CO.
(MEDIEVAL CHRISTIAN MANUSCRIPTS)

In July 1999, another Nazi-stolen artworks case was filed in New York. The case, *Warin v. Wildenstein & Co.*,[81] involves eight rare medieval Christian manuscripts valued at approximately $15 million, and the parties are well-known personalities in the art world.

The manuscripts allegedly belonged to Alphonse Kann, a renowned Jewish art collector in France. The manuscripts are Books of Hours, compilations of devotional prayers handwritten on parchment with elaborately designed color illustrations of religious subjects. Commissioned by wealthy European families during the Middle Ages, they date back to the fifteenth through the seventeenth centuries. The manuscripts are now in the possession of Wildenstein & Co., a legendary Manhattan art gallery. The Wildensteins hold more masterpieces than any other gallery in the world, and their collection of art holdings is estimated to be worth billions of dollars.

The lawsuit, filed in New York state court, alleges that the manuscripts were part of Kann's collection of twelve hundred artworks stolen by the Nazis from his villa in 1940 on the outskirts of Paris, after Kann left France for England.[82]

Kann remained in London after the war and died there in 1948. The plaintiffs are Kann's heirs, Francis Warin, the surviving son of Kann's nephew, and En Memoire d'Alphonse Kann, a French association composed of Kann's other heirs, beneficiaries, and descendants.

The manuscripts reappeared at Wildenstein & Co. in 1996, bearing a Nazi inventory marking, "ka" (standing for "Kann, Alphonse") and a number. According to the heirs, these markings indicate that the manuscripts were from the Kann collection. Wildenstein & Co. sold one of the eight manuscripts, but the other seven are still in its collection. Again, Hector Feliciano is playing a role in the controversy by supporting Warin and the other Kann heirs in their claim. Interestingly, in 1999, shortly before filing this action, the Wildensteins filed suit in France against Feliciano for defamation, claiming that in *The Lost Museum*, Feliciano wrongfully accused the Wildenstein family of dealing in Nazi-stolen artworks during the war. The French trial court dismissed the lawsuit, and the Wildensteins are appealing that ruling.

The defendants in the New York litigation, then the eighty-one-year old (and now deceased) Daniel Wildenstein and his two sons, Alec and Guy, maintained that the manuscripts did not belong to Kann. The Wildensteins claimed that the medieval prayer books were part of the personal collection of Georges Wildenstein, their family patriarch, also Jewish, whose Paris art gallery was likewise looted by the Nazis. When Alphonse Kann fled in 1940 from France to England, Georges Wildenstein came to New York, where he reestablished his art empire.

The Wildensteins argue that the Kann heirs' claim to the manuscripts is based on a mixup committed by the Nazis after both families' collections were looted. According to the Wildensteins, the Nazis housed their family's collection in the same building as the looted Kann collection and mistakenly marked the manuscripts, which came from the Wildenstein collection, with "ka."

In September 2001, Judge Marilyn Diamond of the New York Supreme Court, the trial judge presiding over the case, denied Wildenstein's motion for summary judgment on the grounds that the action was filed too late. In April 2002, the appellate division affirmed her ruling.[83] The case is now back before Judge Diamond proceeding through the pretrial process.

Photo of Maria Altmann
with painting of Adele
Bloch-Bauer I, by
Lawrence K. Ho. *Courtesy
of the Los Angeles Times.*

ALTMANN V. REPUBLIC OF AUSTRIA

In addition to the Schiele litigation, Austria also is a party to another infamous Holocaust art lawsuit involving six paintings by the Austrian
painter Gustav Klimt. The claimant is Maria Altmann, in her late eight-
ies and living in Los Angeles.[84]

Altmann is the niece and heir of Adele Bloch-Bauer. Adele and her
husband Ferdinand Bloch-Bauer were prominent Austrian Jews who
lived in Vienna before the war. A story about the case epitomizes the
prewar Jewish community in Vienna:

> A community of a few thousand Jews had swelled to nearly 1 in 10 Vi-
> ennese. Wealthy Jews were among the city's most prominent citizens
> and generous philanthropists. A few, like the Rothschilds, were even
> given titles by the Hapsburg monarchy. They were, in the words of
> Czech novelist Milan Kundera, the "intellectual cement" of Middle
> Europe.[85]

Adele's father, Moriz Bauer, was a Jewish financier who became
general director of the seventh-largest bank in the Austro-Hungarian
Empire. Ferdinand, a man twice her age that Adele married at seventeen, was a Czech sugar magnate.[86] The couple were friends of Klimt,
and Adele posed as one of his models, even being the subject of some of
the paintings in dispute. The paintings have the following titles: *Adele
Bloch-Bauer I, Adele Bloch-Bauer II, Beechwood, Apple Tree I, Houses in Un-
terach am Attersee,* and *Amalie Zuckerkandl.* They are presently valued at
approximately $150 million.

The paintings are now hanging in the Belvedere Gallery (the Austrian National Gallery) in Vienna. One of the reasons that the litigation over these paintings has been so bitter is that the paintings are considered significant works of art in the gallery's collection. According to Austria, "They . . . are national treasures and part of the cultural heritage of the Republic [of Austria]."[87] All but one have been hanging in the Belvedere Gallery for more than fifty years. *Adele Bloch-Bauer I*, painted by Klimt in 1907, even appears on the cover of the gallery's official guidebook to the museum. The painting has been described as "a shimmering, gold-encrusted work treasured as an early landmark of Austrian modernism."[88]

Adele Bloch-Bauer died of meningitis in 1925 at age forty-three. In her will, executed two years earlier, she named five of the Klimt paintings in dispute (and one other) and asked that Ferdinand donate them to the Austrian Gallery upon his death. "I kindly ask my husband to bequeath my two portraits and four landscapes by Gustav Klimt after his death to the Austrian National Gallery in Vienna," In 1936, Ferdinand delivered one of the six paintings named in the will (and not subject to this litigation) to the gallery.

In 1938, in the aftermath of the Anschluss, Ferdinand fled Austria to Switzerland. The plaintiff Maria Altmann, the niece of Ferdinand and Adele, likewise that same year fled Austria to England with her husband after he was taken to and then released from Dachau. In 1942, Maria and her husband arrived as Jewish refugees in Los Angeles, and three years later they became American citizens.

After Ferdinand left, the Germans raided and stole his possessions, including his home, his business, and his artwork. Some of the Klimt paintings went to the Austrian Gallery and others to other Austrian museums. High-ranking Nazis, including Hitler and Goering, helped themselves to some of the other artworks in the Bloch-Bauer collection. Dr. Erich Fuehrer, an Austrian lawyer appointed by the Nazis to liquidate Ferdinand's art collection, also stole some of the art, which he was forced to return after the war.

Ferdinand died in 1945, several months after the war ended. In his last will, written shortly before he died, he did not make any bequests to the gallery or to any other Austrian institution. Considering how he was treated by his native country, this is not surprising. In his will, Ferdinand left all his possessions to Maria Altmann, her brother, and her sister. According to Maria Altmann,

He died alone and lonely, a broken man. Adele's wishes were a request, not an obligation, to share her love of the Klimts with her beloved Viennese. What love could my uncle have for Austria after they robbed him of everything? He had no intention of giving the Klimts to these people.[89]

As for Adele, she added, "This art was dragged out of the house by people who murdered their friends. Would Adele want the things she treasured left [in Austria] after that?"[90]

After the war, Ferdinand hired Dr. Gustav Rinesch, an Austrian lawyer and family friend, to locate the family property seized by the Nazis. After Ferdinand died, the four Bloch-Bauer heirs (Maria, her brother, and her two first cousins) continued to retain Rinesch to recover their family's possessions, including the stolen artworks. Maria's brother also traveled to Vienna from the United States for this purpose.

In 1946, Austria made all wartime "Aryanizations" null and void. Nevertheless, the Austrian government's postwar policy impeded the return of artworks to their owners, as explained by the American judge now presiding over this litigation:

> However, the Republic [of Austria] often required the original owners of such property, including works of art, to repay to the purchaser the purchase price before an item would be returned. Austrian law also prohibited the export of artworks that were deemed to be important to Austria's cultural heritage. It was the policy after the war to use the export license law to force Jews [living abroad and unwilling to return to Austria and] who sought export of artworks to trade artworks for export permits on other works.[91]

This is what happened here. In 1948, Rinesch negotiated a deal by which the heirs "donated" the Klimt paintings mentioned in Adele's will to the Austrian Gallery in exchange for receiving an export license to bring out of Austria other artworks of the family. Rinesch also acknowledged in writing the validity of Austria's claims to the paintings. According to Maria, neither she nor the other three heirs were ever aware of this deal. She always believed that her aunt and uncle had donated the other Klimt paintings to the Austrian Gallery before the war.

Fifty years later, in 1998, Maria Altmann is now a widow, still living in Los Angeles. That year, in the midst of the *Schiele* controversy, the

Austrian government opened the Austrian Gallery's archives to private researchers to independently confirm that Austria did not possess wartime-looted artworks. An Austrian journalist, Hubertus Czernin, doing research in the archives, discovered some surprising facts about the Klimt paintings, which he then published. For instance, the Austrian Gallery had always publicly claimed that it had acquired its show-piece, *Adele Bloch-Bauer I*, as a donation from Ferdinand Bloch-Bauer in 1936. The archival records show, however, that the "donation" was made in 1941, when Dr. Erich Führer, the liquidator, transferred *Adele Bloch-Bauer I* to the Austrian Gallery, accompanied by a letter signed "Heil Hitler." Czernin also discovered postwar correspondence between Dr. Karl Garzarolli, then the director of the Austrian Gallery, and his predecessor expressing concern that Adele's will did not legally transfer the paintings to the Austrian Gallery and that the Austrian Gallery never obtained "even during the Nazi era an incontestable declaration of gift in favor of the [Austrian] state from Ferdinand Bloch-Bauer."[92] The letter ended in a conspiratorial tone:

> In any case, the situation is growing into a sea snake. . . . I am very concerned that up until now all of the cases of restitution have brought with them immense confusion. In my opinion it would be also in your interest to stick by me while this is sorted out. Perhaps that way we will best come out of this not exactly danger-free situation.[93]

Last, Czernin discovered and later provided Altmann with details of the deal that the Austrian lawyer was forced into in 1948 by which the three Klimt paintings that came to the Austrian Gallery during the war were allowed to stay there and the others could remain in Austria and later came to the Austrian Gallery. This included another letter from Dr. Garzarolli to the head of the Austrian agency in charge of export permits, suggesting that the permits for Ferdinand's collection be delayed "for tactical reasons."[94] Shortly thereafter, in April 1948, the lawyers entered into the deal with Austria and "executed a document purporting to acknowledge the intention to donate the paintings [to the Austrian Gallery] expressed in Adele's will."[95]

In December 1998, a new Austrian restitution law was enacted aimed at returning artworks that had been donated to Austrian museums after the war under this coercive policy of withholding export permits. The Austrian government has since returned thousands of artworks and other cultural objects under this program. Among them are a collection of 250 artworks, including three portraits by the Flemish artist Frans Hals, to the Rothschild family; nearly 2,000 items to the heirs of the nineteenth-century composer Johann Strauss, whose last wife was Jewish—the wife's daughter was forced to hand over the family's collection to the Nazis—and two other Klimt paintings to the heirs of Hermine Lasus, who was forced to sell them because she was Jewish. Altmann, as the sole surviving Bloch-Bauer heir named in Ferdinand's will, contacted Austria for the return of objects that were kept by the postwar Austrian government under the coercion program, including the Klimt paintings.

In June 1999, the Advisory Board created under the law issued its decision with regard to the works taken from the Bloch-Bauer estate. The board recommended that sixteen Klimt drawings and nineteen pieces of porcelain donated under coercion by the Bloch-Bauer family to Austria after the war, in exchange for the export permits, be returned to Maria Altmann and the other heirs. (According to Austria, these objects are currently valued at approximately $1 million.) The board rejected, however, Altmann's claim to the Klimt paintings, deciding that the Klimt paintings were not coerced from the family but legally came to the Austrian Gallery under Adele's 1923 will and Ferdinand's orally expressed intentions before he fled Austria that the paintings would go the Austrian Gallery upon his death, in accordance with Adele's wishes. Maria Altmann asserted that "the entire commission proceeding was a sham and the outcome was politically pre-ordained."[96] In her decision, the American judge essentially agreed with the details of the Advisory Board's proceedings as they were laid out in Altmann's lawsuit:

> There was political opposition to the return of the Klimt paintings. The Committee received an incomplete report regarding the Klimts, and some members did not receive an expert's opinion regarding the invalidity of the purported bequest to the Gallery. On June 28, 1999, the committee met and affirmed a recommendation that the Klimts not be returned. The vote on the return of the paintings was predetermined, and one member of the committee eventually resigned in protest.[97]

Altmann's attorney proposed to Austria that the matter be resolved by private arbitration between the Austrian Gallery and Altmann. Austria

declined. Altmann then prepared to sue in Austria. Here a major practical problem arose. Under Austrian law, as in many other countries, the
party filing a lawsuit is required to deposit with the court a filing fee
amounting to a percentage of the amount sued. (This is another reason
why the United States remains the forum of choice for Holocaust restitution suits.) The filing fee in Austria is 1.2 percent of the value of the
plaintiff's claim. Because the artworks were worth approximately $150
million, Altmann was required to deposit a filing fee of $1.8 million
with the court in order to have her lawsuit heard. A retired dress shop
owner, she was unable to do so and asked for special relief from the
Austrian court. The Austrian court granted her a partial waiver, but the
reduced fee still amounted to all her available assets, approximately
$200,000, a sum she insisted that she could not pay. The court also held
that she could be forced to use all her savings to file the suits, since "savings accounts may not be spared to the disadvantage of the general
public."[98]

Altmann decided to drop her lawsuit in Austria and, in August
2000, filed her lawsuit in federal court in Los Angeles. Her filing fee was
$150. Her attorney is the thirty-three-year-old Los Angeles attorney E.
Randol Schoenberg, a grandson of the famous Austrian composer
Arnold Schoenberg who, like Altmann and her husband, also fled the
Nazis, from Berlin in 1933, and settled in Los Angeles. Schoenberg took
the case on a contingency basis, and according to him,

> Maria is an old family friend on my mother's side. Her late husband
> Fritz and my maternal grandfather were friends in Vienna before the
> war. Maria has known me since I was born. In 1998, Maria asked me to
> assist her, which I agreed to do. I had seen the paintings frequently in
> Austrian Gallery since my first trip to Vienna when I was just eleven
> years old. My mom had pointed them out to me as "Maria's aunt
> Adele Bloch-Bauer."[99]

At this point, a familiar figure came into the picture. By sheer coincidence, the case was assigned to federal judge Florence-Marie Cooper
(see chapter 3). Judge Cooper, while a California state judge and before
her appointment to the federal bench by President Bill Clinton, had
presided a few years earlier over the *Stern* insurance litigation. She was
instrumental in settling that case when she denied the motion of the defendant, the Italian insurance company Generali, to dismiss it.

Austria and the Austrian Gallery's position in the suit was straight-forward. In their own words, they "maintain, as they have for over 50 years, that, under Austrian law, the [1923] Will [of Adele] and subsequent conduct of Ferdinand gave the Republic [of Austria] ownership of the paintings."[100] However, rather than having the case heard on its merits, the Austrian defendants, as did the Italian insurer Generali, asked Judge Cooper to dismiss this lawsuit on the ground that she lacked the jurisdiction to hear it. Austria and the gallery, however, had an argument not available to the private defendant Generali. The defendants in this case pointed to the rule in the United States, codified under federal law in the Foreign Sovereign Immunities Act (FSIA),[101] that as sovereigns, foreign nations and their affiliated entities are generally immune from litigation in American courts. For this reason, with a few exceptions, the various Holocaust restitution suits discussed in the other chapters have been against private European actors (the Swiss and French banks, German corporations, European insurance companies) rather than against the European governments themselves (Switzerland, France, Germany, Italy). Here, Altmann had no choice but to sue Austria and the Austrian Gallery, which under the FSIA, is considered "an agency or instrumentality" of a foreign state.

Much to the surprise to those of us watching the litigation, on May 4, 2001, Judge Cooper ruled in favor of Altmann.[102] Like her earlier ruling in the *Stern* insurance case, likewise denying a motion to dismiss, this ruling also was monumental. Its effect was that for the first time in the United States a foreign country was being forced to go to trial in an American court on a claim alleging failure to return to its proper owners a Nazi-stolen artwork. Judge Cooper found that Austria and the Austrian Gallery were not entitled to the foreign sovereign immunity defense under the FSIA. After indicating a general presumption that foreign states and their affiliated entities are immune from litigation, the FSIA then enumerates various exceptions when such immunity should be denied. One of those exceptions provides that that a foreign state is not immune from suit in an action concerning (1) property taken in violation of international law, (2) property that is owned or operated by an agency or instrumentality of the foreign state, and (3) that agency or instrumentality is engaged in commercial activity in the United States.[103] In this case, Judge Cooper found, Altmann's factual allegations met all three requirements of the exception. First, the Nazis' taking the paintings (the "property" in question under the FSIA) solely because of Ferdinand's Jewish heritage was a clear violation of international law. Judge Cooper also found the "second taking" in 1948 to be in violation of international law, "when the paintings were 'donated' to the Austrian Gallery in 1948 in order to secure export licenses for other works of art."[104] Second, the paintings were "owned or operated" by the gallery, an "agency or instrumentality" of Austria. Finally, the Austrian Gallery was engaged in commercial activity in the United States. In 2000, the Austrian Gallery published a book in the United States, *Klimt's Women,* in conjunction with Yale University Press. In fact, the book reproduces some of the Klimt paintings in dispute. The Austrian Gallery also published an English-language guidebook featuring some of the paintings (including *Adele Bloch-Bauer I* on the cover) that can be purchased in the United States. The Austrian Gallery has lent *Adele Bloch-Bauer I* to museums in the United States and advertises its exhibitions in the United States. Judge Cooper found all these to be commercial activities conducted by the Austrian Gallery in the United States.

In another surprise to the court watchers of this case, Judge Cooper also rejected various other procedural arguments made by Austria and the Austrian Gallery regarding why Altmann's suit should be dismissed. Their other major contention was that Altmann had to pursue her claims in Austrian courts. According to Austria, a proper "adjudication of [Altmann's] claims will depend on an understanding and application of, among other things, Austrian probate, succession, property, restitution, contract and fraudulent concealment laws,"[105] and therefore only Austrian courts were capable of hearing this suit. Judge Cooper rejected this argument, since as she held, "Austrian courts provide an inadequate forum for resolution of Plaintiff's claims."[106] Not only does Austrian law require Altmann to file a fee that she cannot afford,[107] but even if the case were heard by an Austrian court, Judge Cooper found, her suit would be time barred under Austria's thirty-year limitations period. Austria, therefore, does not provide an adequate forum for Altmann's claims. In contrast, Judge Cooper found that the limitations period that she would apply began only when plaintiff discovered the truth about how the Austrian Gallery obtained the paintings.

Moreover, Austria did its best to make Austrian courts as inhospitable to Altmann as possible. Altmann's attorney was willing to go back to Austrian courts if Austria would, in turn, agree to drop the limitations period defense and allow the claims to be heard by an Austrian judge on its merits. Lawyers often make such an agreement as a condition for having a lawsuit subject to U.S. jurisdiction but, more appropriate to a foreign forum, moved to the foreign court. Under such an agreement, the American judge dismisses the lawsuit, on the express condition that defendants waive the procedural defense in the foreign court and allow the case to proceed immediately to trial. Austria refused. As for the issue of filing fees, Judge Cooper noted that "Austria has appealed the reduction in filing fees [granted to her by an Austrian judge], and contends that Plaintiff should be required to pay an even greater amount."[108]

Austria and the Austrian Gallery appealed Judge Cooper's denial of their motion to have the case dismissed. Under American law governing litigation against foreign nations, a foreign nation is granted the right to an immediate appeal upon the denial of its motion to dismiss on grounds of sovereign immunity. Because of Altmann's advanced age, the Ninth Circuit, in August 2001, granted an expedited review of the appeal.

Before the Ninth Circuit, Austria argued that in denying Austria's motion to dismiss, Judge Cooper essentially did not treat Austria fairly, that is, in the same manner that the United States would be treated if it and one of its museums were sued in Austrian courts. Austria postulated:

> The United States would not expect itself and the Smithsonian Institution to be hauled into court in a foreign country by a foreign litigant over a painting in the Smithsonian on the basis of an assertion that the Smithsonian is engaged in commerce abroad because one of its publications can be obtained there. Austria and the Gallery are not subject to jurisdiction in the United States for the same reasons.[109]

The Ninth Circuit's ruling brought another surprise. After reviewing the parties' briefs and hearing oral arguments, the three-judge appellate panel, rather than deciding whether to affirm or reverse Judge Cooper, took the unexpected step of ordering Altmann and Austria to enter into mediation. This decision broke new ground, as it was the first time that a federal appellate court had ordered a foreign nation to take part in mediation proceedings. "Mediation could bring a resolution that would serve the parties better than results achieved through litigation," wrote the panel in its March 20, 2002, order. The court asked the mediator to report to it "every 30 days as to the status of the mediation."

Austria, however, was not ready to budge. In the week before the first mediation meeting, the Austrian press reported that the Austrian government would refuse to make any concessions. As a result, only one mediation conference was held. The case was then resubmitted to the three appellate judges for a decision.

In December 2002, the Ninth Circuit unanimously upheld Judge Cooper's ruling, forcing Austria to proceed to litigation. The eighty-six-year-old Altmann may yet get her day in court.

CASES SETTLED WITHOUT LITIGATION:
THE EXAMPLE OF THE NORTH CAROLINA MUSEUM OF ART

Many more Holocaust looted art claims have settled without resorting to litigation than through lawsuits. The lawsuits may dominate the headlines, but in the last seven years, quiet diplomacy and private negotiations have led to the return of some significant artworks to their rightful owners. Of course, while litigation may not have expressly led to the resolution of these claims, both in the United States and abroad, the threat of American litigation remains a powerful incentive for possessors of Holocaust looted art, whether they be museums, art galleries, or private collectors, to find an out-of-court resolution. Since the Holocaust restitution campaign began in the mid-1990s, more than two thousand artworks have been returned to their rightful owners around the world without litigation.

I will illustrate with one such successful resolution, because it presents a scenario unlike the bitterly fought battles just described.

In contrast to the position taken by the possessors of looted artworks in the preceding lawsuits, when the North Carolina Museum of Art (NCMA) was presented with a claim of having in its collection a Holocaust looted artwork, *Madonna and Child*, a 1518 painting by the German Renaissance artist Lucas Cranach, one of eighty-five artworks confiscated by the Nazis in 1940 from Dr. Philipp von Gomperz. The Nazis lionized Cranach as the quintessential Aryan painter. In the early 1950s, the painting ended up in Beverly Hills, California, bought by an unsuspecting collector who later donated it to the NCMA. In November 1999, two sisters living in Austria, the grandnieces of von Gomperz and his sole surviving heirs, laid claim to the painting. They filed a claim with both CAR and HCPO. CAR located the painting in the NCMA and informed HCPO of its discovery. The museum did not stonewall the claim. Instead, shortly after being informed that the painting might have been stolen, the North Carolina museum conducted with HCPO a thorough investigation of the provenance of the *Madonna and Child*, akin to the investigation conducted by HARP for the Seattle Art Museum regarding the *Odalisque*. In February 2000, when the investigation revealed the accuracy of the claim, the museum announced that it would return the painting to the Gomperz heirs, currently living in Austria.[110] The sisters did not have to file suit or even hire an attorney. Instead, the agreement was negotiated by Monica Dugot, deputy director of New York State's HCPO. Even though the agreement had no connection to New York, Dugot, acting on behalf of the two Austrian nationals, settled the claim for them. Howard Spiegler, the attorney who—in contrast to the amicable resolution of the Cranach painting— is still fighting for the claimants in the Schiele saga, summarized the surprising but happy ending to the story:

> The heirs were so taken with the Museum's beneficence that they agreed to sell the painting back to the Museum at substantially below the market price, reflecting what they called a "partial donation" because, as they put it, "the public should know that the heirs of Phillip Gomperz appreciate the sense of justice shown by the [Museum's] decision to restitute the painting." And the State of North Carolina was so impressed with the whole affair that it presented Ms. Dugot with a special state medal, never before given to a non-resident of North Carolina.[111]

NONLITIGATION ALTERNATIVES TO RESOLVING HOLOCAUST LOOTED ART CLAIMS

This discussion of litigating Holocaust looted art cases illustrates that as with every other Holocaust restitution claim, American courts provide the best—and often the only viable—forum in which such claims can be litigated. Unlike in Europe, as the *Altmann* case shows, claimants in the United States can initiate a lawsuit with minimal costs and retain a competent attorney who can take the case on a contingency basis. *Altmann* also showed one reason why a Holocaust looted art lawsuit cannot be pursued in continental Europe: the much stricter time period under which such claims can be brought. In these jurisdictions, the time period for filing a lawsuit starts at the time of the wrongful act, that is, when the artwork was stolen. Even in Germany, which has a thirty-year limitation period for filing suits for stolen objects, the time for filing such suits for Nazi-stolen art has long expired. As the *Goodman* case showed, in the United States the discovery rule in many states does not begin the time period for filing the lawsuit until the plaintiff actually discovers that defendant possesses the stolen artwork. In New York, the limitation period does not even begin to run until the claimant demands the return of the art and the possessor refuses. Most Holocaust looted art claims, therefore, are not time barred in the United States. The plaintiff's ability in the United States to conduct discovery before trial also allows the claimant to obtain helpful evidence—even directly from defendant—to buttress the case.

As Thomas Kline, the Goodman heirs' attorney, attested, "my observation is that . . . [Holocaust looted art] claims can be pressed successfully to conclusion, or the current possessors of stolen art can be compelled to negotiate a suitable compromise resolution of such a claim, if a claimant has sufficient resources to mount a credible claim."[112] Kline also added, "I do not believe that our legal system needs tinkering with in the interest of advancing claims by Holocaust art victims; meritorious Holocaust-related theft claims can be brought and pursued to [a] satisfactory result under our system, if backed by sufficient resources."[113]

Kline's statement contains an important qualifier. The plaintiff must possess "sufficient resources"—translation: must be wealthy—to be able to mount a successful suit, even if the claim is meritorious. On another occasion, Kline stated, "I am almost at the point where I would say that if the art is worth less than $3 million, give up."[114] His clients agree. "Winner-take-all litigation, only cost-effective for the most expensive art, is a terrible waste of money, no matter how it comes out, " Simon Goodman admitted.[115] In the *Goodman* litigation, the costs of the case were so great that the Goodman brothers, originally hailing from London, resorted to placing an ad in the Anglo-Jewish press asking for

donations for a legal defense fund. "We are limping into court,"[116] admitted Simon Goodman days before the case settled. Kline, their attorney, estimates that defendant "Searle spent a million dollars trying to
hold us off, and we didn't even go to trial."[117]

In the *Rosenberg* case, the plaintiffs also were unhappy to have been
forced by the Seattle Art Museum to litigate the matter. Plaintiff Elaine
Rosenberg lamented, "There is no justification for the Seattle Art Museum forcing the Rosenberg family to incur the expense and delay of
bringing a lawsuit."[118] According to Ronald Lauder, chairman of the
Museum of Modern Art and head of CAR, "If we treat each case—and
there'll be hundreds—as front page news, with lawyers and seizures,
we'll never succeed in getting this moving in the right direction."[119] An
April 1998 article in the *Jerusalem Post* labeled the job of recovering
Holocaust looted art a "rich man's game."[120]

The experience of taking these stolen art cases to court shows that
their litigation is time-consuming, costly, and emotionally exhausting
for the claimants. As Monica Dugot of New York's HCPO explained:

> Not only is looted art extremely expensive to recover—one must also
> remember that the legal process can be a particularly lengthy and pub-
> lic one. Moreover, it often introduces a rancorous climate not con-
> ducive to amicable resolution and usually results in resolutions that
> are money and expense driven. The reality is that survivors are well
> into their eighties and simply cannot afford the cost of a long drawn
> out battle.[121]

For this reason, two of the cases involving Nazi-stolen art, *Goodman*
and *Rosenberg*, have settled, and more settlements are likely to follow.
The MoMA case is still ongoing, undoubtedly because it was first
brought by the New York district attorney, with far greater resources
than the private plaintiffs in *Goodman* and *Rosenberg*, and is now being
carried on by the U.S. attorney. *Altmann v. Austria* is a good example of
a Holocaust looted art lawsuit in which emotion carried the day. Austria views the case as a matter of defending its national honor, since the
case involves one of its national treasures. Altmann, the elderly plaintiff, sees the case as a matter of family honor, and her efforts, as a struggle to right before she dies a terrible injustice committed by Austria
upon her family. Austria has unlimited resources to defend the case and
so refuses to discuss settlement. Schoenberg, Altmann's attorney who is

taking the case on a contingency basis and is a family friend, likewise refuses to give up.

For claims involving disputes regarding Nazi-stolen art, the adversarial litigation system appears not to be the best method of resolving such disputes. Museums and persons against whom claims have been made, art industry experts, and even lawyers on both sides of the dispute all agree on this point.

Even though there is consensus that Holocaust looted art claims should be resolved without going to court, the problem remains as to what the best alternative to litigation is. To date, no uniform alternative solution has been found, with various—and sometimes even conflicting proposals—made by various parties.

Relying on her experience in helping claimants with Holocaust art claims at HCPO, Dugot recommends discussion between the parties as soon as the artwork is located and the current possessor is known. Rather than "filing suit now and talking later," a strategy often favored by trial lawyers to exert maximum bargaining power for their client, Dugot suggests "talking first and sue only if really necessary." As she observes, "an early dialogue between the claimant and the current possessor (before expenses have been incurred) presents many opportunities to resolve these types of disputes to the benefit and satisfaction of both parties."[122] As an example, she points to her successful resolution of the claim involving Cranach's *Madonna and Child* with the NCMA.

An important element in reaching a successful resolution through dialogue is the involvement of a third-party expert in the proceedings. In the *Madonna and Child* painting controversy, the role played by HCPO in investigating the provenance of the painting and confirming to the North Carolina museum that it was indeed holding a painting stolen by the Nazis, and thereafter Dugot's role as a mediator between the museum and the claimants were critical to resolving the dispute. Dugot's involvement led to a "reasoned dialogue ensur[ing] the painting's return without undue legal expenses being incurred on either side."[123] Similarly, the dispute over Matisse's *Odalisque* was resolved through the involvement of HARP, hired by the Seattle Art Museum to determine the provenance of the painting.

One alternative to litigation, which can be used even after a lawsuit has been filed, is mediation (a neutral third party—sometimes an expert in the field—tries to bring the parties to an agreement but cannot force them to agree); another is binding arbitration (a neutral arbitrator or a panel of arbitrators—sometimes also experts in the field—hears the case and issues an arbitration award, much like a court judgment). Lawyers today call both of these outcomes "alternative dispute resolution," or "ADR" for short. According to Constance Lowenthal of CAR, who works on behalf of claimants,

> One of the reasons we would like mediation to be considered is that then the people who are guiding the negotiations are really familiar with the constraints, the needs, the ethics, and the ways of the art world—which most judges are not. It is very specialized. And while many judges would love to have such a case, it's almost always their first.[124]

James Wood, director of the Art Institute of Chicago, viewing the issue from the collectors' side, agrees.

> These cases are tremendously emotional. They often get tried in the press. When that happens, it introduces other aspects and positions harden. If either party really feels he could win [a lawsuit], mediation will not help. But most cases are pretty gray. And those are the kind of situations that can be resolved through mediation, skillfully applied. With a jury trial, who knows?[125]

Moreover, because all these are individual suits, the cost-spreading benefits of class action litigation are not available for Holocaust looted art cases. Each claimant must bear the total amount of expenses, and unless the work of art is highly prized, an attorney is unlikely to handle the case on a contingency basis.

Attorney Owen Pell of White & Case in New York, who has represented both claimants and defendants in various Holocaust restitution lawsuits, proposes that ADR of Holocaust looted art claims be conducted at the international level. For the last four years Pell has been promoting the creation of an international mediation/arbitration commission promulgated by a treaty which various nations possessing Holocaust looted art can join. Pell outlined the need for an international solution to the problem:

> Looted art cases often turn on the sheer happenstance of where the art has come to rest—with certain [countries] completely precluding re-

covery. This seems particularly unfair to victims of genocide or their heirs who, of course, had no control over the disposition or movement of their art. As a result, the legal system is neither consistent nor predictable, and does not encourage the voluntary or efficient settlement of claims or protect the rights of looting victims seeking recovery of what is rightfully theirs. This confusing web of municipal laws and litigation risks has created an increased need for uniformity, especially with respect to art works looted or stolen in violation of international law and/or in connection with crimes against humanity or genocide.[126]

According to Pell, "A mediation/arbitration commission created pursuant to a treaty or some other form of collective state action would provide the surest, most efficient and most consistent way under international law to resolve claims relating to art works looted or stolen during World War II."[127] Furthermore, he argued,

> a neutral forum with clear rules of law and procedure capable of developing and pooling historical data regarding looted art, providing a means to clear title to art, *and* resolving claims would not only be fairer to victims, but to museums and art dealers seeking repose and/or certainty with respect to their holdings. The existence of such a forum also might deter looting in future conflicts by making it harder to market looted works.[128]

Pell's proposal is worthy of consideration. A multinational Holocaust looted art tribunal could tackle the problem swiftly and comprehensively. Unfortunately, neither the United Nations nor any other regional international organization has taken up the idea.

If standing ADR commissions were more likely to be created country by country or even if an ad hoc mediation/arbitration tribunal were formed whenever the parties in a particular case were ready to mediate or arbitrate their dispute, there still would remain the problem of finding funds to compensate a good-faith purchaser who must give up the looted art to a Holocaust survivor or heir.

The parties in the *Goodman v. Searle* litigation, having gone through the litigation wars over Holocaust looted art, support the idea of ADR but add an interesting twist:

The best approach to these complex issues would be a formal mechanism for mediation or arbitration, balancing the interests of legitimate claimants, innocent owners, and the public that most benefits if those works now in museums can remain there. Ideally, negotiators could draw on a stash of public and private money to compensate legitimate claimants.[129]

According to the last sentence of the Goodman parties' proposal, not only would the claims be settled outside the courtroom, but a remedy also would be created for the loss suffered by the good-faith purchaser or the legitimate claimant. Theoretically, under American law, while the good-faith purchaser who has to give up the stolen good could demand compensation from his or her immediate seller and "the line of purchasers could be traced all the way back to the first dealer who knowingly purchased the work from the Nazis or other looters,"[130] in practice that line of "viable purchasers who can be successfully sued" is often broken because a previous seller may be deceased, no longer in existence, or outside the jurisdiction. In *Rosenberg v. SAM*, for example, the Seattle museum sued the New York art dealer who last sold the stolen *Odalisque*, which the museum was forced to give up. Fortunately, for the museum, Knoedler & Co., the New York dealer, was still in existence and eventually settled by offering the museum any painting in its collection as damages. Knoedler, however, could not in turn sue the Galerie Drouant-David, the French gallery from which it bought the painting. Not only would Knoedler have to pursue the gallery in French courts (itself a dubious proposition, since the French gallery could successfully assert the good-faith purchaser and/or statute of limitations defenses under French law), but the gallery long ago went out of business. A common fund, of the kind suggested by the Goodman litigants, would satisfy the conflicting parties' claims to the disputed artwork. Either the fund would compensate good-faith purchasers for Holocaust looted artwork who must give up the work to heirs of the prewar owners, or the heirs willing to give up the artwork would receive payment for the artwork. The idea of such a "universal solution" involving a pool of money that would be used to pay claimants or good-faith possessors, like the one that the Swiss banks or German industry agreed to establish, would also act as an important incentive to settle the matter quickly and efficiently. As Ori Soltes, former director of the National

Jewish Museum in Washington, D.C., and who originated the HARP project, explains, "'It might be in the interest of the art community—auction houses, dealers, museums—to contribute to the solution. They could justify 'communal reasons' for their participation, perhaps the way industry groups sometimes pay into a fund to settle class-action claims."[131]

Unfortunately, the actual creation of such a fund immediately runs into problems of short-term self-interest and greed. To date, the community of museums, galleries, and art dealers seems unwilling to create such a fund. Instead, the professional art world leaves each defendant who unluckily ends up with a Nazi-stolen artwork to fend for itself, despite the communal responsibility of the art world after World War II in turning a blind eye toward art with a suspicious provenance that suddenly appeared in the marketplace. As a reporter observed, "When the idea of levying a tax on dealers and auction houses, or their transactions, has come up at symposiums and conferences, it has not won resounding support from the art trade, with few people in the business feeling a responsibility for what happened in the war."[132]

Instead of raising communal funds to deal with the problem, American museums have taken a different route. In 1998, the 170-member Association of Art Museum Directors (AAMD) in the United States created the Task Force on the Spoliation of Art during the Nazi/World War II Era. The AAMD's press release announcing the creation of the task force declared:

> The Association of Art Museum Directors recognizes and deplores the systematic unlawful confiscation of art that was one of the many horrors of the Holocaust and World War II. The Association is committed to implementing a mechanism for coordinating full access to the newly available documentation on this wide-scale confiscation of art.
>
> In keeping the AAMD's Code of Ethics, the Association reaffirms the commitment of its members to weigh, promptly and thoroughly, claims of title to specific works. . . . In order to achieve timely resolution of ownership claims relating to art alleged to have been stolen immediately before, during and immediately after World War II, the Association strongly recommends the creation of a mechanism for the resolution of these claims, such as mediation, arbitration or other forms of alternate dispute resolution.[133]

The task force, in turn, issued guidelines to museums to expedite both the discovery and the handling of Nazi-stolen art. The guidelines, contained in a June 1998 report by the task force, mandate that museums respond to "legitimate" claims relating to illegal confiscation by "offer[ing] to resolve the matter in an equitable, appropriate and mutually agreeable manner."[134] They also urge museums to take an active approach by reexamining the provenance of artworks in their collections that were assembled before 1945 and that changed hands between 1933 and 1953. Philippe de Montebello, director of New York's Metropolitan Museum of Art and chairman of the task force, claimed that "by adopting the report, America's museums place themselves on record as committed to acting swiftly and proactively to conduct the necessary research that will enable us to learn as much as possible about the history of works of art for which full ownership records have not been available."[135]

Unfortunately, the AAMD's task force guidelines are vague, no more than statements of aspirations without any specifics or teeth for enforcement. For instance, while two of the guidelines urge resolution of "legitimate" claims, they offer no guidance as to which claims are to be considered legitimate. Another guideline recommends that museums "offer to resolve" the legitimate claim in "an equitable, appropriate, and mutually agreeable manner." Such language is meaningless, providing no specifics as to what a museum should do when faced with a claim that it possesses art stolen by the Nazis during World War II. Rather, the guidelines, and the creation of a museum task force, appear to be more a public relations exercise than a real attempt to deal with the problem. After the task force was created, Manhattan District Attorney Robert Morgenthau agreed that it was a matter of "too little, too late." Referring to his case against MoMA, Morgenthau stated, "I am pleased to learn that 53 years after the end of World War II, museum directors have established a task force to address the question of looted art. Would they have done so if it had not been for our investigation?"[136] Lloyd P. Goldenberg, a Washington, D.C., art law specialist, added, "In the past the museums have clearly not complied with their legal and ethical responsibility to make appropriate title inquiry prior to acquisition."[137] When confronted with a claim, the museums "most often resist."[138] Goldenberg predicted that the guidelines could turn out to be little more than "a public relations effort to make the museums appear godly."[139] Rabbi Abraham Cooper of the Simon Wiesenthal Center agreed:

The energy to finally look at this issue didn't come from the art world. It came from the media, and human rights groups, and a few individuals who said, you know what, this was 50, 60 years ago, it didn't happen on my watch, but it's time to do the right thing. Something's got to be fixed. I'm sure that [museum] lawyers broke out in a sweat—but this is a very welcome development.[140]

In April 2001, the AAMD task force issued a one-sentence addendum to its guidelines:

It should be the goal of member museums to make full disclosure of the results of their ongoing provenance research on those works of art in their collections created before 1946, transferred after 1932 and before 1946, and which were or could have been in continental Europe during that period, giving priority to European paintings and Judaica.[141]

The addendum, like the original guidelines, appears to be more empty verbiage. Member museums are given yet another goal rather than mandated requirements. To date, the guidelines have been ineffective in either uncovering any artworks or returning disputed works to their owners.[142]

In December 1998, the U.S. State Department organized the Washington Conference on Holocaust-Era Assets. Delegates from forty-five countries and thirteen nongovernmental organizations (NGOs) met at the State Department over four days to discuss various Holocaust restitution issues, including looted art.[143] Out of the conference came the so-called Washington principles, dealing specifically with World War II looted art. However, the principles, like the AAMD guidelines, are extremely vague, "call[ing] for such steps as opening museum archives to facilitate provenance research, publicly announcing unrestituted art, and devising a 'just and fair solution' for looted works whose owners cannot be identified."[144] Moreover, like the American museum directors' guidelines, they are not even binding. As explained by Ambassador J. D. Bindenagel, the State Department organizer of the conference, the Washington principles "are moral commitments. . . . How they are applied is up to governments, individual auction houses, galleries, and museums."[145]

In late 1998, in reaction to the *Schiele* case, a proposal began circulating in New York urging the creation of a central register of stolen art. Under the proposal, a victim of an artwork theft would have, in all instances, six years to file suit to recover the theft. The victim must also register the theft with the Art Loss Register (ALR), a privately owned, for-profit computerized database of 100,000 stolen and missing artworks. Failure by a victim to register the stolen artwork with ALR could immunize a good-faith purchaser from suit. Prospective buyers would also be required to check with ALR before making their purchase, to show their "due diligence" as a good-faith buyer. Holocaust victims would be allowed more time—ten years, according to some—to make claims or be forever cut off from claiming looted art.

As the London-based *New Statesman* pointed out, the use of the ALR database has become more popular:

> Some in the art world have been reluctant to accept the register, because to do so would put their exalted business on a par with the second-hand car trade. The availability of stolen cars is so widespread that all reputable dealers, as a matter of course, check every motor vehicle passing through their premises with the police-operated register of stolen vehicles. The art trade seems finally to have accepted that, however a sublime a Fragonard oil sketch, or a Matisse woodcut, in this regard they are no different from a 1988 Toyota with a dodgy clutch. In 1998, the register carried out barely 2,000 searches on behalf of dealers; by [2000] that had shot up to 15,000.[146]

Nevertheless, the proposal was opposed by the various groups dealing with Nazi-stolen art, including HARP and CAR.[147] A major practical problem, Constance Lowenthal of CAR pointed out, was

> how the register will make itself known. . . . [T]heft victims could protect their rights in New York State only by knowing about this law and knowing about this registry. But there's nothing in the proposal about how the registry is going to inform someone who lives in Kiev or Ankara or Beijing or New Delhi that if they don't register their stolen object, and it turns up in New York, they have no chance of reclaiming it.[148]

Another objection, voiced by Willi Korte, vice chairman of HARP, was to the idea that a single database would be adequate for researching

Holocaust claims: "There are hundreds of thousands of missing art-works of all sorts. . . . The great majority of them will never be recovered and claimed because they can't be identified."[149]

In January 1999, the Paris-based International Council of Museums (ICOM), a professional body in existence since 1946 with a membership of approximately fifteen hundred museums worldwide, issued its list of recommendations concerning how members should deal with "the issue of works of art confiscated from Jewish owners during the Second World War and kept in museums or public collections."[150] The four rec-ommendations are brief and seemed more in the nature of "we need to say something about the problem" rather than anything of substance. That is, member museums are to "actively investigate and identify all acquisitions . . . that might be regarded as of dubious provenance"; "make such relevant information accessible to facilitate the research and identification" of looted art; "actively address and participate in drafting and establishing procedures, nationally and internationally, for disseminating information on these objects and facilitating their right-ful return"; and "actively address the return of all objects of art that for-merly belonged to Jewish owners . . . according to national legislation and where the legitimate ownership of these objects can clearly be es-tablished." The recommendations appear to be a shorter version of the guidelines issued more than a year earlier by the American museum di-rectors' task force on Holocaust looted art. The last recommendation, and the only one to deal specifically with the issue, may in fact become an obstacle to returning a Holocaust looted art object. A museum faced with a claim of possessing a Holocaust looted artwork may argue that according to this recommendation, it need not return it because its do-mestic laws ("national legislation") makes the claim time barred or that the museum now holds clear title to the looted artwork under its do-mestic law because the artwork went though the hands of a good-faith purchaser before arriving at the museum. In addition, the museum could assert that in accordance with the ICOM recommendations, it can keep the looted artwork because legitimate ownership by the claimant to the artwork cannot be "clearly established" to the museum's satis-faction. As the HCPO's Dugot remarked,

> The reality is that few cases are . . . well documented and often, after much research has been done gaps in provenance still remain. While it is true that a gap in provenance does not necessarily suggest that a

painting was looted in the Holocaust, the opposite cannot be inferred either. In other words, that same gap does not indicate that a painting was *not* looted. Absolute certainty in cases such as these can be elusive and inferences must be drawn on available information. . . . Often, the quest for perfect and precise answers becomes an impossible barrier to just resolution of claims.[151]

HOLOCAUST LOOTED ART AND THE INTERNET

Everyone agrees that the dissemination of information is essential. Two of the Washington principles deal with this issue. The fifth principle states that "every effort should be made to publicize art that is found to have been confiscated by the Nazis and not subsequently restituted in order to located pre-War owners or their heirs." The sixth principle calls for "efforts . . . to establish a central registry of such information." As with other Holocaust restitution claims, the Internet can play an extremely useful role. Since Holocaust looted art is now dispersed throughout the world and claimants to this art likewise can also appear from anywhere, the worldwide reach of the Web can be helpful in matching such art with its proper owners. The transaction costs of such Internet matching between looted art and rightful owner also are minimal, avoiding the time-consuming and intensive process of searching innumerable art catalogs, books, and other paper resources that can make a search for a missing Holocaust looted art object akin to a search for a needle in a haystack. Art law specialist Lloyd P. Goldenberg imagined the possibilities that the Internet can bring to the problem: "Five years from now somebody sitting at a computer in Budapest will be able to do more mixing and matches, and say: 'Hey, you know what? That was Grandpa's.'"[152] Monica Dugot already has an example of the Internet's ability:

> A painting by the 20th-century German-Jewish artist, Lesser Ury, owned by a German businessman and sold under duress in 1941, was located in an Austrian municipal collection and returned to the grandson of the original owner. This case was resolved as a direct result of the Linz Museum having published a report describing the provenance of their collection and making it available to the public via the Internet. The HCPO was able to successfully match the Lesser Ury

with its rightful owner. . . . [T]his was done relatively quickly and without any monies being expended and could not have been done without the Linz Museum's information.[153]

At the Vilnius Forum, held in October 2000 in the capital of Lithuania as a follow-up to the Washington conference, delegates from thirty-seven countries and seventeen NGOs issued a "Vilnius Declaration" urging "all governments to undertake every reasonable effort to achieve the restitution of cultural assets looted during the Holocaust era to the original owners or their heirs." As a follow-up to Washington principles 5 and 6, the Vilnius Declaration now specifically urges the use of the Internet for this effort:

The Vilnius Forum asks governments, museums, the art trade and other relevant agencies to provide all information necessary to such restitution. . . . Governments and other bodies as mentioned are asked to make such information available on publicly accessible Web sites and further to co-operate in establishing hyperlinks to a centralized Web site in association with the Council of Europe.

Already some museums, both in the United States and abroad, have put up on their Web sites descriptions of art in their collections, including notations about any gaps in provenance. Of course, for a Web site to be helpful, it must be "user friendly." If a claimant or researcher is forced to comb through the entire collection of a museum for pieces with a checkered provenance, the Web site is not very useful. A separate Web page in the museum's Web site listing the suspicious items in the collection, or a search feature on the Web site allowing a search for Holocaust looted art in the collection using particular key words (for example, *Holocaust, provenance, lost art, looted art, spoliation*), is much more valuable.

At the Vilnius Forum, Dugot praised the National Gallery of Art in Washington, D.C., for the information about Holocaust looted art that it posts on its Web site, www.nga.gov. Earlier, in November 2000, the National Gallery had to part with a valuable seventeenth-century painting by the Flemish artist Frans Snyder after concluding that it had been looted by the Nazis from a French Jewish family during the war. Ironically, the painting had been donated to the gallery ten years earlier by a New York art dealer who himself was a Jewish refugee from Nazi

Germany. The National Gallery's action was the first and—to date—the only time that a publicly funded federal institution has relinquished a Nazi-looted artwork. The Getty Museum in Los Angeles also has a comprehensive section on its Web site, www.getty.edu, listing all the works in its collection on which it is conducting provenance research. The Web site allows users to search the Getty's collections not only by artist's name but also by prior owners, auction houses, and dealers, maximizing the capability of the search. Even smaller American museums have gotten into the act. In 2001, two years after its unhappy litigation experience over the *Odalisque*, the Seattle Art Museum posted on its Web site, www.seattlemuseum.org, a list of thirty-five of works in its collection that have gaps in provenance. Even if every American museum created such a category on its Web site or included such a search feature (an unlikely occurrence; although the Getty has the funds to do this, most museums do not), this would still require an individual search of every museum's Web site in the United States.

A more efficient method would be for American museums to create together a central looted or lost art Web site, on which each could post its suspicious artworks. The Lost Art Internet Database created by the German government's Coordination Office of the Federal States for the Return of Cultural Property (Koordinierungsstelle)—www.lostart.de—would be a good model for such a centralized national Web site. At the urging of the London-based Commission for Looted Art in Europe (ECLA), museums in the United Kingdom joined to created a central national registry—www.nationalmuseums.org.uk/spoliation—listing art of dubious provenance that may have been stolen by the Nazis. In France, following the issuance of the Mattéoli Commission's report on assets taken from Jews in wartime France (see chapter 4), the French Ministry of Culture created an electronic database—which can be accessed electronically at http://www.culture.fr/documentation/mnr/pres.htm—listing approximately two thousand works of art seized by Germany and returned to France after the war that remained unclaimed and were designated in 1949 as national cultural assets. These paintings, known as *musées nationaux recupération* (national recovery museums), or MNRs, are in the care of French national museums, including the Louvre. While these paintings carried the special MNR designation while being displayed or stored by French museums, the Mattéoli Commission noted in 2000 that for more than forty years, "no active research was carried out"[154] to find their true ownership. Moreover, the public

Claims Conference's old way of distributing funds—an elite group of insiders making all the decisions (no matter how sensible) behind closed doors during meetings periodically held in New York—is no longer possible now that the voices of the dissenters have grown louder. As Holocaust historian Michael Berenbaum explained,

> Survivors have become more articulate over the years, more active in their own organizations and in the larger Jewish and secular community. And with this newfound role, comes a sense of pride and dignity. They want to fully participate in determining their needs, in pressing for their interests, something they were far less capable of doing in the immediate post-war era, as they were rebuilding their lives, and in the 1950's adjusting to life in America and Israel.[1]

Nevertheless, the current debate bears all the earmarks of the encounter I witnessed in London: one group of elderly European Jews—who survived the Holocaust and have the time, energy, and inclination to focus on Holocaust restitution issues—fighting with another group who have been doing the same thing for the last fifty years. The "outsiders" are claiming that the "insiders" have been doing a poor job and that they can do it better.

Second, distribution issues bring out disputes among aged survivors that reveal an intergenerational rivalry. Many survivors feel that the funds belong only to them, since they were sought on their behalf and in the name of the suffering and degradation they personally experienced. In their view, only they have the right to decide how the new unanticipated billions now flowing in should be distributed. In a *Jerusalem Post* editorial, published after the Swiss bank settlement, I once endorsed this view.[2] This position, however, is strongly challenged by leaders of many Jewish organizations, especially the World Jewish Congress (WJC). These leaders argue that the heirs of the six million murdered are the entire body of worldwide Jewry, or at least the descendants of those killed, many of whom today are running the organized Jewish bodies in the United States, Israel, and Europe. The most forceful proponent of this view is Rabbi Israel Singer, now running the Claims Conference on the heels of his victories as the WJC leader most responsible for the Holocaust restitution settlements. In the June 2002 issue of *Sh'ma*, a respected Jewish monthly, Singer described his position:

Holocaust survivors are not the only persons charged with making decisions for the Jewish people about how to use monies that will not be needed after they die. While our first obligation is to take care of Holocaust survivors, the remainder of any monies should be spent to ensure the existence of the Jewish people—not necessarily the existence of Jewish organizations. These decisions, which are about the future rather than the past, affect the entire Jewish people.[3]

Speaking "as a child of survivors" and as someone who "worked for them [his] entire life," Singer asserts this dual perspective: "The entire Jewish people are the heirs of survivors. . . . Survivors have tremendous institutional memory—without which the Jewish people couldn't understand their existence in this time. However, survivors should not decide all questions about funds restored to the Jewish people from the Holocaust."[4]

Many Holocaust survivors are livid when they hear Singer and others claim that the "entire Jewish people are the heirs of survivors" and that therefore the Holocaust restitution funds belong to all Jews. HSF-USA president David Schaecter, a Holocaust survivor and long-time Jewish activist from Florida, responded to Singer:

> The organizations that negotiated in the name of survivors are pushing to be the organizations that decide how to distribute the "leftover" money. . . . While voicing empty rhetoric about "taking care of survivors first," they have given paltry support for the real social service needs of survivors today. . . . How dare these institutions presume to spend "restituted" funds for their favored "philanthropic" projects into the next century, using money claimed from the most terrorized victims of the past century?[5]

Singer proposed the creation of "a new body that would include the [Claims Conference], the World Jewish Restitution Organization, and the government of Israel, along with Holocaust survivors, Jewish educators, and innovative thinkers," to make all distribution decisions. The mandate of the new organization, which Singer proposed calling the Fund for the Jewish People or the Jewish People's Fund, would be to support the rebuilding of Jewish communal life or, in his words, to address the future needs of the Jewish people; for example, educa-tion—creating an innovative voucher system for every Jewish child to attend Jewish schools—would be a welcome initiative. The purpose of this effort would be to create a new future for the Jewish people. This restitution should be used to rebuild the Jewish soul and spirit. This has never been done effectively in the Diaspora.[6]

I doubt that Singer's proposal will ever be realized, even if it were to receive the complete support of Holocaust survivors. The diversity of the contemporary Jewish community and the panoply of groups claim-ing to represent the Jewish people and their interests contain the seeds of still more bitter disputes. For instance, Chasidic and ultra-Orthodox Jewish organizations, whose origins are in prewar Poland, Lithuania, and other eastern European nations in which Orthodox Jews were pro-portionately a large segment of the prewar Jewish population, claim that only they represent the interests of the murdered, since their entire communities were at "ground zero" (that is, eastern Europe) and so were entirely decimated when the Germans invaded. Using this ration-ale, they are laying claim to a substantial portion of the new funds. Meanwhile, other Jewish umbrella groups are challenging this view and the underlying rationale of the Orthodox groups. They claim that a majority of the European Jewry murdered during World War II were not religious Jews but Jews of various religious backgrounds, some fully or partially secular, and even people whom all but the Nazis would regard as non-Jews, including Christians of Jewish origin.

These various competing interests in the Holocaust restitution funds were summarized in a report by Judah Gribetz, the attorney ap-pointed by Judge Korman as "special master" to work out an allocation plan after the Swiss bank settlement, based on the hundreds of propos-als he received. Agudas Chasidei Chabad, the Chabad or Lubavitcher branch of the Orthodox movement, proposed using the funds to "sus-tain the destroyed and rebuilt communities of Eastern Europe and Rus-sia; continue services to the survivor communities around the world; and compensate communities for their direct losses sustained by the looting of communal assets." Reform Judaism made its claim through the World Union for Progressive Judaism, which likewise asked for an allocation "to provide a measure of justice and dignity for the Liberal Jewish victims of the Holocaust . . . [and] to restore and perpetuate Lib-eral Judaism's unique contribution to modern Jewish life." These are just two groups among dozens claiming to represent Holocaust victims, not to mention their divergent views on what "building a Jewish future" means to their contemporary heirs.[7]

Finally, even if it is decided that only survivors should have a voice in the distribution, there is the unsolvable conundrum of determining who fits the definition of "Holocaust survivor." Those who survived the ghettos and death camps insist that only they can be truly called Holocaust survivors. People who lost their entire families, never mind all their assets, but who managed to escape the Nazi onslaught by emigrating or fleeing vehemently oppose this view. What about Jews like my parents, who survived the war by fleeing East, or Jews who were lucky enough to come to the United States or England in the 1930s but lost their entire families in the Nazi genocide? Then there are the so-called child survivors—infants and older who either were hidden by Gentiles or survived under false identities. They passionately—and also correctly—claim the status of "Holocaust survivor," although they were not in labor or death camps. Who would deny Anne Frank the status of survivor if she and her family had survived the war without being betrayed and arrested? As for the assertion by camp survivors that the hidden ones "had it better" during the war, those who survived in hiding point to their daily fear of being exposed, arrested, and shipped off to death.

The dilemma of definition becomes even more complex when the children of survivors—born in displaced persons (DP) camps after the war or where their survivor parents settled as new immigrants—enter the debate. Helen Epstein, among others, has documented the experiences of "second-generation survivors" who grew up in families that sustained heavy losses and deep scars from the Holocaust.[8] My own experience as a child of survivors, which I described in the preface, personally confirms this fact. My parents were never in the death camps; imagine the burden carried by children whose parents survived Auschwitz, Treblinka, Buchenwald, and the like. My friend Bill Elperin, president of The "1939" Club and the first "second-generation" head of the organization, whom I also discuss in the preface, told me soon after I became a member that I could rightly call myself a "Holocaust survivor."

Even if the sons and daughters of those European Jews who survived the war reject this title, that still does not solve the definitional dilemma. In his attack in the book *The Holocaust Industry*[9] (see chapter

7), Norman Finkelstein makes much of the fact that the figures currently being published for the number of Holocaust survivors still alive today had actually increased since his parents came out of the death camps. He cites this inconsistency as proof of some conspiracy by Jewish organizations to manufacture nonexistent survivors as a means to promote their agendas. In fact, the numbers change because the definition is inconsistent. On this point, I tend to agree with Gabriel Schoenfeld's assessment of Finkelstein's claims, published in *Commentary:* "These are crackpot ideas, some of them mirrored almost verbatim in the propaganda put out by neo-Nazis around the world."[10]

Putting aside the question of who decides and turning to the question of how the money should be distributed also presents an endless debate. Immediately after the Swiss bank settlement, various individuals and institutions, both Jewish and non-Jewish, began suggesting how the funds should be distributed. An article in the *New York Times* described the growing controversy:

> A battle is flaring between Jewish humanitarian groups, plaintiffs' lawyers and concentration camp survivors over the $1.25 billion paid by Swiss banks to settle Holocaust-related lawsuits and potentially billions more from claims against companies in Germany, Austria and other countries.
>
> At the core of the dispute is the emotionally charged question of how to divide the bulk of the settlement, because only a small fraction of it will go to the heirs of Jews who had Swiss bank accounts on the eve of World War II and were killed by the Nazis. As a result, up to $1 billion may be up for grabs.[11]

Since that time, the $1 billion figure has increased to $8 billion (and even that number is nothing more than a gross estimate; the WJC, for instance, has thrown out the figure of $11 billion as the amount of new funds pledged or collected in the Holocaust restitution campaign). There seems to be general agreement that the legal claimants—whether heirs to the Swiss and French dormant accounts, beneficiaries of traceable Holocaust-era insurance policies, or slave laborers uncompensated for their labor—should be paid first. What about any remainder? This is not a hypothetical question, since it appears now that at least in the Swiss and German settlements, perhaps tens or even hundreds of millions of dollars may be left over after all the eligible applicants are paid.

The first proposal is that any leftover money should go only to Holocaust survivors. The National Association of Jewish Child Holocaust Survivors (NAHOS), a New York–based group of child survivors of the Holocaust (whose leaders also were founders of HSF-USA), expressed its views in a sample letter that it urged its members to send to Judge Korman and Judah Gribetz, the court-appointed "special master" in charge of allocation plans:

> No amount of money, neither in bulk dollar figures nor in percentages, should be taken from any restitution proceeds that have been obtained in the name of Holocaust victims. Any proposed allotments, no matter how worthwhile the cause, be it for Holocaust education, support of religion, erection of monuments, or any other reason, must be entirely voluntary on our part.[12]

Gizella Weisshaus, the lead plaintiff in the first Holocaust restitution suit brought by Edward Fagan and Robert Swift, also argued at the time that the money should go only to those who had suffered. Weisshaus was vehement that the WJC and the Claims Conference should have no role in the allocation and that they receive none of the funds.

The objection to spending money for Holocaust education or other social causes was made by NAHOS, Weisshaus, and others in reaction to a proposal made by the WJC and the Claims Conference that an 80/20 formula be adopted: 80 percent of the proceeds going directly to Holocaust survivors and 20 percent allocated to Jewish organizations for social causes. While both Gribetz and Korman rejected the WJC/Claims Conference proposal, the NAHOS advocates, Weisshaus, and other critics of the WJC and Claims Conference, as discussed in the earlier chapters, lost the battle to prevent the two organizations from playing a major role in distributing the later-acquired funds from Germany, France, and other sources. Nevertheless, the critics continue to insist that the Claims Conference, now in charge of distributing a major portion of the restitution money, spend the funds only on and directly for elderly survivors.

The contention that all money collected, including any undistributed funds, should only be used directly to benefit aged survivors is based on a strong moral premise. Throughout the entire restitution campaign, the major cry of the advocates, including representatives of the WJC and Claims Conference, was that this campaign was being waged on behalf of the aging survivors, more and more of whom were dying every day. This argument was made in the courts, in the halls of Congress and state capital offices, in press conferences, and in bulletins. Now that the money has been collected, using the funds for other purposes would create the impression of a cynical "bait and switch."

A second proposal for the excess funds is that they should go to the state of Israel, where the majority of the survivors live. The head of the Anti-Defamation League (ADL), Abraham Foxman, made this argument in his December 1998 editorial:

> I believe, first and foremost, that those who have claims should receive payment. Holocaust survivors without specific claims should be included in the disbursement of funds. After claims are satisfied and after needy survivors, who are mostly in Eastern Europe, are provided for, I suggest the remainder go to Israel. Not only would this make an important statement, but Israel has the greatest number of Holocaust survivors who need support. Israel has proportionally more children and grandchildren of survivors than any other nation.[13]

To date, Foxman's suggestion has not been acted on, although it may be resurrected again once the slow process of distributions to the actual claimants is completed. A July 2002 article in the *Jerusalem Report*, entitled "Israel Stakes a Claim," reports that "against this cash-rich backdrop [of Holocaust restitution settlements], Israeli officials and survivor group leaders have recently began demanding increasing control of the [Claims] Conference," where the major distribution decisions of the Holocaust restitution money are most likely to be made.[14] Nevertheless, the cry of "give the money to Israel" also has strong opponents. According to Roman Kent, a Holocaust survivor on the board of the Claims Conference,

> As a group, Holocaust survivors are the strongest supporters of Israel. . . . But this money does not belong to Israel. It doesn't belong to the Jewish community. This money is being returned in the name of survivors, so it belongs to the tens of thousands of needy survivors around the world who are not being helped enough, by the Jewish community or anyone else.[15]

Third, various proposals have been made to spend the money on Holocaust remembrance and education. Miles Lerman, then the chair of the U.S. Holocaust Memorial Council and himself a Holocaust survivor, made this proposal in the aftermath of the Swiss settlement. "Survivors are entitled to get what was stolen from them or their parents," he said. "But we believe Holocaust education is more important; we believe the last chapter of the Holocaust cannot be gold and it cannot be bank accounts."[16] Two years later, as additional funds were pledged by German, French, and other European concerns and governments, Susan Glazer (a writer responding in *Commentary* to Gabriel Schoenfeld's critique of Holocaust restitution; see chapter 7), echoed Lerman's proposal:

> No one would dispute that the money should be given to the remaining victims and their heirs. But a second concern should be to provide funds for additional research and to create educational programs for teaching about the Holocaust. This would help take the focus away from the purely monetary considerations that have clouded perceptions and place it back on the issue of morality of justice.[17]

In his response to Glazer, Schoenfeld criticized the plan to use the excess funds for Holocaust education:

> Let me just say that I would question [the] call for more money to be directed to Holocaust studies. There appears an iron law that the more funds flow to a given field, the more rapidly it is in danger of becoming populated by specialists in grantsmanship and worse. This is fully evident in the recent downward spiral of Holocaust research into "gender studies" and other well-funded forms of intellectual frivolity.[18]

Another category of Holocaust education is supporting remembrance and educational programs in Europe. Since one of the implicit goals of the restitution movement was to force European nations to confront their wartime pasts, it would seem that educational projects in Europe dealing with anti-Semitism and the persecution of Jews would be a worthy use of the excess funds. In the German slave labor settlement, the German payers insisted that DM 700 million (approximately $325

million) of the DM 10 billion fund go to Holocaust education and remembrance, especially since they titled their foundation the Remembrance, Responsibility, and the Future Foundation. Count Lambsdorff
defended this allocation by explaining that this money, while not going
directly to the survivors, would still benefit them, albeit indirectly after
they died. "When the survivors have passed away, their memory and
their legacy can be kept alive with projects financed by the interest that
has accrued on the Future Fund's capital."[19] Likewise, in the French
bank settlement, a portion was allocated, at the banks' insistence and
with the support of the French government, to perpetuate the memory
of the Shoah and other historic examples of man's inhumanity to man.

Allocations for Holocaust education and remembrance remain controversial. As I have stated, critics view them as a means for organized
Jewish groups to create a "slush fund" to perpetuate their existence and
for academics and others, applying for financial support from the
groups controlling the flow of the funds, as parasites taking money that
rightfully belongs to the surviving victims. I understand their concern.
As long as there are elderly survivors anywhere in the world in need of
assistance, it seems unreasonable to channel newly found funds to more
Holocaust museums, to support the publication of more Holocaust
books, or to hold additional Holocaust conferences. I speak as an academic who could directly benefit from such funds but would gladly
give them up if they were to be used to support people like my mother's
elderly survivor cousin in Odessa.

Related to the proposal to spend the money on Holocaust education
and remembrance are proposals to use the funds, as Rabbi Singer put it,
"to revitalize and create a renaissance for the Jewish people."[20] Speaking specifically about the Swiss funds, Rabbi Shmuel Bloom, then the
executive vice president of Adugath Israel of America, a major Jewish
orthodox organization, echoed this proposal. "Some individuals clearly
are entitled to compensation. But . . . money left over . . . 'should be used
to rebuild and continue the Jewish people. The way to rebuild the Jewish people primarily is through education'"[21] This again, however, has
the makings of a "slush fund" by which the same insiders and their successors, who have been doling out the German reparation payments
over the last fifty years, would continue to perpetuate the existence and
power of their organizations. HSF-USA president David Schaecter
made a case for the needs of elderly survivors:

There are between 80,000 and 110,000 survivors in the United States (about 400,000–500,000 worldwide). . . . Many are dying alone, without home or health care in their last years. No one is paying attention, especially the leaders of the American Jewish community . . . despite the headlines over the past few years suggesting that "billions of dollars" have been recovered for Holocaust victims. . . . The truth is that the restitution process has largely been a disaster for Holocaust survivors and their families.[22]

Schaecter pointed out that of the twenty-four organizations comprising the Claims Conference, only two represent survivor organizations. As a result, he noted that Holocaust funds have not been used for Holocaust survivors.

Large amounts of funds recovered in the name of Holocaust victims are not necessarily used for survivor needs. The funds have become a source of "worldwide Jewish philanthropy" and millions of dollars have been earmarked for non-survivor projects dear to the hearts of individual board member organizations throughout the world. While of many of these projects are worthy, they are not related to the needs of survivors. For example, millions of dollars are currently being committed by the Claims Conference to care for Russian Jews in the former Soviet Union. While 55 percent of those Jews are said to be survivors, 45 percent are not. In the year 2000, the Claims Conference allocated $775,000 to the organizations of Jews in Bulgaria, where there was no Holocaust, and $1.45 million to the Yiddish Theatre in Tel Aviv. Shouldn't the General Jewish community take responsibility for these allocations rather than use funds recovered in the name of survivors?[23]

Schaecter is correct in asserting that the needs of elderly survivors should not be put aside in the interest of developing some unspecified "Jewish renaissance." The governing motto for distribution should be money for "persons, not projects." However, the examples he cites to prove his point are misguided. Elderly Jews in Bulgaria who survived World War II are certainly Holocaust survivors, even though they were lucky not to have been deported to Auschwitz. Moreover, their needs are as great, if not greater, as those of the Jews in Schaecter's Miami Beach, especially now with the economic collapse of Bulgaria after the fall of Communism. Schaecter maintains that many elderly Holocaust survivors in the United States need money for "home or health care in their last years," but a great many more elderly Holocaust survivors in Bulgaria lack even a home, daily meals, or basic medicines. (There is no Social Security or Medicare in Bulgaria or in any of the other eastern European nations or the former Soviet Union.) As for the allocation to the Yiddish Theatre in Tel Aviv, we have to ask, who are the major beneficiaries of these funds? They are not the younger generation of Israelis, for whom Yiddish is a foreign language, but Israeli Holocaust survivors from eastern Europe whose mother tongue is Yiddish and for whom the Yiddish Theatre remains both a major source of pleasure and a link to their prewar past. The allocation seems perfectly proper. Last, I take issue with Schaecter's conclusion that "the restitution process has largely been a disaster for Holocaust survivors and their families." This has not been my experience. The distribution process is just getting under way, and whether it will be a disaster or not remains to be seen.

A final distribution proposal, first raised with the Swiss bank settlement, deserves at least some mention: to use the money to assist victims of more recent genocides. Columnist Jeff Jacoby offered this suggestion in the *Boston Globe*:

> All Jews, including Holocaust survivors, should reject the funds; instead, the moneys should be distributed to survivors of other, more recent human rights tragedies (such as to the victims of the Rwandan massacres and the Bosnian conflict of the 1990's, and the Khmer Rouge Cambodian auto-genocide of the 1970's).[24]

Jacoby explained the rationale for his proposal, which he says originated in a conversation with Dennis Prager, a Los Angeles broadcaster known for his writings on ethics and Judaism:

> Once the cheated depositors have been paid, let the Jewish people relinquish any claims to the balance of the money. Let it be used instead to help human beings whose lives have been shattered by genocide and ethnic slaughter. Rather than earmarking the money for Jewish causes, spend it to heal the still-suffering survivors of the Rwandan massacre. Or the deeply scarred victims of the Cambodian holocaust. Or the Bosnian women brutalized in Serbia's rape camps. "We Jews wanted to awaken the world to what the Swiss did," Prager says. "We don't want to profit by it."[25]

Jacoby's and Prager's suggestions did not go anywhere but still mustered some support from those who felt that at least some portion of the received funds could be used to help survivors of later genocides. In their view, it would be better to spend money on these living victims of other genocides than to build another Holocaust museum or memorial, since this would fit the governing motto of "money for persons, not projects." Moreover, it would also send the message that Jews and, foremost among them, survivors of the Holocaust, are ready to help others who suffered as they did. "Never again," they maintain, is not just a calling cry to prevent another genocide to Jews but "never again" to humankind.

Individuals in the restitution movement with whom I have shared Prager's and Jacoby's suggestion to give away the funds have gone ballistic on hearing it. Leo Rechter, a child Holocaust survivor and the head of NAHOS, wrote,

> Astounding! Jacoby has empathy for the formerly wealthy survivors; he has empathy for the victims of other genocides, but to try and ameliorate the final days of needy Shoah survivors does not cross his mind. . . . It is of course easy to be magnanimous with someone else's money, even though it is plainly evident that it is often desperately needed by the latter.[26]

The "never again" to humankind theme was also reflected in two proposals made to Special Master Judah Gribetz on how to allocate the Swiss bank settlement funds. The Campaign against Genocide, a Washington, D.C., nongovernmental organization (NGO) devoted to fighting the continuing threat of genocide and mass murder, asked for "$3 million to help it become a self-sustaining organization to mobilize the U.S. and the international community against the threat of genocide wherever in the world it may arise."[27] The Salzburg Seminar, of Middlebury, Vermont, an NGO with similar purposes, proposed that "six million dollars of the Settlement Funds should endow [its] Seminar Project on Reconciliation to convene annual series of symposia to review unresolved issues relating to the Holocaust, explore viable and equitable solutions to these unresolved issues and help frame policy guidelines for dealing with similar post-conflict situations."[28]

It appears, therefore, that claims that "only Holocaust survivors should receive the funds now flowing in" or, the fallback position, that "at the least only Holocaust survivors should decide how the money should be distributed" do not begin to address all the complex issues raised by the question of allocation. As Holocaust historian Michael Berenbaum summed it up in *Sh'ma*:

> The struggle over these funds pits Israel against the Diaspora, impoverished East European Jews against their more affluent and powerful Western—and particularly American—brethren. It pits the heirs of Holocaust survivors no longer alive against the survivors who are still alive. And it demands that we assess the responsibilities that we have to the Jewish past against our responsibilities to the Jewish future.[29]

While Berenbaum agrees with the importance of Jewish education and the need to build a Jewish future, he also cautions that these new-found moneys should be spent first on the living. "I fear that we have not yet discharged the responsibilities that we have toward the Holocaust survivors who are still with us. . . . Let us not fight over the *yerushah* [inheritance] while the survivors are still with us and while people in need are still in need."[30]

Burt Neuborne, in his court-appointed role as lead settlement counsel in the Swiss bank settlement, also made an important point regarding the distribution of the Swiss funds. In a July 2002 letter to NAHOS president Leo Rechter (replying to Rechter's plea to Judge Korman that some of the Swiss funds be immediately released to pay for home health care of elderly American Holocaust survivors), Neuborne reminded him that the funds were not charity to be doled out for any and all programs to benefit elderly survivors. Rather, they are the result of class action litigation that resulted in a settlement of specific legally recognized claims. As a result, in return for dismissing the suits against them, the money received from the Swiss banks could be used only to satisfy those claims for which the Swiss banks were sued in the first place. Neuborne asserted:

> The first, and most prevalent, misconception about the Swiss Bank settlement is that it is not a charitable fund for the benefit of Holocaust survivors generally. Rather, as I noted at the November 20, 2000 hearing on the Special Master's Proposed Plan of Allocation and Distribution of Settlement Proceeds, the fund is the result of the settlement of a lawsuit involving precisely defined legal claims against Swiss banks.

In working out a plan of allocation and distribution, Judge Korman, Special Master Gribetz and I are under a legal duty to attempt to distribute the funds to persons who have valid legal claims against the Swiss bank defendants. We have attempted to cast that net widely in order to benefit as many persons as possible, but the process is not without limits.[31]

These legal parameters limit Korman, Gribetz, and Neuborne regarding their choices of how to distribute any funds remaining after all the outstanding dormant account bank claims are satisfied. For this reason, Neuborne was forced to decline, at least for now, Rechter's request to aid all elderly Holocaust survivors:

I hope you understand, therefore, that the Swiss settlement fund cannot be converted into a general relief fund. Even if we wanted to shift funds from one category of Holocaust victim to another in a search for moral justice or a response to pragmatic need, we would be violating our legal duties to attempt such moral triage. None of us doubt that there are people in need, and that many praiseworthy uses can be found for the Swiss settlement funds. If, as I believe, it proves impossible to find the owners of a significant number of Swiss bank accounts, a secondary distribution process can take place during which morality and pragmatic need will play a significant role.[32]

The German slave labor, French bank, and Holocaust-era insurance funds, in contrast to the Swiss bank settlement, are not strictly class action settlements administered through the American court system. While bearing in mind that in deciding on the distribution of these settlements, the net should be cast as widely as possible to benefit as many persons as possible, any distribution of residual funds from these settlements should nevertheless have some reasonable relation to the claims made in those suits.

A final observation: We should realize that the distribution of money will always produce discord, especially when the payouts are the consequence of a tragedy, man-made or natural. Witness the heated debate, false starts, and sad tribulations surrounding the distribution of benefits to the families of those killed in the September 11 terrorist attacks. As Rabbi Irving Greenberg, former chair of the U.S. Holocaust Memorial Museum, explained,

When you . . . try to put a cash value on human beings, that creates the greatest tension in life. . . . In the real world, when someone is killed, you might say there is no amount of money to make up for the loss. But families have to live on. In the ideal, there is no limit. In the real world, there is. . . . You end up making the best choice under the circumstances. In all ethical systems, it is necessary to live with compromises. . . . The killing during the Holocaust was so widespread and so devastating that there was never even a concept to pay for the lives wiped out, only to pay for the crippling effect on the survivors.[33]

The real questions of how to serve justice and concurrently balance the claims of memory, responsibility, and group survival will inevitably produce competing visions. How much more so with an event that changed the lives of entire generations.

7

The Legacy and Consequences
of Holocaust Restitution

IN EARLY 2001, as the Clinton presidency was entering its final days, both President Clinton and Stuart Eizenstat, his special Holocaust restitution adviser, looked back with satisfaction at the achievements made by the Holocaust restitution movement during Clinton's second term. Beginning in 1995, the movement had yielded by the end of 2001 agreements with European corporations and governments to pay more than $8 billion to Holocaust survivors around the world. Although the money was coming mostly from Europe and the recipients also would be mostly Europeans and other foreigners, the movement was essentially a U.S.-based and U.S.-coordinated operation. In its heyday, numerous Clinton officials worked almost full time on Holocaust restitution issues. Through the work of Alan Hevesi's Executive Committee and the state insurance commissioners, nearly one thousand state and local officials in every state joined the campaign to get the Europeans to pay for their wartime financial misdeeds. Leading the charge were the American litigators, who were pushing hard to get the cases to trial so that their elderly clients would have their day in court to tell their stories to sympathetic jurors.

Yet for all their successes, their victories were not unambiguous. Almost from the beginning, the movement produced strong controversy, which was not a surprise considering, as one writer observed, the "minefield of passions that lies beneath this issue."[1]

CRITICISM OF THE RESTITUTION MOVEMENT

The first publicly raised misgivings over the litigation appeared in December 1998, with two prominent commentaries appearing almost at the same time. Abraham Foxman, head of the U.S.-based Anti-Defamation League and himself a child survivor who had been hidden by a Polish Catholic family, wrote an opinion piece for the *Wall Street Journal*, labeling the litigation against the Swiss banks as undignified. He deplored the fact that this struggle for restitution from the private defendants had made money the "last sound bite" of the Holocaust. According to Foxman, this is a "desecration of the victims, a perversion of why the Nazis had a Final Solution, and too high a price to pay for justice we can never achieve."[2] In a later interview, he explained that the litigation "trivialized the Holocaust, skewed it and made it to be that Jews didn't die because they were Jews but because they had Monets, Swiss bank accounts, Stradivarius violins. The fact is that a tiny, tiny, tiny, tiny, tiny percentage had Swiss bank accounts." For the perpetrators, he argued, "this was a perk of the genocide, not the cause of it. I am worried that the last sound bite of the century not be that the Jews were killed for their gold teeth."[3]

In an even stronger tone, nationally syndicated columnist Charles Krauthammer published his widely distributed critique of the litigation that same month under the title "Reducing the Holocaust to Mere Dollars and Cents."[4] Krauthammer suggested that "it should be beneath the dignity of the Jewish people to accept [money], let alone to seek it." To him, the villains were the lawyers. He accused attorneys representing Holocaust victims of being "shysters" out to commit a "shakedown of Swiss banks, Austrian industry, [and] German auto makers." Krauthammer warned that "the scramble for money by lawyers could revive anti-Semitism [in Europe]."

Foxman and Krauthammer were not alone in their criticisms. A year after the two critiques appeared, literary critic and writer Leon Wieseltier published an angry piece in *The New Republic*, likewise disparaging lawyers and other activists who sought restitution for wartime financial losses:

> The authority of the philosophers and the historians is being usurped by the authority of the lawyers and the museum directors; and the subject, more and more, is money. . . . [I]n the matter of what transpired between 1933 and 1945 there will be no justice. There is no class action that is possible for this class.[5]

Wieseltier talked about telling his mother, a Holocaust survivor, to "spit at it" when she showed him the application she had received for benefits from the Swiss needy fund, the limited fund created by the Swiss before the Swiss bank settlement, which eventually paid $502 to each eligible "needy" survivor in the United States (see chapter 1). In a tone of moral outrage, Wieseltier exclaimed,

> I am sick of hearing about the fate of gold Holocaust assets. I am sick of hearing about those Schiele paintings. . . . I understand that the money that is the object of this litigation is "our" money, but what has litigation to do with sorrow? I really cannot bring myself to care about where the Monets of the martyrs will hang. I would rather grieve than sue. It seems more lucid.[6]

In September 2000, *Commentary* published a feature story by Gabriel Schoenfeld likewise blasting the movement: "Holocaust Reparations—A Growing Scandal."[7] A few years earlier in another article, Schoenfeld had taken on the entire academy of Holocaust historians, accusing them of diluting the significance of the genocidal tragedy inflicted by Nazi Germany by wallowing in unnecessary details surrounding the events.[8] This time, Schoenfeld went after the plaintiffs' lawyers, Jewish leaders, politicians, and other activists pursuing Holocaust restitution.

Unlike Foxman and Krauthammer, Schoenfeld did not question the legitimacy of seeking Holocaust restitution payments from the European wrongdoers. Rather, he expressed concern about how the movement was being conducted. Specifically, Schoenfeld accused the World Jewish Congress (WJC) and other Jewish community leaders involved in the restitution efforts of ignoring the concerns of individual survivors, their frequent lack of adherence to historical truth in making their accusations, and their failure to see the impact that the movement was having on other vital Jewish interests, primarily the security of Israel. Schoenfeld also agreed with Foxman and Krauthammer that the restitution campaign tended to promote anti-Semitism in Europe ("stoking the fires of anti-Semitism on the far Right" is the way Schoenfeld put it), where the position of Jews is not as secure as it is in the United States.

In 2001, as the movement was winding down and the focus was turning to how to distribute the billions of dollars being collected, Foxman's earlier worry that money and not human losses would become the "last sound bite" of the Holocaust was raised again, this time in Israel. Efraim Zuroff, director of the Israeli office of the Simon Wiesenthal Center, wrote in the *Jerusalem Post:* "I think this is a dangerous thing, that people are getting hung up on the financial aspects. This is not what the Shoah is about. People are going to think: Why are Jews so obsessed with the Holocaust? Because they want to give them a bill at the end of the day."[9] Referring to the billion-dollar settlements, Zuroff explained,

> These are deals that have far-reaching implications, way beyond the dollars and cents that are being obtained. And I'm not always so sure that the success in getting money will be translated into success in getting the idea across. The thing that scares me more than anything else is that people will really get the wrong idea about all of this, and will increasingly think of the economic aspects of this, which is not what this is all about. This is a secondary, or tertiary byproduct of the crimes of the Holocaust.[10]

The harshest critique, however, came a year earlier, in a book with the sensational title *The Holocaust Industry.*[11] The author, American academic Norman Finkelstein, accused Jewish organizations in the United States of using the Holocaust to perpetuate their existence. Angrily, he claimed that these organizations were extorting money from European concerns that were vulnerable to blackmail because they had dealt with the Nazis during the war. A self-avowed anti-Zionist, Finkelstein also branded the movement part of the campaign to justify what he considered to be illegitimate policies of the Israeli state.

Finkelstein's book was largely ignored in the United States but received extensive publicity in Europe. He was interviewed by the BBC when the book was launched in England, and the London-based daily *The Guardian* serialized portions of it. *The Economist* labeled it a "provocative new book," and it became a best-seller in many European countries, including Germany and Switzerland. Finkelstein was able to reap much of his publicity from the fact that, as Schoenfeld aptly pointed out, "first that he himself is Jewish and, second, as he repeats shamelessly at every opportunity, that he is the son of Jews who suffered in the Holocaust."[12]

I had an opportunity to observe Finkelstein in action in New York at the October 2001 Fordham Law School conference on the morality of Holocaust restitution. Taking umbrage for not being invited to speak,

Finkelstein flew in from Chicago and stood outside the conference door handing out a flyer entitled "ACADEMIC CONFERENCE OR HUCKSTER LOVEFEST? An Open Letter to Conference Attendees." In the flyer, he accused the conference organizers of not including among the speakers "a single dissident voice," which was inaccurate, since among the speakers that day were Count Otto Graf Lambsdorff, the chief German negotiator in the slave labor talks; an elderly Jewish survivor who used his time to point out the problems of distribution; and other speakers who wrestled with the difficult moral issues raised by Holocaust restitution. The conference organizers chose a format in which audience participation would be through written questions submitted to the panel speakers. Before his arrival, Finkelstein apparently had been informed of this, and his flyer called this format "a shocking departure from academic norms." He would have none of it. Setting himself down in the aisle seat of the second row, he appeared poised to strike at any moment. That moment came when Professor Burt Neuborne appeared on the late morning panel (I was on the same panel). Finkelstein chose to make Neuborne his main nemesis (His Web site, www.normanfinkelstein.com, labels Neuborne as the "lead blackmailer for the Holocaust Industry"). During the speakers' commentary section, Finkelstein suddenly yelled out to Neuborne to defend the $4.3 million attorney's fee awarded to him in the German slave labor settlement (see chapter 2). Neuborne replied, citing the fact that the fees awarded by the two arbitrators in the German settlement were substantially below the amounts usually granted by American judges to lawyers working on class action suits and that he, like most of the lawyers, was not seeking fees for his work in the Swiss bank settlement. But Finkelstein was not satisfied, continuing to rage at Neuborne until a security guard came to his side ready to usher him out of the room.

Other critics, in more responsible tones, are also raising important questions about the restitution movement. Does the survivors' acceptance of money demean the memory of the deceased victims? Does it allow the perpetrators or their heirs to claim that their debt has now been paid, their moral guilt extinguished? Such questions are being asked whenever monetary damages are sought from those responsible for genocide or other massive human rights abuses. What the critics fail to realize is that they are reinventing the wheel. In fact, the very same issues were hotly debated by an earlier generation of Jews at the end of World War II.

Moreover, besides criminal punishment, the only other remedy that can be imposed on a wrongdoer, even one committing or collaborating in genocide, is to make the wrongdoer pay. As Eizenstat asked in his rebuttal to Schoenfeld, why should victims of the Holocaust accept less?

> In every developed nation on earth, the accepted method of compensating the victim when a civil wrong has been committed, a contract breached, or labor extracted under duress is the award of money. Victims of negligent and reckless acts of all types, including radiation exposure, oil spills, medical malpractice, and smoking-related illness routinely bring lawsuits asking for money damages for themselves and for others who have suffered the same injuries. . . . Why should the victims [of the Holocaust] not have the same right to sue for justice as victims of other and lesser catastrophes?[24]

Richard Cohen, in the same *Washington Post* opinion column quoted earlier, appropriately entitled "The Money Matters," also answered criticism that seeking compensation and making the wrongdoers pay demeaned the memory of the Holocaust: "An immense calamity was committed in Europe, a moral calamity that left a black hole in the middle of the 20th century," he wrote.

> Money is the least of it. But money is part of it. Holocaust victims paid once for being Jewish. Now, in a way, they or their heirs are being asked to pay again—a virtual Jewish tax, which obliges them not to act as others would in the same situation. But in avoiding one stereotype, they adopt a worse one—perpetual victim.[25]

Commenting on his own motivations for entering the restitution battles, Israel Singer also talked about overturning a history of victimhood:

> I don't want to enter the next millennium as the victim of history. . . . Himmler said you have to kill all the Jews because if you don't kill them, their grandchildren will ask for their property back. The Nazis wanted to strip Jews of their human rights, their financial rights and their rights to life. It was an orderly progression. I want to return to them all their rights.[26]

Elie Wiesel went even further, indicating that a failure to deal with the monetary losses from the Holocaust would amount to a suppression of history. Quoted in a 1997 *Time* magazine article, he stated:

> If all the money in all the Swiss banks were turned over, it would not bring back the life of one Jewish child. But the money is a symbol. It is part of the story. If you suppress any part of the story, it comes back later, with force and vengeance.[27]

As for the danger that the restitution campaign would fuel anti-Semitism in Europe, it could be argued that anti-Semites seize every opportunity to promote their hate message. The monetary restitution campaign may have become a useful vehicle for them to portray Jews once again as avaricious and the demand for compensation as a plot to exploit the Holocaust for pecuniary gains. Fearing the wrath of the anti-Semites is never a good reason, however, to avoid doing what is right and just. Here, Foxman and his compatriots offered this rationale as a reason not to seek justice. As *Jerusalem Post* columnist Hirsh Goodman put it, "The anti-Semites looking for reasons to hate the Jews call us Shylocks. Who cares? . . . If those living in countries now under scrutiny feel uncomfortable, that is the price of living with thieves. As one [survivor has] said: 'I will not allow the anti-Semites to dictate our agenda.'"[28]

Eizenstat illustrated the anomalous and simply unjust result of using the fear of anti-Semitism as a reason not to seek restitution:

> Polish Catholics who worked in a Nazi munitions factory under terrible conditions . . . should be repaid for their forced labor, but the Jews who worked beside them should not. Why not? Because it is crass, unseemly—in short "bad for the Jews," as the saying goes—to seek compensation for Holocaust injuries; because doing so exacerbates anti-Semitism by reinforcing the age-old stereotypes that equates Jews with greed.[29]

Foxman, Krauthammer, and Schoenfeld, all supporters of Israel, would not tone down their support for Israel for fear of an anti-Semitic backlash.

Unfortunately, overlooked and underplayed in this debate is the fact that Jews are not the only beneficiaries of the restitution movement. While the Holocaust restitution movement is viewed as a campaign "by

Jews for Jews," the latter part of the formulation is simply inaccurate. Most of the beneficiaries of the restitution money are non-Jewish wartime survivors or their heirs. For example, 80 percent of the recipients of the DM 10 billion German slave labor settlement money are elderly Slavs from eastern Europe forced to work for Nazi Germany. Whatever the Jewish activists accomplished, they did it not just for Jews, but for all victims of World War II in Europe. This was not an unintended consequence of the campaign. From the outset, both the Jewish and non-Jewish lawyers and some of the Jewish organizations wanted to help all who were entitled to restitution from the corporate wrongdoers. Gypsies and other victim groups are benefiting today from the Swiss bank settlement. Elsa Iwanova, the lead slave labor plaintiff in the first slave labor suit filed, *Iwanova v. Ford*, is a former non-Jewish slave from Russia. A number of the heirs to prewar insurance policies or living family members receiving restituted Nazi-stolen art are not Jews. It is unfortunate that so little attention has been paid to this aspect of the restitution movement, which may account for the inaccurate impression in the eyes of most Europeans that this was all about Jews getting money from non-Jews.

Finally is there a danger that once the European governments and private firms make a settlement, they will see themselves as being absolved of all moral responsibility? As Roman Ziegler, a Jewish slave for the German firm Telefunken who now resides in Thornhill, Canada, worries, "I don't want them to wash their hands and say 'We're clean, we've paid.' Their consciences should remember forever."[30] To avoid this, as each monetary settlement was reached, Eizenstat, the Jewish leaders, and sometimes even the representatives of the defendants always hastened to add that no amount of money could atone for the horrors committed. Despite this standard disclaimer, an unspoken belief seemed to hover in the air after each settlement—at least in Europe—that since restitution has been made, the ledger has been balanced. Are the payments nothing more than hard-nosed business decisions by corporations that it is less expensive to pay than to fight the accusations and the attendant negative publicity that flows from them? The Swiss banks settled once they realized that their financial losses would be higher from the lost banking business in the United States than the billion-and-a-quarter dollars that they would have to pay to close the issue. Other European defendants likewise settled to prevent the suits and the attending claims from hampering their abilities to do business in the United States. As Naftali Bendavid explained in the Chicago *Tribune*,

> The lawsuits carry for some the whiff of extortion, as though companies and nations are buying off survivors to avoid bad publicity. No firm can stand to have its image associated with the Nazis, after all, and many have coughed up cash with the same apparent calculus that they might use to ward off some other PR disaster, like the pollution of a nearby river.[31]

But we have also seen that the European governments and private concerns did not get away with just shelling out money. Besides obtaining long-overdue restitution, the litigation also forced European governments to create various historical commissions that have unearthed new and valuable information about the insidious wrongs committed against their Jewish citizens during the war.

The first historical commission, created by Switzerland and headed by Swiss historian Jean-François Bergier, was charged with reevaluating the role of Switzerland during World War II.[32] In its 1999 and 2002 reports, the Bergier Commission criticized both the private Swiss banks and the Swiss government for their dealings with the Nazis and corroborated most of the allegations made in the Holocaust lawsuits filed in the United States. Without the accusing finger of litigation being pointed at the Swiss, as well as the historical findings issued by the Eizenstat report in the United States and the incriminating evidence found by historians working in conjunction with the plaintiffs' lawyers and Jewish groups, the Swiss never would have reexamined their wartime history. In the wake of the Holocaust restitution campaign, the Swiss government in 1998 also commissioned a study of anti-Semitism in Switzerland, and the body conducting the study made specific recommendations to combat it.[33] Seeking to justify his criticism of the campaign to get the Swiss to recognize their wartime misdeeds and make recompense, Abraham Foxman asserted, "I don't care what they say, Switzerland hasn't done a thing since they wrote the check. They haven't taught their people; they haven't invested in tolerance or in fighting anti-Semitism."[34] This discussion shows that Foxman is wrong.

Switzerland is not the only country to reexamine its wartime history as a consequence of the Holocaust restitution litigation. The historical commission created by France, headed by the former cabinet minister and Resistance hero Jean Mattéoli, undertook to study the long-suppressed record of the looting of Jews' assets in wartime France.[35] While the Mattéoli Commission was created before the American litigation against the French banks began, the pressure of the litigation forced the commission to conduct a more thorough study than it would have done otherwise.

Sweden, like Switzerland, also a wartime neutral, created a commission in 1997 to determine the fate of Jewish assets that made their way to Sweden in the prewar and war years. In March 1999, the commission submitted its final report.[36] To its surprise, the commission found that Sweden's wartime role as a haven for Jewish assets and as a possible but unintended accomplice to the Nazi atrocities had never before been examined in Sweden. The commission called for further research in three areas: (1) whether Sweden's trade with Nazi Germany prolonged the war and the persecution of the Jews, (2) the relation of Swedish industry to Jews and Jewish businesses at the time of the Nazi persecutions, and (3) the persecution in wartime Europe of the non-Jewish victims of Nazi Germany.

An Italian government commission created in 1998 issued its final report in mid-2001. It determined that both Italian Fascists and Nazis systematically plundered Jewish assets in Italy. The then Italian premier, Guiliano Amato, stated that the report's findings left him "breathless."[37]

These are a few examples of the historical reexaminations conducted by various countries in the shadow of the Holocaust restitution movement. In all, almost fifty governments created either commissions of inquiry or other, less formal governmental historical bodies in the aftermath of the Holocaust restitution campaign in order to research and publish new studies of their wartime conduct.[38]

Two international conferences held during the Holocaust restitution campaign dealt with wartime monetary issues: the London conference on Holocaust assets in December 1997, which focused on tracing gold looted from the victims; and the Washington conference held a year later, at which delegates from forty-five countries and thirteen nongovernmental organizations (NGOs) met at the State Department for four days to discuss the Holocaust restitution and to draft the so-called Washington principles concerning art stolen by the Nazis. The Washington conference also included a one-day session at the U.S. Holocaust Memorial Museum on Holocaust education. This initiative was followed up with the first-ever international conference of its kind, held in January 2000 in Stockholm, at which prime ministers and education ministers from forty-three countries gathered to discuss how to teach the younger generation the lessons of the Holocaust.

Finally, with the newly discovered historical facts has come a new round of mea culpas. As Israel Singer summed it up:

> After 55 years, President Johannes Rau of Germany wrote letters of forgiveness to every Holocaust survivor that benefited from the Slave Labor agreement. Chancellor Franz Vranitzky spoke in the Knesset putting to rest once and for all the canard that Austria was the first victim of Nazism rather than its first willing accomplice. And French president Jacques Chirac realized that not all of France was in the resistance with Charles de Gaulle. . . . These were the achievements of the struggle for moral and material restitution in the period of the 1990's.[39]

These historical reexaminations are not being limited to governments. Private companies, against whom similar accusations have been made, are likewise putting Holocaust historians on retainer and, for the first time ever, opening up some of their wartime files for inspection. As reported in 1999 by the *New York Times*, "the lawsuits have also created a mini-boom for . . . [World War II-era] historians and research [scholars]."[40] I noted that many of the reports commissioned by the companies have been nothing more than glorified public relations exercises, with the hired historians being given access only to limited documents in the companies' archives and having little or no say on the final product. The final product is then trumpeted by the company to justify, or at least minimize, its wartime activities. As a Holocaust historian related to me with bitter irony after reviewing one such report, "These are the happiest group of slave laborers I have ever seen." While much more needs to be done, even these commissioned reports provide new, and sometimes valuable, information about the role played by private companies during the war.

Some of the reports have been historical blockbusters. Chapter 1 discussed the Volcker Committee created by the Swiss Bankers Association in the aftermath of accusations about the wartime role of the Swiss banks. The examination conducted by the Swiss banks of its dormant accounts proved to be the most costly audit in history. By mid-2002, the

Swiss banks paid out to four leading accounting firms (Arthur Andersen, KMPG, Price Waterhouse, and Coopers & Lybrand) nearly $700 million to track down the wartime dormant accounts of Holocaust victims. As critics point out, this amount is likely to exceed the actual payouts made to dormant account claimants. The three-year investigation required the hiring of more than six hundred forensic accountants and the return to service of retired Swiss accountants, because they were the only ones capable of understanding old German script. All of this would have been unnecessary if the Swiss banks had confronted the problem of dormant accounts immediately after the war instead of burying it.

Chapters 2 and 3 discussed the private reports commissioned by various German companies to fill in the blanks in their wartime histories, among them Deutsche Bank, Allianz A.G., and Bertlesmann. As with the Swiss banks, the German concerns were forced to do this because of the litigation. The London-based *Guardian* wryly noted that "the words 'independent critical review' have become a mantra for German companies attempting to cope with the past. . . . Constructive self-criticism has in itself become something of a growth industry in Germany"[41] as a consequence of the Holocaust restitution litigation.

AMERICAN INDUSTRY AND THE RESTITUTION MOVEMENT

The Holocaust restitution campaign also caught the United States in its net. As accusations of wartime wrongdoing began to be made against various European concerns, the role of the U.S. government and American firms during the war was receiving greater scrutiny. In April 1998, Senator Alfonse D'Amato introduced legislation creating the Presidential Advisory Commission on Holocaust Assets in the United States, whose job would be to ferret out Nazi-stolen loot that may have gotten into U.S. government hands in the aftermath of the war. President Clinton signed the legislation and in December 1998 appointed Edgar Bronfman to chair the twelve-member body. In proposing the U.S. Holocaust Assets Commission, D'Amato remarked:

> While we have sought answers from Switzerland and other nations
> on the disposition of dormant accounts and Nazi gold, we have not
> pursued the issue here in the United States. . . . The United States has

a moral responsibility to address the same issues to which we have sought answers from Switzerland and other nations of Europe. The spirit of American decency demands no less.

The commission issued its final report in December 2000,[42] which included a study of the plunder by American troops of a train loaded with gold, artworks, and other valuables stolen from the Hungarian Jews by the Nazis. The Allies captured the train on May 16, 1945, a week after V-E Day. According to the report, in a notable exception to the generally good effort of American troops to restore property to its rightful owners, both high-ranking U.S. Army officers and lower-level personnel may have helped themselves to these valuables rather than returning them to the Hungarian Holocaust survivors or the postwar Hungarian Jewish community.[43]

In May 2001, a group of Holocaust survivors from Hungary filed suit in the United States, seeking restitution for the American military's complicity in the so-called Hungarian gold theft.[44] According to one plaintiff's attorney, "This is the first case of its type—a class action brought on behalf of Holocaust survivors that charges the U.S. government with improperly disposing of assets."[45]

Earlier that year, IBM was sued for its wartime dealings with the Nazis after the publication of a sensational study by Edwin Black, *IBM and the Holocaust*,[46] examining IBM's role in supplying the Nazis with custom-made IBM-created punch cards and tabulating machines (precursors of modern computers). According to Black, the IBM equipment enabled the Nazis to identify and categorize their Jewish victims. Black's two-year investigation of IBM's involvement with the Nazis began with a visit in 1993 to the United States Holocaust Memorial Museum with his Holocaust survivor parents. There, on exhibit was an IBM Hollerith D-11 sorting machine used in 1933 by the Nazis to conduct a national census that first identified the Jews living in Germany. The IBM suit, which, like the Ford litigation discussed in chapter 2, named both the parent company and IBM's German subsidiary as defendants, was filed by the Hausfeld team of lawyers. The lawyers subsequently were forced to drop the suit after German companies threatened to scuttle the German slave labor settlement if the IBM litigation continued. To date, Hausfeld has not reinstated his suit. However, in mid-2001 a group of Roma (Gypsies) filed suit against IBM in Switzerland, where the company maintains its European headquarters, claiming that its machines helped Adolf Hitler identify and send 600,000 Roma to their deaths.

In 2002, Black issued an updated version of his book.[47] In the new volume, he provides new evidence showing that IBM's New York headquarters directly controlled the subsidiary in Nazi-occupied Poland. While the connection between IBM's U.S. headquarters and its operations in wartime Europe was less evident in the first edition, Black and his researchers claim to have uncovered additional information proving IBM's knowledge of its European subsidiaries and their connection to these activities. For example, Black says that during the war a senior IBM representative in the United States traveled to Europe to meet with executives there and arrange for IBM machines to be leased in Poland to "calculate exactly how many Jews should be emptied out of the ghettos each day" and to transport them efficiently on railways leading to the camps. According to Black, after the Nazis invaded Poland in September 1939, IBM New York established a special subsidiary, Watson Business Machines (named after the then president of IBM, Thomas Watson), in Poland for the sole purpose of servicing the Nazi authorities there. Black also writes that after the war, "IBM recovered all its Polish profits and machines."[48]

IBM did not directly dispute Black's allegations but instead attacked his methodology. According to an IBM spokesperson, "The research behind the book and the conclusions drawn have been questioned."[49] Added the representative, "IBM looks to historians and other experts to evaluate the book. The company has said that if any of the allegations prove to be true, we would be the first to condemn any actions that assisted the Nazi regime."[50]

While the new revelations about IBM's wartime role may be shocking, just as serious is its failure both to acknowledge its past and to remedy the injustice. In response to the latest furor, IBM stated that in 1999 it turned over records connected to its German subsidiary to New York University. Black, however, maintains that IBM did not hand over all of its World War II–related records. Moreover, unlike some German companies confronted with their wartime past, IBM has not commissioned historians to produce an independent historical study of its dealings with the Nazis. In effect, IBM has failed to provide the data to "historians and other experts" to confirm or discredit what Black and his team have been able to piece together through their own research.

The previous chapters also discussed the lawsuits against the

American financial concerns Chase Manhattan and J. P. Morgan for their theft of Jews' assets in wartime France, where these banks had branches, and against the Ford Motor Company for the use of slave laborers by its German subsidiary. Accusations have also been made against General Motors, which, through its German subsidiary Opel A.G., produced the "Blitz" truck used by the Nazis for its "blitzkrieg" attacks. In late 1998, GM became the first American company to allow Holocaust historians to examine its wartime records. GM hired Yale University historian Henry Turner to research its activities in Germany during World War II. According to the then chairman of GM, John F. Smith, "Dr. Turner's work will help us achieve our goal of a complete accounting of GM's and Opel's activities during World War II and to assess our responsibilities."[51] While Opel A.G. was one of the companies contributing to the German fund for Nazi slave laborers, Turner has yet to release his study of the GM/Opel activities in Nazi Europe.

Another company receiving greater scrutiny of its corporate activities is the American photography giant Eastman Kodak. An investigative report in *The Nation*, published in 2001, revealed U.S. archival documents confirming that subsidiaries of Kodak traded with Nazi Germany after the United States entered the war.[52] Apparently, American officials did not recommend that Kodak halt its business but instead allowed it to continue in order to preserve its market position. At its plant in Stuttgart, Germany, Kodak used at least eighty slave laborers and, at its Berlin-Kopenick factory, more than two hundred.[53] In the German settlement, Kodak contributed $50,000 to the German fund for victims of forced labor.[54] Yet after making its contribution, a Kodak spokesman stated, "I have every confidence that Kodak did not do business with any enemy country during the war and that it cooperated fully with U.S. government regulations and sanctions. At no time was Kodak in violation of any proscriptions from the U.S. or U.K. war offices."[55]

On May 1, 2000, amid the Holocaust restitution battles, Eizenstat announced a plan by American companies to establish a fund for Holocaust survivors.[56] The fund would be set up by the U.S. Chamber of Commerce, which, like the German Foundation, would solicit voluntary donations from American companies. The details of the fund were still unclear; it would assist needy Holocaust survivors as well as victims of other tragedies, including natural disasters. How the two would go together was never explained. Nevertheless, at a press conference, Eizenstat proudly announced:

The U.S. Chamber is again showing its leadership and foresight by moving ahead with the establishment of a humanitarian fund of a Center for Corporate Citizenship and a special institution to create a fund for a variety of humanitarian purposes: to assist in natural disaster relief and to relieve the suffering of survivors of one of the greatest human disasters of our time, the Holocaust, and the travails of slave and forced laborers.[57]

Unfortunately, the U.S. Chamber of Commerce Holocaust Fund went nowhere. It failed to receive a single contribution, or even a pledge, for the first eighteen moths of its existence.[58] In December 2001, Ford made the first pledge to donate $2 million.[59] Eizenstat responded that he hoped this move would inspire other U.S. corporations to make their own donations.[60] But nothing happened. My own inquiries led to only vague answers. Apparently, there is now talk of using the fund for aging American POWs who have, to date, been unsuccessful in obtaining compensation for their slave labor at private Japanese companies during the war (see chapter 8) or even for victims of natural disasters.

By most accounts, the U.S. Holocaust Assets Commission headed by Bronfman also was a failure. After spending $2.7 million, the commission failed to meet even its primary goal: assembling a database of Holocaust-era assets still in the United States. Moreover, given its limited mandate to look at only the activities of the federal government and thus not the activities of American industry during the war, the commission could not ask the same questions about American corporate complicity with the Nazis that similar government-created historical commissions had asked in Europe.

Nevertheless, even if only to a limited extent, the litigation against European companies has forced American companies to confront their own questionable wartime dealings. The Holocaust restitution movement, which originated in the United States to determine wartime financial misfeasance in Europe, now encompasses both the U.S. government and corporate America. The finger of blame that was first pointed from the United States to Europe is now being pointed back at us. Unfortunately, there seems to be a double standard here. The demands that we have made on European governments and corporations about honestly confronting and documenting their wartime financial dealings and other activities are not being followed in the United States.

One surprising consequence of the Holocaust restitution campaign is that even Israel has not been immune from the controversy. In the face of accusations that Israeli banks, like the Swiss banks, are holding dormant funds deposited in prewar Palestine by European Jews who perished during the war, the Israeli Knesset created in April 2001 a commission of inquiry to search for such funds. Estimates have placed the value of these accounts in Israeli banks at $40 million. The commission will also search Israeli property records to determine which landholdings may have belonged to Holocaust victims and also European Zionists who purchased land in Palestine and then perished in the Holocaust. The Israeli custodian-general estimates the value of this unclaimed land at a minimum of $90 million. The commission chair stated that the goal of the one-year probe is to "arrive at the truth about the assets in Israel of Holocaust victims."

Truth is what Holocaust survivors want most of all—not only so that their losses and suffering are acknowledged and recognized while they are still alive, but also so that what happened to them never happens again. Quoting again Roman Kent: "We survivors have never talked just in terms of dollars and cents; we have spoken primarily of justice, and of the need for Holocaust education. Only by exposing the historical facts, and educating the next generations, can we avoid a repetition of the past."[61]

The most significant legacy of the Holocaust restitution litigation may be that it has now become a model for dealing with injustices stemming from other historical wrongs. When I hear Holocaust survivors or heirs complaining about the imperfect results achieved by the campaign for Holocaust restitution, I urge them to speak to still-living survivors of other historical injustices or their heirs—whether aging American POWs and civilians used as slaves by private Japanese companies during World War II, the sex slaves (so-called comfort women) of the Japanese Imperial Army, or African Americans seeking an official apology from the United States for slavery. These people would very much like to be in the shoes of the Holocaust claimants. The ongoing struggle of these victims and their representatives is to obtain the results achieved by the Holocaust restitution campaign: some form of monetary compensation coupled with historical recognition and apology. The greatest tribute to the Holocaust restitution movement is that it is now being emulated worldwide.

8

The Post–Holocaust Restitution Era

Holocaust Restitution As a Model
for Addressing Other Historical Injustices

ONE OF THE ENDURING LEGACIES of the Holocaust restitution movement is the precedent it has set for addressing other injustices of the past. In determining the costs and benefits of the Holocaust restitution campaign, we should not consider just the movement's direct impact on Holocaust survivors and their heirs. We should also consider the impact of Holocaust restitution on other movements to right other historical wrongs. Other campaigns—among them, POW and civilian claims against Japanese companies that used slave labor during the war, heirs of victims of the Armenian genocide, and the campaign for restitution for descendants of African American slaves—were launched as a direct outgrowth of the Holocaust litigation, inspired by its successes and sometimes led by the same lawyers. Only by considering these campaigns can the full scope of the movement's legacy be assessed.

SLAVE LABOR CLAIMS AGAINST JAPANESE COMPANIES

The successful suits for Holocaust restitution led formerly captured soldiers and civilians to file claims against Japanese corporations for their use of slave labor during World War II. Without a doubt, the claims against the Japanese multinationals are a direct result of the litigation previously brought against their European counterparts. Aging victims of Japan's wartime activities began filing their lawsuits in American courts only after the Holocaust litigation was successful. Their lawyers are the same as those who prosecuted the Holocaust restitution suits: Edward Fagan and Robert Swift, Michael Hausfeld and Melvyn Weiss (though no longer working with each other), and Morris Ratner of Lieff Cabraser, who is still aligned with Hausfeld. New legal faces include Russ Herman and David Casey, personal injury attorneys who made their name in tobacco litigation.

More than 36,000 American soldiers became Japanese prisoners of war during World War II, and the Japanese also captured nearly 14,000 American civilians.[1] Approximately 25,000 American prisoners were then shipped to Japan and Japan-occupied Asia to work as slave laborers for private Japanese companies. These companies are now among the largest corporate entities in the world: Mitsubishi, Mitsui, Nippon Steel, Kawasaki Heavy Industries, and at least forty others. In addition, the Japanese captured tens of thousands of British, Canadian, Australian, and New Zealand soldiers, who were sent to work for Japanese industry, as well as local Chinese, Korean, Vietnamese, and Philippine civilians who were also used as slaves by these companies.

The litigation against private Japanese industry stemming from these wartime acts began quietly and without much fanfare. In July 1999, while the slave labor suits against the German companies were in full swing, former American POW Ralph Levenberg, seventy-eight years old, filed suit seeking compensation and other damages for being a slave of Japan's Nippon Shary Ltd.,[2] one of Japan's biggest producers of railroad cars. He was represented by a small law firm in San Francisco, where the elderly American veteran resides, and the suit was filed in federal court in San Francisco.

The media paid little attention to the suit at the time. Levenberg's lawyers were not the media-savvy attorneys from the Holocaust restitution arena, or the tobacco lawyers who later came to dominate the litigation. The only significant coverage was an article in *Time Asia* entitled "Striking Back at Japan, Inc." The story noted in passing the parallel to the ongoing slave labor litigation against German industry, commenting that "Imperial Japan Inc.'s wartime track record is just as bad as corporate Germany's."[3]

Other lawsuits by POWs soon followed, filed in various jurisdictions throughout the United States. For maximum publicity, some of the latter suits were filed on December 7, 2000, to coincide with Pearl Harbor Day. These suits received extensive media attention, with major media outlets featuring stories profiling the aging POWs who showed up at press conferences wearing their military insignia. Press conferences were held outside the courthouses where the suits were filed. One of the "Pearl Harbor Day" suits was filed by Fagan and Swift, and Fagan, with his flair for publicity, did one better: he held his press conference outside the Japanese consulate in Los Angeles, where his suit was filed, and demanded entrance to the consulate to personally deliver the papers to Japan's consul general. The media took notice: *Dateline NBC* and *20/20*, in the footsteps of their earlier stories about Holocaust survivors and their restitution claims, likewise profiled these suits.

Eventually, all such litigation gravitated to California because of a state law enacted in July 1999. The California statute permits the filing of a suit by a "prisoner-of-war of the Nazi regime, its allies or sympathisers" to "recover compensation for labor performed as a Second World War slave victim . . . from any entity or successor in interest thereof, for whom that labor was performed."[4] Moreover, the statute extends the limitations period for filing such lawsuits until 2010.

As discussed in chapter 2, the California statute was part of the political campaign being conducted by local politicians to get the German companies being sued for wartime slave labor to come to the bargaining table. The California legislature passed the statute at a time when negotiations with the German companies were stalled. The statute's primary and most immediate goal was to allow these lawsuits to proceed in California.

This legislation had a curious history, which actually began with William Shernoff and Lisa Stern, the Holocaust insurance lawyers who were conducting an aggressive campaign against Italy's Generali Insurance for Holocaust-era insurance claims. Shernoff and Stern wrote and lobbied successfully in Sacramento for the passage of the HVIA (the Holocaust Victim Insurance Act), which extended the limitations period to 2010 for filing suits in California against European insurers doing business in the state. They then used the law to ram their suits down the throat of Generali, forcing the Italian insurer to settle the litigation.

Shernoff and Stern now decided to use the same tactic against the German companies, against whom they had recently filed a slave labor suit. They recruited California State Senator Tom Hayden, of the Chicago 7 trial fame (he had been a defendant), to carry the bill. Over the years, Hayden had transformed himself into a successful politician, representing a liberal district in West Los Angeles. Still always ready to help the underdog, the non-Jewish politician with Irish roots (as he liked to remind his audiences) took up the cause of the aging Jewish survivors introduced to him by Shernoff and Stern.

I first met Hayden at a briefing at Bet Tzedek Legal Services, the Jewish-based legal aid organization in Los Angeles that helped Holocaust survivors apply for benefits from Germany. Hayden had recently introduced the "slave labor" bill (Senate Bill [SB] 1245) in the California legislature. The bill's official summary stated its purpose:

> Thousands of elderly California residents are survivors of slave labor exploitation carried out by the Nazis during the Holocaust, living victims of the "real profiteers" of Hitler's Third Reich. These slave laborers and their heirs are entitled to seek just compensation from their oppressors. SB 1245 would allow for victims to attempt to seek such compensation.[5]

At the briefing, Hayden spoke about how the bill would help Bet Tzedek's clients go after their former German masters, the large German multinationals that did extensive business in California.

I had read about Levenberg's suit, and after our meeting, I wrote to Hayden suggesting that he not forget the wartime slaves of the Japanese companies. I also mentioned my concern to Lisa Stern. Thereafter, the bill was amended to include not only former slaves of private companies in Nazi Germany but also the World War II slaves of the Nazi regime's "allies or sympathisers," meaning, of course, Japan (if Italian firms during Mussolini's rule had used slave labor, they, of course, also could be sued under the California law). To make sure there would be no question that private Japanese corporations would be liable to the same extent as German firms, the final working of the bill stated that compensation would be recoverable "for labor performed as a Second World War slave victim . . . from *any* entity or successor in interest thereof, for whom that labor was performed" (emphasis added).

Ironically, SB 1245, which, when enacted, became California Code of Civil Procedure (CCP) 354.6 (with its predecessor, HVIA, being CCP 354.5), was never used for its original purpose. Shortly after its enactment, the German companies entered into an all-inclusive settlement of the claims against them, rendering the law moot, at least for the German slave labor litigation. As a result, every use of the statute has been by victims of the Pacific conflict in suits against Japanese private companies.

In November 1999, I held a follow-up forum to the March 1998 conference, "Nazi Gold," focusing this time on the outstanding Japanese claims. Aging American POWs vividly related to the audience how they had been wartime slaves of Japanese industry, laboring for, among others, such companies as Mitsui, Mitsubishi, and Kawasaki, all household company names in America today. To my mind, there was a complete moral equivalency between the claims for compensation made by Holocaust survivors and other slaves of German multinationals and the claims of these American and Allied POWs and civilians who had worked for Japanese private firms. Taking to heart Eizenstat's remark, quoted in the last chapter, about the inequity of seeking compensation for a non-Jewish slave of the Germans but foregoing the same claim for a Jewish slave working next to the non-Jew, I saw the same inequity in denying compensation to military or civilian prisoners of the Japanese corporations. These slave laborers were working at the same time across the Pacific Ocean in a mine owned by Mitsui or a factory owned by Mitsubishi (to use actual examples).

While I declined to join any of the Holocaust restitution suits as a lawyer (the subject was too close to home), after the conference I offered to help the lawyers who appeared at Whittier Law School that day in filing their suits against the Japanese companies. At present, while not a counsel of record in any of the cases, I am advising plaintiffs' counsels in this litigation. Eventually, victims of Japanese industry's slave labor filed more than two dozen lawsuits against the corporations that had exploited them during the war.[6] The plaintiffs include American POWs, Allied POWs, and civilians, both U.S. citizens and foreign nationals. As with the Holocaust restitution litigation, all the companies sued do extensive business in the United States, usually through wholly owned American subsidiaries. To cite just one example, mentioned by Linda Goetz Holmes in her study of the issue,

> Kawasaki Heavy Industries used at least 250 American POWs for slave labor at its shipyard in Kobe. . . . The company was awarded a $190 million contract in December 1998 by the Metropolitan Transit Authority of New York to build 100 new subway cars. Kawasaki was awarded even larger contracts by transportation departments in Maryland and Boston, but our ex-POWs never got a dime from their former employer.[7]

The lawsuits were being filed in various jurisdictions throughout the United States. To avoid inconsistent rulings, a centralized federal judicial panel in Washington, D.C., in June 2000 consolidated the various lawsuits before Judge Vaughn Walker, the San Francisco federal judge presiding over the *Levenberg* case, the first Japanese slave labor lawsuit.

Unfortunately, Judge Walker did not take kindly to this litigation, eventually dismissing all the suits. On September 21, 2000, he granted the motion of the Japanese companies to dismiss the lawsuits filed by American POWs and Allied POWs.[8] The basis of his dismissal was the Treaty of Peace signed by Japan and its former enemies in 1951. (The treaty formally ended the conflict and aimed to resolve outstanding issues between defeated Japan and the victorious powers.) Judge Walker cited article 14(b) of the peace treaty:

> Except as otherwise provided in the present Treaty, the Allied Powers waive all reparations claims of the Allied Powers, other claims of the Allied Powers and their nationals arising out of any actions taken by Japan and its nationals in the course of the prosecution of the war, and claims of the Allied Powers for direct military costs of occupation.[9]

Relying on this language, the judge held that the United States and its Allies had waived, on behalf of itself and its nationals, all claims arising out of actions taken by Japan and its nationals (including private Japanese corporations) during the war.

Judge Walker also dismissed the claims of the British, Australian, and New Zealand POWs, since they came from nations that were signatories to the 1951 treaty. In issuing his ruling, the judge left open the claims of Chinese, Filipino, and Korean civilian internees, since "these plaintiffs are not citizens of countries that are signatories of the 1951 Peace Treaty."[10] Walker then asked the parties to file supplemental briefs on these claims. After receiving the briefs in September 2001, he dismissed these claims as well. For the Filipino plaintiffs, the court found that their claims were indeed covered by the 1951 treaty, since the Philippines ratified it in 1956.

For the plaintiffs from the nonsignatory states, Judge Walker found other reasons to dismiss their claims. In a forty-four-page opinion, he held that the California law, CCP 354.6, was unconstitutional. According to Judge Walker, the state law amounted to an infringement on the powers of the federal government to conduct foreign policy. Without the aid of the California law, which extended the statute of limitations to 2010, the claims, stemming from activities conducted by the Japanese companies during World War II, were time barred.[11]

Critical to the court's rulings was the appearance of the U.S. government in the litigation. In a Statement of Interest filed with the court, the United States agreed with the Japanese corporate defendants' position that the language of the peace treaty barred claims of the Allied POWs. In his rulings, Judge Walker emphasized the "significant weight" given to the U.S. government's Statement of Interest.[12]

The position taken by the U.S. government in the Japanese litigation differed significantly from the position it took in the Holocaust litigation. In the Holocaust slave labor litigation, the U.S. government was specifically asked for its position regarding the impact of the various postwar treaties with Germany on the slave labor litigation. In those cases, the government did not file a Statement of Interest on behalf of the private German companies. Rather, it only advised the court that negotiations regarding the creation of a German foundation to compensate the former slave laborers were under way with the aim of fully resolving such claims. The U.S. government continued to play an active role as a party to the German slave labor negotiations, even after the courts dismissed the slave labor cases as precluded by the postwar German treaties (see chapter 2). Similarly, in the French bank litigation, the U.S. government could have intervened in the litigation but did not, allowing the court process to move forward without its influence. For the Japanese slave labor claims, however, the U.S. government not only sided with the Japanese companies but, to date, has failed to press Japan and its private industries to recognize the same type of claims that it forced both Germany and its private industries and France and its banks to resolve.

On the eve of his departure from the U.S. government, Eizenstat was asked for his views on the Japanese slave labor litigation. According to the *New York Times,* he replied that "one of his regrets" was his inability to get Japan to make a similar commitment to Chinese, Koreans, and others whose assets had been seized or who had been forced into slave labor. "The 1951 treaty with Japan clearly foreclosed a lot of options to seek redress," he was quoted as saying. "In the end we never heard back from the Japanese government or companies."[13] Eizenstat, however, did not explain why he continued negotiating with Germany and its industries even after the U.S. courts held that the postwar

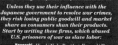

Ad placed in the *New York Times* by the Rape of Nanking Redress Coalition calling for compensation from Japanese companies for wartime slave labor.
Courtesy of Rape of Nanking Redress Coalition, ad produced by Public Media Center.

treaties with Germany also precluded the claims of the slave laborers from Nazi-occupied Europe.

The Bush administration likewise continued to actively oppose the Japanese slave labor claims. In a *New York Times* editorial, Iris Chang, author of a treatise on Japanese wartime atrocities committed during the rape of Nanking,[14] severely criticized the U.S. government's position:

> The decision of the Bush administration to wage a legal fight against its own veterans is short-sighted as well as morally insupportable. A sustained assault against terrorism will require men and women who believe their country and their commander in chief stand behind them. Americans should be ashamed that the government is now prepared to sacrifice the interests of a previous generation of soldiers in order to woo their former enemy. Our leaders in Washington must not be permitted to sell out the men who gave so much to fight for freedom. Otherwise, what shall live in infamy will be not only Pearl Harbor and September 11, but this unjust betrayal. If we are to have another "greatest generation" we must duly honor the rights of the first one.[15]

Concerned with the disparity in the U.S. government's treatment of the German restitution and the Japanese restitution claims, the Senate Judiciary Committee held a hearing in June 2000 on the matter.[16] At the hearing, the State Department continued to maintain that the 1951 peace treaty barred the POWs' claims. At the urging of the committee chairman, Senator Orrin Hatch, the State Department promised to reevaluate the government's position. The promise turned out to be a ploy. Subsequently, the U.S. government filed two more Statements of Interest, urging that cases filed by (1) alien civilians against private Japanese companies similar to the claims of the allied POWs[17] and (2) former sex slaves of the wartime Japanese army—the so-called comfort women—also be dismissed.[18] The second suit was filed by Hausfeld and Lieff, Cabraser. In October 2001, the federal district court in Washington, D.C., like Judge Walker in San Francisco, followed the government's recommendation and dismissed Hausfeld's and Lieff Cabraser's lawsuit filed by the "comfort women" against Japan. All the cases are now on appeal.

In an article in the *Berkeley Journal of International Law*,[19] I explained the legal reasons why Judge Walker was wrong in dismissing the cases.

I showed that although the waiver language of article 14(b) may appear broad, it is not clear that it in fact bars the type of damages sought in the Japanese litigation: private POWs' and civilians' claims against private Japanese companies for uncompensated labor.

To summarize my legal position, the first clause of article 14(b) speaks of a waiver of "reparations," but the POW and civilian victims are not seeking reparations from the Japanese companies, since reparations are government-to-government payments for damages during war, and not claims for private compensation. I also point out that the second clause of article 14(b), which speaks of a waiver of "other claims of the Allied Powers *and their nationals* arising out of any actions taken by Japan *and its nationals in the course of the prosecution of the war*," also contains an important qualifier. While appearing to extinguish the individual claims of U.S. nationals and the nationals of U.S. allies (the plaintiffs in these suits) against the nationals of Japan (the private Japanese corporations named as defendants), not all claims for any wartime actions taken by Japanese nationals are waived. Rather, only those wartime "actions taken . . . in the course of the prosecution of the war." The latter, while never defined in the peace treaty, can reasonably be interpreted to exclude actions taken by private Japanese companies for profit (that is, the use of unpaid slave labor), since profit-making activities are not "actions taken . . . in the course of the prosecution of the war." Private, profit-making enterprises do not prosecute war; governments do. In fact, in a postwar appeal of a treason conviction of a dual U.S.-Japanese national who worked for a Japanese mining company—and brutally abused U.S. POWs who worked there—the U.S. Supreme Court opined that Japanese companies during the war should be viewed as nothing more than private, profit-making ventures.[20]

Finally, article 26 of the treaty states that if Japan ever entered into a war claims settlement agreement with any other country that provided terms more beneficial than those extended to the Allied Power signatories to the peace treaty, then those more favorable terms would have to be extended to the Allied Powers.[21] In fact, Japan entered into subsequent bilateral treaties with Sweden, Spain, Burma, Denmark, the Netherlands, and Russia, in which it agreed to pay compensation to the nationals of those countries. Therefore, even if article 14(b) of the peace treaty is interpreted so as to bar compensation claims by nationals of the Allied Power signatories against Japan or its nationals, that bar was by implication lifted, pursuant to article 26, when Japan agreed to make payments to the nationals of other countries under the subsequent peace treaties it signed.

In his opinion, Judge Walker held that article 26's "more favorable treatment" clause cannot be asserted by private individuals. Rather, since it is part of a treaty entered into between Japan and the Allied signatory nations, the provision can be asserted against Japan only by a signatory nation. With this in mind and given the strong legal arguments in favor of allowing restitution, in March 2001 a bill was introduced in Congress specifically for that purpose.[22] The bill, with more than forty cosponsors, is winding its way through Congress. If the bill passes, it remains unclear, however, what the Bush administration's position will be on it.

As this discussion demonstrates, the restitution movement against the Japanese companies (and Japan) is not achieving the same favorable results as those achieved in the restitution movement against the European companies for their wartime activities. No doubt, the hostile position taken by both the Clinton and Bush administrations to these Japanese claims, unlike those taken by the U.S. government to the Holocaust restitution claims, has been the key difference. While millions of aging Jewish and non-Jewish survivors, both in the United States and abroad, are finally receiving some measure of justice for the wrongs committed against them during World War II by European enterprises, the aging POWs and civilians who suffered at the hands of Japanese industry are being denied the same treatment.

INSURANCE CLAIMS FROM THE ARMENIAN GENOCIDE

While the Japanese slave labor claims have not, to date, done well in court, another historical claim was filed in the aftermath of the Holocaust restitution litigation and used that litigation as a model: insurance claims arising out of the Armenian genocide. It has been more successful. In turn, the Armenian genocide litigation has now created its own legacy, pushing back the time line for when historical wrongs can be recognized by the U.S. justice system by another fifty years, to the beginning of the twentieth century.

The Ottoman Empire was a multiethnic state with a sizable non-Muslim population of mostly Armenian, Greek, and Assyrian Christians as well as prosperous Jewish communities. In the late nineteenth century, the Ottoman government adopted an Islamic state policy and increased the pressure on its non-Muslim subjects. Between 1894 and 1896, this policy culminated in the infamous Armenian massacres. Tens of thousands of Armenians, mostly men, were ruthlessly slaughtered. The ensuing misery induced the ravished Armenian communities to look for ways to prepare for similar future occurrences. In this context, life insurance seemed to be at least a partial solution to the problem. European and American insurance companies were already active in the Ottoman Empire and quickly grasped the emerging business opportunity. The New York Life Insurance Company, for instance, specifically targeted the empire's Armenian population through Armenian-language ads and sales agents, even in remote provincial centers. Thousands of Armenians bought life insurance from these companies. Often the customers were men belonging to the elite of the local business community. Others had received a modern education and were associated with foreign companies working in the Middle East.

In 1915, after the Ottoman Empire's entry into World War I on the side of Germany, the Armenians' worst fears became reality. Within four months, the Ottoman government deported into the empire's Syrian desert almost the entire Armenian population. The deportations were accompanied by large and frequent massacres. In the beginning of the death marches, mostly men and boys were murdered. Later, women and children became the principal targets. The majority of those who survived the death marches were put in concentration camps and soon died from disease, exposure, and famine. In the summer of 1916, the Ottoman government decided to accelerate the extermination and organized the massacre of well over 100,000 Armenians within a few weeks.[23]

In 1918, the Allies defeated the Ottoman army and advanced deep into enemy territory. Soon, they encountered Armenians who had survived under indescribable circumstances in remote areas or as work slaves for Muslim landowners or military factories. Many children had survived because the Ottoman government had tried to assimilate them forcibly into Muslim households. Miraculously, some of these survivors managed with the help of others to contact the companies who had sold life insurance policies to their fathers, mothers, or husbands. The payments were desperately needed to buy food and clothing and for the treatment of the many diseases the survivors had contracted. Soon, however, it became apparent that almost no payments would be forthcoming. Under a series of pretexts, the insurance companies delayed and, in most cases, refused to pay the destitute survivors their money. The badly needed payouts never came.

The insurance companies' abandonment of their clients left a deep impression on the families that made their way to the United States and other parts of the world. For generations, the Armenian diaspora carefully preserved the knowledge about their insurance claims. Now very senior citizens, who as young children had experienced the poverty and desperation of the genocide and the Armenian postwar slums, decided to seek justice in American courts. Twelve of them brought the first and, to date, only lawsuit filed with regard to these insurance claims against the American insurance giant, New York Life Insurance Company. All but one of the claimants reside in the United States. The claimants filed the suit, *Marootian v. New York Life Ins. Co.*,[24] akin to the Holocaust restitution and Japanese slave labor litigation, as a class action and sought payment on the policies issued by New York Life.

In response, New York Life filed motions to dismiss. The insurance company did not dispute that it had sold such policies to the Armenian population in Ottoman Turkey. In fact, it combed its archives and located records, including aged insurance cards, for 2,300 Armenian policyholders from that time period. It argued, however, that the suit should be dismissed because all the policies contained "forum-selection" clauses mandating that if there were ever a dispute about the policies, the parties would resolve it before either French or English courts. An additional problem was the limitations period. Since the policies were written and allegedly unpaid almost a century ago, New York Life could argue that the lawsuits were time barred.

California again came to the rescue. In 2001, the California legislature enacted a statute similar to those it had passed in response to the World War II–era insurance and slave labor litigation, using the previous statutes as a model. (Following the numerical sequence of the previous two statutes, the statute is designated CCP 354.7.) Like the World War II–related statutes, this statute similarly (1) allows suits on Armenian genocide–era policies to be heard in California courts, despite the forum-selection clauses in the policies, and (2) extends the limitations period of such suits to 2010.[25]

In an attempt at damage control, New York Life tried to settle the case, offering $15 million. While the media initially reported that the case had settled for that amount,[26] the plaintiffs ultimately rejected New York Life's offer as being insufficient.

Failing to settle, New York Life pressed on with its motion to dismiss. In a significant victory for the plaintiffs, in December 2001, Los Angeles federal judge Christina Snyder denied New York Life's dismissal motion. In her decision, Judge Snyder held that despite the English and French forum-selection clauses in the policies, the case could be tried in federal court in California. "The Court finds that enforcement of the forum-selection clauses in the NYLIC life insurance policies which are the subject of this action would be fundamentally unfair."[27] In June 2002, the case entered the discovery stage, and trial is set to begin in the spring of 2003.

The legacy of the Holocaust restitution cases was critical to the successes achieved so far in the Armenian genocide litigation. The effective use of the U.S. litigation system, coupled with political pressure, in the Holocaust arena to bring justice to long-forgotten historical wrongs inspired the victims of Armenian genocide to seek the same for their historical inequities.[28] As plaintiffs' lead attorney, Vartkes Yeghiyan of Los Angeles, himself a child of survivors of the Armenian genocide, declared in an interview with the Los Angeles Times, "For the first time [the Armenian community] has gone beyond lamentation and liturgy to litigation, from 'going to church every April 24 [the Armenian Day of Remembrance, commemorating the massacre on April 24, 1915] and mourning' to taking legal action."[29] Paying homage to the Holocaust restitution movement, Yeghiyan commented: "Holocaust victims' heirs' showed me the way." He meant his remarks literally. Following in the footsteps of Lisa Stern five years earlier, Yeghiyan had hired William Shernoff to serve as one of his co-counsels on the case.

THE AFRICAN AMERICAN REPARATIONS MOVEMENT

One of the most interesting consequences of the Holocaust restitution litigation has been to give fresh impetus to the call for payments to African Americans by the U.S. government and American private enterprise for pre–Civil War slavery. The so-called African American reparations movement is now being taken seriously as a direct result of the achievements made in the Holocaust restitution arena. Reparation proponents specifically point to the payments now being made for World War II wrongs as the precedent for their cause. If the American legal system can be used to obtain $8 billion in compensation from European entities for slavery and other wrongs committed in another part of the world more than a half-century ago, they argue, why can't similar compensation be made for slavery that occurred here in the United States, which ended more than a century ago but whose consequences still reverberate in the African American community?

Holocaust survivors and their heirs have been seeking restitution for more than fifty years. The African American slavery reparations movement is well over a century old. Every year since 1989, Michigan Representative John Conyers Jr. has unsuccessfully introduced legislation in Congress to study the issue of slavery reparations.

An important precedent for African American reparations was the success of the so-called redress movement for the internment of American citizens of Japanese ancestry in the United States during World War II. The redress movement resulted in the 1998 passage of the Civil Liberties Act, which authorized a one-time lump-sum payment of $20,000 to each of the approximately 60,000 still-living Japanese American survivors of the wartime internment. Equally significant, in 1990, President George H. W. Bush issued an apology to the Japanese Americans on behalf of the U.S. government for the wartime imprisonment.

> A monetary sum and words alone cannot restore lost years or erase painful memories; neither can they fully convey our Nation's resolve to rectify injustices and to uphold the rights of individuals. We can never fully right the wrongs of the past. . . . In enacting a law calling for restitution and offering a sincere apology, your fellow Americans have, in a very real sense, renewed their traditional commitment to the ideals of freedom, equality and justice.

In 1999, prominent African American activist Randall Robinson published a book entitled *The Debt*, which forcefully argues for slavery reparations.[30] The book did not gain much interest outside the African American community until Robinson and others began to use the Holocaust restitution movement as a model for their cause. Robinson was then able to entice superstar attorney Johnnie Cochran to join him. Robinson and Cochran are currently putting together another "dream team" of lawyers to file suit for African American slavery restitution. Joining their Reparations Coordinating Committee is Alexander Pires Jr., a Washington, D.C., lawyer who in 1999 won a $1 billion settlement for black farmers who were discriminated against in obtaining federal farm loans, and such intellectual heavyweights as professors Manning Marable of Columbia University and Charles Ogletree of Harvard University (the latter was named in an *American Lawyer* magazine article in June 2002 as "the rajah of reparations").[31]

Such a suit would face a variety of procedural legal obstacles. Foremost, of course, would be the statute of limitations. Slavery in the United States ended in 1865, and the suit appears to be time barred. As with the Holocaust restitution and Japanese slave labor litigation, this can be overcome by the passage of a federal or state law extending the statute of limitations. A more difficult problem is finding the proper class of aggrieved claimants. In both the Holocaust restitution and Japanese slave labor lawsuits, the plaintiffs were the actual slaves or their immediate heirs. Similarly, in the Japanese American internment movement, the claimants also were individuals who were actually interned by the U.S. government during the war. No former American slaves are alive today to serve as plaintiffs. Third, the acts complained of were fully legal at the time they were committed. Slavery, which began in the New World with the arrival of the first slave ship in 1619, was the law of the land in the United States until abolished in 1865 by the Thirteenth Amendment. Until that time, it was enshrined in the U.S. Constitution, where it is mentioned on three occasions. As explained by Wayne State University constitutional law professor Robert Sedler,

> I think it's just very important that we understand that, whether we like it or not, slavery was not some aberration in American history, the way the Holocaust may be seen as an aberration in German history. This country was founded on the institution of slavery. It was fully legal in every respect in the United States, and there was no prohibition against profiting from slavery, even in states that were not slave states.[32]

Finally, there is the very real problem of identifying and thereby certifying a class of plaintiffs who could recover from any settlement. Pires himself readily admits this problem: "Class certification itself is a problem. Because everybody says: 'My God, who would the plaintiffs be? Who is this class? Is Oprah Winfrey a plaintiff? Is Michael Jordan a plaintiff? Is Tiger Woods a plaintiff? Tiger Woods isn't even pure black.'"[33] In 2001, after leaving public office, Eizenstat was asked about the parallels between Holocaust restitution and African American reparations claims. He commented on the difference between the claimants in the two movements:

> For slavery *qua* slavery, I think the appropriate remedy is affirmative government action in general, rather than reparations. . . . And if 100 years from now the great-great-grandson of a Holocaust laborer asked for reparations, I don't think that would be appropriate, unless there was some specific property that had been confiscated that they wanted to recover.[34]

Anthony Sebok, professor at Brooklyn Law School, disagrees about the viability of such suits: "The fact that the Holocaust suits gained support of so many parts of the mainstream society makes it harder for those very same components of mainstream American society to ignore these lawsuits."[35]

Most likely, suits seeking such damages will be summarily thrown out of court based on the time factor alone. In fact, in 1995, the Ninth Circuit affirmed the dismissal of two suits, brought by African American plaintiffs against the U. S. government, seeking $100 million in reparations.[36] The court of appeals held in *Cato v. United States*, to date the only case examining the issue, that (1) the United States possesses sovereign immunity to such claims, (2) the claims are time barred, and (3) the claimants lack standing to pursue such claims, since they themselves were never slaves.[37]

However, when the first Holocaust restitution lawsuit was filed in October 1996 against the Swiss banks, it also was viewed by most legal observers as a "sure loser"; less than two years later, the Swiss banks were ready to pay $1.25 billion to end the litigation. Similarly, in the face of the slave labor litigation, Germany and its industries agreed to pay 10 billion German marks ($5.2 billion) in December 1999, just months after two New Jersey federal courts ruled that German companies were immune from such litigation in the United States.

One of the most important lessons to be learned from the Holocaust restitution movement is that once momentum is created for a cause, which is then embraced by the public and the media, a favorable resolution, through either a court settlement or the political arena or both, becomes much more likely. The call for African American reparations currently has such momentum. The issue has been featured on all the major American television networks. The print media have written lengthy and incisive articles about the issue. The *ABA Journal*, the lead-ing American law magazine, published a cover story on the subject.[38] In 2000, the Chicago City Council passed a resolution calling for federal hearings on the issue. Cleveland, Detroit, and Dallas also passed simi-lar resolutions. In August 2002, a "Millions for Reparations" march was held in Washington, D.C., with thousands of African Americans de-scending on the Mall to demand reparations from the U.S. government.

California, again leading the way, enacted a law in 2001 forcing American insurance companies who sold policies insuring slaves as chattel to disclose information about such policies.[39] In May 2002, fol-lowing the mandate of the California law, five American insurance companies reported that they had insured slaves: Aetna, Inc.; American International Group, Inc. (AIG); Manhattan Life Insurance Company; New York Life Insurance Company; and Royal & Sun Alliance.[40] Earlier, in March 2000, Aetna Insurance issued an apology for having issued policies to slave owners insuring slaves as property.[41] Two years later, concurrently with issuing the slave insurance policy reports, Aetna and several other companies issued statements saying they regretted their past involvement in slavery. As with culpable insurers from the Holo-caust era and in the Armenian genocide, public pronouncements of contrition appear not to have been enough to stem the growing stream of suits.

This momentum set the stage for the next step: filing suits against Aetna and other corporate defendants for compensation and the dis-gorgement of profits, similar to the earlier Holocaust-era lawsuits. The first lawsuit came in March 2002, but not by Robinson and Cochran. Stealing the thunder again from the "big boys," as he did in the Holo-caust restitution litigation, was Ed Fagan. Joining Deadria Farmer-Paellmann, a thirty-six-year-old longtime African American repara-tions activist who went to law school in 1995 specifically to arm herself for such litigation and who in 2000 exposed Aetna's slave insurance policies, Fagan filed his class action lawsuit in Brooklyn federal court, the same courthouse where almost seven years earlier he began the Holocaust restitution litigation with the class action lawsuit against the Swiss banks. Upon filing the suit along with other lawyers, Fagan com-mented:

> The legal question is: Should the [defendant corporations] be entitled
> to hold on to money that's the functional equivalent of ill-gotten gains

or stolen money or fruit of the poisonous tree. These guys, their predecessors, were dirty. They built their companies on the backs of en-
slaved African-Americans. And they shouldn't be allowed to hold on
to it.[42]

Fagan also made clear the connection of this suit to the Holocaust restitution movement: "This is simply the logical continuation of the Holocaust lawsuits."[43]

Playing also the role of lead plaintiff, Farmer-Paellmann, on behalf
of herself and nearly forty million African Americans in the United
States, sued Aetna and two other name-brand corporations, Fleet
Boston Financial Corp. and CSX Corp. (the largest railroad on the East
Coast), claiming that they had profited from slave labor. Apparently,
Fleet and its predecessor, the Providence Bank, provided financing for
the ships that brought the slaves to the New World. CSX's predecessors
used slaves to construct railways across the United States. The suit
sought unspecified damages, but Fagan and Farmer-Paellmann declared that they would be asking for $1.4 trillion, the figure alleged to
represent the current value of unpaid African slave labor and interest.
"We're finally going to hold corporations accountable for the crimes
against humanity they committed against my ancestors,"[44] Farmer-
Paellmann announced at the press conference held immediately after
filing of the lawsuit. At the press conference, Fagan explained that
Farmer-Paellmann approached him in 2000 but that he "asked her to
hold off [filing the suit] until the Holocaust cases were over."[45]

The next month, the Fagan team filed a second lawsuit, in a New
Jersey federal court, adding as defendants New York Life, the investment firm Brown Brothers Harriman & Company, and the railroad Nor-
folk Southern Corporation. In Fagan's characteristic style, the suits
were filed with a maximum amount of publicity.

The litigation prompted even more publicity and debate on the subject. The *Hartford Courant*, which itself became embroiled in the controversy after acknowledging that it used to carry ads for the sale of slaves,
predicted that "the unsettling question of compensating African- Americans for the atrocity—and the legacy—of slavery . . . may become the
most divisive issue in the nation."[46] A fair amount of the publicity was
negative, with many prominent African Americans speaking out
against the litigation as a waste of valuable energy that could be channeled toward more productive legal efforts to help African Americans.

Perhaps the most critical comment came from Canada. Echoing the theme found in the Holocaust restitution movement of blaming the lawyers for creating all this trouble, the Toronto-based *National Post* commented in a lead editorial:

> Slavery exists today—except ironically, in some African countries—only as an abhorrent chapter of human history. It belongs, alongside the Scottish clearances, the Spanish conquest, the Babylonian captivity and the Huguenot eviction, as an example of man's capacity for inhumanity. It should be studied. It should be taught. It should be remembered. But it should not pay handsome dividends to plaintiffs and their lawyers.[47]

Even Johnnie Cochran was not happy about the way the litigation began: "We're somewhat distressed about that [referring to Fagan's lawsuits]. If somebody jumps out of the umbrella and goes to trial and it gets dismissed, all you need is for one judge to throw a case out and this thing doesn't go anywhere."[48] Cochran came up with a better game plan. His Reparations Coordinating Committee persuaded Hausfeld to join its cause, and it now meets in Hausfeld's law offices. Hausfeld's original blueprint for the litigation against the Swiss banks, conceived in 1996 and fine-tuned during the next five years in the various legal battles with the Swiss, German, Austrian, French and Japanese multinationals, is now being applied to the legal struggle against American corporate interests with ties to slavery. Much against their will, Hausfeld and Fagan are now being forced to work together again. The Holocaust restitution players, with new supporting legal actors on their side, are now ready to take on corporate America and seek rough justice and recognition for another long-neglected historical wrong.

What next? Cochran predicts, "We thought this was an idea whose time has come. But it's going to be so hard. I think it's going to take the next five or 10 years. There'll be some settlements [and] some victories along the way, but this will be a long battle."[49] His Reparations Coordinating Committee colleague, Florida lawyer Wille Gary, concurs:

> Look, nobody ever said it was going to be easy. If you're not ready to get in the trenches and fight, if you're not ready to get knocked down, kicked out of court and everything else—then it's not the type of issue you want to pursue because it will be a struggle.[50]

Attorneys Johnnie Cochran and Michael Hausfeld. *Courtesy of Cohen, Milstein, Hausfeld & Toll, P.L.L.C.*

Fagan, though, remains optimistic:

> People will come to a point of deciding, do they think a settlement is more appropriate than a trial? And in the Holocaust cases, that's what we thought. If the defendants behave in a responsible way and documents are produced so that we can serve the historical imperatives of the case and there's a meaningful financial gesture by the defendant companies, then I would encourage the clients to financially consider it.[51]

In other words, as soon as the defendants throw some money their way and make a gesture of contrition, which could be soon, Fagan will declare victory and recommend to his clients to settle. In June 2002, *Black Enterprise*, a leading African American magazine, remarked about the lawsuits: "Whether Cochran and company fight this war in the courtrooms, Congress or the court of public opinion, it's possible that these suits could represent the final chance to prompt corporations into acknowledging and accepting penance for their sins of the past."[52]

In the final analysis, the Jewish activists who were instrumental in obtaining the Holocaust restitution funds and who now claim that the "entire Jewish people" are proper heirs to those funds have provided an important philosophical underpinning for the African American reparations movement. Rabbi Israel Singer of the World Jewish Congress claimed that the Holocaust restitution settlements represent money stolen from deceased Holocaust victims, to whom all Jews are heirs. He then proposed that the money be used "to address the future needs of the Jewish people; for example education." According to

Singer's vision, "The purpose of this effort would be to create a new future for the Jewish people. This restitution should be used to rebuild the Jewish soul and spirit."[53]

The African American reparations activists are making exactly the same claims in their struggle. Save for a few dissenters, the activists are not looking for individual payouts to every living African American. Rather, like Singer, they seek the funds to address the future needs of African Americans, especially the critical needs in education. Like Singer's goal for the Jews, they aim to "rebuild the soul and spirit" of the African American community. And like Singer, they argue that any money obtained through these efforts properly belongs to deceased victims, with the entire African American community today being the heirs of those victim-slaves. Analogous to Israel Singer's mission for the Jewish people, the reparation lawsuits seek to create a "Fund for the African American People," which could be used to ensure the existence of a vital African American community in the future.

LEX AMERICANA: OTHER MOVEMENTS ADOPTING THE HOLOCAUST RESTITUTION MODEL

The new trend by governments and corporations to finally "come clean" about the wrongs they committed in the past would not be occurring without the spotlight being shone on their activities through the lawsuits in the United States. American law, in the words of Professor Burt Neuborne, has become *Lex Americana*, imitated throughout the world, with the Holocaust restitution cases becoming the principal model for victims and their representatives seeking to right past wrongs.

Currently, more than a half-dozen campaigns are being waged in both the United States and abroad for recognition and some measure of compensation for past historical injustices. All are claiming inspiration from the American litigation model represented by the Holocaust restitution movement and are seeking to emulate the results achieved by the Holocaust restitution activists, including

- Claims for unpaid wages by Mexican nationals who worked as temporary guest workers (*braceros*) in the United States during

World War II, when an estimated 400,000 Mexican nationals helped fill jobs left vacant by U.S. workers fighting the war. The class action lawsuit, filed in 2001 in federal court in San Francisco, against the Mexican and U.S. governments, along with four banks, claims that the *braceros* are owed at least $500 million, including interest, for a portion of the wages withheld from them by the defendants. The attorneys for the *bracero* plaintiffs are specifically pointing to the compensation obtained by the former German slave laborers as precedent for their suit. Attorneys (which include former Clinton administration civil rights chief and now Morris Ratner's partner at Lieff Cabraser, Bill Lann Lee) say the cases "are similar because they involve not reparations but assets withheld through alleged complicity of foreign governments and financial institutions."[54]

- Claims by victims of apartheid in South Africa, seeking compensation from Swiss, German, and American institutions that did business in South Africa during the apartheid years and directly benefited from the apartheid system. Already, Fagan has allied himself with a group of South African lawyers, and this legal team filed a series of class action lawsuits in the summer of 2002 in federal court in New York and in Swiss courts. Named as defendants are the Holocaust class action lawyers' old nemeses: Switzerland's UBS and Credit Suisse; Germany's Deutsche Bank, Dresdner Bank, and Commerz Banks; and also American corporate giants Citibank and IBM. In a throwback to the accusation against IBM for its dealings with Nazi Germany, IBM is accused of supplying South Africa with computer technology as early as 1952, used to perpetuate the system of institutionalized racial discrimination and repression in apartheid South Africa. In a repeat of the Holocaust restitution scenario, Hausfeld has aligned himself with different group of South African lawyers and activists to pursue a similar litigation.

- Claims by Sudeten Germans expelled from Czechoslovakia after World War II as being "enemies of the Czechoslovak people" for properties lost in the aftermath of their expulsion. These former Czechoslovak citizens and their heirs—a significant number of whom were Nazis or benefited from Nazi Germany's occupation of Czechoslovakia and who were driven from Czechoslovakia en masse at the end of World War II as revenge for the horrors of the

Nazi regime—are claiming that like the Holocaust survivors and heirs, they are entitled to compensation and restitution.[55]

- Claims by the famed Gurkhas from Nepal, known for their ferocity on the battlefield and serving in the British military, for discrimination in pay, promotion, and other benefits that they claim were denied to them during their military service in the British army. Their lawyer is Cherie Booth, Q.C., wife of British Prime Minister Tony Blair, and a leading human rights advocate of her own right. In its story on the suit, the *New York Times*, recognizing that the Gurkhas' method of achieving justice had been inspired by the American litigation model, changed the Gurkhas' famed battle cry from "The Gurkhas have come!" (*Ayo Gurkhali!*) to "The Gurkhas have come with [their] lawyers!"[56]

As the Holocaust restitution movement was reaching its peak in 1999, ADL leader Abraham Foxman already was pondering its long-term consequences. "Where does it end? World War I? The Indians? The slave trade? We'll be at this forever."[57] Human rights activists and lawyers filing these suits respond with, "And why not?" As Norbert Frei, a historian at Bochum University in Germany, explains, "The atmosphere has changed [after the Holocaust restitution litigation]. Where once willful ignorance prevailed, now it is desirable to make good what can be made good.[58]

If the ultimate goal of the Holocaust restitution cases is to serve as a template for a new era of financial relief and recognition for the victims of crimes against humanity, the challenge this time is to implement them without the fifty-year delay for justice. As a result of the victories by the victims of the Holocaust in the U.S. courts, individuals and corporations presently engaged in human rights abuses anywhere in the world are essentially put on notice: eventually you too will be held responsible for your misdeeds.

POINTING TOWARD THE FUTURE: HOLOCAUST RESTITUTION AND THE MIDDLE EAST CONFLICT

Not long after the onset of the Holocaust restitution campaign, I had a conversation with an Israeli official involved in the Holocaust restitution negotiations. After talking about how the negotiations were going, the official expressed a serious concern. The official was worried that the presentation of these claims, and especially the claims for lost land and other real estate by European Jews from prewar eastern Europe, would now open the door for Palestinians who lost property in modern-day Israel in the aftermath of the 1948 war, in which the state of Israel was created, or after the 1967 Six-Day War, when Israel conquered the West Bank and Gaza, to likewise seek restitution.

My Israeli friend exhibited prescience. In February 1999, Edward Said, an Arab American professor at Columbia University, spoke at the University of Minnesota. At the talk, Professor Said strongly suggested that the Holocaust restitution movement had now created a precedent for Palestinian Arabs to make claims on lost property in Israel. Stephen Feinstein, director of the Center for Holocaust and Genocide Studies at the University of Minnesota, noted at the time: "I think you will hear more of this question in the near future as [there is] more discourse about 1948[,] and it seems obvious that Palestinians will use the restitution issue." Later that same year, an article on a Palestinian American Web site urged that

> a broad campaign for the Palestinian right to restitution must be launched so that World Jewish Congress Secretary-General Israel Singer can no longer state, "The return of that which was his, and which belonged to his and her community is a human right which every man deserves" without being taken by [sic] his word.[59]

In 2000, the Council for Palestinian Restitution and Repatriation (CPRR) was established for this purpose. Headquartered in Washington, D.C., its aims are straightforward: "In short, what lawyers for the Jewish survivors of the Holocaust have succeeded in doing for their clients, CPRR is determined to do for Palestinians driven from their homes in 1948 and 1967."[60] Professor Said serves on the advisory board of the organization, and its legal advisers include a number of international law professors in the United States, including Cherif Bassouni at DePaul University, Francis Boyle at the University of Illinois, and John Quigley at Ohio State University, the latter two often associated with pro-Arab causes.

Norman Finkelstein also weighed in on the issue in a contribution to a recent book entitled *Palestinian Refugees and Their Right to Return.*[61]

After briefly summarizing the Holocaust restitution campaign, Finkelstein wrote:

> For our purposes, the merits of the case against Switzerland (dubious at best) are less important than the legal and moral precedents it set. The chairman of the House Banking Committee, James Leach, maintained that states must be held accountable for injustices even if committed a half-century ago: "History does not have a statute of limitations."

Quoting other notables making similar statements in support of Holocaust restitution, Finkelstein commented:

> Noble sentiments all, but nowhere to be heard—unless they are being actively ridiculed—when it comes to Palestinian compensation for the dispossession of their homeland. . . . Apart from the moral link joining Jewish claims against Europe, on the one hand, and Palestinian claims against Israel, on the other hand, a direct material link potentially joins the respective demands.[62]

Just as the activists involved in Holocaust restitution are reluctant to speak about the effect of their movement on Palestinian restitution claims, so are proponents of Palestinian restitution loath to bring up a related restitution issue: Jews who were expelled from Arab lands after creation of the state of Israel and lost their property as a result. The properties of these Sephardic Jews (Jews whose roots are in Spain before their expulsion in 1492) are in Algeria, Egypt, Iraq, Lebanon, Libya, Morocco, Syria, Tunisia, and Yemen, where more than 870,000 Jews resided in 1948 (constituting approximately 2 percent of the population of Arab countries). As these Jews fled these Arab lands, 600,000 of whom came to Israel, they left behind houses, businesses, bank accounts, and communal property such as synagogues, schools, and cemeteries. After the Six-Day War, there was a second expulsion and more theft of property as remnant communities of Jews in Arab lands were either ordered to leave or fled when violence broke out against them.

In May 2002, Israel launched a major initiative to preserve, collect, and computerize claims of Jewish refugees from Arab lands. The project is headed by Israel's Morocco-born justice minister, Meir Sheetrit, with the assistance of the WJC and the American Sephardi Federation in the United States. Sheetrit made plain why Israel is now belatedly asking Jews with yellowing property deeds and other documentation of assets in Arab lands to come forward and provide the information on registration forms entitled "Jewish Property That Remained in Arab Countries."[63] "'The goal of the Ministry of Justice is to gather information regarding the loss of Jewish property in the Arab states' to counter Palestinian claims to lost property in future [Middle East] negotiations," reported the *Jerusalem Post*, also summing up the position of Justice Minister Sheetrit. "The world needs to understand that the number of Jewish refugees exceeds the number of Arab refugees, who are 'exploited by their brethren,' said Sheetrit, referring to Palestinians who have been mired in refugee camps since Israel's independence."[64] Bobby Brown, one of the Israeli negotiators on Holocaust restitution, likewise revealed why Israel is now interested in this restitution issue:

> An injustice was committed to the Jews from Arab countries, and for 50 years we've been saying it's not the right time to deal with this issue. But in a month, or a year, we will be sitting with the Palestinians . . . and negotiating. The issue of restitution will come up. The Palestinians are going to say, "You owe us X-amount." That's the moment that the Jewish side must say, "There was a war. We also have claims. And these must act as a counterbalance." We have to find a rough justice on both sides.[65]

The details and complexities of these competing claims, not to mention those of the Middle East conflict, are beyond the purview of this study. Nevertheless, I point out that the Palestinian demand of the "right to return"—which would effectively turn Israel into another Arab state—was one of the primary reasons for the collapse of negotiations between Israelis and Palestinians at the Camp David talks. The Holocaust restitution settlements may point to a solution to the deadlock of this issue. If the Palestinians were willing to accept financial compensation in a lump sum, based on the rough-justice model concluded in the Holocaust restitution negotiations that Brown referred to, rather than seeking a full-scale return of their properties within Israel proper, the deadlock, at least on this issue, conceivably could be broken. Jews who formerly resided in Arab lands and their heirs do not seek to return to those Arab lands, but only recognition of their claims and financial compensation. If the dispute is boiled down to one of restitution, the issue perhaps could be resolved. It would be a magnificent legacy if the Holocaust restitution movement were to play a role in resolving the conflict between Israel and the Palestinians and thereby finally bring peace to the state created out of the ashes of the Holocaust.

Notes

NOTES TO PREFACE

1. Bill Eichenberger, "Lowdown Highbrows," *Columbus* (Ohio) *Dispatch*, February 18, 2001, F1.

2. At the 1998 Whittier conference, I organized a panel entitled "The Survivors Speak." Unfortunately, it was the least-attended panel on the program.

NOTES TO CHAPTER I

1. Amos Elon, "Switzerland's Lasting Demon," *New York Times Magazine*, April 12, 1998, 40.

2. Ibid. (quoting Swiss economist Gian Trepp).

3. Clare Nullis, "Swiss at Loss Losing 2006 Bid," *AP Online*, June 22, 1999.

4. Tom Bower, *Nazi Gold: The Full Story of the Fifty-Year Swiss-Nazi Conspiracy to Steal Billions from Europe's Jews and Holocaust Survivors* (New York: HarperCollins, 1997); Isabel Vincent, *Hitler's Silent Partners: Swiss Banks, Nazi Gold and the Pursuit of Justice* (New York: Morrow, 1998); Adam LeBor, *Hitler's Secret Bankers: How Switzerland Profited from Nazi Genocide* (New York: Simon & Schuster, 1999)); Itamar Levin, *The Last Deposit: Swiss Banks and Holocaust Victims' Accounts* (Westport, CT: Greenwood Press, 1999); Gregg J. Rickman, *Swiss Banks and Jewish Souls* (New York: Transaction Books, 1999); Jean Ziegler, *The Swiss, the Gold and the Dead: How Swiss Bankers Helped Finance the Nazi War Machine* (New York: Harcourt Brace, 1997) (first published in German as *Die Schweirz, das Gold und die Toten* [Gütersloh: Bertelsmann Verlag, 1997]).

5. Elizabeth Olson, "Swiss Truth-Teller, or Lying Traitor," *New York Times*, February 16, 1999, 4.

6. Johanna McGeary, "Echoes of the Holocaust," *Time*, February 24, 1997, 36.

7. "U.S. and Allied Efforts to Recover and Restore Gold and Other Assets Stolen or Hidden by Germany during World War II," Preliminary Study, coordinated by Stuart E. Eizenstat and prepared by William Z. Slany. Washington, D.C.: U.S. Department of State, May 1997 (hereafter, First Eizenstat Report). The report can be located at www.giussani.com/holocaust-assets/welcome.html,

which is maintained by Swiss journalist Bruno Giussani. The U.S. State Department also maintains a Web site that contains the Eizenstat reports, press releases, and other U.S. government documents on Holocaust restitution. See www.state.gov/www/regions/eur/holocausthp.html.

Eizenstat, appointed in July 1999 as the number two person at the Treasury Department, became the chief American envoy on Holocaust issues, working on settling Holocaust restitution claims until the very last day of the Clinton administration. For Eizenstat's account of his involvement in the Holocaust restitution story, see Stuart E. Eizenstat, *Imperfect Justice: Looted Assets, Slave Labor, and the Unfinished Business of World War II* (New York: Public Affairs, 2003).

8. First Eizenstat Report, iv.

9. In June 1998, the Eizenstat team issued its second report, this time focusing on other neutral nations' financial dealings with Nazi Germany. "U.S. and Allied Wartime and Postwar Relations and Negotiations with Argentina, Portugal, Spain, Sweden, and Turkey on Looted Gold and German External Assets and U.S. Concerns about the Fate of the Wartime Ustasha Treasury, Supplement to the Preliminary Study on U.S. and Allied Efforts to Recover and Restore Gold and Other Assets Hidden by Germany during World War II," coordinated by Stuart E. Eizenstat and prepared by William Z. Slany. Washington, D.C.: U.S. Department of State, June 1998. The Swiss were quite pleased to see this second report, since it also blamed the so-called other neutrals of profiting from their dealings with the Nazis.

10. The report applied an almost ten-point multiplier (9.74) to determine the current value.

11. First Eizenstat Report.

12. Ibid.

13. Neil M. Sher, "Switzerland's Hole Keeps Getting Deeper," *Jewish Journal*, July 25, 1997, 16. Sher, the former lead Nazi hunter in the U.S. Department of Justice, later served as the chief of staff of the International Commission on Holocaust-Era Insurance Claims. His statement about the Swiss was actually a variation of a statement made years earlier by Abba Eban in reference to the Palestinians and the Middle East conflict. Sher applied it to the Swiss banks.

14. The symposium proceedings are published in "Nazi Gold and Other Assets of the Holocaust: A Search for Justice," *Whittier Law Review* 20 (1998): 1.

15. Their satisfaction, no doubt, came from remarks made at the conference by Victor Comras, Eizenstat's deputy, urging state and local officials not to impose sanctions on the Swiss for failing to negotiate a settlement of the claims. "Switzerland has been moving in the right direction. . . . [T]he United States continues to believe that state and local sanctions against the Swiss banks are not only unwarranted, but at this point, counterproductive. . . . [T]he United States Government sees little wisdom in increasing pressure just when

progress is being made." "American Government Officials Speak," *Whittier Law Review* 20 (1998): 34–35. The Swiss reprinted Comras's remarks. See DIALOGUE, *Latest News from the Task Force on Switzerland—World War II*, no. 4, March 1998, 1.

16. The postscript proceedings are published in "Nazi Gold and Other Assets of the Holocaust: A Search for Justice—A Postscript," *Whittier Law Review* 20 (1999): 649–76.

17. In May 2002, this fund made its final distribution and closed up shop. The Swiss government, as with later Holocaust claims settlements, turned over the fund's administration to local Jewish groups. Ultimately, more than 300,000 Jewish survivors worldwide received a payout from the fund. In the United States, the World Jewish Restitution Organization (WJRO) was responsible for the distribution. To receive funds, the WJRO required that a survivor have been under Nazi occupation during the war and self-declare a financial need. Each such survivor received $502. Even the distribution of this paltry sum created a passionate debate among the survivors, a sign of bigger disputes to come (see chapter 6). Some survivors, though in financial straits, refused to apply on principle. Others, though clearly financially secure, applied anyway. As put to me by one survivor, "I am needy—needy for revenge."

18. The Web site for ICEP is www.icep.iaep.org.

19. The Web site for the Bergier Commission is www.uek.ch. Its official name is Independent Commission of Experts: Switzerland—Second World War.

20. See, e.g., J. J. Goldberg, "Turning Fagan into Shylock," *Jewish Journal*, September 12, 1998, 14; Steve Chambers, "Holocaust Lawyer Inspires Range of Emotions—Some See Strong Fighter against Swiss Banks, but Others View Him As an Ambulance Chaser," *Star-Ledger* (Newark, N.J.), December 20, 1998, 2; Barry Meier, "Lawyer in Holocaust Case Faces Litany of Complaints," *New York Times*, September 8, 2000, A1. The last was published concomitantly with a segment on ABC's *20/20* television program.

21. Susan Orenstein, "Gold Warriors," *American Lawyer*, September 1998, 64.

22. The law firm of Cohen, Milstein, Hausfeld & Toll proudly displays this quotation on its Web site (www.cmht.com). In 1989, the *National Law Journal* named Hausfeld as one of the top ten civil litigators in Washington, D.C. (March 29, 1989). The March/April 2001 issue of *Regardies Power*, in its "Washington's Ten Most Feared Lawyers," listed Hausfeld as the most feared lawyer in Washington, D.C.

23. *Handel v. Artukovic*, 601 F. Supp. 1421 (C.D. Cal. 1985). A few years later, the U.S. Department of Justice's Office of Special Investigations, in charge of ferreting out Nazis and Nazi sympathizers living in the United States, succeeded in having Artukovic's citizenship revoked. Artukovic was deported to Yugoslavia, where he died while awaiting trial for his wartime acts.

24. Desson Howe, "A Wealth of New Information on Holocaust," *Washington Post*, November 18, 1998, B1.

25. In 1999, the *National Law Journal* reported that Milberg Weiss, as the firm is popularly known, had earned nearly $700 million in profits since 1988 and that Weiss was earning approximately $12 million per year. "Squirm Time for Milberg Weiss," *National Law Journal*, April 5, 1999, A1.

26. Orenstein, "Gold Warriors," 65. Both lawyer teams soon realized that they would need to amend their lawsuits. Hausfeld's original complaint combined into one case the Holocaust survivors living in the United States and abroad. Subsequently, he separated the two classes of plaintiffs, filing one lawsuit on behalf of U.S. citizens and another on behalf of foreign plaintiffs. All of Fagan's named plaintiffs were U.S. citizens.

27. In his autobiography, Bronfman details his journey of rediscovering his bond to Judaism and thereafter becoming a major Jewish activist: *The Making of a Jew* (New York: Penguin Books, 1996).

28. The journey that Singer began in the Holocaust restitution claims arena landed him eight years later, in 2002, the job of president of the Conference on Material Claims against Germany (hereafter the Claims Conference) (see chapter 6).

29. Paul Erdman, *The Swiss Account* (New York: Tor Books, 1993).

30. Arthur L. Smith Jr., *Hitler's Gold: The Story of the Nazi War Loot* (Oxford: Berg, 1989). The first book to discuss the issue of Nazi-stolen gold and its postwar whereabouts was published in England in 1956: Stanley Moss, *Gold Is Where You Hide It: What Happened to the Reichsbank Treasurers?* (London: Andre Deutsch, 1956).

31. Smith, *Hitler's Gold*, xiii.

32. McGeary, "Echoes of the Holocaust," 39.

33. Ibid.

34. Anne Louse Bardach, "Edgar's List," *Vanity Fair*, March 1997, 269.

35. McGeary, "Echoes of the Holocaust," 39. In 1999, D'Amato's legislative director wrote a book on his experiences in dealing with the issue: Gregg J. Rickman, *Swiss Banks and Jewish Souls* (New York: Transaction Books, 1999).

36. New York, is of course, was the Swiss banks' most important location outside Switzerland. In 1997, for example, 191 foreign banks had branches in New York City, with assets of $659 billion. More than 70 percent of foreign banking establishments in the United States are located in New York City. See www.banking.state.ny.us (Web site of the New York Banking Department).

37. On September 11, 2000, the WJC held a tribute dinner at the Waldorf Astoria Hotel in New York to honor the people who had been critical to the successes achieved by Holocaust restitution movement. Hillary Rodham Clinton was one of those honored, ostensibly because she brought the matter to the attention of President Clinton.

38. In 1999, Eizenstat acquired a second title in addition to deputy treasury secretary. As Clinton's chief envoy to the Holocaust restitution movement, he was made "special representative of the president and the secretary of state for Holocaust issues." Eizenstat worked on Holocaust issues literally to the very last day of the Clinton presidency. On January 19, 2001, he brokered a settlement between the French banks and the claimants' lawyers for claims arising out of wartime accounts in France. Two days earlier, he convinced the Austrians to settle their outstanding wartime claims. In March 2001, he was back in government. The Bush administration asked him to return on special assignment to handle the Holocaust settlements with Germany, Austria, and France, which began to unravel soon after Clinton left office.

39. To process the claims arising from the publication of these account names, the SBA established the Claims Resolution Tribunal (CRT) within Volcker's ICEP. See www.crt.ch (Web site of the CRT). Seventeen arbitrators, selected from both inside and outside Switzerland, were hired to adjudicate the dormant account claims presented to the Swiss banks.

40. Meredith Berkman, "Private Torment of the Woman Who Broke the Swiss Banks," *New York Post*, May 20, 1999, 26.

41. Elaine Woo, "Estelle Sapir, First Holocaust Survivor to Recover Wartime Claim from Swiss Bank," *Los Angeles Times*, April 16, 1999, A30 (obituary).

42. Richard Fish, "At 71, She's Still Trying to Redeem Swiss Holdings," *New York Daily News*, October 31, 1997, 40.

43. David Sanger, "Crack in the Vault: Swiss Bank Yields to a Nazi Victim's Daughter," *New York Times*, May 5, 1998, A27.

44. See ibid.

45. Ibid.

46. Ibid.

47. Quoted in the obituary for Estelle Sapir, *New York Times*, April 16, 1999, A20.

48. Tom Brazaitis, "Digging for Gold," *Cleveland Plain Dealer*, June 1, 1997, 12.

49. Christoph Meili, "Christoph Meili Tells His Story," *Whittier Law Review* 20 (1998): 45.

50. Margot Hornblower, "Of Mercy, Family and Hate Mail," *Time*, May 25, 1998, 4.

51. "Reward for a "Righteous Gentile," *Time*, December 14, 1998, 20.

52. Hevesi's office periodically issued a Holocaust restitution newsletter, *International Monitor*, which provided "an update on the progress in seeking restitution for Holocaust survivors." The newsletter can be accessed electronically at www.comptroller.nyc.gov. The quotations in the text, setting out the Executive Committee's mission, come from the newsletter.

53. Eric Schmitt, "U.S. Backs off Sanctions, Seeing Poor Effect Abroad," *New York Times*, August 1, 2000, A1.

54. John J. Goldman, "Pressure Rises for Holocaust Fund Pact," *Los Angeles Times*, July 3, 1998, A1.

55. Marilyn Henry, "Eizenstat Slams Idea of Swiss Sanctions," *Jerusalem Post*, July 23, 1998, 4. At the same hearing, Eizenstat added: "I regret to say there is no realistic short-term prospect of a broad settlement." William Hall, "Eizenstat Sees No Early Nazi Gold Settlement," *Financial Times*, July 23, 1998, 4. Eizenstat was wrong on both counts. Less than thirty days later, after Hevesi's moves, the Swiss banks settled.

56. Lisa Anderson, "Jewish Leader Hail Decision by Swiss on Stolen War Assets," *Chicago Tribune*, August 13, 1998, A1.

57. John Authers and Richard Wolffe, "When Sanctions Work," *Financial Times*, September 9, 1998, 14.

58. James D. Besser, "Behind the Scenes: A Curious Synergy," *Jewish Journal*, August 21, 1998, 14.

59. *Crosby v. National Foreign Trade Council*, 530 US 363 (2000).

60. The Bergier interim report and the subsequently issued final report can be located at www.uek.ch (Bergier Commission's Web site).

61. Richard Capone and Robert O'Brien, "What's Right with the Swiss Banks' Offer," *New York Times*, June 30, 1998, A33.

62. Letter from Ambassador Alfred Defago to Judge Edward R. Korman, June 3, 1997.

63. Susan Orenstein, "The Gold War," *American Lawyer*, September 1998, 62.

64. E-mail from Morris Ratner to me, June 14, 2002.

65. Henry Weinstein, "Search Opens for Holocaust Claimants," *Los Angeles Times*, June 29, 1999, A3.

66. E-mail from Morris Ratner to me, June 14, 2002.

67. Marilyn Henry, "Swiss Banks Reparations Expected in One Year," *Jerusalem Post*, June 6, 1999, 3.

68. *In re Holocaust Victim Assets Litigation*, 105 F. Supp. 2d 139 (E.D.N.Y.2000).

69. The court-created Swiss banks settlement Web site, www.swissbankclaims.com, summarizes the various suggestions and reproduces some suggestions in full. See chapter 6.

70. In addition, a set of "Frequently Asked Questions" and answers were posted on the Swiss bank settlement's Web site.

71. Morris Ratner is proud to have been among the strongest supporters of including the first group in the settlement. According to Ratner, as the only openly gay (and Jewish) attorney on the plaintiffs' litigation team, he wanted to make sure that homosexual victims would be included because they have been

among the least compensated victims of Nazism. E-mail from Morris Ratner to me, April 10, 2002.

72. In the late stage of the litigation, to increase the pressure on the Swiss banks, a parallel lawsuit was filed against the Swiss banks in California. That lawsuit contained one named plaintiff who was not Jewish, an elderly Romani (Gypsy) victim of the Nazis, now living in California. This was the only non-Jewish named plaintiff in any of the suits against the Swiss banks. Moreover, none of the suits ever contained any of the other three classes of VTNP claimants.

73. For instance, the press release from Hausfeld's law firm announcing the August 13, 1998, settlement stated: "In an historic, unprecedented legal settlement, Swiss private banks will pay Holocaust survivors $1.25 billion to settle legal claims arising from the banks' conduct during and after World War II." Cohen, Milstein, Hausfeld & Toll, *E-Journal* www.cmht.com/ipsltmt.htm.

74. Of the more than 19 million persons murdered by the Nazis, 12.2 million came from the Soviet Union and 5.4 million from Poland. R. J. Rummel, *Death by Government* (New York: Transaction Books, 1997), 112.

75. Henry Weinstein, "Holocaust Survivors, Swiss Banks OK Settlement," *Los Angeles Times*, January 23, 1999, A13.

76. *In re Holocaust Victim Assets Litigation* (Swiss Banks), Frequently Asked Questions, April 17, 2001, 10, available at www.swissbankclaims.com.

77. Individuals applying as Slave Labor II claimants—those claiming to have performed slave labor for a Swiss-run company—could receive payment even if they did not fit one of the VTNP categories. For example, a non-Jewish Pole or Russian would be eligible, but only if the claimant could show that he or she had performed labor for such a Swiss company. To assist in the process, Switzerland submitted a list of Swiss companies that used slave or forced labor in Nazi Germany or Nazi-occupied Europe.

78. The date chosen was linked to the date of the comprehensive German Foundation settlement. In that settlement, only the heirs of former German slave laborers who were alive on February 15, 1999, could receive a payout due to their deceased relative (see chapter 2).

79. Plan of Allocation and Distribution, 111, *In re Holocaust Victim Assets Litigation*. The plan is available on the Swiss bank settlement Web site and is also published in Judah Gribetz and Shari C. Reig, "Special Master's Proposed Plan of Allocation and Distribution of Settlement Proceeds," *Fordham International Law Journal* 25 (2001): S-307 (symposium issue on Holocaust restitution).

80. Even the figure issued by the Volcker Committee (53,886 accounts) is probably underestimated. As the Israeli newspaper *Ha'aretz* pointed out, the committee's auditors were "able to examine only four million out of a total of 6.7 million accounts in Swiss banks at the end of the war. Details of the remaining accounts were not kept." Yair Sheleg, "Israel: Volcker Panel Numbers Too

Low," *Ha'aretz*, December 7, 1999, 1. The auditors then matched the names of holders of the discovered dormant accounts with the lists of those who perished in the Holocaust kept by the U.S. Holocaust Museum and the Yad Vashem Holocaust Center in Israel. Both these victims' lists, however, are incomplete. For example, "the list of victims maintained by Yad Vashem includes only about half of all those who died in the Holocaust" (ibid.).

While the Volcker Committee report cleared the Swiss banks of any criminal wrongdoing, the actions of the banks "led the Committee to question whether their duty of due care in their dealings with customers was observed by a number of banks and their officers in the special situations following World War II" (Independent Committee of Eminent Persons, report, 14).

81. *In re Holocaust Victim Assets Litigation*, 105 F. Supp. 2d 155–57.

82. Ibid., 158.

83. The CRT was changed into a court-sanctioned body and is now called CRT II, with CRT I being the tribunal created by the SBA in 1997 to process the claims submitted in response to the SBA's original publication that year of the two lists of dormant account names. The Web site for CRT II is www.dormantaccounts.ch or www.crt-ii.org.

84. *In re Holocaust Victim Assets Litigation*, 225 F. 3d 191 (2d Cir. 2000).

85. See *In re Holocaust Victim Assets Litigation*, 2001 WL 868507 (2d Cir. 2001). Several other appeals were filed but later withdrawn.

86. Claims Resolution Tribunal, In re *Accounts of Otto Fuchs and Maria Fuchs*, claim no. 210775/AH. The entire text of the Certified Award is available on the CRT-II Web site, www.crt-ii.org.

87. See *In re Holocaust Victim Assets Litigation*, 2001 WL 868507 (2d Cir. 2001) (unpublished opinion rejecting the appeal of three claimants that Gribetz made an improper distribution); *In re Holocaust Victim Assets Litigation*, 225 F. 3d 191 (2d Cir. 2000) (published opinion rejecting an appeal by a group of ethnic Poles who objected to the exclusion of ethnic Poles from the Swiss bank settlement).

88. E-mail from Burt Neuborne to me, November 27, 2001.

89. Declaration of Burt Neuborne Concerning the Award of Attorneys' Fees, *In re Holocaust Victim Assets Litigation*, February 22, 2002.

90. Ibid. According to Neuborne, "I believe that the lawyers who prosecuted this litigation have exhibited extraordinary generosity and commitment . . . by foregoing literally hundreds of millions of dollars in fees. . . . Repeated, inaccurate press reports stressing lawyers feuding over fees have irresponsibly fostered the stereotypical image of greedy lawyers seeking to profiteer at the expense of Holocaust victims. I urge the Court to make clear that this litigation is an example of counsels' unselfish commitment, not an exercise in greed. . . . I am confident in asserting that this is the lowest fee structure ever adopted in a case of comparable complexity and success."

91. The Bergier Commission's six-hundred-page Final Report can be

found at www.uek.ch (Bergier Commission's Web site). The Web site also contains the Bergier Commission's Interim Report, issued in May 1998.

92. Bergier Commission Final Report, 448.

93. Ibid., 446.

94. Ibid., 445.

95. Ibid.

96. Ibid., 15.

97. Ibid., 455.

98. Ibid., 277.

99. Ibid.

100. Ibid.

101. Ibid.

102. Ibid., 447.

103. Ibid., 448.

104. According to the Final Report's findings, Switzerland knowingly sent thousands, mostly Jews, to their deaths through its "excessively and uselessly restrictive" wartime refugee policy. The report concluded: "We are obliged to sustain the affirmation, perhaps provocative in form, but nonetheless in conformity with the facts: The refugee policy of our authorities contributed to the most atrocious of Nazi objectives—the Holocaust."

105. Elizabeth Olson, "Commission Concludes That Swiss Policies Aided the Nazis," *New York Times*, March 23, 2002, A4. From 1996 to 1998, the same story undoubtedly would have made page 1 of the *Times*.

106. This is a standard clause in a legal release.

107. Bergier Commission Final Report.

108. *Rosenberg v. Swiss National Bank*, case no. 98CV01647 (U.S. District of Columbia, filed June 29, 1998).

109. Declaration of the Swiss Federal Council, August 13, 1998.

110. Elizabeth Olson, "Swiss Are Relieved, but Sour, at Banks' Holocaust Accord," *New York Times*, August 16, 1998, A8.

111. Sanbar later put his criticisms in a monograph, published in Israel and translated into English. Raul Teitelbaum and Moshe Sanbar, *Holocaust Gold— From the Victims to Switzerland: Trails of the Nazi Plunder* (Tel Aviv: Moreshet, 2001).

112. Freddy Rom, "Swiss President Retreats on Vow Made to Help Holocaust Survivors," *JTA On Line*, July 9, 2002.

113. Ibid.

114. As I discussed earlier, the Swiss government's sole effort in restitution was the creation in 1997 of the $200 million for "needy" Holocaust survivors, of which a little more than half was funded by the Swiss government, including the SNB, with the other portion coming from private industries in Switzerland.

115. Michael Ollove, "Museums Tracing Nazi-Looted Art," *Pittsburgh Post-Gazette*, April 18, 2000, A4.

116. Information about Bank Leumi's Holocaust-era dormant accounts and the claims process for Bank Leumi and other Israeli institutions can be located at www.unclaimedassets.com/israel.html.

117. Sometimes Hevesi would resort to bluffing. Thus in 1998, he announced that the Executive Monitoring Committee would examine the proposed purchase by Deutsche Bank of the New York–based Banker's Trust, in light of Deutsche Bank's failure to resolve its Holocaust-era claims. Even though New York had no authority to review this purchase—a matter wholly within the province of the U.S. Federal Reserve Board—Hevesi's rumblings led Deutsche Bank to renew its efforts to settle the claims.

118. 630 F. 2d 876 (2nd Cir. 1980). Since the Swiss banks' lawsuits were filed in the Second Circuit court, the *Filartiga* decision was binding precedent for any decision issued by Judge Korman.

119. Thus, Rodovan Karadzic was served with court papers when he came to the United States as part of the Serbian delegation invited to the United States to end the war in Bosnia. *Kadzic. v. Karadzic*, 70 F. 3d 232 (2nd Cir. 1995). In the mid-1990s, a Guatemalan general was sued and served with court papers while on a visit to Harvard University. *Xuancax v. Gramajo*, 886 F. Supp. 162 (D. Mass. 1995). It turned out that the general was also a torturer and was sued by his victims, both Guatemalan and American, when they learned of his U.S. visit. In 1999, Chinese President Jiang Zemin likewise was served with a lawsuit filed under the *hostis humani* principle during a visit to the United States. The case is still in litigation.

120. *Restatement of Foreign Relations Law of the United States* (Third), §404.

121. See *Jota v. Texaco, Inc.*, 15 F.3d 153 (2d Cir. 1998); *Wiwa v. Royal Dutch Petroleum*, 226 F.3d 88 (2d. Cir. 2000); *Doe v. Unocal Corp.*, 110 F. Supp. 2d 1294 (C.D. Cal. 2000); *Bowoto v. Chevron Corp.*, Civ. No. C99-2506 (N.D. Cal. 1999); *Doe v. ExxonMobil Corp.*, Civ. No. 1:01CV01357 (D.C. 2001)

122. In September 2002, the Burmese plaintiffs achieved a significant victory over Unocal when the Ninth Circuit Court of Appeals overturned the dismissal of the suit by the federal trial judge two years earlier. *Doe v. Unocal*, 2002 U.S. App. LEXIS 19263 (9th Cir. September 18, 2002).

123. Neela Banerjee, "U.S. Lawsuit Snares Exxon, Oil Firm Is Cited in Indonesian Human Rights Abuses," *International Herald Tribune*, June 22, 2001, 19.

124. David Corn, "Corporate Human Rights," *The Nation*, July 15, 2002, 31.

125. Ibid.

NOTES TO CHAPTER 2

1. House Committee on Banking and Financial Services, *World War II Assets of Holocaust Victims*, testimony by Deputy Treasury Secretary Stuart E. Eizenstat, September 14, 1999, quoting Count Lambsdorff.

2. House Committee on Banking and Financial Services, *World War II Assets of Holocaust Victims*, testimony by Burt Neuborne, September 14, 1999, 4.

3. This dark legacy of German industry reemerged in the United States in 2001, entirely outside the context of the Holocaust restitution. Shortly after the groundbreaking of the new World War II memorial in Washington, D.C., it was discovered that the American company hired to construct the monument for our "greatest generation" was the American subsidiary of Phillip Holzmann A.G., a German construction firm that used slave labor during the war. Despite a public outcry over this revelation and a campaign by some former slaves of Phillip Holzmann to have the U.S. government cancel the contract, the company is being allowed to build the monument.

4. In March 2001, the German Catholic Church acknowledged that it knew the identities of about 1,200 of 10,000 laborers who were forced by the Nazi regime to work for the church. By then, most of the victims had already died. As a measure of some restitution, German Cardinal Karl Lehmann announced that those still alive would receive a one-time payment of DM 15,000 (approximately $ 7,500) from the church. In addition, the church would contribute DM 5 million (approximately $2.5 million) to the German Foundation for former slave laborers. *Reuters Online*, March 5, 2001.

5. Richard Wolffe, "Putting a Price on the Holocaust," *Irish Times*, March 16, 1999, 15.

6. The program was known in Nazi Germany as *Vernichtung durch Arbeit* (extermination through work), sometimes labeled today as Germany's death-through-work program.

7. Benjamin B. Ferencz, *Less Than Slaves: Jewish Forced Labor and the Quest for Compensation* (Cambridge, Mass.: Harvard University Press, 1979), xvii. In 2002, Indiana University Press reprinted Ferencz's classic work, and Ferencz, still quite active at eighty-four in the area of human rights (see his Web site www.benferencz.org), wrote a new introduction to the book. Benjamin B. Ferencz, *Less Than Slaves: Jewish Forced Labor and the Quest for Compensation* (Bloomington: Indiana University Press, 2002).

8. At one time, Eizenstat proposed a different formulation, calling those "who lived in concentration camps or similar facilities while they worked" as "Category A Forced Laborers" and those "who lived under different conditions" as "Category B Laborers." This formulation never caught on. See Remarks of Stuart E. Eizenstat at the annual meeting of the Conference on Jewish Material Claims against Germany and Austria, July 14, 1999, 12.

9. Adam Lebor, "Holocaust Slaves Set to Gain Compensation," *The Independent*, August 22, 1998, 15.

10. The Schroeder government is a coalition government, consisting of Schroeder's Social Democratic Party and the Green Party, with its leader Joschka Fischer, the former radical firebrand, as Schroeder's foreign minister.

Since the 1980s, the Greens have advocated that German firms pay their wartime slave laborers. Consequently, the Coalition Agreement of October 20, 1998, establishing the Schroeder government, included such a commitment in the new government program.

11. "Battle Brews on Insurance Pact," *Forward*, August 28, 1998, 3.

12. For example, in September 1998, Volkswagen announced the establishment of a private $12 million fund to compensate its former slave laborers. The effort was not well received. Bobby Brown, then Prime Minister Benjamin Netanyahu's adviser for diaspora affairs, commented, "$12 million? Why not 85 cents?" Brown called the $12 million "a book-keeping correction for Volkswagen." See "Peres' Role in VW Restitution Draws Ire of Netanyahu Aide," *Forward*, September 18, 1998, 1. A year later, I.G. Farben, the notorious German chemicals concern that worked thousands to death in Nazi camps and manufactured death gas, announced the creation of a $1.6 million fund to compensate wartime slave laborers. See "IG Farben to Set up Holocaust Fund," *Wall Street Journal*, August 19, 1999, A10. A spokesperson for the I.G. Farben survivors' group called the amount "laughably small" and demanded that the company, ordered by the Allies to be liquidated after the war, complete its liquidation and distribute to survivors the $11 million in assets that it still holds. "Survivors Want Gas Co. Liquidated," *AP Online*, August 16, 1999.

13. "Companies and the Holocaust: Industrial Actions," *The Economist*, November 14, 1998, 75.

14. Thomas S. Mulligan, "Lawsuit Alleges Ford Profited from Forced Labor in WWII," *Los Angeles Times*, March 5, 1998, D1.

15. On its Web site, Ford sets out its side of story. See http://media.ford.com/events/fw_research.cfm.

16. Allan Hall, "Holocaust Survivors Sue Designer Hugo Boss in Slave Labour Case," *The Scotsman*, May 15, 1999, 17.

17. Beata Pasek, "Nazi Slaves Still Feel Victimized," *AP Online*, April 5, 1999.

18. Ibid.

19. Frances A. McMorris, "Milberg Weiss Lawyer Focuses on Cases for Holocaust Survivors," *Wall Street Journal*, May 19, 1999, B7.

20. Ibid.

21. Daniel Kurtzman, "Holocaust Survivors Want Firms in Germany to Pay Compensation," *Jewish Telegraphic Agency*, September 2, 1998.

22. Jonathan Weisman, "Redress Sought in Nazi-Era Labor," *Baltimore Sun*, August 23, 1999, 1A.

23. Henry Ford, the founder of the Ford Motor Company, was well known for his anti-Semitic activities in the 1920s and 1930s, including the first American publication of *The Protocols of the Learned Elders of Zion* and *The International Jew*, a collection of anti-Semitic articles from Ford's own newspaper, the *Dear-*

born Independent. See Neil Baldwin, *Henry Ford and the Jews* (New York: Public Affairs, 2001).

24. Lynda Hurt, "Decades of Delay: Wages of Nazi Slavery," *Toronto Star,* August 28, 1999, A1.

25. "Slave Labor," *60 Minutes Transcript,* November 29, 1998.

26. Andrew Quinn, "Calif. Suit Filed over Holocaust-Era Slave Labor, *Seattle Times,* April 1, 1999, A16.

27. The German companies argued that the lawsuits against them cannot be maintained in the United States because of (1) the existence of alternative resolution mechanisms for resolving the suits; (2) nonjusticiability (meaning that the lawsuits raise political questions not capable of being handled by the courts); (3) lack of jurisdiction, both personal and subject matter; (4) *forum non conveniens;* and (5) the statute of limitations. The German companies referred to various treaties between defeated Germany and the victorious Allies that they claim do not allow litigation against them in the United States for their wartime wrongs.

28. Gerald M. Steinberg, "The Holocaust Did Not 'Just Happen,'" *Jerusalem Post,* October 23, 1998, 9.

29. Ibid.

30. The Germans are fond of using other euphemisms when dealing with World War II. The term "Nazi" is best avoided; the preferred formulation is the "National Socialist" regime. The German program of working slave laborers to death is labeled "forced labor . . . performed under particularly harsh conditions." The regime of sanctions either imposed on or threatened by New York, California, and other states for the German companies' failure to settle the claims of the slave laborers is called "administrative and legislative measures against German companies . . . in various U.S. states." And finally, the dropping of all lawsuits against Germany and German firms arising from their activities during the war is called "legal peace."

31. Information about the German fund and the subsequent DM 10 billion ($5 billion) settlement can be found at the foundation's Web site, www.stiftungsinitiave.de.

32. Sara Silver, "Germany to Push Cos. on Restitution," *AP Online,* March 3, 1999.

33. Roger Cohen, "German Companies Set up Fund for Slave Laborers under Nazis," *New York Times,* February 17, 1999, A1. According to the *New York Times,* the announcement of the fund "was clearly aimed at stopping a wave of lawsuits in American courts against German companies that used slave labor and forced labor during World War II" (ibid.).

34. The original twelve were three German automotive giants, Daimler-Chrysler, Volkswagen, and BMW; two German banks, Deutsche Bank and Dresner Bank; two German chemical and pharmaceutical concerns, Bayer and

Degussa; one German insurance company, Allianz; and three other blue-chip German industrial companies, Krupp, BASF, and Hoechst. The twelve participants invited other German companies to join the fund and make a contribution. In August 1999, four more German companies agreed to join: Siemens, Commerzbank, Veba, and RAG, making a total of sixteen German companies participating.

35. Contrast this with the talks on Holocaust-era insurance claims (see chapter 3), in which important parties, such as the trial lawyers, were kept out of the negotiation sessions. The insurance talks accordingly failed.

36. House Committee on Banking and Financial Services, *World War II Assets of Holocaust Victims*, testimony by Burt Neuborne, September 14, 1999, 8, quoting Count Lambsdorff.

37. Weisman, "Redress Sought," 1A.

38. House of Representatives Committee on Banking and Financial Services, statement of Dr. Otto Graf Lambsdorff, February 9, 2000.

39. Henry Weinstein, "Firms Offer Fund for WWII Slave Labor," *Los Angeles Times*, June 11, 1999, A1.

40. Ibid.

41. Ibid.

42. "German Companies Withhold Payments," *Sun-Sentinel* (Fort Lauderdale, Fla.), June 11, 1999, D3.

43. House Committee on Banking and Financial Services, *World War II Assets of Holocaust Victims*, testimony by Burt Neuborne, September 14, 1999, 4.

44. Weisman, "Redress Sought," 1A.

45. Roger Cohen, "Germany: Schroeder on Slave Talks," *New York Times*, September 8, 1999, A11.

46. *Iwanowa v. Ford Motor Co.*, 67 F. Supp. 2d 424 (D.N.J. 1999).

47. *Burger-Fischer v. Degussa AG*, 65 F. Supp. 2d 248 (D.N.J. 1999) (hereafter Degussa/Siemens).

48. I discuss in detail those earlier claims in my "Nuremberg in America: Litigating the Holocaust in American Courts," *University of Richmond Law Review* 34 (2000): 19–30.

49. Degussa/Siemens, 255. In the conclusion of the opinion, the court reaffirms these findings: "The plaintiffs' accounts of the wrongs they suffered at the hands of the Nazi government and the defendants are deemed to be completely accurate. The historical events recited herein are established either by undisputed submissions in the record or are of common knowledge."

50. Degussa/Siemens. In response to the popular misconception that the German corporations were complying with German law (albeit enacted by the Nazis) at the time they used slave labor, the plaintiffs' German law expert pointed out that "slavery and involuntary servitude have been prohibited in Germany since 1871 and that Section 234 of the German Civil Code prohibits

slavery and involuntary servitude under penalty of imprisonment" (ibid., 257).

51. *Iwanova v. Ford Motor Co.*, 65 F. Supp. 2d 424, 440 (D.N.J. 1999).

52. Ibid.

53. Degussa/Siemens, 254–55.

54. Ibid., 282.

55. Ibid., 285. Judge Debevoise also lamented that "were the court to undertake to fashion appropriate reparations for the plaintiffs in the present case, it would lack any standards to apply." The court continued: "Wrongs were suffered not only by the classes of persons represented in these proceedings, however, but also by many other classes of persons in many lands. They, too, had claims against resources among all the deserving groups. By what practical means could a single court acquire the information needed to fashion such a standard? This was a task which the nations involved sought to perform as they negotiated the Potsdam Agreement, the Paris Agreement, the Restitution Agreement and the 2 + 4 Treaty. It would be presumptuous for this court to attempt to do a better job" (ibid., 284).

56. See Bazyler, "Nuremberg in America," 209–32. I believe that if the judges' dismissals had been heard on appeal, they would have been overturned. However, the parties settled all claims three months later, and the appeals were dropped. Consequently, the rulings were never reviewed by a higher court.

57. Tom Hayden, "Ex-slave Laborers Deserve Far Better; Holocaust: Rich Firms Get Good Press with Token Payments, but What about the Victims?" *Los Angeles Times*, December 30, 1999, B11.

58. House Committee on Banking and Financial Services, *World War II Assets of Holocaust Victims*, testimony by Deputy Treasury Secretary Stuart E. Eizenstat, September 14, 1999, 8.

59. Ibid., 9.

60. Roger Cohen, "Nazi Slave Labor Talks Halt over Payments," *New York Times*, November 4, 1999, A12.

61. David R. Sands, "Stall Tactics Charged over Holocaust Legal Claims," *Washington Times*, October 6, 1999, A12.

62. See Holman W. Jenkins Jr., "Once More into the Dock with 'Nazi' Companies," *Wall Street Journal*, March 24, 1999, A27.

63. Mel Weiss had this to say about the new $3.3 billion figure: "The world will judge the morality of this offer and . . . will condemn it." Pauline Jelinek, "Nazi Victims Snub Offer," *Chicago Sun-Times*, October 8, 1999, 44.

64. In a November 1999 interview, Stuart Eizenstat commented on the difficulty of getting the plaintiffs' lawyers to agree to the DM 10 billion settlement figure. I "had to battle long and hard to persuade plaintiffs' lawyers . . . to lower their proposals from well-above the range of 10 billion to 15 billion marks." See

Roger Cohen, "Talks on Compensating Nazi-Era Slaves Turn to Sour Haggling," *New York Times*, November 18, 1999, A7.

65. Unlike the Swiss bank settlement, which was in U.S. dollars, the German settlement, at Germany's insistence, was in German marks. As a result, the value of the settlement fluctuated according to the value of the mark. Unfortunately, after December 1999, when the tentative deal was reached, the mark steadily lost value, about 20 percent. By 2002, when the first payments to the survivors went out, the deal was worth $4.8 billion.

66. German Foundation Law, article 9(4).

67. Burt Herman, "WWII Slave Labor Deal Sought," *AP Online*, August 27, 1999. See also chapter 6 for a discussion of the definition of "Holocaust survivor."

68. Herman, "WWII Slave Labor Deal Sought."

69. Roger Cohen, "Accord Reached on Forced Labor; Germany Settles Allocation of $5B to Survivors, Others," *New York Times*, March 24, 2000, A1.

70. German Foundation Law, sections 9(1), 11(1), and 12(1). The Germans also took a credit for any payments received by former slave laborers from the German companies which, before the fund was established, had already made payments to their slaves (ibid., section 15[2]). For instance, in 1998 Volkswagen began a $12-million private relief effort for its former slave laborers. Former slaves who received payment from the Volkswagen private fund were not eligible for payment from the German Foundation.

71. House Committee on Banking and Financial Services, prepared statement by Treasury Deputy Secretary Stuart E. Eizenstat, February 9, 2000, 6.

72. On October 19, 2000, the U.S. and German governments exchanged diplomatic notes putting the Executive Agreement into effect.

73. The formal law establishing the foundation is known as Gesetz Zur Errichtung Einder Stiftung "Erinnerung; Verantwortung und Zukunft" (Law on the Creation of a Foundation "Remembrance, Responsibility and Future") (hereafter German Foundation Law). In accordance with the German Foundation Law, the foundation is governed by a twenty-seven-member board of trustees (Kuratorium) and administered by a three-member board of directors that reports to the board of trustees. Prominent German political figures were asked to head the two bodies. As part of the deal, one trustee on the foundation board had to be chosen from the American class action lawyers involved in the litigation. The natural choice was the lawyer most trusted by all sides: Professor Burt Neuborne.

74. House Committee on Banking and Financial Services, *Hearing*, 106th Cong., 2d sess., February 9, 2000, 6.

75. The term *historic responsibility* was used in the preamble to the German law creating the German Foundation. As for the responsibility of the German people for Nazi-era crimes, the preamble stated that "the German Bundestag

acknowledges political and moral responsibility for the victims of National Socialism. The Bundestag intends to keep alive the memory of the injustice inflicted on the victims for coming generations as well."

76. Cohen, "German Companies Set up Fund," A1.

77. See www.stifttungsinitiative.de (preamble of the German Economy Foundation Initiative Steering Group). The Germans meant what they said. As discussed later, when one American judge, Judge Shirley Wohl Kram, refused to dismiss the litigation against the German banks until some details were resolved, she suggested that payments to the elderly survivors not be held up, urging that the Germans begin making interim payments to the survivors. The Germans would not budge; until all U.S. litigation against them was dismissed, not one German pfennig would be forthcoming.

78. As the Joint Statement of Principles declares, this condition will be achieved only "once all lawsuits against German companies arising out the Nationalist Socialist era and World War II pending in U.S. courts . . . are finally dismissed with prejudice by the courts" (Joint Statement of Principles, article 4). The German Foundation Law, promulgated by the Bundenstag, confirms this ironclad condition. Article 17(2) of the Foundation Law deferred the "allocation" of any of the funds to the survivors until the "establishment of adequate legal security for German enterprises."

79. "No Deal Yet on Holocaust Payments," *Reuters Online*, June 3, 2000.

80. According to article 17(2) of the German Foundation Law: "The first allocation of funds to the Foundation requires as a precondition . . . the establishment of adequate legal security for German enterprises. The German Bundestag shall determine whether these preconditions exist." Explained one of the American attorneys defending the German companies, "It's for the German Bundestag and government to decide what is adequate legal security." See Mark Hamblett, "Second Circuit Rejects Judge's Holocaust Settlement Conditions," *New York Law Journal*, May 18, 2001, 1.

81. "Germany Criticises U.S. on Slave Labour Talks," *Reuters Online*, June 5, 2000.

82. Executive Agreement, section 2(1). Of course, the executive branch's filing a Statement of Interest urging dismissal of a lawsuit does not guarantee that a court in the United States would follow the executive branch's suggestion and automatically dismiss.

83. In re *Nazi Era Cases against German Defendants Litigation*, 198 F.R.D. 429 (D.N.J. 2000). One Holocaust survivor, Si Frumkin of Los Angeles, refused to dismiss his lawsuit, preferring to continue his case against his former German master, the German construction company Phillip Holzmann A.G. Judge Bassler would not allow him to do so. In March 2001, Bassler dismissed Frumkin's suit, along with all the others, forcing Frumkin to accept the DM 15,000 from the foundation as his only remedy. *Frumkin v. J.A. Jones*, 129 F. Supp.

2d 370 (D.N.J. 2001). Frumkin has not given up. He has filed a lawsuit against the United States, *Frumkin v. USA*, before the Court of Federal Claims in Washington, D.C., seeking now to have the U.S. government pay what his former German master owes him.

84. Steve Chambers, "Dismissal of Other Suits Clears Way for Slave-Labor Reparations," *Star-Ledger* (Newark, N.J.), November 14, 2000, 7.

85. John Schmidt, "Deutsche Bank Says It 'Regrets' Nazi Deals," *International Herald Tribune*, August 1, 1998, 1.

86. Jenkins, "Once More into the Dock," A27.

87. An Austrian bank representative, John Rees of Creditanstalt, testified at the November 1, 1999, fairness hearing that the assigned claims for mismanagement and plunder involved securities valued at $300 million.

88. George John, "Bank Offers $92M for Holocaust Role," *AP Online*, January 31, 1999.

89. In re *Austrian and German Holocaust Litigation*, 80 F. Supp. 2d 164 (S.D.N.Y. 2000). As with the Swiss bank settlement, Judge Kram authorized the creation of a Web site to chart the progress of the settlement, www.austrian-bankclaims.com. The Second Circuit court, likewise relying on representations of additional money becoming available for the Austrian Holocaust claimants from the Austrian bank assignment, subsequently upheld Judge Kram's decision that the Austrian settlement was fair. *D'Amato v. Deutsche Bank*, 236 F. 3d 78 (2nd Cir. 2001).

90. While Judge Kram's denial of the dismissal appeared to have delayed the payments to the survivors, in fact it had the effect of speeding up the resolution process. Besides the extinguishment of the Austrian banks' assigned claims, Judge Kram was also concerned that she was being asked to dismiss the survivors' claims, even though the foundation still had not yet been fully funded. The German companies were dragging their feet in fully funding their portion (DM 5 billion) of the foundation. In her ruling, the judge said she could not dismiss the lawsuit without assurance that the foundation had the money to pay the claimants. Five days after Judge Kram's ruling, the Germans miraculously solved the funding problem. The original sixteen founding German companies put up a *Burwechaft*, the German equivalent of a letter of credit, guaranteeing any shortfall in the German industry's contribution.

91. In a press release following Judge Kram's ruling, the U.S. State Department asserted that her "decision is contrary to the recommendations of all parties having an interest in the case and will delay justice and payments to Holocaust victims, a significant number of whom are dying each month" (press release 2001/179, March 7, 2001). The characterization was both untrue and unfair, as not all interested parties recommended dismissal. The Austrian survivors and their representatives urged that the suits not be dismissed until their claims were properly handled.

92. Henry Weinstein, "Holocaust Survivors Settlement Hits Snag," *Los Angeles Times*, March 10, 2001, A15.

93. Mark John, "Germany Seeks Disqualification of Nazi Slaves Judge," *Reuters Online*, March 29, 2001.

94. Ibid.

95. Mark Hamblett, "Second Circuit Rejects Judge's Holocaust Settlement Conditions," *New York Law Journal*, May 18, 2001.

96. Ibid.

97. The German Foundation's Web site proudly announced that more than 6,000 German firms contributed to the fund, many of whom did not exist during the war or did not use slave labor. These included subsidiaries of American companies, some that did use slave labor, such as Ford Werke, and some that did not, such as Coca-Cola Essen, the German unit of the American soft drink giant, and Esso Deutschland, a unit of ExxonMobil.

98. Imre Karacs, "Germany Clears the Way for Nazi Slave Payments," *The Independent*, May 31, 2001, 15. One excuse used by the German companies was that under the Berlin Accords they were not obligated to fully fund the foundation until "legal peace" was achieved. However, even after all the dismissals were obtained, not all the funds were delivered to the foundation.

99. "[German] Firms Urged to Pay Nazi Slave Fund," *CNN.com*, March 8, 2001. According to the *Times of London*, Hans Eichel, the finance minister, reacted angrily, saying: "It's up to business to pay up, and be very quick about it." Roger Boyes, "US Court Puts Nazi Slave Deal in Peril," *Times of London*, March 9, 2001, 1. Chancellor Schroeder put it more diplomatically, "German industry knows what its responsibilities are." Markus Krah, "German Firms Raise Share of Nazi Slave Reparation." *Reuters Online*, March 13, 2001. At a speech in March to trade unionists in Berlin, Schroeder was interrupted by a protester who interrupted his speech by coming onto the stage carrying a banner reading, "Immediate payment for every forced labourer instead of closure for the culprits." Emma Thomasson, "Germany to Fight New Legal Hurdle to Holocaust Fund," *Reuters Online*, March 21, 2001.

100. "Israel President Asks German Firms to Pay Slaves," *Reuters Online*, March 10, 2001.

101. Burt Herman, "Poland Wants Slave Money Released," *AP Online*, April 6, 2001. To help their survivors, Poland, before even receiving the funds from Germany, sent to eligible survivors in Poland older than eighty an interim payment of $350. Approximately 50,000 such checks were sent (ibid.).

102. Burt Herman, "Germans Raise Compensation Fund," *AP Online*, March 13, 2001.

103. Ibid.

104. Because of the German companies' miserliness, the suggested

amount that each German firm should contribute had to be raised. Originally, voluntary industry contributions were set at a rate of 0.1 percent of the 1998 turnover. It was then raised to 0.15 percent to make up the shortfall, and the sixteen founding members were forced to increase their contribution to 0.2 percent of the turnover.

105. Imre Karacs, "Germany Clears the Way for Nazi Slave Payments," *London Independent*, May 31, 2001, 15.

106. Ibid.

107. Ibid.

108. Peter Ford, "Europe's Halting Path to Resolve Nazi Era," *Christian Science Monitor*, June 4, 2001, 1.

109. Roger Cohen, "Last Chapter: Berlin to Pay Slave Workers Held by Nazis," *New York Times*, May 31, 2001, A1.

110. Besides the former slave laborers, those persons on whom the Nazis performed medical experiments also began receiving money in 2002, most of whom also qualified for payments as slave laborers. Approximately 4,400 claimants sought compensation under the Medical Experiments portion of the German Fund. Non-Jewish forced laborers claiming compensation under the *Kinderheim* portion of the German Fund received their first checks in 2003. The *Kinderheim* were the "Nazi nurseries" set up to take care of those infants and small children whose mothers were shipped to Germany and Austria and forced to work there. Under the horrid conditions in these nurseries, most of the infants and children perished. I discuss the claims of the victims of the medical experiments and the still-living mothers (all non-Jewish from eastern Europe) against German companies in "Nuremberg in America," 249–56 (medical experiments claims) and 256–58 (*Kinderheim* claims).

111. The German Foundation Law states that "the approval and disbursement of one-time payments to those persons eligible . . . will be carried out through partner organizations. The Foundation is neither authorized nor obligated in this regard." Foundation Law, section 10 (1). Translation: The Germans are not responsible for the payment or distribution of this money. If something goes wrong, we are not to blame, and you cannot sue us.

112. The governments themselves of Russia, Ukraine, Belarus, Moldova, Estonia, Poland, and the Czech Republic wanted to distribute the fund money owed to their citizens and so created their own partner organizations. Sometimes this proved to be not such a good idea. For instance, the Polish government's insistence that it be in charge of distribution in Poland led to the poor "German marks for Polish zlotys" exchange deal, discussed later, which resulted in the Polish beneficiaries' receiving less than their counterparts in other countries.

113. For the IOM Web site on the German settlement program, see www.compensation-for-forced-labour.org.

114. German Foundation Law, section 9(7).

115. This is a common scenario in American litigation. Upon settlement of a case, the costs of the litigation are taken care of at the outset, including the fees due to the lawyers who successfully prosecuted the suits.

116. Yair Sheleg, "Profits of Doom," *Ha'aretz*, June 29, 2001, 1.

117. Sheleg, "Profits of Doom."

118. Daniel Wise, "$60 Million in Fees Awarded to Lawyers Who Negotiated $5 Billion Holocaust Fund," *New York Law Journal*, June 15, 2001, 1.

119. Ibid.

120. Toby Axelrod, "Lawyers for Nazi-Era Slave Laborers Urged to Use Fees to Help Survivors," *JTA Newswire*, June 26, 2001.

121. Ibid.

122. Ibid.

123. Ibid.

124. E-mail from Morris A. Ratner to me, June 17, 2002.

125. Weisman, "Redress Sought," 1A.

126. Marilyn Henry, "Slave Labor Pact Reached with Germany," *Jerusalem Post*, March 24, 2000, 7A: "British survivors said yesterday that they would pursue their claims in European courts." Daniel Johnson, "Comment: Germany Must Pay the Nazis' Slaves," *Daily Telegraph*, December 7, 1999, 14: "Even if their lawyers agree to a deal, dissident survivors could refuse to accept it. . . . The rebels could open up a new front by initiating proceedings at the European Court of Human Rights. Their legal advice, I understand, is they would stand an excellent chance of success."

127. "Restitution Deal with Austria Likely," *Jerusalem Post*, February 28, 2000, 6.

128. Michael Adler, "Eizenstat Says Key Agreement Reached on Slave Labor Payments," *Agence France-Presse*, February 16, 2000.

129. "Nazi Slave Labor Talks Adjourn in Dispute," *Reuters Online*, March 3, 2000.

130. Ibid.

131. Neuborne's lawsuit listed the breaches of the agreement by the German companies just discussed. In addition, Neuborne sued the Austrian banks and their current owner, Germany's Hypo Vereinsbank, to honor the representations made by the Austrian banks regarding the purported value of the Austrian banks' assignment in the Austrian bank settlement deal.

132. *Ukrainian National Association of Jewish Former Prisoners of Concentration Camps and Ghettos v. United States*, 182 F. Supp. 2d 305 (E.D.N.Y. 2001).

133. Edmund L. Andrews, "Germans, Citing Suits, Say They're Holding War Slaves' Fund," *New York Times*, March 15, 2001, A1.

134. *Ukrainian National Association of Jewish Former Prisoners of Concentration Camps and Ghettos v. United States*, 178 F. Supp. 2d 312 (E.D.N.Y. 2001).

135. Henry Weinstein, "Holocaust Insurance Claim Deadline Gets Pushed Back," *Los Angeles Times*, January 27, 2002, A16.

136. *Gross v. The German Foundation Industrial Initiative*, no. 02-CV-2936 (WGB), filed June 20, 2002.

137. The Germans made the fund payments "strictly personal and individual" (German Foundation Law, section 13[2]). Heirs of survivors were not entitled to payment, and so the payments came too late to help the millions of former slave laborers and their families who died before the funds were distributed. The Germans made one exception: if an eligible survivor was alive on February 15, 1999, when the fund proposal was first announced by Chancellor Schroeder, the "surviving spouse and children shall be entitled to equal shares of the award." In the event there was no surviving wife or children, other heirs of such a recently deceased survivor could receive the funds.

138. Toby Axelrod, "Lawyers for Nazi-era Slave Laborers Urged to Use Fees to Help Survivors," *JTA Newswire*, June 26, 2001 (quoting Jewish survivor Gunter Nobel of Berlin).

139. Burt Herman, "Nazis' Slave Laborers to Get $7,500 Each," *AP Online*, March 24, 2000.

140. William Drozdiak, "Payments Set for Ex-Slaves of Nazi Germany," *Washington Post*, March 24, 2000, A13.

141. Bob Mims, "Holocaust Survivor Waits for News after Filing Compensation Claim," *Salt Lake City Tribune*, January 28, 2002, A1.

142. Cohen, "Last Chapter," A1.

143. Weinstein, "Holocaust Survivors Settlement Hits Snag," A15.

144. Ibid.

145. Laura Mecoy, "Some Nazi Camp Laborers Attack Compensation Plan," *Sacramento Bee*, December 18, 1999, A1.

146. Ibid. Both Frumkin and Deutsch called me soon after the settlement was announced, looking for some way they could opt out of it. I could not offer them any hope, telling them that if they pursued their suits, they would be necessarily dismissed as soon as the U.S. government filed a Statement of Interest recommending dismissal. Frumkin and Deutsch nevertheless pushed on. On March 1, 2001, the federal district judge, following the submission of the U.S. Statement of Interest urging the dismissal of Frumkin's lawsuit, dismissed it along with all the others (see preceding discussion). In an ironic, but tragic twist, Frumkin's wartime master was Phillip Holzmann, A.G., whose U.S. subsidiary, J.A. Jones, Inc., received the contract to built the World War II memorial in Washington, D.C. Deutsch's suit, filed in federal court in Los Angeles, likewise was dismissed a year later at the urging of the U.S. government.

147. Matt Miller, "Holocaust Survivors Await Amends," *Patriot-News Harrisburg*, June 24, 2001, B4.

148. Daniel Kurtzman, "Holocaust Survivors Want Firms in Germany to Pay Compensation," *Jewish Telegraphic Agency*, September 2, 1998.

149. Herman, "WWII Slave Labor Deal Sought."

150. Roger Cohen, "Germany Adds $555 Million to Offer in Nazi Slave Cases," *New York Times*, November 16, 1999, A8.

151. Marilyn Henry, "Germans Announce Fund for Holocaust Slaves," *Jerusalem Post*, February 17, 1999, 4.

152. Weiss justified his change of strategy as follows: "The Germans fell far short of the mark in terms of an expression of humanity or generosity. Unfortunately, we have an aging clientele. We are getting a lot of pressure from the governments of Israel and the United States to provide money quickly because of the circumstances. But it's far from adequate." See Norman Kempster, "Agreement Reached on Nazi Slave Reparations," *Los Angeles Times*, December 15, 2001, A1.

153. Hayden, "Ex-Slave Laborers Deserve Far Better," B11.

154. Ibid.

155. Ibid.

156. House Committee on Banking and Financial Services, *Hearing*, 106th Cong., 2d sess., February 9, 2000, 6.

157. Declaration of Stuart E. Eizenstat, paragraph 30, attached as exhibit 1 to Statement of Interest of the United States in In re *Nazi Era Cases against German Defendants*.

158. Eizenstat gave another reason why an overall settlement with the entire German industry was preferable to U.S. court judgments against specific German companies: A settlement benefits all who have been injured by German industry during the war, whereas a court judgment helps only those survivors who worked as slaves for German companies that (1) are still in existence today and (2) do business in the United States, so as to be subject to the jurisdiction of American courts.

159. Kempster, "Agreement Reached on Nazi Slave Reparations," A1.

160. "Laborers Lost Money Can't Buy Justice for Nazi-Camp Survivors," *Pittsburgh Post-Gazette*, December 17, 1999, A30 (editorial).

161. "Practicality, Not Justice," *Jerusalem Post*, March 26, 2000, 6 (editorial).

162. In the early 1990s, with the fall of the Iron Curtain and the unification of East and West Germany, Germany made payments to some of these "double victims" in Belarus, Poland, Russia, Ukraine, and the Czech Republic. Approximately 1.5 million survivors received an average payment of $600. House Committee on Banking and Financial Services, *Hearing*, testimony by Dr. Otto Graf Lambsdorff, 106th Cong., 2d sess., February 9, 2000, 6.

163. "What has to be done now is . . . for the Federal Government [of Austria] to provide rapid compensation to the victims of forced labour during the

Nazi regime by taking into account the responsibility of the enterprises concerned. The new Government will ensure that the former forced labourers, who are now of an age in which they urgently need help, get their rights" (www.reconciliationfund.at).

164. See the Web site of the Austrian Reconciliation Fund (the Austrian slave labor fund), www.reconciliationfund.at.

165. Ibid.

166. For the Austrian nonslave labor settlement Web site, providing details of this deal, see www.nationalfonds.org.

167. Kenneth R. Timmerman, "Austria Confronts Its Dark Past" (special report), *Insight on the News*, August 12, 2002, 24, available at www.insightmag.com.

168. Peter Ford, "Europe's Halting Path to Resolve Nazi Era," *Christian Science Monitor*, June 4, 2001, 1.

NOTES TO CHAPTER 3

1. Steven Sullivan, "Marta's List: The Pursuit of Holocaust Survivors' Lost Insurance Claims," *Contingencies* (Journal of the American Academy of Actuaries) (July/August 1998): 18 (quoting Elan Steinberg, WJC executive director).

2. Deborah Senn, "Private Insurers and Unpaid Holocaust Era Insurance Claims," *Washington State Insurance Commission Report*, April 30, 1999, 3–4 (hereafter Senn Report). The full report can be located on the Washington State Insurance Web site, www.insurance.wa.gov.

3. Alan Gersten, "Making Amends—European Insurers Are Finally Accepting Some Liability for Unpaid Holocaust Victims' Claims," *Life Insurance International*, October 1, 1998, 7.

4. LeeAnn Spencer, "Quest for Holocaust Insurance Benefits: Survivors, Heirs Testify about Their Unpaid Claims," *Chicago Tribune*, November 11, 1997, 1.

5. Senn Report, 8.

6. George Raine, "Recovering Nazi Plunder," *San Francisco Examiner*, November 16, 1997, D1.

7. Greg Steinmetz and Anita Raghavan, "Big Insurer Calls Shots in Germany, Inc.," *Wall Street Journal*, November 1, 1999, A41.

8. Fay Cashman, "Grapevine," *Jerusalem Post*, August 21, 1998, 18. By the late 1930s, Generali's Jewish directors and managers in Italy had been removed from their positions under Italian Fascist laws. These laws paralleled those enacted in the Reich and were enforced less strictly until the Germans pressured Mussolini for stricter enforcement.

9. Marilyn Henry, "A Holocaust Paper Trail to Nowhere?" *Jerusalem Post*, May 12, 1999, 11.

10. Ibid.

11. Senn Report, 4, table 1.

12. Senn Report, 16.

13. "Agency Finds Nazi-Era Document," *Jerusalem Post*, April 11, 2001, 9.

14. A detailed discussion of the scheme concocted in the aftermath of *Kristallnacht* can be found in Gerald D. Feldman, *Allianz and the German Insurance Business, 1933–1945* (Cambridge: Cambridge University Press, 2001), 190–235 (chapter entitled "The 'Night of Broken Glass' and the Insurance Industry"). Another discussion can be found in the Senn Report, 16–17.

15. "Life Insurance and the Holocaust," *Insurance Forum*, September 1998, 84.

16. John Marks and Jack Egan, "Insuring Nazi Death Camps: History Catches up with Another German Corporation," *U.S. News & World Report*, February 22, 1999, 52 (citing the German magazine *Der Spiegel*).

17. Brendan Noonan, "On a Grand Scale," *Best's Review: Life-Health Insurance Edition*, December 1, 1999, 41.

18. Ibid.

19. Feldman, *Allianz and the German Insurance Business*, vii.

20. Ibid.

21. Ibid.

22. Michael Maiello and Robert Lenzner, "The Last Victims," *Forbes*, May 14, 2001, 112.

23. Ibid.

24. Greg Garland, "Holocaust Heirs Fight 'Resistance' over Reparations," *Baltimore Sun*, February 3, 2002, 1A.

25. Ibid. Kadden was instrumental in writing the reports by the Washington insurance commissioner cited in this chapter.

26. Garland, "Holocaust Heirs Fight," 1A.

27. U.S. Office of Strategic Services, Board of Economic Warfare, Enemy Branch, "Axis Penetration of European Insurance," June 15, 1943.

28. Greg Steinmetz and Anita Raghavan, "Big Insurer Calls Shots in Germany, Inc.," *Wall Street Journal*, November 1, 1999, A41.

29. *Stern v. Assicurazioni Generali S.p.A.*, First Amended Complaint, para. 31, BC 185376 (Cal. Superior Ct., filed February 5, 1998).

30. Exhibit B to First Amended Complaint, *Stern v. Assicurazioni Generali S.p.A.*

31. Ibid.

32. House Committee on Banking and Financial Services, *Hearing*, 105th Cong., 2d sess., September 10, 1998, 175. Generali is now back doing business in post-Communist eastern Europe, with offices in the Czech Republic, Slovakia, Hungary, Romania, and Poland.

33. *Cornell v. Assicurazioni Generali, S.p.A.*, 97 Civ. 2262 (S.D.N.Y. 1997).

34. *Winters v. Assicurazioni Generali, S.p.A.*, 98 Civ. 9186 (S.D.N.Y. 1998) (later renamed *Schenker v. Assicurazioni Generali, S.p.A.*).

35. For a summary of federal and state laws regarding Holocaust restitution, see Michael J. Bazyler, "Nuremberg in America," *University of Richmond Law Review* 34 (2000): 272–83, app. B.

36. Alan Abrahamson, "Searching for Justice," *Los Angeles Times Magazine*, June 20, 1999, 20.

37. David Lyons, "Holocaust Claims Get a New Boost," *National Law Journal*, May 18, 1998, A6; Aurora Mackey, "Settling Old Scores: Victims of the Third Reich Mount a New Legal Challenge," *California Lawyer*, April 1999, 17.

38. "Defendants' Memorandum of Points and Authorities Supporting Motion by Specially Appearing Defendants to Quash Summons and/or Dismiss or Stay," *Stern v. Assicurazioni Generali, S.p.A.*

39. "Declaration of Federico Baroglio," submitted in Support of "Generali's Motion to Quash and/or Dismiss or Stay," *Stern v. Assicurazioni Generali S.p.A.*

40. California Code of Civil Procedure, section 354.5.

41. The enacting legislation to the HVIA explained why California was promulgating the law:

(a) The [California] Legislature recognizes that thousands of Holocaust victims and the heirs of Holocaust victims are residents or citizens of the State of California. . . .

California has an overwhelming public policy interest in assuring that its residents and citizens who are claiming entitlement to proceeds under policies issued to Holocaust victims are treated reasonably and fairly and that those specific contractual obligations are honored.

(b) It is the specific intent of the Legislature to assure Holocaust victims be permitted to have an expeditious, inexpensive, and fair forum in which to resolve their claims for benefits under these policies by allowing actions to be brought in California courts and subject to California law, irrespective of any contrary forum selection provision contained in the policies themselves.

It is the finding of the Legislature that enforcement of forum selection provisions in those policies would work an undue, unreasonable, and unjust hardship on Holocaust victims who are residents of California and that those provisions are unenforceable with respect to the policies as to which this act applies.

42. Judge Cooper is a graduate of Whittier Law School, my home institution. In 2000, she was appointed to the federal bench and in 2002 decided another significant Holocaust restitution case, dealing with Nazi-stolen art (see chapter 5).

43. Judge Cooper's decision is available at 1999 WL 167546, and all quotations are from the decision.

44. Ibid.

45. Ibid.

46. Transcript of hearing, *Stern v. Assicurazioni Generali S.p.A.*, June 16, 1999.

47. Ibid.

48. Ibid.

49. "Holocaust Insurance Settlement Reported," *New York Times*, November 25, 1999, A4. See also Henry Weinstein, "Holocaust Victim's Heirs Settle Suit," *Los Angeles Times*, November 25, 1999, A1.

50. *Cornell v. Assicurazioni Generali S.p.A.*, 2000 U.S. Dist. LEXIS 2922 (S.D.N.Y. March 16, 2000) (dismissing UAP-Vie); *Cornell v. Assicurazioni Generali S.p.A.*, 2000 U.S. Dist. LEXIS 11004 (S.D.N.Y. August 7, 2000) (dismissing *Der Anker Allgemeine*). LEXIS legal citations are available at www.lexis.com.

51. *Cornell v. Assicurazioni Generali S.p.A.*, 2000 U.S. Dist. LEXIS 118193 (S.D.N.Y. December 19, 2000).

52. *Schenker v. Assicurazioni Generali, S.p.A.*, 2002 U.S. Dist. LEXIS 12845 (S.D.N.Y. July 11, 2002). In September 2002, however, Judge Mukasey denied the motions of Generali and Zurich to be dismissed from the litigation as well. See In re *Assicurazioni Generali S.p.A. Holocaust Insurance Litigation*, 2002 U.S. Dist. LEXIS 18127 (S.D.N.Y. September 25, 2002).

53. California Insurance Code, section 13800–807 (1999). The Registry Law was approved unanimously by both houses of the California legislature in September 1999 and signed by Governor Gray Davis on October 8, 1999. As chapter 2 discusses, Davis also filed a suit in his personal capacity against the German companies to force settlement of the German slave labor claims.

54. Quoted in George Raine, "State Takes on Major Insurers," *San Francisco Examiner*, November 14, 1999, B1.

55. Ibid.

56. Ibid.

57. George Raine, "State Goes after Insurers Despite Officials' Pleas," *San Francisco Examiner*, December 2, 1999, A25.

58. *Gerling Global Reins. Corp. v. Low*, 240 F. 3d 739 (9th Cir. 2001).

59. *Gerling Global Reins. Corp. v. Low*, 2001 U.S. Dist. LEXIS 16072 (E.D. Cal. October 2, 2001).

60. *Gerling Global Reins. Corp. v. Low*, 296 F. 3d 832 (9th Cir. July 15, 2002).

61. *Gerling Global Reins. Corp. v. Nelson*, 123 F. Supp. 2d 1298 (N.D. Fla. 2000).

62. "Probe into Insurance Pay-Outs," *Financial Times*, October 31, 1997, 5.

63. Current information about ICHEIC can be found at its Web site, www.icheic.org.

64. Letter from Bruno Dallo, general counsel of Basler-Lebens-Versicherungs-Gesellschaft, to Lawrence S. Eagleburger, January 11, 1999.

65. Avi Machlis and John Authers, "Jewish Groups Warn of Holocaust Deal Crisis," *Financial Times*, April 23, 1999, 3.

66. Ibid.

67. Quackenbush, along with Deborah Senn, the Washington State commissioner of insurance, took the most aggressive and principled stances against the European insurers in the Holocaust restitution arena. Both are now out of the picture. The next year Quackenbush was forced to resign from office after revelations that he had entered into "sweetheart" deals with other insurance companies he was regulating. Senn, who ran for the U.S. Senate, failed in her election bid. As a result, the claimants of the Holocaust insurance restitution movement lost two of their most effective government supporters.

68. Avi Machlis and John Authers, "Holocaust Compensation: Talks 'Heading for Crisis,'" *Financial Times*, April 23, 1999, 14.

69. Standard of Proof (B) states that "in assessing a claim by claimant, the participating insurance companies have agreed:

(1) not to reject any evidence as being insufficiently probative of any fact necessary to establish the claim if evidence provided is plausible in the light of all the special circumstances involved, including but not limited to the destruction caused by World War II, the Holocaust, and the lengthy period of time that has passed since the Insurance policy under consideration was obtained;

(2) not to demand unreasonably the production of any document or other evidence which, more likely than not, has been destroyed; lost or rendered inaccessible to the claimant;

(3) to consider all information submitted by the claimant together with all information recovered by the insurers and the ICHEIC during their search of insurer and other appropriate archives and at all times consider the difficulties of proving a claim after the destruction caused by World War II and the Holocaust and the lengthy period of time that has passed since the insurance policy under consideration was obtained.

70. Denise Levin, "Judge Questions Constitutionality of Holocaust Law," *Los Angeles Daily Journal*, September 8, 1999, 1.

71. Pauline Jelinek, "Insurance Claims Being Accepted from Holocaust Survivors," *AP Online*, February 15, 2000.

72. Press release, February 15, 2000.

73. "Allianz-Holocaust Claims Review in Line with Criteria," *Reuters Online*, June 2, 2000. Allianz issued a statement disputing ICHEIC's assertions: "It is very important for us that all eligible claimants are processed quickly and generously. But it is in the interest of all claimants that we do not settle claims which are not backed by any documentation" (ibid.).

74. As stated at the outset of this chapter, Jews were required to file such forms with the Nazis listing all their assets, including insurance policies. It would be irrational for a Jewish applicant to file such a form and list assets that the applicant did *not* have. The forms, therefore, serve as credible proof of existence of an insurance policy.

75. "Holocaust Claims Seen Wrongly Rejected," *Reuters Online*, June 1, 2000.

76. Ibid.

77. See Henry Weinstein, "Spending by Holocaust Claims Panel Criticized," *Los Angeles Times*, May 17, 2001, 1; Michael Maiello and Robert Lenzer, "The Last Victims: As the Jews Fled the Holocaust, European Insurers Pocketed Their Premiums," *Forbes*, May 14, 2001, 112. According to Eagleburger, $9 million was needed for worldwide advertising alerting potential beneficiaries of the ICHEIC's existence.

78. Maiello and Lenzer, "The Last Victims."

79. Yair Sheleg, "Profits of Doom," *Ha'aretz*, June 29, 2001, 1.

80. Letter from Chairman Lawrence Eagleburger to Representative Henry Waxman, April 11, 2002, 7.

81. Sheleg, "Profits of Doom," 1.

82. Letter from William M. Shernoff to Hon. Michael B. Mukasey, May 15, 2002.

83. Weinstein, "Spending by Holocaust Claims Panel Criticized," 1.

84. Statement by Bobby Brown, the Israeli government's representative to ICHEIC, made in court declaration and quoted in Henry Weinstein, "Insurers Reject Most Claims in Holocaust Cases," *Los Angeles Times*, May 9, 2001, A1.

85. Deborah Senn, Washington State insurance commissioner, "A Status Report on Holocaust-Era Insurance Claims," December 2000, 6.

86. *Buxbaum v. Assicurazioni Generali*, 33 N.Y.S. 2d 496 (Sup. Ct. 1942).

87. Elli Wohlgelernter, "Kleiner Calls for Release of Holocaust Insurance Holders Names," *Jerusalem Post*, June 23, 1999, 5.

88. Stewart Ain, "Rejected Claims Anger Jewish Groups," *Jewish Week*, May 12, 2000, 37.

89. Remarks by Deputy Treasury Secretary Stuart Eizenstat at signing ceremony establishing the Foundation for the Remembrance, Responsibility, and the Future, July 2000.

90. Stuart Eizenstat, "Justice Remains beyond Grasp of Too Many Holocaust Victims," *Forward*, October 18, 2002, 1.

91. As I show in chapter 4, the French banks made substantially the same privacy argument in the class action litigation again them, but without success. Both the federal judge and the federal magistrate presiding over the French bank cases held that under existing American discovery rules involving international litigation, European privacy laws are not an obstacle to a European

defendant's obligation to reveal information considered confidential under foreign law but not confidential under American law. See *Bodner v. Banque Paribas*, 202 F.R.D. 370 (E.D.N.Y. 2000).

92. Statement by Jorg Allgauer, representative of Alllianz, quoted in "Eagleburger Asks Quackenbush to Excuse Five Companies from Hearing," *Best Wire*, December 1, 1999.

93. Ibid.

94. "International Holocaust Commission under Fire for Lack of Claims Payment," *Best Wire*, November 16, 2001.

95. Statement by Andrew Frank, Allianz spokesperson, quoted in Weinstein, "Insurers Reject Most Claims," A1.

96. E-mail from Danny Kadden to me, July 1, 2002.

97. See www.house.gov/reform (Web site containing hearings statements and follow-up correspondence, maintained by Rep. Henry Waxman's office).

98. Sharon Samber, "Show Us the Money," *Jewish Journal*, November 12, 2001, 23.

99. Ibid.

100. Ibid.

101. Garland, "Holocaust Heirs Fight," 1A.

102. "Eagleburger Wants 'Policing' of Insurance Companies, Extended Filing Deadline," *Agence France-Presse*, November 9, 2001.

103. The leader of the pack appeared to be Generali. By October 2002, Generali had offered to pay 1,285 of the 6,834 claims that ICHEIC had received specifically naming Generali.

As of October 2002, the figures for the other ICHEIC insurers were as follows (ICHEIC, *Claims Review*, no. 19, October 18, 2002):

- Allianz: Made 103 offers and an additional 341 offers for its Italian subsidiary Reunione Adriatica on 2,691 claims received.
- Axa: Made 61 offers on 333 claims received.
- Winterthur: Made 16 offers on 86 claims received and 3 claims settled before ICHEIC's establishment.
- Zurich: Made 24 offers on 153 claims received.

104. Philip Shenon, "Holocaust Claims Commission Falling into Turmoil over Finances," *New York Times*, January 25, 2002, A4.

105. Molly Hennessy-Fiske, "Regaining Losses of Holocaust," *News & Observer* (Raleigh, N.C.), February 12, 2002, B1.

106. Ibid.

107. Garland, "Holocaust Heirs Fight," 1A.

108. Si Frumkin, "A Legacy of the Holocaust: Sealed Insurance Lists," *International Herald Tribune*, May 26, 2000, 5.

109. Ibid.

110. "Graffiti for Intellectual—Simon Says," February 25, 2002, 1 (Frumkin's self-published newsletter).

111. Interestingly, more information can be gleaned about ICHEIC's operation and the issues it is facing from the Web site created by Congressman Henry Waxman on Holocaust-era insurance than on the official ICHEIC Web site. Unlike the ICHEIC Web site, Waxman's contains every piece of correspondence between his office and the ICHEIC and also transcripts of the hearing held on the issue. See www.house.gov/reform/min/maj/maj _holocaust.htm.

112. Letter from Sam Dubbin to Attorney General Janet Reno, September 18, 2000 (italics in original).

113. "Time to Settle," *Financial Times*, January 25, 2002, 12 (editorial).

114. Ibid.

115. Ibid.

116. Sharon Samber, "Intrigue at Holocaust Insurance Commission," *Jewish Press*, February 1, 2002, 9.

117. Quoted in Amanda Levin, "Holocaust Panel Head Ends Negotiations," *National Underwriter*, August 9, 1999, 29.

118. Henry Weinstein, "Holocaust Insurance Claim Deadline Gets Pushed Back," *Los Angeles Times*, January 27, 2002, A16.

119. "Regulators Frustrated by Stalled Holocaust-Era Claims," *Best Wire*, February 25, 2002.

120. Ibid.

121. Weinstein, "Holocaust Insurance Claim Deadline," A16.

122. "Insurers with Unresolved Holocaust-Era Claims May Face Lawsuits," *Best Wire*, February 25, 2002.

123. "Former Official Defends Record on Shoah Envoy," *Forward*, February 22, 2002 (letter to the editor from Stuart Eizenstat).

124. Weinstein, "Holocaust Insurance Claim Deadline," A16.

125. John Authers and Richard Wolffe, "A Web of Disgust," *Financial Times*, June 21, 2002, 1 (parentheses in original).

126. Memorandum from Lawrence S. Eagleburger to ICHEIC Companies, June 7, 2002.

127. Ibid.

128. Ibid.

129. E-mail from Nat Shapo to me, October 29, 2002. Looking into the future, Shapo struck a cautionary note. "The [September 2002] agreement [with the German insurance companies] holds a lot of promise but will be a severe test for ICHEIC, which hasn't operated smoothly in the past as it should have. . . . It's got great potential for survivors, but at this time, it's just potential." See "Holocaust Commission to Distribute $275 Million from German Companies," *Best's Insurance News*, October 21, 2002, 3.

130. Greg Garland, "Agency Turmoil Hinders Claims from Holocaust," *Baltimore Sun*, July 7, 2002, 1A.

131. "The Holocaust Endures," *Baltimore Sun*, July 14, 2002, 4F (editorial).

132. "Battle Brews on Insurance Pact," *Forward*, August 26, 1998, 3.

133. Denise Levin, "Judge Questions Constitutionality of Holocaust Law," *Los Angeles Daily Journal*, September 8, 1999, 1.

134. Ibid. Eizenstat continues to defend ICHEIC. In "Justice Remains beyond Grasp," his October 18, 2002, article in the *Forward* Eizenstat wrote,

I believe Eagleburger and ICHEIC have gotten a bum rap from critics. For sure, ICHEIC has not been a model of efficiency. But its problems were caused largely by internal dissension. Its high costs resulted from an expensive but necessary worldwide outreach program to notify potential claimants, establishing a claims process that would be free to victims and subsidizing costly travel to meetings in Jerusalem, New York and Washington. None of these costs would come out of the benefits to claimants. The delays resulted largely from the German companies trying to disregard obligations we felt they had made two years earlier.

135. Adam Lebor, "The Final Insult," *Times of London*, October 28, 2000, 24. Eizenstat even insisted that the meetings be moved to a new date if one of the plaintiffs' attorneys could not appear at one of the negotiating sessions with Germany.

136. Lebor, "The Final Insult."

137. Ibid.

138. Tom Tugend, "Holocaust Claims Are Rejected," *Jewish Chronicle*, May 12, 2000, 4.

139. Yair Sheleg, "No General Agreement on the Generali Agreement," *Ha'aretz*, June 20, 2000, 1.

140. Ibid.

141. *Agence France-Presse*, November 9, 2001.

142. Tim Boxer, "With the Bushes, Son Shines," *Jewish Week*, May 10, 2002, 47.

143. Letter from ICHEIC Chairman Eagleburger to forty-five congressional representatives, October 11, 2000.

144. Weinstein, "Spending," 1.

145. Garland, "Holocaust Heirs Fight," 1A.

146. ICHEIC press release, February 15, 2000.

147. Under the West German monetary reform law of 1948, there was a ten-to-one devaluation (ten Reichmarks would be worth one West German deutsche mark).

148. Garland, "Agency Turmoil," 1A (quoting Steven Pridham).

NOTES TO CHAPTER 4

1. On the history of Vichy France and French collaboration with the Germans, see Susan Zucotti, *The Holocaust, the French and the Jews* (Lincoln: University of Nebraska Press, 1993); and Michael. R. Marrus and Robert O. Paxton, *Vichy France and the Jews* (Stanford, CA: Stanford University Press, 1981). For legal discussions, see Richard H. Weisberg, *Vichy Law and the Holocaust in France* (New York: New York University Press 1996); and Vivian Grosswald Curran, "The Legalization of Racism in a Constitutional State: Democracy's Suicide in Vichy France," *Hastings Law Journal* 1 (1998): 50. Professors Weisberg and Curran spoke at the Fordham Law School symposium in November 2001 on the morality of Holocaust restitution. Their remarks can be found in "Symposium—Holocaust Restitution: Reconciling Moral Imperatives with Legal Initiatives and Diplomacy," *Fordham Law Journal* 25 (2001): S-107–32, 154–62.

2. See Mattéoli Commission, "Summary of the Work by the Study Mission on the Spoliation of Jews in France," April 17, 2000, 10, 25.

3. See House Committee on Banking and Financial Services, *World War II Assets of Holocaust Victims*, testimony by Professor Richard Weisberg, September 14, 1999.

4. Both Professors Weisberg and Curran provide good summaries of the recent historical findings. Professor Weisberg's overview can be found in his congressional testimony for the House Banking Committee just cited. See also Vivian Grosswald Curran, "Competing Frameworks for Assessing Contemporary Holocaust-Era Claims," *Fordham International Law Journal* 25 (2001): S-121.

5. House Committee on Banking and Financial Services, *World War II Assets of Holocaust Victims*, testimony by Professor Richard Weisberg, September 14, 1999.

6. Crédit Lyonnais, Paris agencies department, circular of November 21, 1940, quoted in Mattéoli Commission Interim Report, 181.

7. Ibid.

8. Curran, "Competing Frameworks," S-125. Curran summarizes the findings of French historian Lacroix-Riz as follows: "Professor Lacroix-Riz discovered records of depositions and other evidence that show a pattern of intentional falsification of past events by the banks."

9. *Bodner v. Banque Paribas*, no. 97 CV 07433 (E.D.N.Y. December 17, 1997), para. 77.

10. *Benisti v. Banque Paribas*, no. 98 CV 07851 (E.D.N.Y. December 23, 1998).

11. *Mayer v. Banque Paribas*, no. 302226 (Cal. Super. Ct. March 24, 1999). The lawsuit was filed by one plaintiff, Lily Mayer, an elderly Holocaust survivor residing in California.

12. House Committee on Banking and Financial Services, *World War II*

Assets of Holocaust Victims, statement by Professor Claire Andrieu, member of the Mattéoli Commission, September 14, 1999.

13. Mattéoli Commission, "Summary," 6. The report is available online at www.ladocfrancaise.gouv.fr.

14. Mattéoli Commission, "Summary," 5.

15. Ibid.

16. Ibid., 23.

17. Ibid., 6.

18. Ibid.

19. Ibid., 14.

20. Ibid.

21. Mattéoli Commission, "Newsletter of the Study Mission into the Looting of Jewish Assets in France," September 1999.

22. "French Panel to Pay Jews Persecuted during War," *Chicago Tribune*, September 12, 1999, 10 (quoting Henri Hadjenberg, then president of the Representative Council of French Jewish Organizations, known by its French acronym, CRIF).

23. Anne Swardson, "French Jews and Banks Fight Holocaust Lawsuits," *Washington Post*, September 14, 1999, A26.

24. Memorandum of Law of the Republic of France, 2.

25. House Committee on Banking and Financial Services, *World War II Assets of Holocaust Victims*, testimony by Elan Steinberg, September 14, 1999.

26. House Committee on Banking and Financial Services, *World War II Assets of Holocaust Victims*, testimony by Adolphe Steg, September 14, 1999.

27. See New York City's Comptroller's Proposed Brief *Amicus Curiae* in Opposition to Defendants' Motions to Dismiss (April 26, 1999) (hereafter Hevesi Brief). For a discussion of the critical role played by the Executive Committee in Holocaust restitution, see chapter 1.

28. Hevesi Brief (footnote omitted).

29. Ibid., 10.

30. Ibid., 11.

31. James Bone, "Barclays Settled with Nazi Victims," *Times of London*, August 4, 1999, 15.

32. Notice of Pendency of Class Action, Proposed Settlement of Class Action and Settlement Hearing, 3.

33. After the two federal judges in New Jersey issued their ruling, I also came to the conclusion that their rulings were in error. See the discussion in Michael J. Bazyler, "Nuremberg in America: Litigating the Holocaust," *University of Richmond Law Review* 20 (2001): 1, 209–36.

34. Defense lawyers, of course, claim that Judge Johnson ruled incorrectly and that his decision would have been overturned on appeal if the litigation had continued.

35. See *Bodner v. Banque Paribas*, 114 F. Supp. 2d 117 (E.D.N.Y. 2000).

36. Ibid., 138.

37. *Bodner v. Banque Paribas*, 202 F.R.D. 370 (E.D.N.Y. 2000).

38. The only money that came from the French government involved accounts stolen from Jews by French government-owned banks (such as the Trésor Public and Caisse des Dépots et Consignations) and for direct spoliation by the Germans of Jewish assets in French banks, such as safe-deposit boxes.

39. See www.ambafrance-us.org/news/statmnts/2001/civs2.asp for the text of the agreement.

40. United States–France Bank Agreement, annex B, section B.

41. House Committee on Banking and Financial Services, *World War II Assets of Holocaust Victims*, testimony by Elan Steinberg, September 14, 1999, 62.

42. United States–France Bank Agreement, annex B, section E.

43. E-mail from Harriet Tamen to me, June 27, 2002.

44. As discussed earlier, approximately 75,000 Jews—men, women, and children—were deported from France during World War II. In a decree dated July 13, 2000, the French government established a compensation program for survivors who were made orphans by this deportation or other acts of wartime anti-Semitic persecution in France.

45. E-mail from Morris Ratner to me, June 18, 2002.

46. E-mail from Harriet Tamen to me, June 27, 2002.

47. Curran, "Competing Frameworks," 122 (citations omitted).

48. Ibid., 121.

49. Professor Weisberg points out that this fear does not exist with regard to the Germans. Regardless of whatever our criticisms are of present-day Germany, one of them is not that Germany will try to forget, or deny, its ignoble wartime past.

NOTES TO CHAPTER 5

1. This is the estimate given by Professor Jonathan Petropoulos, historian and former research director for art and cultural property, U.S. Presidential Commission on Holocaust Assets, in his testimony before Congress in February 2000. Breaking down this figure by country, "this includes some 200,000 works in Germany and Austria, some 100,000 in Western Europe and 300,000 objects from Eastern Europe and the Soviet Union." House Committee on Banking and Finance, written comments by Jonathan Petropoulos, February 10, 2000, 2.

2. Petropoulos, however, cautions, that all "these figures are often highly speculative. At some level, it is impossible to obtain precise statistics. This stems part from the wide variation in figures provided by different countries: statistics have significant (and often political) implications, and they have been calculated in different ways. . . . Over fifty years after the end of World War II, we

do not know precisely how many objects were looted, restituted, or remain missing" (House Committee, 2).

3. Henry Bondi, quoted in Gaby Wood, "Profits and Loss," *The Guardian,* February 14, 1998, 6.

4. Jonathan Petropoulos, *Art As Politics in the Third Reich* (Chapel Hill: University of North Carolina Press, 1996), 184. Citing another expert, Petropoulos gives the figure of RM (Reichmarks) 163,975,000 spent by Hitler on art.

5. Petropoulos, *Art As Politics.*

6. See "The Art Trade under the Nazis: The Not So Secret List," *Art Newspaper,* www.theartnewspaper.com/articles/for record/jan 99. More complete information, containing not only the names but also background data on the individuals listed, has now been compiled by the U.S. National Archives and Records Administration (NARA). See www.archives.gov/research_room/holocaust_era_assets/art.

7. "The Art Trade."

8. Lynn Nicholas, "The Rape of European Art," *American University International Law Review* 14 (1998): 237, 238.

9. Colleen Smith, "Stolen 'Letter' Sparks Review of DAM Collection," *Denver Post,* September 24, 2000, 1.

10. For a study discussing art confiscated by the Soviets after the war and its fate, see Konstantin Akinsha, Gregorii Kozlov, and Sylvia Hochfield, *Beautiful Loot: The Soviet Plunder of Europe's Art Treasures* (New York: Random House, 1995).

11. Nicholas, "The Rape of European Art," 241.

12. Press release of the Herrick, Feinstein, law firm representing Jen Lissitzky in this transaction, located at firm's Web site, www.herrick.com.

13. Nicholas, "The Rape of European Art," 242.

14. Petropoulos, *Art As Politics.*

15. Opening statement by Thomas R. Kline to the Committee on Art and Cultural Property, Presidential Commission on Holocaust Assets in the United States, April 12, 2000.

16. Eliahu Salpeter, "Guilty Exhibits," *Ha'aretz,* March 8, 2000, 10.

17. Petropoulos, *Art As Politics.*

18. Ibid.

19. Aharon Appelfeld, "Buried Homeland," *New Yorker,* November 23, 1998, 48, quoted and cited in Petropoulos, *Art As Politics.*

20. Petropoulos, *Art As Politics.*

21. Peter Ford, "Europe's Halting Path to Resolve Nazi Era," *Christian Science Monitor,* June 4, 2001, 1 (estimate made by the WJC's Elan Steinberg).

22. Hector Feliciano, *The Lost Museum: The Nazi Conspiracy to Steal the World's Greatest Works of Art* (New York: Basic Books, 1997).

23. Lynn H. Nicholas, *The Rape of Europa: The Fate of Europe's Treasures in the Third Reich and the Second World War* (New York: Knopf, 1994).

24. Monica Dugot of the New York Holocaust Claims Processing Office pointed out correctly that "it is important to keep in mind that a 'Holocaust art success story' should not simply be defined as 'a claimant obtaining the return of Holocaust looted artwork'—these cases can be resolved in other ways that are 'fair' which does not necessarily result in the painting being returned or restituted, there have been many other creative solutions" (e-mail from Monica Dugot to me, August 2, 2002).

25. B. J. Davis, "See No Evil," *California Lawyer*, October 1999, 36.

26. Monica Dugot, "Holocaust Era Looted Art: Legal and Ethical Issues and Possible Solutions," presentation to the ABA Section of International Law and Practice, May 10, 20002, New York City.

27. One exception is Los Angeles attorney E. Randol Schoenberg, who was involved in the Austrian settlement negotiations and is counsel in the *Altmann v. Austria* art case.

28. Dugot, "Holocaust Era Looted Art."

29. Comments by Lloyd P. Goldenberg, a Washington, D.C., art law specialist: "I do not agree that it would be 'impossible' to get looted art back into proper hands. It might be difficult and labor intensive but now that so many archives in Eastern Europe are available for inspection the main issue is—as always—money" (e-mail from Lloyd P. Goldenberg to me, August 18, 2002).

30. Presentation by Monica Dugot to the Vilnius International Forum, October 4, 2000.

31. Petropoulos, *Art As Politics*, quoting and citing the National Archives, College Park, Md., record group 260, entry 1, box 373, Office of the Military Government for Bavaria, Monuments, Fine Arts, and Archives Monthly Consolidated Field Report, March 1948, 52.

32. Norman Kempster, "Tracking the Nazi Plunder," *Los Angeles Times*, November 30, 1998, F1.

33. Ibid.

34. Howard N. Spiegler, "Recovering Nazi-Stolen Art: Report from the Front Lines," *Connecticut Journal of International Law* 18 (2001): 297. There is one exception: if a good-faith purchaser undertakes a reasonable due diligence search before purchasing the good, for any competing claims to the good, and does not learn of a competing claim because the owner failed to provide notice that the good was stolen, then good title can pass to a good-faith purchaser.

35. W. Page Keeton et al., *Prosser and Keeton on the Law of Torts*, 5th ed. (St. Paul: West Publishing, 1984), 93–94.

36. Eric Gibson, "De Gustibus: The Delicate Art of Deciding Whose Art Is It," *Wall Street Journal*, July 16, 1999, 11.

37. CAR's Web site is www.comartrecovery.org. The Web site contains updates on Holocaust looted art issues in the United States and across the world. It also provides useful links; see www.comartrecovery.org/resources/organizations.htm.

38. HARP's Web site is www.lostart.org.

39. HCPO's Web site is www.claims.state.ny.us.

40. ECLA's Web site is www.lootedartcommission.com.

41. ALR's Web site is www.artloss.com.

42. Gibson, "De Gustibus," 11. The so-called Elgin Marbles, dating back to Greek antiquity, were taken from Athens in 1812 by the earl of Elgin and are now held by the British Museum in London. Greece has long demanded their return, but Britain has refused.

43. After the war, a number of Holocaust looted art cases were decided in American courts, including the important *Menzel v. List* case, discussed later. For a description of these early looted art cases, see Michael J. Bazyler, "Nuremberg in America: Litigating the Holocaust in United States Courts," *University of Richmond Law Review* 34 (2000): 1, 28–30.

44. *Goodman v. Searle*, Plaintiffs' Mem. of Law in Opp. to Defendant's Motion for Summary Judgment, January 27, 1998, 3.

45. *Menzel v. List*, 267 N.Y.S. 2d 804 (1966).

46. *Goodman v. Searle*, Defendant's Mem. of Law in Support of Motion for Summary Judgment, 11.

47. *Goodman v. Searle*, Plaintiffs' Mem. of Law in Opp. to Defendant's Motion for Summary Judgment, January 27, 1998, 4.

48. Marilyn Henry, "Holocaust Victims' Heirs on Stolen Art," *Jerusalem Post*, August 16, 1998, 3.

49. In 2000, after the case concluded, Howard J. Trienes, Searle's attorney from the powerhouse Chicago law firm Sidley & Austin, published a short study giving "his take" on the case. See Howard J. Trienes, *Landscape with Smokestacks: The Case of the Allegedly Plundered Degas* (Evanston, Ill.: Northwestern University Press, 2000).

50. Conversation with Nick Goodman, July 23, 1999.

51. Robin Updike, "'Odalisque' Project Was Lengthy, Thorough," *Seattle Times*, June 16, 1999, E6.

52. Robin Updike, "SAM to Return Matisse Stolen during WWII," *Seattle Times*, June 15, 1999, A1.

53. Karen Lowe, "Matisse Painting Stolen by Nazis to Be Returned," *Agence France-Presse*, June 15, 1999.

54. Updike, "SAM to Return Matisse," A1.

55. Patrick McMahon, "Matisse Stolen by Nazis to Be Returned," *USA Today*, June 15, 1999, 10A.

NOTES TO CHAPTER 5 373

56. "Museum, Gallery Reach Settlement over Painting," *Dallas Morning News*, October 15, 2000, 39A.

57. Martha Lufkin, "Author Seeks Finder's Fee for Recovered War Loot," *Art Newspaper*, September 2001, 9.

58. Martha Lufkin, "Trying to Be Paid Twice," *Art Newspaper*, October 2001, 8.

59. Feliciano, *The Lost Museum*.

60. Celestine Bohlen, "Judge Revives Case of Nazi-Looted Art," *New York Times*, April 27, 2002, A1. Howard Spiegler, attorney for the Bondi heirs, responded to Feliciano: "I share Mr. Feliciano's frustration; we would have of course been happy to have resolved this matter early on if at all possible. But it must be remembered that all parties must be willing to do so and it is not uncommon for defendants in these kind[s] of cases to attempt to have the case dismissed on some technical grounds before they turn to a serious examination of how the case can be resolved" (e-mail from Howard N. Spiegler to me, August 19, 2002).

61. *United States v. Portrait of Wally*, 2002 U.S. Dist. LEXIS 6445 (S.D.N.Y. 2002).

62. Niles Lathem and Laura Italiano, "New York's Other Art Controversy," *New York Post*, September 30, 1999, 30.

63. ACAL, Section 12.03, the antiseizure law, reads: "No process of attachment, execution, sequestration, replevin, distress or any kind of seizure shall be served or levied upon any work of fine art while the same is en route to or from, or while on exhibition or deposited by a nonresident exhibitor at any exhibition held under the auspices or supervision of any museum, college, university, or other nonprofit art gallery, institution or organization within any city or county of this state for any cultural, educational, charitable or other purpose not conducted for profit to the exhibitor, nor shall such work of fine art be subject to attachment, seizure, levy or sale, for any cause whatever in the hands of authorities of such exhibition or otherwise."

64. See In re *Application to Quash Grand Jury Subpoena Duces Tecum* (*People v. The Museum of Modern Art*), 688 N.Y.S. 2d 3 (1998).

65. Ibid.

66. *People v. The Museum of Modern Art*, 93 N.Y.S. 2d 729 (1999).

67. The U.S. government decided that it would not take action to stop the return of *Dead City* to Vienna, since some of the facts regarding the claim were in dispute. The Bondi heirs' claim to *Wally* was more straightforward.

68. 18 U.S.C. Section 2314 (2000).

69. 18 U.S.C. Section 545, 19 U.S.C. Section 1595a (c), 22 U.S.C. Section 401(a).

70. *United States v. Portrait of Wally*, 105 F. Supp. 2d 288 (S.D.N.Y. 2000).

71. *United States v. Portrait of Wally*, 2000 WL 1890403 (S.D.N.Y. December 28, 2000).

72. Ibid.

73. *Portrait of Wally*, 2002 U.S. Dist. LEXIS 6445 (S.D.N.Y. 2002).

74. *United States v. Portrait of Wally*, 105 F. Supp. 2d at 294.

75. Ibid.

76. For an excellent criticism of Judge Mukasey's original decision holding that *Wally* was no longer stolen when recovered by the U.S. Army, written by a nonlawyer but an art expert, see Milton Esterow, "The Law Is an Ass," *ARTnews*, September 2000, 192. Esterow is the editor and publisher of *ARTnews*.

77. Martha Lufkin, "U.S. Court Throws out Arguments about Nazi-loot Schiele," Art Newspaper.com, April 13, 2002.

78. Celestine Bohlen, "Judge Revives Case of Nazi-Looted Art," *New York Times*, April 27, 2002, A1.

79. 22 U.S.C. Section 2459 (2000).

80. Peter Watson, "If It's Art, It Must Be Fake," *The New Statesman*, April 23, 2001, 23. Watson points out a second factor for the "change in attitude": in the world of antiques, up to 80 percent of the objects have no provenance.

81. *Warin v. Wildenstein & Co.*, no. 115413-99 (N.Y. Sup. Ct. July 27, 1999).

82. *Warin Compl.*, para. 32. After the war, Kann remained in London and died there in 1948 (para. 7).

83. *Warin v. Wildenstein & Co., Inc.*, 740 N.Y.S. 2d 331 (2002).

84. Altmann's attorney, E.. Randol Schoenberg, created a Web site, www.adele.at, devoted specifically to the case. It contains court pleadings and other relevant documents.

85. Ann Marie O'Connor, "Whose Art Is It Anyway?" *Los Angeles Times*, December 16, 2001, 12.

86. "Adele's betrothal was viewed as a joining of dynastic families, an impression strengthened by the fact that Adele's sister, Therese, had married Ferdinand's brother Gustav. Adele's and Therese's four brothers had died—of tuberculosis, cancer, even a duel—so the Bloch brothers agreed to a joint surname" (ibid.).

87. Appellants' Opening Brief at 7, *Altmann v. Republic of Austria* (no. 01-56003, U.S. Ct. of Appeals, Ninth Circuit).

88. Ann-Marie O'Connor, "Mediation Ordered in Suit over Klimt Paintings," *Los Angeles Times*, March 27, 2002, B1.

89. Ibid.

90. Ibid.

91. *Altmann v. Republic of Austria*, 142 F. Supp. 2d 1187 (C. D. Cal. 2001).

92. Letter from Dr. Kurt Garzolli of the Austrian Gallery to his predecessor, Dr. Bruno Grimschitz, March 8, 1948, quoted in *Altmann v. Republic of Austria*, 142 F. Supp. 1187 (C. D. Cal. 2001).

93. Ibid.

94. Letter from Dr. Kurt Garzolli to Dr. Otto Demus, president of the Austrian Federal Monument Agency (in charge of export licenses), March 31, 1948, quoted in *Altmann v. Republic of Austria.*

95. *Altmann v. Republic of Austria.*

96. Appellee's Opposition Brief on Expedited Appeal, *Altmann v. Republic of Austria* (no. 01-56003, U.S. Ct. of Appeals, Ninth Circuit), 8.

97. Ibid.

98. Appellee's Opposition Brief on Appeal, *Altmann v. Republic of Austria* (no. 01-56003, U.S. Ct. of Appeals, Ninth Circuit), 8.

99. E-mail from E. Randol Schoenberg to me, July 24, 2002.

100. Appellants' Opening Brief, *Altmann v. Republic of Austria* (no. 01-56003, U.S. Ct. of Appeals, Ninth Circuit), 15. When I asked Peter Moser, the Austrian ambassador to the United States, about the case, he made the same point. "This is not a case at all about restitution of Nazi-looted art," he told me. Rather, he explained, it is a case involving a donation of artworks made in Austria and its legal effect under Austrian law. The case has nothing to do, he maintained, with World War II or the Holocaust.

101. 28 U.S.C. Section 1602 et seq.

102. *Altmann v. Republic of Austria.*

103. FSIA, 28 U.S.C. Section 1605 (a) (3) (known as the "takings in violation of international law" exception).

104. *Altmann v. Republic of Austria.*

105. Appellants' Opening Brief, *Altmann v. Republic of Austria* (no. 01-56003, U.S. Ct. of Appeals, Ninth Circuit), 17.

106. Ibid.

107. Judge Cooper noted: "Plaintiff is not indigent. Nevertheless, the Court finds that the filing fee required by the Austrian courts is oppressively burdensome. Paying even the reduced amount would force an 85-year-old woman to expend a great majority, if not at all, of her liquid assets" (142 F. Supp. at 1210).

108. 142 F. Supp. at 1210.

109. Appellants' Reply Brief, *Altmann v. Republic of Austria* (no. 01-56003, U.S. Ct. of Appeals, Ninth Circuit), 3.

110. The press release of the North Carolina museum announcing its return of the painting can be found at www.museum-security.org/00/120 .html.

111. Spiegler, "Recovering Nazi-Stolen Art," 297.

112. Opening statement by Thomas R. Kline to the Committee on Art and Cultural Property, Presidential Commission on Holocaust Assets in the United States, April 12, 2000.

113. Ibid.

114. Marilyn Henry, "Holocaust Victims' Heirs Reach Compromise on Stolen Art," *Jerusalem Post*, August 16, 1998, 3.

115. See Lee Rosenbaum, "Nazi Loot Claims: Art with a History," *Wall Street Journal Europe*, January 29, 1998, 14.

116. Henry, "Holocaust Victims' Heirs Reach Compromise on Stolen Art," 3.

117. L. J. Davis, "See No Evil," *California* Lawyer, October 1999, 36.

118. Tunku Varadarajan, "Gallery Is Sued over 'Looted' Art," *Times of London*, August 5, 1998, 11.

119. Judith H. Dobrzynski, "Man in the Middle of the Schiele Case," *New York Times*, January 29, 1998, E1.

120. Marilyn Henry, "Recovering Looted Art: A Rich Man's Game," *Jerusalem Post*, April 3, 1998, 17 (discussing the costs of litigating the *Goodman* case).

121. Monica Dugot, "The Holocaust Claims Processing Office's Handling of Art Claims," *Fordham International Law Journal* 25 (2000): S-134–35.

122. Ibid., S-135.

123. Ibid.

124. Alan G. Artner, "Ethics and Art Museums Struggle for Correct Response to Stolen Art Claims," *Chicago Tribune*, August 16, 1998, 6.

125. Ibid.

126. Owen C. Pell, "The Potential for a Mediation/Arbitration Commission to Resolve Disputes Relating to Artworks Stolen or Looted during World War II," paper delivered at the annual meeting of the Swiss Arbitration Association, Zurich, January 22, 1999.

127. Ibid.

128. Ibid. (underline in original).

129. See Rosenbaum, "Nazi Loot Claims," 14.

130. Michelle I. Turner, note, "The Innocent Buyer of Art Looted during World War II," *Vanderbilt Journal Transnational Law* 32 (1999): 1511, 1541.

131. Judith Dobrzynski, "Loot-Holders Learn That Honesty Can Be Tricky," *Raleigh* (N.C.) *News & Observer*, September 13, 1998, G3.

132. Ibid.

133. See press release, Association of Art Museum Directors, February 3, 1999, available at www.aamd.org.

134. Report of the AAMD Task Force on the Spoliation of Art during the Nazi/World War II Era (1933–1945), part II, Guidelines D.2 ("Discovery of Unlawfully Confiscated Works of Art") and E.2 ("Response to Claims against the Museum"), June 4, 1998, available at http://www.aamd.org./guideln.shtm.

135. Walter V. Robinson, "17 Museums to Review Collections for Stolen Art," *Boston Globe*, June 5, 1998, A1.

136. Walter V. Robinson, "Judge Rejects Seizure of Disputed Paintings from a N.Y. Museum; DA Rebuffed on Art Nazis May Have Looted," *Boston Globe*, May 14, 1998, A4.

137. Robinson, "17 Museums," A1.

138. Ibid.

139. Ibid.

140. Diane Haithman, "Where Were These Paintings between 1933 and 1945?" *Los Angeles Times*, September 3, 2000, 1 (Sunday Calendar) (brackets in original).

141. Addendum to the report of the AAMD Task Force on the Spoliation of Art during the Nazi/World War II Era (1933–1945), available at www.aamd.org.

142. The AAMD claims credit, however, for the return of Matisse's *Odalisque* to its rightful owners. See Lowe, "Matisse Painting": "The Seattle Art Museum did the right thing. They followed the guidelines set out for handling these cases," said a spokesperson for the AAMD.

143. Proceedings of the Washington Conference on Holocaust-Era Assets can be located at www.state.gov/www/regions/eur/holocaust/heac.htm.

144. Marilyn Henry and Hubertus Czernin, "Owning Up," *ARTnews*, May 1, 1999, 68.

145. Ibid., quoting J. D. Bindernagel, State Department senior coordinator of the Washington Conference.

146. Watson, "If It's Art," 23.

147. The proposal was backed by Ashton Hawkins, general counsel to the Metropolitan Museum of Art, and Ronal S. Tauber, chairman of the ALR.

148. Sylvia Hochfield, "Statute with Limitations?" *ARTnews*, November 1, 1998, 10.

149. Ibid.

150. International Council of Museums (ICOM) Recommendations concerning the Return of Works Belonging to Jewish Owners, January 1999, available at www.icom.org.

151. Dugot, "Holocaust Era Looted Art."

152. Haithman, "Where Were These Paintings."

153. Dugot, presentation to Vilnius International Forum, 2.

154. "Report on Art Theft in France during the Occupation and the Situation of 2,000 Works of Art Entrusted to the French National Museums: The MNRs," *Mattéoli Commission Report*, April 17, 2000, 35.

155. Ron Grossman, "Key to Art Nazis Stole May Be Locked Away in Commission's Plan to Publish Postwar Loss Claims in Peril," *Chicago Tribune*, December 17, 2000, 1.

156. Ibid.

157. Ibid.

158. E-mail from Monica Dugot to me, July 24, 2002.

159. E-mail from Lloyd P. Goldenberg to me, August 18, 2002.

160. E-mail from Lucille Roussin to me, August 29, 2002.

161. "Israelis Suggest Museums Admit Some of Their Art Was Nazi Loot," *AP Online*, March 2, 2000.

162. Ibid.

163. Ibid.

164. Spiegler, "Recovering Nazi-Stolen Art," 298.

165. Davis, "See No Evil."

NOTES TO CHAPTER 6

1. E-mail from Michael Berenbaum to me, July 17, 2002.

2. Michael J. Bazyler and William Elperin, "Holocaust Justice and Financial Accountability," *Jerusalem Post*, January 29, 1999, 9.

3. Israel Singer, "Transparency, Truth, and Restitution," *Sh'ma*, June 2002, 1.

4. Ibid.

5. David Schaecter, "Use Restituted Funds for Urgent Survivors' Needs," *Sh'ma*, June 2002, 7.

6. Singer, "Transparency," 1.

7. Gribetz summarized the hundred of proposals in annex A of his Plan of Distribution, and many appear in their original complete form at the Swiss banks' class action Web site, www.swissbankclaims.com.

8. Helen Epstein, *Children of the Holocaust: Conversations with Sons and Daughters of Survivors* (New York: Putnam, 1979).

9. Norman Finkelstein, *The Holocaust Industry: Reflections on the Exploitation of Jewish Suffering* (New York: Verso, 2000).

10. Gabriel Schoenfeld, "Controversy: Holocaust Reparations," *Commentary*, January 2001, 20. Danny Kadden, an activist for Holocaust survivors who is also a sociologist, pointed out to me that "defining and counting Holocaust survivors is at best an imprecise science. Survivors' views of themselves have shifted over time. Many who rejected that label ten years ago are likely to adopt that identity now. It makes estimating the survivor population and their mortality patterns a tremendous challenge."

11. Barry Meier, "Jewish Groups Fight for Spoils of Swiss Case," *New York Times*, November 29, 1998, A1.

12. NAHOS, The Newsletter of the National Association of Jewish Child Holocaust Survivors, Sample Letter to Object to Any Deduction from Restitution Proceeds, May 5, 1999.

13. Abraham H. Foxman, "The Dangers of Holocaust Restitution," *Wall Street Journal*, December 4, 1998, A18.

14. Nelly C. Gross, "Israel Stakes a Claim," *Jerusalem Report*, July 1, 2002, 14.

15. Michael J. Jordan, "Debate over Restitution Funds Leads to Internal Jewish Struggle," *JTA On Line*, January 14, 2002.

16. James D. Besser, "Seeking Moral Restitution," *Jewish Journal*, December 4, 1998, 22.

17. Susan Glazer, "Controversy: Holocaust Reparations," *Commentary*, January 2001, 17.

18. Schoenfeld, "Controversy," 20.

19. House Committee on Banking and Financial Services, *Hearings*, testimony by Dr. Otto Graf Lambsdorff, 106th Cong., 2d sess., February 9, 2000, 6.

20. Jordan, "Debate."

21. Henry Weinstein and John J. Goldman, "Cutting the Cloth of Atonement," *Los Angeles Times*, September 7, 1998, A20.

22. Schaecter, "Use Restituted Funds," 7.

23. Ibid.

24. Jeff Jacoby, "Jews Can Set a Moral Example with Holocaust Funds," *Boston Globe*, December 7, 1998, A15.

25. Ibid.

26. E-mail from Leo Rechter to me, July 10, 2002.

27. Plan of Allocation, annex A, A-6, In re *Holocaust Victim Assets Litigation* (Swiss Banks), available at www.swissbanks.com.

28. Ibid.

29. Michael Berenbaum, "Let Us Not Fight over the *Yerushah*," *Sh'ma*, June 2002, 5.

30. Ibid.

31. Letter from Burt Neuborne to Leo Rechter, July 9, 2002.

32. Ibid.

33. Valerie Kellogg, "Facing the Impossible Question: How Much Is Life Worth?" *Newsday*, January 27, 2002, B4 (interview with Rabbi Irving Greenberg).

NOTES TO CHAPTER 7

1. Roland Stephen, "Controversy: Holocaust Reparations," *Commentary*, January 2001, 17.

2. Abraham H. Foxman, "The Dangers of Holocaust Restitution," *Wall Street Journal*, December 4, 1998, A18.

3. Naftali Bendavid, "Is the Meaning Lost in Court," *Chicago Tribune*, August 12, 2001, 1 (quoting Foxman).

4. Charles Krauthammer, "Reducing the Holocaust to Mere Dollars and Cents," *Los Angeles Times*, December 11, 1998, 26.

5. Leon Wieseltier, "Assets," *New Republic*, November 8, 1999, 98.

6. Ibid.

7. Gabriel Schoenfeld, "Holocaust Reparations—A Growing Scandal," *Commentary*, September 2000, 1. Schoenfeld is the senior editor of the magazine.

8. See Gabriel Schoenfeld, "Auschwitz and the Professors," *Commentary*, June 1998, 10. My own view is that his attack was unfair. The historians were bringing to light important historical facts not studied before and opening a new chapter in the historiography of the Holocaust to be explored by the next generation of Holocaust scholars.

9. Elli Wohlgelernter, "Compensation Issue Clouds Holocaust Message," *Jerusalem Post*, January 19, 2001, 6A.

10. Ibid.

11. Norman Finkelstein, *The Holocaust Industry: Reflections on the Exploitation of Jewish Suffering* (New York: Verso, 2000).

12. Schoenfeld, "Controversy," 20.

13. Elazar Barkan, *The Guilt of Nations: Restitution and Negotiating Historical Injustices* (New York: Norton, 2000), 3. An excellent discussion of the debate about accepting restitution from postwar Germany can be found in Tom Segev, *The Seventh Million: The Israelis and the Holocaust* (New York: Henry Holt, 2000), 189–252.

14. Barkan, *The Guilt of Nations*, 9, 23–27.

15. Richard Cohen, "The Money Matters," *Washington Post*, December 8, 1998, A21.

16. Stuart Eizenstat, "Controversy: Holocaust Reparations," *Commentary*, January 2001, 20.

17. Ibid.

18. Roman Kent, "Controversy: Holocaust Reparations," *Commentary*, January 2001, 12.

19. Letter to the editor, *Pittsburgh Post-Gazette*, December 26, 1998, A14.

20. Jonathan Weisman, "Redress Sought in Nazi-Era Labor," *Baltimore Post*, August 23, 1999, 1A.

21. Ibid.

22. Ibid.

23. Richard Wolffe, "Putting a Price on the Holocaust," *Irish Times*, March 16, 1999, 15.

24. Eizenstat, "Controversy," 10.

25. Cohen, "The Money Matters," A21.

26. Ibid.

27. Lance Morrow, "The Justice of the Calculator," *Time*, February 24, 1997, 45.

28. Hirsh Goodman, "Atrocities beyond Compensation," *Jerusalem Post*, October 22, 1999, 8B.

29. Eizenstat, "Controversy," 10.

30. Lynda Hurst, "Decades of Delay: Wages of Nazi Slavery," *The Star*, August 28, 1999, A1.

31. Bendavid, "Is the Meaning Lost in Court," 1.

32. The Bergier Commission reports are available on its Web site, www.uek.ch.

33. See Swiss Federal Commission against Racism, "Anti-Semitism in Switzerland: A Report on Historical and Current Manifestations with Recommendations for Counter-Measures," November 1998.

34. Bendavid, "Is the Meaning Lost in Court," 1.

35. The Mattéoli Commission's reports are available on its Web site, www.civs.gouv.fr/uk/commission/commission01.htm.

36. See "Sweden and Jewish Assets: Final Report from the Commission on Jewish Assets at the Time of the Second World War," 1999. Available at www.ess.uwe.ac.uk/genocide/Sweden1.htm.

37. Allesandra Rizzo, "Italy Panel Finds Asset Plundering," *AP Online*, May 2, 2001.

38. The following countries created commissions of inquiry into Holocaust issues: Argentina, Austria, Belgium, Brazil, Republic of Croatia, Czech Republic, Estonia, France, Germany, Greece, Hungary, Israel, Italy, Latvia, Lithuania, The Netherlands, Norway, Portugal, Slovak Republic, Spain, Sweden, Switzerland, Turkey, and the United States. The following countries began conducting new research as a consequence of the new scrutiny of the wartime role of governments and private entities during the Holocaust: Albania, Australia, Belarus, Bosnia and Herzegovina, Bulgaria, Canada, Chile, Cyprus, Denmark, Finland, Iceland, Ireland, Luxembourg, Macedonia, Moldova, Poland, Russia, Slovenia, South Africa, Ukraine, United Kingdom, and Uruguay. See U.S. Presidential Commission on Holocaust Assets, "Final Report, Appendix D"; U.S. Holocaust Memorial Museum "List of Government-Appointed Historical Commissions concerning the Holocaust," available at www.taskforce.ushmm.org/combody.htm.

39. Israel Singer, "Transparency, Truth, and Restitution," *Sh'ma*, June 2002, 1.

40. Barry Meier, "Chronicles of Collaboration: Historians Are in Demand to Study Corporate Ties to Nazis," *New York Times*, February 8, 1999, C1.

41. Dan Glaister, "Shadow of Shame," *The Guardian*, December 22, 1998, 17.

42. The report, "Plunder and Restitution: The U.S. and Holocaust Victims' Assets—Report to the President of the Presidential Advisory on Holocaust Assets in the United States," December 2000, is available on the commission's Web site, www.pcha .gov.

43. Israeli Holocaust historian Ronald Zweig recently published a book on this subject: *The Gold Train: The Annihilation of the Jews and the Looting of Hungary* (New York: Morrow, 2002).

44. *Rosner v. United States*, no. 01-1895-Civ. (S.D. Fla. Filed May 27, 2001).

45. Henry Weinstein, "Hungarians Sue U.S. over Seized Holocaust Loot Reparations, *Los Angeles Times*, May 8, 2001, A14. In August 2002, Florida federal district judge Patricia A. Seitz denied the U.S. government's motion to dismiss and allowed the lawsuit to go forward (*Rosner v. U.S.*, 2002 U.S. Dist. LEXIS 17632 [S.D. Fla. August 28, 2002]). The plaintiffs' lawyers hailed the ruling, but Stuart Eizenstat labeled it "legal[ly] . . . suspect." Stuart Eizenstat, "Justice Remains beyond Grasp of Too Many Holocaust Survivors," *Forward*, October 18, 2002, 1. Nevertheless, Eizenstat, now in private practice, maintained that "the American government is morally obliged to provide an accounting for what was lost, an apology if wrongdoing is found, and some token payment to the Hungarian Jewish community." Why a token payment? If the U.S. Army stole in 1945 what rightfully belonged to the Hungarian Jews, damages should be paid on the same scale as that used today by the European wrongdoers. Justice requires no less.

46. Edwin Black, *IBM and the Holocaust: The Strategic Alliance between Nazi Germany and America's Most Powerful Corporation* (New York: Random House, 2001).

47. Edwin Black, *IBM and the Holocaust: The Strategic Alliance between Nazi Germany and America's Most Powerful Corporation*, 2d ed. (New York: Crown Books, 2002).

48. Ibid.

49. Dominic Rushe, "IBM Faces Fresh Revelations of Nazi 'Collaboration,'" *Sunday Times of London*, March 31, 2002, 3.

50. Ibid.

51. "GM Probing Former Ties to Nazis," *New York Post*, December 23, 1998, 34.

52. John S. Friedman, "Kodak's Nazi Connections," *The Nation*, March 26, 2001, 40.

53. Ibid.

54. Ibid.

55. Ibid.

56. "Treasury Deputy Secretary Stuart E. Eizenstat's Remarks to the United States Chamber of Commerce, Office of Public Affairs," *Treasury Department's Treasury News*, 1, available at www.treas.gove/press/releases/ps586.htm.

57. Ibid.

58. "Germany Fears Rivalry from U.S. Holocaust Fund," *AP Online*, May 2, 2000.

59. Henry Weinstein, "Ford Says WWII Study Clears Firm History," *Los Angeles Times*, December 7, 2001, C1.

60. Ibid.

61. Kent, "Controversy," 12.

NOTES TO CHAPTER 8

1. A good historical discussion of these claims can be found in Linda Goetz Holmes's *Unjust Enrichment: How Japan's Companies Built Postwar Fortunes Using American POWs* (Mechanicsburg, PA: Stackpole Books, 2001).

2. *Levenberg v. Nippon Sharyo Ltd.*, case no. C-99-1554 (N.D. Cal., filed July 16, 1999).

3. Donald MacIntyre, "Striking Back at Japan Inc.," *Time Asia*, August 16, 1999, 10.

4. California Code of Civil Procedure (CCCP), section 354.6.

5. SB 1245 Senate Bill—Bill Analysis.

6. For a list of lawsuits filed to date in the United States against Japanese companies (which I have maintained), see www.law.whittier.edu/sypo/final /lawsuit.htm.

7. Goetz Holmes, *Unjust Enrichment*, xix. In July 2002, the New York City Transit Authority ordered an additional 1,700 subway cars from Kawasaki, an order worth more than $3.3 billion, the largest subway car contract in the city's history. See Randy Kennedy, "1,700 Subway Cars to Be Built, Order Largest," *New York Times*, July 31, 2002, B1.

8. In re *World War II Era Japanese Forced Labor Litigation*, 114 F. Supp. 2d 939 (N.D. Cal. 2000).

9. Treaty of Peace with Japan, September 8, 1951, 3 UST 3169, 136 UNTS 45.

10. In re *World War II Era Japanese Forced Labor Litigation*, 114 F. Supp. 2d, at 945.

11. In re *World War II Era Japanese Forced Labor Litigation*, 164 F. Supp. 2d 1160 (N.D. Cal. 2001).

12. Ibid., 948.

13. David Sanger, "Report on Holocaust Assets Tells of Items Found in the U.S." *New York Times*, January 17, 2001, A3.

14. Iris Chang, *Rape of Nanking: The Forgotten Holocaust of World War II* (New York: Viking, 1998).

15. Iris Chang, "Betrayed by the White House," *New York Times*, December 24, 2001, A15.

16. Senate Committee on the Judiciary, *Former U.S. World War II POWs: A Struggle for Justice*, hearing, 106th Cong., 2d sess., February 9, 2000, 14 (hereafter Sen. Judiciary Comm. Hearing).

17. Statement of Interest of the United States of America, In re *World War II Era Japanese Forced Labor Litigation* (*Sun Yoon Kim v. Ishikawajima Harima Heavy Industries*), Master MDL Docket No. 1347 (N.D. Cal., filed December 13, 2000).

18. Statement of Interest of the United States of America, *Hwang Geum Joo v. Japan*, Case No. 00-CV-288 (D.D.C., filed April 27, 2001); see also Bill Miller, "U.S. Resists Comfort Women' Suit," *Washington Post*, May 14, 2001, A1.

19. Michael J. Bazyler, "The Holocaust Restitution Movement in Comparative Perspective," *Berkeley Journal of International Law* 20 (2002): 11.

20. *Kawakita v. United States*, 343 U.S. 717 (1952). Defendant Kawakita defended his actions on the ground of coercion. He argued before the Supreme Court that as an employee of Oeyama Nickel, which used soldiers captured by the Japanese military as captive labor, he was part of the Japanese war effort. The Supreme Court rejected this characterization of his status and that of Oeyama Nickel:

> The Oeyama Nickel Industry Co., Ltd., was a private company, organized for profit. . . . The company's mine and factory were manned in part by prisoners of war. They lived in a camp controlled by the Japanese army. Though petitioner [Kawakita] took orders from the military, he was not a soldier in the armed services. . . . His employment was as an interpreter for the Oeyama Nickel Industry Co., Ltd., a private company. The regulation of the company by the Japanese government, the freezing of its labor force, the assignment to it of prisoners of war under military command were incidents of a war economy. But we find no indication that the Oeyama Company was nationalized or its properties seized and operated by the government. The evidence indicates that it was part of a regimented industry; but it was an organization operating for private profit under private management (ibid., 727–28).

21. Article 26 provides: "Should Japan make a peace settlement or war claims settlement with any State granting that State greater advantages than those provided by the present Treaty, those same advantages shall be extended to the parties to the present Treaty."

22. Justice for United States Prisoners of War Act of 2001, H.R. 1198 (introduced in the U.S. House of Representatives on March 22, 2001). Section 3(a) (2) of the bill also would specifically construe section 14(b) of the 1951 Peace Treaty as *not* "constituting a waiver by the United States of claims by nationals of the United States, including claims by members of the United States Armed Forces, so as to preclude [litigation of such claims]."

23. For studies of the Armenian genocide, see Richard G. Hovannisian, "Remembrance and Denial: The Case of the Armenian Genocide" (Detroit: Wayne State University Press, 1999); and Richard G. Hovannisian, "The Armenian Genocide in Perspective" (New York: Transaction Books, 1986).

24. Case No. 99-12073 (C.D. Cal. 1999, filed January 17, 2000).

25. California Code of Civil Procedure, section 354.4.

26. Nathan Vardi, "Settling a Case—After 85 Years," *Forbes*, May 14, 2001, 120. See also Beverly Beyette, "He Stands up in the Name of Armenians," *Los Angeles Times*, April 27, 2001, E1.

27. *Marootian v. New York Life Ins. Co.*, 2001 U.S. Dist. LEXIS 22274 [*53] (November 30, 2001).

28. In April 2001, NPR's *All Things Considered* featured a segment on the suit. NPR host Linda Wertheimer introduced the segment by commenting that the Armenian litigation "is modeled on similar efforts by survivors of the Nazi Holocaust." See "Class Action Lawsuit against New York Life Filed by Heirs of Armenian Policyholders during the First World War," *NPR: All Things Considered*, April 9, 2001.

29. Beyette, "He Stands Up," E1 (brackets in original).

30. Randall N. Robinson, *The Debt: What America Owes to Blacks* (New York: Dutton/Plume, 1999).

31. Paul Braverman, "Slavery Reparations: The Opening Shots," *American Lawyer*, June 2002, 22.

32. Comments by Robert Sedler, Distinguished Professor of Law, Gibbs Chair in Civil Rights and Civil Liberties, Wayne State University Law School, made on the *NPR: Talk of the Nation* radio program, April 3, 2002, transcript available at 2002 WL 3296890.

33. Mathew Kauffman and Kenneth R. Gosselin, "Slavery Reparations Effort Just Beginning," *Hartford Courant*, April 2, 2002, E1.

34. Tamar Levin, "Calls for Slavery Restitution Getting Louder," *New York Times*, June 4, 2001, 1.

35. Kauffman and Gosselin, "Slavery Reparations Effort," E1.

36. *Cato v. United States*, 70 F. 3rd 1103 (9th Cir. 1995).

37. Ibid., 1107–11.

38. Jeffrey Ghannam, "Repairing the Past," *ABA Journal*, November 2000, 38.

39. California Insurance Code Sections, 13811–13.

40. "AIG . . . located a replica of a $550 policy issued on the life of a slave named 'Charles'—including a lengthy list of exclusions, including death by suicide. Aetna said it had uncovered seven life insurance policies, some of which covered multiple lives." "Calif. Law Forces Firms' Disclosures," *Reuters Online*, May 2, 2002.

41. According to one of the plaintiffs' attorneys in the African American reparations lawsuits, "Aetna insured slaves for slave owners. They insured them against injury. They insured them against death to two-thirds of their value, I guess with the view that if they insured them for their full value, their full purchase price, there would be no incentive at all for the slave owner to just not work them to death and replace them." Comments by Robert Wareham, made on the *NPR: Talk of the Nation* radio program, April 3, 2002, transcript available at 2002 WL 3296890.

42. Kauffman and Gosselin, "Slavery Reparations Effort," E1.

43. Michael Moutot, "U.S. Descendants of Slaves Launch Historic Lawsuit against Private Industry," *Agence France-Presse*, March 27, 2002.

44. Ibid.

45. Ibid.

46. Kauffman and Gosselin, "Slavery Reparations Effort," E1.

47. "Ancient Injustice, Modern Shakedown," *National Post,* March 30, 2002, A19 (editorial).

48. K. Terrel Reed, "Sins of the Past," *Black Enterprise,* June 1, 2002, 35 (quoting Johnny Cochran).

49. Ibid.

50. Kauffman and Gosselin, "Slavery Reparations Effort," E1.

51. Ibid.

52. Ibid.

53. Israel Singer, "Transparency, Truth and Restitution," *Sh'ma,* June 2002, 1.

54. Oscar Avila, "Mexican Workers Seek Full Pay for Labor in U.S. during World War II," *Chicago Tribune,* May 6, 2002, A3.

55. After World War II, some fifteen million ethnic Germans were driven from their ancestral homes in central Europe, from both southern Czechoslovakia and parts of western Poland and Hungary. The claims of these Germans for compensation have reawakened old wartime wounds, with critics mocking the claims of those they consider to have been "traitors" and "Hitler's Fifth Column." In January 2002, Czech Prime Minister Milos Zeman, labeling the Sudeten Germans as such, suggested that they could have been given the death penalty for their treachery, and so expulsion was an act of mercy. See Kate Swoget, "Zeman Starts War 'with' Vienna," *Prague Post,* January 30, 2002. For more information, see *Sudetendeutche Landsmannschaft/Sudeten German Heritage Union,* at www.sudeten.de.

56. See Sarah Lyall, "Look out, the Gurkhas Have Come! With Lawyers," *New York Times,* May 23, 2002, A4.

57. Jonathan Weisman, "Redress Sought in Nazi-Era Labor Claims," *Baltimore Sun,* August 23, 1999, 1A.

58. Peter Ford, "Europe's Halting Path to Resolve Nazi Era Claims," *Christian Science Monitor,* June 4, 2001, 1.

59. See www.rightofreturn.org (article entitled "The Right to Restitution Is Universal! Call for a Broad Campaign for the Restitution of Palestinian Refugees").

60. See www.rightofreturn.org (article by Sherri Musher).

61. Norman Finkelstein, "Lessons of Holocaust Compensation," in *Palestinian Refugees and Their Right to Return,* edited by Naseer Aruri (London: Pluto Press, 2001).

62. Ibid.

63. The form can be downloaded on the Web site of the American Sephardi Federation, www.asfonline.org.

64. Melissa Radler, "Campaign to Record Claims of Jewish Refugees from Muslim Lands," *Jerusalem Post*, May 12, 2002, 1. Two months later, a new organization was formed, Justice for Jews from Arab Lands, headed by a heavyweight, former U.S. ambassador to the United Nations, Richard C. Holbrooke. See Melissa Radler, "Group Seeks Justice for Jewish Refugees," *Jerusalem Post*, October 2, 2002, 1.

65. Peter Hirshberg, "Private Property Keep Out!" *Jerusalem Report 10th Anniversary Issue*, 1999, available at www.jrep.com/Info/10thAnniversary/1999/Article-11.html.

Relevant Web Sites

CHAPTER 1

Claims Resolution Tribunal (CRT): www.crt.ch; www.dormantaccounts.ch or www.crt-ii.org.

Holocaust Victims Assets Litigation: www.swissbankclaims.com.

Independent Commission of Experts Switzerland—Second World War (Bergier Commission): www.uek.ch.

Independent Committee of Eminent Persons (Volcker Commission): www.icep-iaep.org.

New York Banking Department: www.banking.state.ny.us.

New York City Comptroller's Office: www.comptroller.nyc.gov.

Swiss Special Task Force on World War II: www.switzerland.taskforce.ch.

Switzerland and the Holocaust Assets: www.giussani.com/holocaust-assets.

U.S. State Department, Holocaust Issues: www.state.gov/www/regions/eur/holocausthp.html.

CHAPTER 2

Austrian Fund for Reconciliation, Peace and Cooperation: www.reconciliation-fund.at.

Benjamin B. Ferencz Web site: www.benferencz.org.

Ford Motor Company Newsroom: http://media.ford.com/events/fw_research.cfm.

German Economy Foundation Initiative Steering Group: www.stiftungsinitiative.de.

Holocaust Era Claims Litigation: www.unclaimedassets.com/austria.htm.

International Office of Migration, German Forced Labor Compensation Program: www.compensation-for-forced-labour.org.

National Fund of the Republic of Austria for Victims of National Socialism: www.nationalfonds.org.

CHAPTER 3

International Commission on Holocaust Era Insurance Claims: www.icheic.org.
U.S. House of Representatives Committee on Government http://reform.house
.gov/min/maj/maj_holocaust.htm.
Washington State Insurance Commissioner: www.insurance.wa.gov.

CHAPTER 4

Barclays Bank and J. P. Morgan & Co. French Bank Settlements: www.
barclaysfrenchclaims.org.
Commission for the Compensation of Victims of Spoliation (France):
http://www.civs.gouv.fr/uk/commission/commission01.htm.
Mattéoli Commission's Final Report: www.ladocfrancaise.gouv.fr.

CHAPTER 5

Altmann v. Republic of Austria: www.adele.at.
Art Loss Register: www.artloss.com.
Association of Art Museum Directors: www.aamd.org.
Commission for Art Recovery: www.comartrecovery.org.
Commission for Looted Art in Europe: www.lootedartcommission.com.
Holocaust Art Restitution Project: www.lostart.org.
Holocaust Claims Processing Office: www.claims.state.ny.us.
International Council of Museums (ICOM): www.icom.org.
Washington Conference on Holocaust-Era Assets (proceedings):
http://www.state.gov/regions/eur/wash_conf_material.html

CHAPTER 7

List of Government-Appointed Historical Commissions concerning the Holocaust: http://taskforce.ushmm.org/combody.htm.
Presidential Advisory Commission on Holocaust Assets in the United States:
www.pcha.gov.
"Sweden and Jewish Assets: Final Report from the Commission on Jewish Assets at the Time of the Second World War" (1999): www.ess.uwe.ac.uk
/genocide/Sweden1.htm.

CHAPTER 8

American Sephardi Federation: www.asfonline.org.
Council for Palestinian Restitution and Repatriation: www.rightofreturn.org.

Japanese Litigation: www.law.whittier.edu/sypo/final/lawsuit.htm.
National Coalition of Blacks for Reparations in America: www.ncobra.com.
Sudetendeutschen Landsmannschaft (in German): www.sudeten.de.

OTHER USEFUL WEB SITES

Simon Wiesenthal Center, Los Angeles: www.wiesenthal.com.
United States Holocaust Memorial Museum (Holocaust Victims' Assets):
www.ushmm.org/assets/index.html.

Bibliography

CHAPTER I

Bazyler, Michael J. "www.swissbankclaims.com: The Legality and Morality of the Holocaust-Era Settlement with the Swiss Banks." *Fordham International Law Journal* 25 (2001): S-64.

Bower, Tom. *Nazi Gold: The Full Story of the Fifty-Year Swiss-Nazi Conspiracy to Steal Billions from Europe's Jews and Holocaust Survivors.* New York: Harper-Collins, 1997.

Bronfman, Edgar M. *The Making of a Jew.* New York: Penguin Books, 1996.

Erdman, Paul. *The Swiss Account.* New York: Tor Books, 1993.

Gribetz, Judah, and Shari C. Reig. "A Special Master's Proposed Plan of Allocation and Distribution of Settlement Proceeds." *Fordham International Law Journal* 25 (2001): S-307.

LeBor, Adam. *Hitler's Secret Bankers: How Switzerland Profited from Nazi Genocide.* New York: Simon & Schuster, 1999.

Levin, Itamar. *The Last Deposit: Swiss Banks and Holocaust Victims' Accounts.* Westport, CT: Greenwood Press, 1999.

Meili, Christoph. "Christoph Meili Tells His Story." *Whittier Law Review* 20 (1998): 45.

Moss, Stanley. *Gold Is Where You Hide It: What Happened to the Reichsbank Treasurers?* London: Andre Deutsch, 1956.

Rickman, Gregg J. *Swiss Banks and Jewish Souls.* Somerset, NJ: Transaction Books, 1999.

Rummel, R. J. *Death by Government.* Somerset, NJ: Transaction Books, 1997.

Smith, Arthur L. Jr. *Hitler's Gold: The Story of the Nazi War Loot.* Oxford: Berg, 1989.

Teitelbaum, Raul, and Moshe Sanbar. *Holocaust Gold—From the Victims to Switzerland: Trails of the Nazi Plunder.* Tel Aviv: Moreshet, 2001.

Vincent, Isabel. *Hitler's Silent Partners: Swiss Banks, Nazi Gold and the Pursuit of Justice.* New York: Morrow, 1998.

Ziegler, Jean. *The Swiss, the Gold and the Dead: How Swiss Bankers Helped Finance the Nazi War Machine.* New York: Harcourt Brace, 1997. First published in

German as *Die Schweirz, das Gold und die Toten*. Gütersloh: Bertelsmann Verlag, 1997.

CHAPTER 2

Baldwin, Neil. *Henry Ford and the Jews*. New York: Public Affairs, 2001.
Eizenstat, Stuart E. *Imperfect Justice: Looted Assets, Slave Labor, and the Unfinished Business of World War II*. New York: Public Affairs, 2003.
Ferencz, Benjamin B. *Less Than Slaves: Jewish Forced Labor and the Quest for Compensation*. Bloomington: Indiana University Press, 2002.

CHAPTER 3

Feldman, Gerald D. *Allianz and the German Insurance Business, 1933–1945*. Cambridge: Cambridge University Press, 2001.
Gersten, Alan. "Making Amends: European Insurers Are Finally Accepting Some Liability for Unpaid Holocaust Victims' Claims." *Life Insurance International*, October 1, 1998, 7.

CHAPTER 4

Grosswald Curran, Vivian. "Competing Frameworks for Assessing Contemporary Holocaust-Era Claims." *Fordham International Law Journal* 25 (2001): S-121.
———. "The Legalization of Racism in a Constitutional State: Democracy's Suicide in Vichy France." *Hastings Law Journal* 50 (1998): 1.
Marrus, Michael. R., and Robert O. Paxton. *Vichy France and the Jews*. Stanford, Calif.: Stanford University Press, 1995.
Mattéoli Commission. "Summary of the Work by the Study Mission on the Spoliation of Jews in France." April 17, 2000.
Weisberg, Richard H. *Vichy Law and the Holocaust in France*. New York: New York University Press, 1996.
Zucotti, Susan. *The Holocaust, the French, and the Jews*. Lincoln: University of Nebraska Press, 1999.

CHAPTER 5

Akinsha, Konstantin, Gregorii Kozlov, and Sylvia Hochfield. *Beautiful Loot: The Soviet Plunder of Europe's Art Treasures*. New York: Random House, 1995.
Dugot, Monica. "The Holocaust Claims Processing Office's Handling of Art Claims." *Fordham International Law Journal* 25 (2001): S-134.

Feliciano, Hector. *The Lost Museum: The Nazi Conspiracy to Steal the World's Greatest Works of Art*. New York: Basic Books, 1997.

Nicholas, Lynn H. *The Rape of Europa: The Fate of Europe's Treasures in the Third Reich and the Second World War*. New York: Knopf, 1994.

———. "The Rape of European Art." *American University International Law Review* 14 (1998): 237.

Petropolous, Jonathan. *Art As Politics in the Third Reich*. Chapel Hill: University of North Carolina Press, 1996.

Spiegler, Howard N. "Recovering Nazi-Stolen Art: Report from the Front Lines." *Connecticut Journal of International Law* 18 (2001): 297.

Trienes, Howard J. *Landscape with Smokestacks: The Case of the Allegedly Plundered Degas*. Evanston, Ill.: Northwestern University Press, 2000.

Turner, Michelle I. "The Innocent Buyer of Art Looted during World War II." *Vanderbilt Journal of Transnational Law* 32 (1999): 1511.

CHAPTER 6

Epstein, Helen. *Children of the Holocaust: Conversations with Sons and Daughters of Survivors*. New York: Putnam, 1979.

Finkelstein, Norman. *The Holocaust Industry: Reflections on the Exploitation of Jewish Suffering*. New York: Verso, 2000.

CHAPTER 7

Barkan, Elazar. *The Guilt of Nations: Restitution and Negotiating Historical Injustices*. New York: Norton, 2000.

Black, Edwin. *IBM and the Holocaust: The Strategic Alliance between Nazi Germany and America's Most Powerful Corporation*. New York: Crown Books, 2002.

Segev, Tom. *The Seventh Million: The Israelis and the Holocaust*. New York: Henry Holt, 2000.

Zweig, Ronald W. *The Gold Train: The Annihilation of the Jews and the Looting of Hungary*. New York: Morrow, 2002.

CHAPTER 8

Bazyler, Michael J. "The Holocaust Restitution Movement in Comparative Perspective." *Berkeley Journal of International Law* 20 (2002): 11.

Chang, Iris. *Rape of Nanking: The Forgotten Holocaust of World War II*. New York: Viking Press, 1998.

Goetz Holmes, Linda. *Unjust Enrichment: How Japan's Companies Built Postwar Fortunes Using American POWs*. Mechanicsburg, PA: Stackpole Books, 2001.

Hovannisian, Richard G. *The Armenian Genocide in Perspective.* New York: Transaction Books, 1986.

———. *Remembrance and Denial: The Case of the Armenian Genocide.* Detroit: Wayne State University Press, 1999.

Robinson, Randall N. *The Debt: What America Owes to Blacks.* New York: Dutton/Plume, 1999.

ADDITIONAL SOURCES

Authers, Richard, and John Wolffe. *The Victims' Fortune.* New York: HarperCollins, 2002.

Bazyler, Michael J. "Nuremberg in America: Litigating the Holocaust in American Courts." *University of Richmond Law Review* 34 (2000): 1.

Brooks, Roy L., ed. *When Sorry Isn't Enough: The Controversy over Apologies and Reparations for Human Injustice.* New York: New York University Press, 1999.

Chesnoff, Richard Z. *Pack of Thieves: How Hitler and Europe Plundered the Jews and Committed the Greatest Theft in History.* New York: Doubleday, 1999.

James, Harold. *The Deutsche Bank and the Nazi Economic War against the Jews.* Cambridge: Cambridge University Press, 2001.

Junz, Helen B. *Where Did All the Money Go? Pre-Nazi Wealth of European Jewry.* Berne: Staempfli Publishers, 2002.

Pross, Christian. *Paying for the Past: The Struggle over Reparations for Surviving Victims of the Nazi Terror.* Baltimore: Johns Hopkins University Press, 1998.

"Symposium Holocaust Restitution: Reconciling Moral Imperatives with Legal Initiatives and Diplomacy." *Fordham International Law Journal* 25 (2001): S-1.

Zweig, Ronald W. *German Reparations and the Jewish World: A History of the Claims Conference.* London: Frank Cass, 2001.

Index

NOTE: Cases are not indexed individually by name. A comprehensive list is found under the main heading "cases."

About the Author

Michael J. Bazyler is Professor of Law at Whittier Law School, Costa Mesa, California; a research fellow at the Holocaust Education Trust in London; and for 2003 the holder of a fellowship at the Center for Advanced Holocaust Studies, United States Holocaust Memorial Museum, Washington, D.C. An international law litigator and human rights activist, he is the son of Holocaust survivors who was raised in postwar Poland.